James M. Le Moine

The Chronicles of the Saint Lawrence

James M. Le Moine

The Chronicles of the Saint Lawrence

ISBN/EAN: 9783337729387

Printed in Europe, USA, Canada, Australia, Japan

Cover: Foto ©Thomas Meinert / pixelio.de

More available books at **www.hansebooks.com**

Seaside Series.

THE

Chronicles of the St. Lawrence.

BY

J. M. LeMOINE,

AUTHOR OF MAPLE LEAVES ; QUEBEC, PAST AND PRESENT, ETC.

PUBLISHED BY DAWSON BROS., Montreal; DAWSON & CO., Quebec;

JOHN W. LOVELL, Rouses Point, N. Y.

1878.

"THERE is in North America a mighty river, having its head in remote lakes, which, though many in number, are yet so great that one of them is known as the largest body of fresh water on the globe,—with a flow as placid and pulseless as the great Pacific itself, yet as swift in places as the average speed of a railway train. Its waters are pure and azure-hued, no matter how many turbid streams attempt to defile them. It is a river that never knew a freshet, nor any drying-up, no matter how great the rain or snow-fall, or how severe the drought on all its thousand miles of drainage or of flow—and yet that regularly, at stated intervals, swells and ebbs within certain limits, as surely as the spring tides each year ebb and flow in the Bay of Fundy—a river so rapid and yet so placid as to enchant every traveller—so grand and yet so lovingly beautiful as to enthral every appreciative soul,—which rises in a great fresh-water sea, and ends in the greater Atlantic—some places sixty miles wide, at others less than a mile—a river that never has yet had a respectable history, nor scarcely more than an occasional artist to delineate its beauties. It lies, for a thousand miles, between two great nations, yet neglected by both, though neither could be as great without it —a river as grand as the LA PLATA, as picturesque as the RHINE, as pure as the LAKES OF SWITZERLAND. Need we say that this wonderful stream is the ST. LAWRENCE, the noblest, the purest, most enchanting river on all God's beautiful earth."

INTRODUCTION.

It has been a frequent subject of surprise, nay of disappointment, to tourists and strangers visiting each summer the noted spots on the Lower St. Lawrence, that, with abundance of material at command, no history had yet been attempted of the majestic stream which for some thousands of miles winds its course to the ocean.

What, indeed, would be Canada without this main artery of commerce ? For six months, the wilderness of snow, jeered at by the great scoffer, Voltaire, one hundred years ago ;—for the rest of the year a parched-up desert, closed to European shipping, with tropical heats and a stunted vegetation.

Embracing on both banks more than one thousand miles of sea board from Quebec to Cape Gaspé ; lined by innumerable settlements, thriving villages, rising towns ; dotted in its whole length with numberless, fertile and picturesque islands, each having its peculiar history, its wild legend of the forest or the sea, its thrilling incident of naval warfare, possibly its harrowing tale of shipwreck and death.

What a rich harvest here for the antiquarian, the historian or the novelist ? Conflicts on sea and on land between the ferocious aborigines, those mysterious wanderers, some of whom had totally disappeared without the faintest trace, between Cartier's visit, in 1535, and Champlain's day, legends of their ferocity towards the white man, the disturber of their forest home; scarcely a bay, a cape, a headland without a trace, a souvenir, of the deadly feud, which for centuries arrayed in hostile conflict Old and New England against Old and New France, in 1628–1632; 1690; 1759-1760; 1775-1783.

If the distant past of the great river has so many teeming memories, how much of interest does it not possess in the recent settlements on its banks, for every class of readers?

What sources of information are now available? a few common-place guide-books, repeating each year monotonous, stale, scanty, stereotyped bits of gossip.

It is this want I have attempted to supply. Having once spent an entire summer on the Gaspé coast; made several successive land and sea voyages to the most noted centres on the Lower St. Lawrence, including a visit to the leading cities of the Maritime Provinces; had the advantage of a study, extending over many years, of the old and modern French and English works on Canada; communicated freely with the best informed Gaspesians, I have got to believe I possessed some qualifications to perform successfully the task I had laid out. My labor was much facilitated, having at command, in a copious journal I have kept, a daily entry of my peregrinations. It is less fine writing and elaborate sentences, I aim at, than a familiar narrative, a fresh, a spontaneous, (*negligé* at times, perhaps,) statement of daily sights and incidents. To prevent repetitions, each paper covers a portion of the St. Lawrence left out of the others; the last paper of all, relating a pleasant excursion, undertaken with a sporting friend and party in the harbor of Quebec, affords incidents of the three SIEGES. I gave it a light, sketchy form as a relief to *ennui*, after so many historical facts, and closed it with the humorous description of the tribulations which befel my sporting friend, from his having speculated on a dead whale. Special attention has been given to the historical portion of these annals, intended to complete the series of sketches of Canadian History, the MAPLE LEAVES, ALBUM DU TOURISTE, and QUEBEC PAST AND PRESENT. The work is specially intended for the information and amusement of summer tourists visiting, either by steamer or by railway, the shores of the Lower St. Lawrence.

J. M. LeMOINE.

SPENCER GRANGE, 17th May, 1878.

The Chronicles of the St. Lawrence.

PART I.

PART II.

THE

CHRONICLES OF THE ST. LAWRENCE.

—

PART I.

CHAPTER I.

THE GULF PORT STEAMERS — FATHER LOFTUS — GASPÉ — ITS
SCENERY AND AMUSEMENTS.

ON BOARD THE "GASPÉ," *12th Sept.,* 1871.

ON a soft and hazy afternoon the good steamer "Gaspé," Commander Baquet, was gliding noiselessly past the many lovely
isles of the St. Lawrence, past the Traverse, past the Pilgrims;
so noiselessly, in fact, that, to one standing on shore, it might
have seemed that she had returned to her old trade, viz.:
secretly carrying cotton from the land of Dixie to the white
cliffs of Old England, in spite of the screeching of the American
Eagle. Though a good sea boat, she is not by any means a fast
one; as blockade runners are expected to show at times a pair
of heels, and this she failed to do, she was forced, on receiving
two shot holes in her bow, to alter her ways. It is owing to
this that she became a respectable Canadian craft—one of the
Gulf Port Steamers.

After enjoying a substantial meal, the passengers, one and all, ascended to the deck; some to smoke—others to talk politics — some to crack jokes : a motley assembly from every part of the Dominion, with a sprinkling of foreigners. Amongst the latter, was a big-fisted *padre*, who persisted in cracking ponderous jokes. There was in his behavior something peculiar; some made him out an Armenian Deacon—others said he belonged to the Greek dispensation. As he was fierce at times—as fierce, in fact, as a Greek when " Greek meets Greek "—we all agreed a Greek he should be, and such he remained to us, under the historic name of " Father Tom Loftus."   *   *   *   *   *   Soon the wind sprung up; the ship rocked; a storm was brewing. Was it owing to having clergymen on board? An irreverent joker advised to throw one of them overboard ; it was, however, mildly suggested to " wait until morning." No clergyman was thrown overboard, and next morning—why, it was calm. At 9 a.m. a boat came alongside, and took ashore the passengers for Father Point and Rimouski, including Mr. W——, a most jovial Quebec broker.

On all that day our brave steamer kept her course, under steam and sails, amidst the gorgeous scenery of the St. Lawrence. In the distance were visible the blue peaks of mountains bathed in autumnal sunshine, their wooded valleys and green gorges all aglow with the blaze of the colors which September drops on the foliage of our maple and oak trees,—gold, crimson, red, maroon, amber, pale green, brown—a landscape such as neither Claude Lorraine, nor Landseer, ever dared to attempt in their brightest day dreams ; a spectacle which invests the most humble Canadian cot with hues and surroundings denied to the turreted castle and park of the proudest English baron. On we steamed, past Cape Chatte, a name borrowed two centuries back and more from the Commander de Chatte, a French nobleman,—and mentioned as such by Champlain in his map as early as 1612. A beacon for ships was lighted on it, on the 11th August last.

On the opposite side, where the Laurentian chain seems to end, is Pointe des Monts, (the Point of the Mountains), and not

Point Demon (the Devil's Point) as some geographers have been pleased to inscribe on the charts; others, however, say that M. de Monts, more than two centuries ago, bequeathed it his name. Antiquarians, there is a nut for you to crack!

We had on board several "choice spirits" of an enquiring turn of mind—ever ready to make experiments in order to ascertain what was the best cure for sea-sickness. As the steamer rolled heavily at times, the enquiry had a practical bearing. Was "hot Scotch" a specific in all cases? Or was "Irish potheen" to be resorted to when the patient felt a kind of sinking sensation at the pit of the stomach? Here, as well as at the Vatican,* the opinions were divided, as on the question of infallibility. After steaming thirty-eight hours, the "Gaspé" was securely moored at Lowndes' wharf, Gaspé Basin, one of the most snug harbors in all British North America.† The beach below is occupied by stores, warehouses, offices; the heights where the O'Harras, Perchards and Arnolds formerly lived are now held by the modern aristocracy of Gaspé and officials, on both sides of the Basin. On the south side, amidst trees, frowns Fort Ramsay with its cannon. The new and substantial residence of the Hon. John Leboutillier, M.L.C., ‡ is conspicuous from afar, amongst the less showy dwellings of the other members of the clan.

On the corresponding shore sits the roomy dwelling of the respected Collector of the port, J. C. Belleau, Esq., a true-hearted patriot of 1837, who, with the Vigers, DeWitts, and other men of note, were consigned to dungeons most dismal, for having dared to suspect that under the Family Compact there were

---

° The famous Œcumenical Council had just closed.

† Gaspé Bay is well described by Champlain, pages 1085-90, &c. The name itself, it is suggested by his commentators, is borrowed from the picturesque rock, detached from the shore, three miles higher than Cape Gaspé, known to seamen as "Ship Head," or the "Old Woman," from the singular transformation by mirage; the Indian name being *Katsepiou*, which means *separate* (abridged into Gaspé.)—*See Champlain's Voyages.*

‡ This gentleman has since died.

some abuses in Canada. Adjoining the Collector's residence, and facing the spot where the Royal squadron anchored in 1860, with the Prince of Wales on board, flourishes the temple of Roman Catholic worship. They were grand times, indeed, these gala days of 1860, when Albert of Wales visited his Royal mother's lieges, the Gaspesians. The officials, military and civil, turned out in tremendous force. Plumes, cocked hats, long-tailed coats, short-tailed coats, coats without tails, spurs, swords, helmets, every device, in fact, calculated to lend *éclat* to the pageant, was brought to the front.

Amongst other items of news, we heard it talked of to restore to Gaspé an office of high rank and ancient creation—the office of Lieut.-Governor of Gaspé. Major Cox, in 1775, appears to have been the resident Lieut.-Governor. We were shown a hickory chair that belonged to him. This seat did not seem firm, nor very durable, though it was a century old; we felt, on sitting down on it, just like a Governor—pardon, a Lieut.-Governor— as Lieut.-Governors *sit* less secure and luxuriously. In the good old Tory days, many offices existed with emoluments well defined and duties very problematical. The Lieutenant-Governorship of Gaspé, with a salary of £1,000 and perquisites ?— why, there were many things worse than that!

Messrs. Joseph and John Eden own extensive wharves and stores on the beach; but, alas, the Free Port system, which in 1864, crammed the Gaspé stores with goods, and deluged the coast with cheap gin and St. Pierre de Miquelon brandy, is a dream now—a melancholy dream of the past. We have to thank the aforesaid active Government officers for their courtesy to us as strangers. The old Coffin Hotel, now much enlarged, is beautifully located on the hill, and merely requires an experienced " Russell " to render it profitable, and a source of pleasure to the many tourists who will hereafter wind their way each summer to Gaspé Basin.*

---

* This hostelry was burned down in March, 1878.

Higher up than their wharves, the Messrs. Lowndes have in operation an extensive saw-mill, which provides daily bread for many, many Gaspé families. Let us hope it may flourish !

One of the chief amusements at Gaspé Basin, during the summer months, is yachting and bobbing for mackerel, just outside the Basin, in the Bay. It is a most exciting and invigorating pastime. The worthy American Consul counts on numerous American craft entering the basin so soon as the new Washington Treaty goes in force.

CHAPTER II.

GASPÉ BASIN—DOUGLASTOWN—POINT ST. PETER'S—MAL BAIE
—NEW CARLISLE—PASPEBIAC—THE GREAT JERSEY FIRMS.

THERE is something singularly striking when, on a bright Saturday morning, at break of day, with the far-reaching Bay of
Gaspé before you lit up with amber sunshine, your ear catches
the boom of the heavy guns fired by the two Gulf Port steamers
—the one from Pictou, the other from Quebec; their usual
signal on nearing the placid waters of the Basin. They are so
well timed that both frequently arrive together. Hark! to the
wild echo bounding over the waters, and then leaping from peak
to peak in this weird, mountainous region. Three centuries ago
and more, other echoes no less wild disturbed the quiet of this
forest home—the shouts of joy of Jacques Cartier's adventurous
crew, when planting a cross on the sandy point at the entrance,
on the 24th July, 1534; and when taking possession in the
name of Francis I of France; not, however, without an energetic protest being then and there made by a great chief, " clad
in a bear skin, and standing erect in his canoe, followed by his
numerous warriors." Hakluyt tells us that the old chief was
enticed on board the French ships, and, on his sons Taiguragny
and Domagaya being decked out in most gorgeous raiment, he
was prevailed to let the vain youths accompany the French captain to the court of the French King. Poor vain lads! had you
been wise you would have jumped overboard and swam ashore
when you passed Ship Head!

　　Look eastward on the dark waving woods hoary with age.
Is this not

　　　. . . . . . the forest primeval! The murmuring pines and the hemlocks
　　Bearded with moss, and in garments green, indistinct in the twilight,

Stand like Druids of eld, with voices sad and prophetic,
Stand like harpers hoar, with beards that rest on their bosoms,
This is the forest primeval; but where are the hearts that beneath it
Leaped like the roe, when he hears in the woodland the voice of the huntsman?

Where are now the descendants of the fierce Indians who then greeted Cartier, and whose huts were located on the rocky ledge where I now stand? There were then no swift steamers churning these glad waters—no golden wheat-fields, as those I can now see at Sandy Beach; but everywhere the forest primeval--its gloom—its trackless wilds—its uselessness to civilized man.

On we sped, with steam and sails. Soon opened on us the extensive old settlement of Douglastown. It was not named after any fierce black Douglas, celebrated in song, but by an unassuming land surveyor of that name. Numerous descendants of the first settlers, of 1785—the U. E. Loyalists—still survive: the Kennedys, Thompsons, Murisons, etc., industrious fishermen all. The whole bay is studded with fishing stations and small villages, in which generally the R. C. church is the most conspicuous object. After passing *Grande Grève* and *Chien Blanc*, both the scenes of awful marine disasters, the steamer hugs the shore towards Point St. Peter's, a large and important fishing settlement, and creeps through a deep channel between the rocky ledge called Plateau and Point St. Peter's, and another thriving fishing location called Mal Baie. According to Champlain and his commentator, the origin of the name is taken from *Moltes* or *Mornes* Baie (Codfish Bay) which the English turned into Mal Baie.

However, don't be surprised at any transformation in these wild regions, as Cat Cape (Cape Chatte) and Devil's Point (Pointe de Monts) sufficiently testify. I might add another queer transmogrification. At St. Luce there is a deep cove and jutting point; in spring, it is infested with mussels, which the French call *des Cocques;* hence the French name *L'Anse aux Cocques*. But the English must have a cock instead; they have named it Cock Point. I know I shall make the mouths

of antiquarians water when I tell them I have at last, after a
deal of research, got hold of the origin of the name of Father
Point, a little higher up than Cock Point ; but of this hereafter.
Let us hurry on to the great, grand, and growing capital on the
Canadian side of Baie des Chaleurs (New Carlisle). All know
why the Bay was called Baie des Chaleurs (Bay of Heat) by
Cartier, though all of us on board the " Gaspé" found the place
extremely cold.

On a high bank, with a southern exposure, lies a fine cham-
pagne country laid out in square blocks of four acres each—for
a town chiefly inhabited by English and Scotch.   It has an
Episcopalian church, a Roman Catholic church, a new court-
house and jail, and no less than two judges, living within view
of each other.   Two resident judges in New Carlisle remind
one of the two rival Roman Catholic churches staring at one
another at Trois Pistoles—one evidently will have to knock under, the place cannot afford such a luxury.   It is said there is
here enough litigation to fatten three resident lawyers, and that
there are three physicians in the place.   It is healthy notwithstanding, and some of the inhabitants have been known to
attain great ages.   Little or no fishing is done at the shire town.
I had no time to find out whether it derives its name from an
Earl of Carlisle, or from Tom Carlyle, the great Essayist and
coiner of words.   From the readiness with which words and
names are altered, one would fain believe it hails from the great
essayist.   One case in point : that of the neighboring fishing
settlement—its commercial emporium—Paspebiac.   This is an
Indian name—the English-speaking population have altered it
into Paspy Jack.   They call themselves Paspy Jacks, and the
French, who get their backs up readily, especially since they
have had Parliamentary elections to manage, call it *Pospillat*
and themselves *Des Pospillats*.   In Bishop Plessis's account of
his mission, here, in 1811, we read that in many instances the
maternal ancestors of the Pospillats were Micmac squaws,
much to the disgust of the neighboring settlements.   These
half-breeds were then accounted fierce and revengeful.   Tom

Carlyle must have had something to do with this word-coining. But let us return to the county town. The view from the heights is most imposing. You notice here and there a better style of dwelling, trim flower-gardens interspersed with the scarlet clusters of the mountain ash or roan berry—comfortable old homesteads, like that of the Hamiltons—splendid new residences, like that of Dr. Robitaille, M.P.*

There are several educated families located at New Carlisle which renders it a most pleasant residence, especially during the summer months; but beware how you utter the word "Election," and keep a dignified reserve on this explosive subject until you are at least past, on your return, Ship Head or Fox River.

Talking of fiercely-contested elections reminds one of the great election of Eatanswill, mentioned in "Pickwick." Forty-five green parasols be it remembered, judiciously bestowed, had turned the scale on that eventful day.

In Canada, barrels of flour and the coin of the realm, are said to be more effective. However, let us hope that in Bonaventure, the election was carried with that lofty patriotism and exquisite purity, the shining characteristic of all Canadian elections, in June last!!! Hem!!

For tourists in quest of health, sea-bathing and good fishing, I

---

* New Carlisle was first settled by American Loyalists: that is, by persons whose loyalty to the British Crown induced them to leave the United States at the period of the Revolution. These persons obtained free grants of land, agricultural implements, seed and provisions for one year. Lieut.-Governor Cox was appointed, in or about 1774, as Governor of the district of Gaspé, and seems to have resided alternately in two shire towns, New Carlisle and Percé. He appears to have been sent for the purpose of settling the Loyalists in New Carlisle and Douglastown, and to have expended between the two places upwards of £80,000 sterling, a large amount when we consider the little progress made in either locality. The Abbé Ferland states that Judge Thompson once jocularly observed to the Roman Catholic Bishop of Quebec, that " this sum can only have been spent in making excavations underground, nothing appearing on the surface to justify such an outlay."—
Pye's Gaspé Scenery.

know few places more eligible than Baie des Chaleurs and Gaspé
Basin.

Paspebiac, with its roadstead running out to a point in the
Bay, is the seaport—the great fishing stand of the Messrs. Robin
and the Messrs. LeBoutillier Brothers. The fishing establishments—a crowd of nice white warehouses, with doors painted
red, comprising stores, offices, forges, joiners' shops, dwellings for
fishermen, even to powder magazines—all stand on a low beach
or sand bar, connected with the shore by a ford for horses, and
a trestlework bridge for foot passengers, which is taken down
every fall and restored in the spring at the expense of the Messrs.
Robin. It seems singular that the business and wealth centered
here cannot afford a bridge. Crossing by ford at night, when
the tide is high, is anything but an agreeable prospect. It is
scarcely safe. Perhaps when some of the magnates of the place
are found drowned in the ford, the Bridge question will assume
a more tangible phase.

Paspebiac is three miles east of New Carlisle. Here the
Custom House is located. The Collector (1871) is J. Fraser, Esq.,
an active, well-informed old Scotchman.* The bar on which the
fishing warehouses stand, is a triangle formed by sand and other
marine *detritus*. The interior of the triangle is gradually filling
up. Here the fishermen dwell in summer ; they remove to their
winter quarters on the heights in rear in December.

It was in 1766 that Charles Robin, Esq., first landed at Paspebiac and explored the coast in a small brig called the " Sea-
Flower." One hundred and forty-six years previous (1620)
other explorers, the Pilgrim-Fathers, were landing a little to the
south in the "May-Flower." On 11th June, 1778, two American
privateers plundered Mr. Robin's store of all his goods, furs,
and seized his two vessels, the " Bee " and the " Hope ; " both
were moored in the Paspebiac Roads. But the " Bee " and the

---

* This worthy, aged official, having since accepted a pension lives in his
old homestead, formerly the residence of the historian, R. Christie, at Cross
Point ; he is Warden of the County.

New England privateers were all recaptured in the Restigouche, by H. B. M. vessels, " Hunter " and " Piper ; " and the heavy salvage Mr. R. was called on to pay, viz. : one-eighth, caused him to fail ; he was off for Jersey.   In 1783 he returned, sailing under French colors, and continued to accumulate wealth until 1802, when he left for Europe.   •

On the green hills in rear, the great Jersey houses have splendid farms, dwellings, gardens, parks.   Fish manure and kelp are bountifully supplied here and largely used.   The winter residences of the Managers of Messrs. Robin, and Messrs. Le Boutillier Bros., are most commodious, most complete.   I was allowed to inspect a large store for the packing of pork on the establishment of the Messrs. Robin—the first I had ever seen on this principle.   The thawing is done in the depth of winter without any artificial heat, and merely by a device which, whilst it excludes the cold air, retains the natural heat generated in the earth.   In about a week the frozen pigs gradually thaw and are fit for salting. The walls of this building, between earth, sawdust, timber, etc., are about twelve feet thick, with a vacuum between each layer.

It is well worth a visitor's attention to examine the vast facilities and arrangements devised to carry on the gigantic trade in fish, oil, etc., of the two wealthy Jersey houses, whose head establishments are at Paspebiac.   The western point of the bar, or beach, is occupied by Le Boutillier Bros., a respectable old Jersey house ; but though a worthy rival of its neighbors, it is not so ancient as the great house of C. R. C. (Charles Robin & Co.)   None of the Robins, however, reside here.   C. R. C. is a mighty name on the Gaspé coast.   It has existed more than a hundred years.   Whether the " Co." is represented by sons, as formerly, I cannot tell ; perhaps, like the great London house immortalized by Dickens, C. R. C. might now mean daughters—it is beyond doubt " Dombey & Son " turned out to be a daughter.*   C. R. C. amongst the Gaspesians represent mil-

* Since these lines were written in 1871, a notice of transfer of commercial rights appeared in the *Morning Chronicle* of Quebec, Oct. 8, 1877, giving the

lions; seven vast establishments rejoice under this mystic combination.

It would be akin to sacrilege to say, at Paspebiac, that they
could be affected by hard times. No one can fathom their
resources : no one dare dispute the principle on which each establishment is carried on. The poor clerks and managers, 'tis
true, cannot own wives or families at their residences at Gaspé ;
the founder of the house ordained it otherwise one hundred
years ago, and their business rules are like the laws of the
Medes and Persians—they alter not. C. R. C. is really a grand,
a glorious name, a tower of strength in Gaspesia, though it may
mean a monopoly. Its credit is calculated to last until the end
of time. Canada Banks may get in Chancery; the Bank of
England may feel tight, hard up; but C. R. C. never. Its credit stands higher on all the range of this vast coast than the
Bank of England. I should be the last to attempt to dim the
lustre of these great Jersey firms ; their word is as good as their
bond, and in times of need, when the fishery fails, the poor fisherman never appeals to them in vain.

I cannot leave Paspebiac without noticing one of the most
prominent elements of progress recently introduced—the exten-
sion of the Electric Telegraph, all the way down from Métis to
Baie des Chaleurs and Gaspé. Times are indeed changed since
those dark ages when a Gaspé or Baie des Chaleurs mail was
made up once each winter and expedited to Quebec on the back
of an Indian on snow-shoes. Thanks to their Parliamentary
Members, thanks to the wealthy Jersey firms, thanks to the
enterprise of the people who furnished the telegraph posts, (the
Montreal Telegraph Co. agreeing to put them up), the wires
place them now in hourly intercourse with every city of America and of Europe.

---

following as the members of the commercial firm of Charles Robin, viz. :
" Messrs. Raulin Robin, Philip Gosset and William Lempriere, all of the
Island of Jersey, in Europe, where is situate the head office."

CHAPTER III.

THE MIC-MACS—PETER BASKET, ESQUIRE, THE GREAT INDIAN
CHIEF—HOPE TOWN—LORD AYLMER AND HIS MIC-MAC
ACQUAINTANCE—NOUVELLE—CHIGOUAC—PORT DANIEL—
THE OLDEST MAYOR IN THE DOMINION.

THE Mic-Mac and other Indians have gradually deserted
many points of the Gaspé coast, which swarmed with them formerly. Some 500 or 600 have congregated at Mission Point, on
the Restigouche, up Baie des Chaleurs. Doubtless the fierce Pospillats will also gradually decrease in numbers as the admixture of
Indian blood is not favorable either to morality or colonization.
Left to their unbridled instincts, what delightful drinking-bouts
these lazy mountaineers, the Mic-Macs, must have! What
wholesale slaughter of the lordly salmon, at all seasons, whether it is spawning or not! How many moose and caribou are
left in the close season to rot on the mountains, with their
tongue, mouffle or hide alone removed? This indiscriminate
slaughter of our finest game has already rendered extinct the
majestic Wapiti, who, one hundred and thirty years ago, roam-
ed in countless droves over a great portion of Lower Canada.
Now, you have to go all the way to Manitoba or to the Rocky
Mountains to get a sight of the Wapiti. I am no admirer of
the red man, though Fenimore Cooper can make a hero of him;
those I have met so far, with some exceptions, I occasionally
felt inclined to see them improved—as Brother Jonathan im-
proves them—off the face of the earth. One of these exceptions
is Peter Basket, Esq., of Restigouche.

Peter Basket is the name of the great Mic-Mac chief who visited Queen Victoria and the Prince Consort, about 1850, and returned loaded with presents. As he seems to delight in courts and great folks, may I ask whether he, or some ancestor of his, was one of the orators who formerly waited on His Excellency Lord Aylmer, of whom an old Chronicler writes :

" When Lord Aylmer was Governor-General, he once went on an excursion to Gaspé. Amongst others who flocked there to welcome the representative of royalty were Mic-Mac Indians, numbering some 500 or 600. When His Excellency landed with a brilliant staff, he was met by this respectable deputation of the aboriginal race. The chief, a fine powerful man, surrounded by his principal warriors, at once commenced a long oration delivered in the usual solemn, sing-song tone, accompanied with frequent bowing of the head. It happened that a vessel had been wrecked some months previously, in the Gulf, and the Indians, proving themselves ready and adroit wreckers, had profited largely by the windfall. Among other ornaments which they had seized, was a box full of labels for decanters, marked in conspicuous characters, Rum, Gin, Brandy, etc. The chief had his head liberally encircled with ornaments of the usual kind, and on this occasion had dexterously affixed to his ears and nose some of the labels as bangles. At the beginning of the interview, these were not particularly discernible amid the novelty of the spectacle ; and it was only while listening to the lengthened harangue of the savage chief that His Excellency began to scrutinize his appearance and dress; and then his ears and nose, with the labels inscribed Brandy, Gin, Rum, etc. Glancing toward his staff, he could no longer maintain his gravity, and was joined in a hearty but indecorous burst of unrestrainable laughter. The indignant chief, with his followers, immediately withdrew, and would neither be pacified nor persuaded to return, although the cause of His Excellency's ill-timed merriment was explained to him."

The road, on leaving Paspebiac beach, reaches the heights—

some nicely-wooded lands, formerly the property of Messrs. Robin & Co., now called Hopetown, a thriving settlement of industrious and economical Scotchmen. Handsome cottages are rapidly taking here the place of the forest. The village of Nouvelle comes next; then a settlement called Chigouac, with a good mill stream, and two grist mills erected on it.

When being jolted in a two-wheeled post stage, without springs, over these villainous roads, the traveller will do well to fix before hand the stopping places (for meals), as hostelries are few and far between. Don't buoy yourself up with the hallucination that on the Gaspé coast, at least, you will have the most savory of its products—fresh fish—always at command. Such would be "a delusion and a snare." On my complaining once of this deprivation, my thoughtful landlady whispered in my ear that she had refrained from giving me, two days in succession, fresh mackerel from fear of hurting my feelings, and lest I should go away with the idea that no other fare could be had but a fish diet. As a rule, you can count on the perpetual "ham and eggs" for breakfast, dinner and supper; but in some portions of these latitudes, the hens, it appears, on strike either for less work or better food, had decided not to lay, and I had to make the most of "ham" solus. This ham regime, when protracted, gets irksome; you long for the egg country, where hens are not on strike. Omelettes, let me tell you, are not a thing to be lightly talked of or despised, my sherry-sipping and plum-pudding eating travelling friend. An epicure of my acquaintance holds as an axiom that it requires three persons to serve up an omelette properly; one to mix—another to fry—a third to turn it in the pan, without lodging it in the fire.

But on this point I found nothing in Hackluyt, nor in Purchas, great travellers though they be.

An hour's drive from Chigouac brings you to a beautiful farming country, a deep, picturesque bay—called Port Daniel —in the Township of Port Daniel, which begins at Pointe-au-Maquereau, a rocky point jutting in the sea. When you reach

the summit of the range of Cap au Diable, the beautiful Bay of
Port Daniel suddenly meets the eye ; a splendid and varied panorama lies before you. As you descend the mountain on a bright
summer afternoon, an interesting, an amusing scene often awaits
you. The innumerable fishing boats having returned, men,
women and children are busily engaged in landing, splitting
and conveying the fish to the stages. At the mouth of Port
Daniel River, we have again the usual lagoon, and *bar* which
prevents the entrance of vessels of any large size ; there is, however, good anchorage under the Cape. On this, the east side of
the river, just at the harbor's mouth, snugly ensconced under
the hill, stands the Roman Catholic church.

"The 'Gaspé Fishery and Coal Mining Company' commenced
an establishment, and built a couple of small vessels on this
river—and their so-called coal-field, a *bed of shale*, is about
three miles up the stream. Crossing the ferry about a quarter
of a mile further, is another river, on which there is a small
saw-mill."—*Pye's Gaspé Scenery.*

I must confess, this picturesque sunlit landscape will dwell
long in my memory.

Possibly, some spots visited for the first time seem to your
enchanted eye still more lovely, from the pleasant associations
which linger around them. A slight act of kindness where you
expected but the cold indifference of the world ; a hospitable
welcome ; the hand of good fellowship, cordially extended by an
utter stranger ; the exchange of cultivated ideas, and intellectual converse, where, at best, you counted merely on the rude
and unsympathizing gaze of the boor or the stranger : such incidents, no doubt, contribute to create vivid, lasting and pleasure-
able emotions, which, being identified with the landscape itself,
leave a delightful record in the haunted halls of memory. It
was my good fortune to experience this welcome at Port Daniel.
The Chief Magistrate of Port Daniel, William Macpherson,
Esq., is a well-informed and warm-hearted Worshipful Mayor,
I should say the Prince and Nestor of Mayors on the Gaspé

coast ; I learn he has graced the civic chair twenty-six years.[*]
He is a Scot, a true Scot. Under what portion of the vault
of Heaven will you not find a canny Scot, prosperous, high
in place, well to do ? The great tea-merchants in China are
Scotch ; the greatest philosophers in the United Kingdom of
Great Britain are Scotch ; the wealthiest companies in Canada are
Scotch—Allan, etc. At the Council Board in the Dominion
Government ; in Ontario ; Quebec—McDonalds, Macdonalds,
Robertsons, McKenzies, all Scots. Am I not then justified in
quoting from the prize poem read at the St. Andrew's meeting
in Montreal, Halloween, 1866 :

> An' sae it is the wide worl' o'er,
> On fair or barren spot,
> Frae Tropic isles to Arctic shore,
> Ye'll fin' the canny Scot.
> All posts o' honor weel he fills,
> Leal subject o' his Queen ;
> For loyalty, an' honesty
> Claim kin wi' Halloween."

Long life then to His Worship of Port Daniel !
Spencer Grange, *Halloween*, 1871.

---

[*] On reviewing these pages after a lapse of several years, our venerable
friend, we find, has added seven more years to his tenure of office.

CHAPTER IV.

HARRINGTON COVE—POINTE-AU-MAQUEREAU—THE LOSS OF THE
COLBORNE IN 1838—AN UNEXPECTED RENCONTRE WITH ONE
OF THE FEW SURVIVORS OF THE SHIPWRECK—HIS OWN
VERSION OF THE DISASTER.

> " Two voices are there—one is of the sea,
> One, of the mountains—each a mighty voice."
>
> —*Wordsworth.*

THE 21st September, 1871, was indeed for me a bleak, gloomy
day on the sea coast; the autumnal equinox was raging.
Scrambling over mountain gorges and dark gullies in a spring-
less, two-wheeled post stage is not cheering at any time; still
less with a raw easterly wind and drizzling rain switching your
face. One feature of the landscape was in marvellous keeping
with the surrounding gloom—the ceaseless roar of the surf on
the iron-bound coast I was skirting.

> " A hollow, hollow, hollow sound,
>   As is that dreamy roar
>   When distant billows boil and bound
>   Along a shingly shore."
>
> —*Hood.*

Never had I heard old Ocean's voice in grander tones—never,
in more impressive majesty. I cannot say it had exactly a
depressing influence; though it certainly made one thoughtful.
Closing in with the dark rocks of Pointe-au-Maquereau, bristling
with their silvery crest of foam, I thought of the horrors of that
awful night of October, 1838, which, at this very spot, con-

signed to the "chambers of the deep" so many brave men, so many loving young hearts. On my way down I had been shown, in the church-yards at Paspebiac and Port Daniel, the graves of the Hudsons, of Capt. Kent, and of several other victims of that shipwreck.

Before the era of light-houses, fog-whistles, beacons, etc., the coast of Gaspé was particularly dreaded by English mariners bound for Montreal or Quebec. Many and heart-rending were the tales of marine disaster, starvation and death, in these localities ; few left a deeper impression than the loss of the ill-fated barque " Colborne," stranded at Pointe-au-Maquereau on the 16th October, 1838.

The extraordinary value of her cargo,—some $400,000 worth of silks, wines, hardware, silver plate, specie, drifting ashore at Harrington's Cove and Port Daniel,—a vast heap of confusion ; the spoils picked up by wreckers ; the sale by auction of such untold wealth, which built up the fortunes of many a nobby family ; the appalling loss of life, exposure and sufferings of the few survivors, all conspired to render the shipwreck of the Montreal trader, a harrowing, a most memorable occurrence. This shipwreck now commemorates an era on the Gaspé coast.

After crossing by the ford at Port Daniel the path winds round a cape of a very rugged aspect. By some it is called *Cap d'Enfer*, by others *Cap au Diable*, and to one ascending these dreary heights, at the gloaming, on a bleak autumn evening, it does seem a haunt not uncongenial to his satanic majesty, An artist might fittingly select Pointe-au-Maquereau to depict the Spirit of Evil hovering over, under the guise of the " Flying Dutchman," looking out for some storm-tossed bark to revel in the death-groans of the drowning mariners.

On we jogged, over rough roads and rougher bridges, until the sombre outlines of the trees in the valley beneath were scarcely visible at all. Evening had fairly set in ; the rain, wind, and moaning of the sea increased. Seeing no dwelling, I at last asked the jehu, who was rather of a bibulous turn,

"Where are we then to stop to-night?" In reply, I was told that we were rapidly nearing l'Anse-au-Gascon; that the hospitable roof of Joseph Jones Acteson, Esq., J.P., would soon shelter us.

"Are there, then, no regular hotels on this coast?" I enquired.

"None, sir, Iam sorry to say. Travellers have to trust to the good-will of inhabitants for food,—and shelter. However, you are, I consider," he added, " rather in luck's way, you, who appear so keen after local traditions, local history, and general information. Soon you will have an opportunity of conversing with a thorough-going Englishman—the father of a numerous family—probably the sole survivor on this side of the Atlantic of the fifty-four human beings who, in 1838, constituted the crew and passengers of the British bark 'Colborne,' stranded close by. Mr. Acteson will, I am certain, take pleasure in relating to you all that took place before and after the loss of this ill-starred ship." I was accordingly introduced to Squire Acteson, J.P., and though he suffered at the time from the effects of a kick from a horse, he turned out so communicative that, tea being dispatched, I asked him for full particulars of the shipwreck, and with his consent, committed them in his presence to paper, as follows :—

THE LOSS OF THE "COLBORNE" AT MAKEREL POINT,

16th October, 1838, as described by Mr. Acteson.

" O ! never may the moon again disclose me such a sight
    As met my gaze when first I looked on that accursed night.
    I've seen a thousand horrid shapes begot of fierce extremes
    Of fever, and most frightful things have haunted in my dreams."
                              The Demon Ship—Hood.

"The 'Colborne' was a bark of about 350 tons, owned by parties in Hull, and commanded by Captain Kent, an experienced seaman. We sailed from London, for Quebec and

Montreal, on the 30th August, with an unusually rich cargo of British merchandise, wines, spirits, sperm oil, spices. There was also on board valuable silver plate for Sir John Colborne; ornaments for R. C. churches, and a number of boxes of specie for the banks, each box containing about £1,000. Our crew consisted of seventeen men and some thirty-eight passengers, amongst whom I can remember Capt. James Elliott Hudson of the British Army, his lady, five daughters and six sons; Mr. Wm. Walker, of the Royal Navy, brother-in-law to Capt. Hudson; Mr. W. Scobell, of Hamilton, Ont.; Mr. J. Scobell, of Devonshire, wife and six children, and four children of his sister's, a Devonshire widow; Capt. Bucket, wife and child; Mr. Gilbert, father of a person of that name in Hamilton; Mrs. Wilson, wife of—— Wilson, Esq., Hamilton; Mrs. Keast, mother of Mr. Hawkins, of Toronto; Mr. Barrows, of Devonshire, and Mr. George Manly, of Quebec, Deputy Sheriff. The day had been overcast, the weather, foggy; a catch of delicious codfish served up for dinner had put us all in prime humor. Our captain had sighted, as he thought, a light on Anticosti, though I strongly maintained to him that at that time no such light was kept up. The light seen was probably on Mount Anne, at Percé. Therein lay our trouble.

"Close to twelve o'clock at midnight of the 15th Oct., whilst Capt. Kent and Capt. Hudson were taking a glass of wine together in the cabin, the watch was called; while aloft reefing topsails, one of the hands sung out, 'Breakers ahead;' before the ship could be put about, she struck heavily, starting stern post and unshipping rudder.

"Everything was tumult in an instant. The ladies rushed about frantic, in their night-dresses, seizing on all the wearing apparel they could, to clothe themselves and their little children —every one of them indeed sobbing and shedding tears. We tried the pumps; eight feet of water in the hold. The chief mate asked the Captain for leave to cut away the masts, and get the boats ready, but Captain Kent replied: ' there is no danger, that he was master, and that the masts would not be cut.' Our ship lost her rudder at the first stroke, but the Captain, by shifting the sails, got the vessel in deep water. Finding her fast filling, he attempted (though she was but a stone's throw from the shore when the ship first struck) to reach the rocks ; she failed, having no helm. In about half an hour, it blowing very fresh, the ship again struck and fell over. In an instant all were in the sea ; the women wild with terror, the poor dear children, whom we, rough sailors, used to play with on deck, uttering piercing cries. When I now recollect the scene I subsequently witnessed on the wreck floating ashore, when we grappled with boat-hooks for their little bodies, and fished them up between the hatches, I could shed tears as if the whole thing had happened but yesterday. I was then young and active and an excellent swimmer ; five seamen and myself had managed to get in the jolly-boat, which was amidships and had served as a roof to protect some live stock deposited in the long-boat. A huge green billow struck her, and making her turn over a somersault, I felt myself sinking to a great depth. At that moment I thought it was all up. I fancied I could see myriads of stars high above my head, shining through the waters—the most secret thoughts of my whole life crowded before my mind, as if I were looking in a mirror. Possibly the stars seen might have been the phosphorus emitted by the waves during the storm ; the whole sea seemed on fire that night. I gradually rose to the surface ; my first thought was to rid myself of my coat ; it was no use trying. I made for the ship's yard, as she was on her beam ends, and with three others who had previously been with me in the jolly-boat when she capsized, I got into the long-boat, which was between the masts in the water. After clearing her from the rigging, we tried to reach the wreck to pick up some of the crew or passengers ; but, having lost our oars, we had to drift at the mercy of the waves. With some boards found in her, we rigged a kind of aft-sail by sitting with our backs to them ; this kept the boat's head to the sea. Thus, we drifted about all night, which was intensely cold. Two of Capt. Hudson's sons who were on board would likely have perished from cold, wet and exhaustion, had we not protected them, by sitting down on them. We were in the neighborhood of the ship, and could hear all night particularly loud and melancholy cries on board ; this was a powerful young sailor, who never ceased moaning untill he sank exhausted about dawn, uttering even from under the waves a loud scream for help ; none ever was to come to him. This strong fellow had shipped just as we started from London, instead of two lads from Hull, who had deserted. Thus had they escaped the fate of the majority of us ; the lad had had just time to jump on board, as we left the London docks. It is now thirty-three years ago since I heard his cries of despair, and many a time have I woke in my sleep, horrified, fancying I heard the same awful screams. At five o'clock next morning our long-boat was towed by the natives into Anse-au-Gascon. Some of us were quite insensible ; the unremitting attention shown to us by the French and English fishermen, after some hours, brought us all round. The ' Colborne' drifted about, water-logged, from Monday night to the following Saturday, when the numerous boats which the news of her shipwreck had attracted, succeeded in towing her ashore in Harrington Cove, a mile and three-quarters distant from Port Daniel harbor. Some of the crew were found in the rigging, dead; some, quite exhausted. Capt. Hudson was fished up with a boat-hook from the wreck, also two children and Mr. Walker ; one sailor, the body of Capt. Kent, and another were picked up amongst the rigging—all were taken on shore at Port Daniel, to the store of Wm. Carter, Esq., where the inquest was held. Of the fifty-four souls on board, the second mate, eight seamen, two sons of Capt. Hudson, and one steerage passenger were alone saved. I am now fifty-seven years of age, and have resided on the coast ever since, having married Isabella Chedor, the daughter of the man who rescued me the morning after the shipwreck.

" Several bodies were picked up. It was reported that the

body of Mrs. Hudson, on whom was found £600 in bank bills, had been found, the same having drifted across the Bay, and a number of vessels had been seen picking up the goods floating in the Bay and Gulf.   I could mention to you many other details, but it is getting late."

> " I dropp'd my pen, and listen'd to the wind
> That sang of trees uptorn and vessels toss'd."

It was indeed, as Squire Acteson well observed, getting late, and I retired to my sleeping-quarters facing the beach, from which broke forth, like a mournful dirge, the ceaseless roar of the sea ; that relentless sea whose foam, like a shroud, had closed over poor Captain Kent and his luckless passengers.   It moaned as of yore, and

> " What were the wild waves saying ? "

Next morning my host told me all about the extraordinary appearance of the bay and beach, strewn with the valuable merchandise of the stranded ship when she broke up ; silver plate put up to auction, and knocked down for a few shillings ; church ornaments of great value used by the natives as wearing apparel ; costly wines and silk dresses sold for a trifle.   Five boxes of specie of £1,000 each were saved.   In spite of the efforts of the auctioneer and authorities, valuable lots disappeared as if by magic.

The $400,000 of the " Colborne " did indeed enrich many wreckers, and some that were not wreckers.

CHAPTER V.

New Port Cove—Pabos—Grand River—Its Ricketty Old
Bridge—Cape Cove—Cap d'Espoir—Curious Transform-
ations of Names—Still more curious Legends.

The reader has no doubt been interested as much as I was at
the time by the graphic description of the loss of the " Colborne,"
as it fell from the lips of my hospitable host, Squire Acteson.
This left us at Anse-au-Gascon, not very far distant from Pointe-
au-Maquereau, the western boundary of the County of Gaspé.
Pointe-au-Maquereau marks the entrance to the Bay des Chaleurs, the Island of Miscou, distant about fifteen miles, being
the boundary of the bay, on the New Brunswick side. From
L'Anse-au-Gascon to Newport Islands, a distance of about
five miles, the road leaves the shore, and runs through the woods.
These Islands are two patches of rock where, we were told, " Captain Philip Dean, of Jersey, once had a fishing stand." Pointe-
au-Maquereau is not visible from the road, so that the traveller
passes the boundary between the two counties without being
aware of it. The land through this portage is rocky and scarcely fit for settlement.

" The seigniory of Pabos joins that of Grand River, to the
east. Next comes Great Pabos, where a chartered English
company, under the name of the ' Gaspé Fishery and Coal Mining
Company,' formerly established their headquarters, and squandered the moneys entrusted to them by the duped shareholders.
Under the French rule this appears to have been a well-settled
locality.

" On a small island, in the middle of the lagoon, traces could be lately seen of what once constituted the foundations and cellar of a large house, said to be that of the Governor or Intendant. The remains of three mill dams on the north side of the river were also visible, and the various articles found from time to time prove that a considerable number of families must have once occupied the front.

"Pabos is a bar harbor and very difficult of access. There are two rivers which empty themselves into the lagoon, at a short distance from each other. A large portion of the land in Great Pabos is unfit for culture.

"Next to Great Pabos is Little Pabos with a river of the same name, which was bridged by the Government in 1844. The river Pabos as well as Grand River, are the resorts of large flocks of wild fowl in the spring and fall. The inhabitants are all sportsmen. Distance from Pabos to Grand River about eight miles ; from Newport to Pabos, three."

Pabos the Great, seemed to me an ordinary French-Canadian parish, with a respectable-looking church. A telegraph office has recently been opened here, in the house of a Scotchman, by the name of Archibald Kerr. From this house, on the heights, where I stopped for dinner, I could notice a point below, where the sea fowl (the *Mouniacs*, I fancied) seemed to congregate and feed in countless numbers. I was told that they never left the spot from May till November, and slept at night on the waters.

Grand River will be remembered by me on account of its long and ricketty old bridge. "It was built out of a loan from the 'Municipal Loan Fund,' and is a standing monument of what local dissension can do. Grand River was conceded, on the 31st May, 1697, by Louis de Buade, Count de Frontenac, (Governor), and John Bochart (Intendant), to Mr. James Cochu, of Grand River,—commencing from the Seigniory of Great Pabos, belonging to Mr. René Hubert, extending towards Cape Hope, near the Island of Percé.

"This Seigniory was purchased by the late Mr. Charles Robin, from Mr. Duncan Anderson, on the 18th June, 1793. The Cape mentioned in the concession as Cape Hope is the Cape Despair of our day."

Abbé Ferland, in his journal, speaks very highly of Grand River, not only as a valuable fishing station, but as regards its soil and agricultural capabilities. He also states "that in consequence of the immense quantity of wild fowl resorting to this vicinity every spring and fall, all the men are sportsmen; that if shooting has its delights, it has also its dangers, as many hands are seen minus a finger or thumb; and that, by a remarkable coincidence, accidents of this kind have universally happened on a Sabbath or other holy day."

The Messrs. Robin are still the owners of the soil. Very few of the settlers on their estate have paid for the land, and the majority can only be viewed in the light of tenants. The land is good, for the most part level, and well-adapted for agricultural purposes. But here, as along the whole coast from New Richmond to Cap Chatte agriculture is a mere secondary consideration when compared with the fisheries. The owners have, nevertheless, set the inhabitants a good example, having a fine farm which is well cultivated and yields abundant crops; next to Percé, Grand River is Messrs. Charles Robin & Co.'s best fishing stand. They generally have about thirty-two boats every season fishing on this establishment. . . Besides this firm, there are three other mercantile establishments in Grand River, namely Messrs. J. O. Sirois, Thomas Tremblay, and Thomas Carbery.

This, like all the rivers on the coast, has a bar which makes it both difficult and dangerous of access in bad weather. Small schooners can enter the harbor at high water and remain in perfect security. The population of the seigniory and township of Grand River, which, by the last census (of 1861) was 879 souls, is rapidly increasing, and a perceptible improvement has taken place in the appearance of the buildings within the last few years.*

---

* Pye's Gaspé Scenery.

"The distance from Grand River to Cape Cove, a large settlement, is ten miles, and eight from thence to Percé; it forms part of the township of that name, which extends about eighteen miles along the sea coast.

"Population of this settlement chiefly Protestant, the church forming a prominent object in the view. There is also a large Roman Catholic church at Cape Despair to the west of Cape Cove.

"Cape Cove, like Percé, is an important fishing station. There are three commercial houses, Messrs. De la Parrelle Brothers, Thos. Savage, and Amice Payne. The two first-named firms are also ship-owners, and all are natives of Jersey. There is excellent land and some good farms in the vicinity. Mr. Savage has an extensive farm, and a very fine grist-mill, which is in a hollow half a mile beyond his barn. The mill is by far the best of its kind in the district; but, unfortunately, the supply of water is not sufficient for such a combination of machinery, which includes all the latest improvements.

"Cape Despair, which shelters the Cove to the westward, is a comparatively low head land, and is said to have been originally called *Cap d'Espoir*, or Cape Hope. The lugubrious change of name is reported to have been caused by the total loss thereon of an English man-of-war, or transport, carrying troops, forming portions of Sir Hovenden Walker's squadron."*

Shortly after the repulse before Quebec, in 1690, of Sir William Phipps (whose expedition had cost the British £100,-000), the Earl of Sunderland, then Secretary of State, determined to make another attempt to dislodge the French from their strong position at Quebec. The armament intended for this object, in 1707, was entrusted to General Macartney; but the defeat of the allied forces at Alamanza compelled Queen Anne to help her ally, Charles III. King of Spain, and General Macartney, instead of sailing for Quebec, was sent to Portugal.

----

* Pye's Gaspé Scenery.

Four years after (1711) General Nicholson, a provincial officer, who had just taken possession of Nova Scotia, having suggested the plan of the campaign, five thousand troops from England and two thousand Provincials were placed under the command of General Hill, brother to the Queen's favorite, Mrs. Masham; the naval force being commanded by Admiral Walker, a dash was made for old Quebec; the great disaster which befell on the 22nd August, 1711, was caused chiefly by fog.

Let us say a word of this famous spot :—Our readers are, no doubt, aware that this stormy cape has furnished food for many antiquarian disquisitions. On some old maps, it is marked as Cape Hope, *Spei;* on more recent ones as Cape Despair. It certainly turned out as the latter to Admiral Hovenden Walker's distracted fleet, in 1711. The English Armada, which that year was going to annihilate French power in Canada, came to grief, like the Spanish Armada, destined to invade the British soil. I have already noticed the curious mutations which many names have experienced on the Gaspé coast. Free translations have played the de-il with more than one. We may add to Pointe de Monts, Cape Chatte ; l'Anse au Gris Fonds—the Cove with the grey bottom, made into Griffin's Cove ; Mille Roches, converted into Mill Rush, &c. A most curious instance of free translation was recently mentioned by the Burlington *Free Press.* That journal, alluding to the murder lately committed at St. Albans, by John Bishop, says :—

"The French-Canadian papers made bad work of the late Bishop tragedy in St. Albans. Finding the announcement in English that 'John Bishop, of St. Albans, in a fit of jealousy, shot his wife and himself,' one of the French papers translated it for its own columns as follows : '*Jean, Evêque de St. Albans, dans un accès de jalousie, a tué sa femme !*' The *Franco-Canadien* took this up, and, as it would never do to have it supposed for an instant that a bishop of the Church of Rome was married, made all plain by making it read, 'The Protestant Bishop of St. Albans,' etc. The *Minerve* next gave this news as direct from St. Albans, as follows: 'The Protestant Bishop of this city shot his wife and himself. He was killed, and his wife is not expected to recover.' And the *Daily News* brought up the rear with the curious version that 'a murder and suicide took place yesterday at St. Albans. In a fit of jealousy, a man killed himself and afterwards killed his wife.' "

———

Legendary as well as antiquarian lore surrounds the hoary and frowning Cape with a maze of romance.

Queen Anne sent in 1711, as aforesaid, a powerful fleet, with seven or eight thousand troops, to kill off forever French power in Canada. A most violent storm arose, dispersed the Armada, and eight of the vessels were lost, with every soul on board, in the Gulf of St Lawrence, chiefly on Egg Island. It is supposed that the fragments of the wreck, generally known as *Le Naufrage Anglais*, seen until of late years on Cap d'Espoir, as related by the Abbé Ferland, belonged to one of these ships. Mr. Pye* sums up this incident as follows: " To this tradition of the sad disaster which probably is substantially correct, superstition has added wild and supernatural visions, which haunted the imaginations of the fishermen of the last, and of the early part of the present century. Something after this style:—When the surface of the treacherous deep was smooth as a mirror, mountain waves would suddenly appear, bearing on their foaming crest a phantom ship crowded with human beings, whose antique military dress denoted that they belonged to a by-gone age. On her bow is seen the tall figure of one whose mien and dress denote that he is a superior officer. One foot resting on the bowsprit, in an attitude as though he were prepared to spring ashore, with his right hand he appears to point out the dark cape to the helmsman, whilst on his left arm he supports a female figure clad in white flowing robes. With wild and light-

———

* Pye's Gaspé Scenery.

ning speed the doomed bark rushes to destruction, as though urged on by some invisible and supernatural agency.   One mighty crash—a wild cry of despair in which is plainly distinguished the voice of a woman—and all is over.   The phantom ship with her living freight has disappeared beneath the roaring surge."

CHAPTER VI.

The Early History of Percé—The Rock as Viewed by Naturalists—Two Rival Republics—What May Lead to War.

A short drive over tolerable roads and rather dangerous bridges brought me from Cape Cove to Percé—the shire town, or *chef-lieu*, of the Gaspé district, a very old settlement.

In 1534, Jacques Cartier visited Percé, and gave the name of "Cap de Pres," either to Percé Rock or to Mont Joli. Ever since the end of the sixteenth century this spot continued to be frequented by the French—most successful fishermen, who there found every species of facility to cure and dry codfish. Probably they followed in the wake of Cartier. Subsequently to the foundation of Quebec, Champlain, on different occasions, sent boats to Percé, either to procure stores and provisions, or to take advantage of the vessels on their return to France each fall, to convey letters.

Jean Nicholas Denys, having obtained from the Company of New France a grant of all the sea coast which skirts the Gulf of St. Lawrence, from Canseau, in Acadia, to Cap des Rosiers, paid a visit to his domains and attempted to turn them to advantage. He sent some vessels to Percé, but with indifferent success, as he could not personally superintend his ventures—in fact, matters turned out so bad that he was ruined. The French Government, in order to help him out of trouble, and also to meet the demands of several shipowners, re-annexed to the royal domain this immense extent of country, and by way of indemnity, granted to his son, Richard Denys de Fronsac, lands in the Bay and on the river of Miramichi. Later on, De Fronsac obtained the grant of Percé and of the adjoining territory, where he induced seven or eight families to establish themselves, but this small population of residents was scarcely noticeable amongst the five or six hundred fishermen who arrive there each summer for the annual catch of fish. The Bishop of Laval deemed it worth his while to look after the spiritual wants of this remote portion of his flock. In 1673 he entrusted this mission to the Recollet Fathers, who erected a chapel at Percé—another at Bonaventure Island, which chapel was called Sainte Claire. To the two first missionaries succeeded, in 1675, Father Chretien Le Clercq, who wrote on Canada two works now scarce : " *La Gaspésie—Le Prémier Etablissement de la Foi dans la Nouvelle-France.*" After William of Orange had assumed the sceptre of his father-in-law, James II., English ship-owners took advantage of the hostile feelings which sprang up between France and England to destroy the French settlements in America, and to attempt to seize on Canada. Percé was attacked without a moment's warning. Father Jumeau relates as follows this thrilling episode of the war, which took place in August, 1690 :

" Two British men-of-war appeared under French colors in the roadstead of Bonaventure Island, and by this stratagem easily captured five fishing vessels, whose captains and crews, entirely engaged with the fishery, had to make for Quebec, not being able to defend their ships. The enemy landed . . . pillaged, sacked and burnt the houses of the inhabitants—some eight or ten families, who, for the most part, had already taken refuge in the woods . . . . I am seized with horror at the bare memory of the impiety . . . . which those miscreants committed in our church, which they had converted into a guard-house. They broke and trampled under feet our images. The paintings representing the Holy Virgin and St. Peter were both pierced by more than one hundred and fifty gun shots . . . . Not a cross escaped their fury, with

the exception of the one I had formerly planted on Rolland's
Table, (*Table à Rolland*) which, from its height on a nearly
inaccessible mountain, still subsists as a monument of our Chris-
tianity . . . . They set fire to the four corners of our
church, which was soon consumed, as well as the church of our
Bonaventure Island Mission."

The Abbé Ferland, to whom I am indebted for these interesting details, draws a lively sketch of the death-like stillness
which pervades the settlement during the lonely winter months,
and the awakening bustle, stir, and cheerfulness which the return of the ships brings with it in May.   A poet's fancy might,
indeed, revel in the sight, and find therein a congenial theme.

" At peep of day," says he, "you see the shore swarming with
stalwart Jersey lads, in their blue smocks, or shirts, worn over
their pants, busy launching their light boats for a long and
sometimes a dangerous day's cruise; in a minute or two the
sunlit ocean seems all studded with snowy specks—a whole
fleet of swift fishing-smacks, with their white sails filling to the
last breath of the land breeze, like a flock of vernal birds winging their flight over the glad waters towards some fairyland in
the blue distance—the return of the venturesome crew from the
dreaded Orphan's Bank*—some three or four hundred, with the
last of the sea breeze, at eventide," each proclaiming his success
with boisterous mirth, loud shouts, love ditties wafted—they
would wish—to that bright isle, their native land, their Eden,
far in the East, where more than one ' black-eyed Susan sighs for
their return, they hope.'

But enough for Percé; as may be observed, it has its lights
and shadows.

Let us again translate from our old friend's journal—the
Abbé Ferland.   Here is one of his delightful chromos of Percé

---

* The Orphan's Bank, which is far out at sea, is not visited by all. A
violent wind from the land may blow out the boats to sea. The fate of
many in the past—a watery grave—must be the result. Hence the name.

Rock and its airy inhabitants—the gulls and cormorants. More than once, have I myself watched their curious proceedings :—

" From the windows of the parish priest's residence one can see distinctly the green plateau of Percé Rock. It is strewed with conspicuous objects, which at times seem to move, at others are stationary—the winged denizens of this retreat ; some are busy hatching their eggs, whilst others are on guard to protect the newly-born young. This airy city is divided into two wards : one is occupied by the Gulls (the Herring Gull) and the other by the Cormorants. If any member of one tribe presumes to wander beyond the boundary of those of his feather, such an encroachment is not silently borne. A formidable outcry, of one thousand voices, pervades the air, and is heard sometimes at a distance of several miles. A cloud like a heavy storm of snow hovers over the spot tainted by the presence of the stranger. If the invaders should be in numbers, a column detaches itself from the innumerable inhabitants of the threatened territory, and describing a half circle rushes to attack the rear of the enemy. As the defenders of the soil are always formidable and fierce on their native land, the strangers are compelled to withdraw and shrink from the blows and shrieks of their adversaries."

This border warfare causes frequent encounters ; scarcely a quarter of an hour elapses without one's being aware from the loud cries that Discord has let fly her shafts.

The two republics, whose territory combined covers about two acres in superficies, were of yore protected by the steepness of the rock, and lived secure far from the reach of man.

The paternal nest was bequeathed from one generation to the next. The Gulls and Cormorants educated their children at the identical spot where they themselves had sprung from the shell into this wicked world.

This world, however, was undergoing changes. It was, 'tis true, above, always the same sky ; around, the same sea, roaring and lashing the solid foundations of their citadel, and covering

with the foam of its mountainous waves, the beaches of the two
adjoining coves. But, close by, a few hundred yards away, the
world was not the same. The forest was cut down; smoke rose
over roofs inhabited by the white man; the shore had ceased to
be solitary; the surf bore on its crest, vessels with white sails
and long masts. The republic was in danger; her fisheries were
invaded by barbarians, who, on more occasions than one, had
shed the blood of the ancient denizens of the rock. After all, if
it did become prudent to go and catch fish at a greater distance,
cormorants and gulls could equally eat it in safety from the
inaccessible summit of their habitation. Fallacious hope! for
gulls as well as for men, nothing on earth exists free from
change. About the year 1805, that is some thousands of years
after the establishment here of the descendant of the first gull,
two foolhardy fishermen resolved to scale the fortress which,
so far, had been considered impreguable. . . . A single point
seemed to offer a chance of success. Near one of the arches,
about forty feet above the base, the rock forms a point, and
underneath the ascent, seems more practicable. But the fearless fishermen chose another, through bravado; it might have
scared a chamois. With oars tied together, and leaning on the
surface of the rock, they managed to climb the most steep portion, and then, by hanging on to projections and shrubs, they ac-
tually got to the top.

It was indeed a glorious feat, this ascent of the rock by Duguay and Moriarty—for the first time. It is true there was a
vague tradition that on certain occasions a youth of herculean
proportions and preternatural appearance had been seen on the
top; but these superstitious tales merely served to exhibit in
more vivid colors the venturesome spirit of the mortals who had
dared to brave the *Genius* of Percé Rock, and beard him in his
inaccessible den.

The feat suggested to these two men by the love of distinction was prompted in others by motives of interest and the rage of
imitation; once the path was known, one-half of the difficulties

disappeared. Each year the eggs and young birds were robbed. At first the presence of man disturbed the old birds so little that they often remained on the nest until removed. Fortunately a by-law of the magistrates of Percé, prohibiting these practices, has restored the peaceable inhabitants of the Rock to their hearths and homes. The loud cries of these birds, heard from afar, have more than once been of great help to boats or ships caught in the fog near Percé; they were excellent fog whistles and beacons to the benighted mariner.

CHAPTER VII.

Percé—The Percé Rock—Mont Joli—Bonaventure Island—Captain Duval—The Celebrated Privateer,
"Vulture."

"The Village of Percé, which derives its name from the Rock,
is most advantageously situated for the cod fishery. It consists
of two small coves, called North and South Beach. The principal
part of the population reside at North Beach, which also contains
the court-house, jail, and Roman Catholic church. South Beach
is chiefly occupied by the important fishing establishment of
Messrs. Charles Robin & Co., who own the principal part of the
land on that side. The two coves are separated by a headland
called Mont Joli, supposed by some to have been once united
with the Rock. On this promontory formerly stood the Protestant Episcopal church, and the graveyard still marks the spot.
The population of Percé does not exceed five hundred souls,
except during the summer months, when it is more than
doubled. It is the shire town of the County of Gaspé.

"Few spots, if any, on the sea-board of Canada possesses greater
attraction for the artist and lover of wild and romantic scenery
than Percé and its environs. Mont Ste. Anne, in rear of the
village, rising almost abruptly to the height of 1300 feet, is the
first land sighted by all vessels coming up the Gulf to the south-
ward of the Island of Anticosti. In clear weather it may be seen
at a distance of sixty to seventy miles, and it is even confidently
asserted by shipmasters worthy of credit that it has been seen by
them at a distance of seventy-five to eighty miles.

"If you ascend the high road towards the settlement called
' French Town,' and stand on the rising ground in rear of Belle-

vue, you have beneath you, and all around, one of the most magnificent panoramas the eye can wish to rest upon. Ste. Anne, rising in all its towering majesty on your left, and extending to the eastward, forms within Barry Head a portion of an amphitheatre, almost enclosing the village on two sides. The Roman Catholic church is a striking object at the foot of Barry Head. Over and beyond this, at a distance of six miles, is seen Point St. Peter and Plateau. To the right of this nothing is seen but the sea as far as the eye can reach. Then comes the Rock, which you overlook from this point. The birds (gulls and cormorants) on its summit can also be distinctly seen."

A romantic legend, alluded to by the Abbé Ferland, attaches to the Percé Rock—we regret we have not space for it.

I have myself seen the snow-white gulls sitting in myriads on their nests on this green summit in July. You might have imagined the froth of the sea or gigantic snow-flakes spread amidst verdant pastures—a most attractive spectacle to the eye of a naturalist.

" The Island of Bonaventure then forms the foreground. But to the westward of that again the sea meets the eye, until it rests on Cape Despair, and you get a bird's-eye view of Cape Cove and L'Anse a Beau-Fils. From this point you have a most extensive sea view down the Gulf and to the entrance of the Bay of Chaleurs, the light on the Island of Miscou, New Brunswick, distant about thirty-two miles, being often seen on a clear night.

" Leaving those lower regions, if you undertake to ascend Mont Ste. Anne—no very difficult task for those who are free from gout and asthma—a view presents itself to the astonished eye, grand beyond description. All that we have just described lies in one vast panorama at our feet. In rear, that is, from west to north, the variegated green of the primeval forest meets the eye, which seeks in vain some oasis, as it were, in the boundless green expanse on which to rest. Hill and dale, mountain and valley, all clad in the same verdant garb, extend as far as the human ken can range. Casting your eye gradually eastward,

you see over the land into the Gaspé Bay, and beyond Ship Head
into the mouth of the St. Lawrence ; then, far away to seaward
down the Gulf; to the right, up the Bay of Chaleurs. If the
weather is clear, besides a number of large vessels, the white sails
of a fleet of schooners, chiefly American, of from 40 to 150 tons,
and amounting sometimes to some two or three hundred sail,
may be seen engaged in the cod and mackerel fisheries. From
this point nothing obstructs the view, which extends over Bonaventure Island and all the headlands on either side, and on a
fine calm day two hundred open boats, spread over the bosom of
the treacherous deep, look like small specks upon the surface of
a mirror. Taken as a whole, we know of no scenery in the British Provinces to equal this.

" The drive or walk round the mountain to the corner of the
beach is most romantic, as well as the sail round the Island of
Bonaventure, and should on no account be omitted by the
excursionist. The road through the mountain gorge, which is
the highway connecting Percé with Gaspé Basin, must have
some resemblance to many portions of Swiss scenery.

" Percé possesses two places of worship. That of the Church of
England is situated on an eminence at the foot of the mountain
on the Irish Town road. It is built in the Gothic style, and
though very small, being only capable of containing one hundred persons, yet it is one of the neatest and most complete
village churches we have seen on this continent. The Protestant
community are mainly indebted to Messrs. Charles Robin & Co.
for its erection. The Roman Catholic Church is a large building, and when the interior is finished off, it will be a very handsome structure.

" Percé is strictly a large fishing-stand—the best in Canada—
and it is here that the Messrs. Robin have their most extensive
fishing establishment. We believe we are justified in stating that
there is nothing to equal it, as a whole, in Canada, New Brunswick, or Nova Scotia. This establishment collects yearly from
14,000 to 15,000 quintals of codfish, fit for shipment, including

what they receive from their planters and dealers throughout the township of Percé.

"Percé was for some time the residence of Lieut-Governor Cox, who was appointed Governor of Gaspé about 1785. The site of the Government House may still be seen."—Pye's *Gaspé Scenery.*

The foregoing is certainly a glowing, and so far as I know, a truthful picture of Percé, with the exception as to what relates to the date of appointment of Lieut.-Governor Cox. According to Colonel Caldwell's letter * to General James Murray, bearing date 15th June, 1776, Major Cox, formerly of the 47th, was at that time Lieut.-Governor of Gaspé.

Percé, notwithstanding its picturesque scenery, never had for me one-half of the attractions of Gaspé Basin. It must, however, have had some attractions, even in ancient days, since Monseigneur St. Vallier, who stopped there on his voyage from France to Quebec in 1685, was induced to revisit it in the spring of 1686. One is quite safe in considering it a large fishing-stand—in fact the grandest on the coast—the kingdom of cod, herring, and train oil—the Elysium of fishermen. During the busy months, codfish in every shape, in every stage of preservation or putrefaction, scents the air—especially in August. The pebbly beach is strewn and begemmed with codfish drying; the flakes glisten with it in the morning sun, whilst underneath plethoric maggots attain a wonderful size. The shore is studded with fish heads and fish offal in a lively state of decomposition. Cod heads and caplin are liberally used to manure the potato fields : the air is tainted with the effluvia ; the land breeze wafts you odors which are not those of " Araby

---

* This old letter, published in 1866, under the auspices of the " Literary and Historical Society of Quebec "—page 10—contains the following passage :—

" On my way I passed by the picket drawn up under the Field Officer of that day, who was Major Cox, formerly of the 47th, and now Lieut-Governor of Gaspé."

the Blest." Well-to-do houses in some localities have a fishy smell. The churches are not proof against it. Not many years back, the R. C. Bishop, visiting the chapel on a fishing station, on entering, exclaimed to the pastor, " Is the chapel used to dry and cure codfish? The smell here is positively dreadful!" "No, my lord," the pastor replied; "but at the news of your approach my parishioners had the floor carefully washed with soap. Unfortunately, the soap was made from fish oil." The historian Ferland relates the anecdote.

Even potatoes chime in with the general homage to the finny tribe; some have been known to grow with bones in them. A lady friend of mine made this her principal grievance against Percé. She left it in high dudgeon. Being a judge's lady, I have often wondered why she did not apply to the Court for a writ of injunction against this intolerable nuisance.

The safest place to be out of the reach of the fishy aroma is out at sea. But though there be fish everywhere—in the sea—on the land—in the churches—in the air, you may feel like the Ancient Mariner,

> " Water, water, everywhere, nor any drop to drink."

It was my ill-fortune once to see fish everywhere, and still none to eat.

My landlady met my repeated enquiry for fresh fish for dinner, with some studied apologies about the weather. " The boats could not go out," " the wind was so high," and so on. I reluctantly came to the conclusion that at times it requires a deal of interest to get fresh codfish for dinner at Percé, unless you are an M. P. P.

It is, notwithstanding, a healthy location. Strong smells, though they may press hard on the olfactory nerves, don't kill. The citizens of Petrolia, 'tis said, are long livers.

Hon. John LeBoutillier,* M. S. C., and Mr. Frs. Lebrun have extensive fishery establishments here. Hon. J. LeBoutillier resides at Gaspé Basin.

° This worthy old Gaspesian closed his career in July, 1872.

Percé has latterly been selected in preference to Gaspé Basin as the shire-town (*chef-lieu*). A new court-house and jail are in process of erection. The most prosy highwayman or debased murderer once duly convicted, will enjoy the privilege of being duly hanged in view of all the magnificent scenery just mentioned by Mr. Pye. I am sorry for it, on account of the genial and educated sheriff (Vibert) of the district, whose acquaintance I had not the good fortune to make.

BONAVENTURE ISLAND.

"This island, in the depth of winter, has the appearance of a vast iceberg, and like the Percé Rock, is one of Nature's wonderful productions, forming a natural break-water between the South Cove, Percé and the Gulf. The whole is one vast mass of reddish conglomerate, from which the term Bonaventure Formation has been derived. It appears as though it had been upheaved from the bottom of the ocean, forming on the seaside, towards the Gulf, a stupendous wall 300 to 500 feet high, with no less than fifty fathoms of water at its base. It slopes gradually towards the mainland, and is well settled, there being a R. C. church, a school-house, and some twenty dwelling-houses. It is two and a half miles long, and three-quarters of a mile broad, and is distant two and a half miles from the mainland. The depth of water is sufficient for the largest ships afloat to beat through the channel. Messrs. LeBoutillier Brothers have a large fishery establishment on the island, at which thirty-eight boats and about 120 men are employed. This was once the property of the late Captain Peter Duval, a native of the island of Jersey, and one whose deeds and prowess would not disgrace the annals of England's history. Yet, strange to say, there appears to be no record preserved by the family of a feat scarcely to be surpassed. The grandson of our hero, who still resides on the island, knows nothing of the leading facts, which are as follows :

"Towards the close of the last war between England and France, Captain Duval commanded a privateer, lugger-rigged,

D

mounting four guns, with a crew of twenty-seven hands, himself included, and owned by the Messrs. Janvrin, of Jersey. She was a small vessel, under 100 tons, and appropriately named the 'Vulture,' having been the terror of the French coast from St. Malo to the Pyrenees. The 'Vulture' was almost as well known along the shores of the Bay of Biscay as in her port of registry, and like a bird of prey was continually hovering along the coast, capturing vessel after vessel. The port of Bayonne had suffered severely from the continued depredations of the Jersey privateer off its entrance, and the merchants of the place resolved to make an effort to capture their tormentor. A joint stock company was formed, and a suitable vessel obtained, a brig of about 180 tons, which being mounted with sixteen guns, and manned by a crew of eighty men, awaited the return of the 'Vulture.' That vessel having been seen off the port one fine afternoon, the brig slipped out during the night, disguised as much as possible, so as to be taken for a merchant-vessel, and being sighted early on the following morning by the lugger's look-out, the latter immediately gave chase and soon came up with what she supposed would be an easy prize. The reader, however, may conceive her astonishment when, on running alongside of the brig, the ports were opened and every preparation made for action. On seeing this the first lieutenant of the 'Vulture,' Captain LeFeuvre, told Captain Duval that having no chance against such perfect odds, their only alternative was to strike. 'Strike!' he exclaimed with an oath. 'So long as I have a leg to stand on we shall fight. If I am knocked off my pins, you take command, and do as you please.' The vessels immediately engaged, the 'Vulture' keeping so close to her antagonist that the shot from the latter could not take effect owing to her great length. Meantime the lugger continued to pour into the brig a well-directed fire of grape-shot, cutting her rigging, and killing and wounding half of the French crew. The captain of the brig, knowing the determined character of his opponent, and expecting that he would attempt to board, made for Bayonne. The lugger gave chase, but night coming on, the brig reached port in safety. Of the lugger's crew, only one was killed and two of them slightly wounded; Captain Duval stating that with ten hands he would have taken the brig by boarding, but he feared to attempt it against such fearful odds. The Protestant burial-ground on Mont Joli contains the remains of this brave man, who attained a ripe old age."—Pye's *Gaspé Scenery.*

CHAPTER VIII.

Point St. Peter—The Light of Other Days—The Irrepressible Memories of the Past—Belle Anse—Douglastown Portage—The Black Pool and its Legends.

The preferable mode of travel from Percé to Gaspé Basin is
decidedly by water in summer—the land route being of a peculiarly primitive order, trying alike to man and beast. On
leaving the great shire-town, the highway winds round the hills
in rear of the Ste. Anne range—a distance of several miles—
until you reach a sand bank, which divides the sea from the
lagoon. It is called the corner of the beach; *vulgo*, "Corny
Beach."

The scenery through the mountain gorge is truly grand, and
the contemplation of its beauties will more than compensate the
tourist for the difficulties of the road. About a mile from the
highest point, you pass immediately by the base of a stupendous wall of conglomerate, which appears as though it had been
upheaved by another Atlas. There are indications all round Percé
that, at some distant period, the mountains have been rent, and
vast masses dislodged from their original position by some
violent convulsion of nature.

A few miles out of Percé the country assumes a level appearance. The mountain ranges gradually disappear from the back-
ground. . . . . . The roads in the Township of Percé
are decidedly the worst in the County of Gaspé, and most of
the bridges are in a very dangerous state, being without railings
or guard of any kind to prevent the traveller from being precipitated into the abyss below.

The bay, at Mal Baie, is a splendid sheet of water, bounded
by Percé on the one side, and Point St. Peter on the other.

. . . . . Before reaching it, one has to cross the Mal
Baie stream—a good river for salmon and trout-fishery—by
means of a scow.

At Belle Anse, in Mal Baie, the high road leads to the portage
at right angles, branching off to Point St. Peter on the right and
towards Douglastown on the left. The same drizzly weather
followed me through this Avernian avenue, called the Portage—
a dismal drive during the silent hours of night.

Reluctantly had I to forego the sweet, though at times melancholy, satisfaction, of revisiting old, familiar places : Point
St. Peter and its hospitable shores. The irrepressible memories
of other days still persisted in enshrining it in a bright halo.
Right well can I recall Point St. Peter; its pebbly beaches; its
symmetric long rows of boats, anchored, at night-fall, in straight
line—in view of each fishing-station—all dancing merrily on the
crest of the curling billows ; its fearless, song-loving, blue-
smocked Jersey fishermen. Can I ever forget its storm-lashed
reef ; its crumbling cliffs ; its dark caves, made vocal at each easterly blow with the wild discord of the sea? Plateau, its foam-
crowned ledges, surrounded by noisy sea fowl ! Where now the
leading men of Point St. Peter I knew of yore ? Where the
Johnstons, Creightons, Packwoods, Collas, Alexanders of thirty
years ago ? Gone, one and all, or nearly so, to their long home.
Some reposing in yonder lone churchyard, on the brow of the
hill in rear; others, placed by loving hands, in their marble
tombs under the shade of their own fairy island of Jersey,
sleeping the long sleep. Of some, scarcely a trace left amongst
men ; of others, stalwart sons worthily perpetuating the names
of their respected sires. Possibly, some yet forgotten behind on
this green earth of ours—a few, a very few.

Point St. Peter brought back vividly to my mind a most
harrowing memory of my youth—the untimely death, under
peculiarly painful circumstances, of an early friend ; it reads thus
in my boyish diary :

" It is the hour of noon on a dreamy August day, 1843. A

loving father is detailing to me long-pondered domestic arrangements, cherished hopes, carefully laid-out plans of family
advancement.   One above others, in the happy family group, he
seems to doat on—though he named him not—a bright boy of
eleven summers, venturesome, full of spirit and intelligence, my
daily companion in the boat or with the gun, though by several
years, my junior.   Of the five blooming children, the lights of his
home, on this one seemed to centre all the hopes of the fond
parent.

The light-hearted youth, humming a song, shot past me—
whilst I remained conversing with his father—on his way to our
oft-frequented fishing-ground, near the wharf, beckoning to me
not to delay ; but I did delay.   I tarried, as I was wont, listening to the frank discourse of his excellent, true-hearted father.
I tarried behind.   .   .   .   Alas ! why had I not followed on.
An hour later and I am re-entering the portals of this once
happy home, helping to carry a livid corpse—that of my late
companion.

It was I who discovered him—dead, quite dead, reclining on
his side—softly sleeping beneath the green, transparent waves,
at the spot where he and I, had so oft enjoyed our favorite
pastime : angling for cod and halibut.   A trusty servant and
myself, in silence, are laying on a little bed, in full view of the
horror-stricken but not unsubmissive father, what now remaines
of so much bright promise, youth and hope.   All this is now
happening at this very spot."

The sorrowing father (he died in 1846) was the late Henry
Bissett Johnston, a highly-educated Scotch gentleman of Point
St. Peter.   I can recall it all as a scene of yesterday, though
it occurred close on thirty years ago ; but let us hie away.   .   .   .

The portage road from Mal Baie to Douglastown, on a murky
September night, reminds one of the Cimmerian gloom with
which Virgil surrounds the abodes of souls in Hades.   If you
are of an enquiring turn of mind, kind reader, gifted with a robust
constitution, unappalled by jolting, it will be worth your while

to go and see for yourself. At midway, a dark bridge spans a brawling brook still darker in aspect. White foam floats about the black pool at your feet, at the sight of which your horse snorts and draws back. More than one goblin story is told of this dreary spot. On my asking my companion whether he could discover the bridge through the gloom which the shadows of the tall surrounding trees deepened into absolute darkness,—

"No," said he, "but I can hear the roar of the brook, and my horse knows the way, though horses have been more than once scared by some awful screams heard here at night."

"You have," I replied, "been the mail-carrier for some time. Have you ever heard these noises?"

"Never," said he, "but my uncle's horse did, some years ago. A murder, 'tis related, occurred at this bridge many years since; and you know," he added, with emphasis, "horses at night can see things which are hidden from men."

"I cannot," I replied, "charge my memory with an instance of the kind happening to me during my travels." I found that Superstition could assert her sway at the Douglastown Portage as well as on Hounslow Heath, near London—wherever a deed of blood in fact dwells in the memory of man.

CHAPTER IX.

Shipwreck of Sir Hovenden Walker's Squadron on Egg Island, 22nd August, 1711—Loss of Eight Transports, with 884 Men—Particulars of the Equipment of this Formidable Armada—Attack on Placentia Projected—Return of Fleet to England—Persecution of the Luckless Admiral—His Death in 1725, in South Carolina.

> There lieth a wreck on the dismal shore
> Of cold and pitiless Labrador,
> Where, under the moon, upon mounts of frost,
> Full many a mariner's bones are tossed.
>
> *Tom Moore*, 1804.

In the path of inward bound ships, on the North Shore of the Lower St. Lawrence, lies a desolate isle—of granite formation—about two miles in length. The lonely summit is surmounted by a white wooden light-house, with a revolving white light, visible at fifteen miles, and completing its evolution in a minute and a half.

Had its fitful glare shone on these waters one hundred and ten years ago, it might possibly, in spite of ignorant pilots, have preserved from a watery grave many hundreds of British tars and soldiers, and saved from pain and humiliation a proud British Admiral. That stormy, disastrous August night (the 22nd) of 1711, has indeed become memorable.*

---

* " A journal, or full account of the late expedition to Canada, with an appendix containing commissions, orders, instructions, letters, &c., by Sir Hovenden Walker, Kt., London, printed by D. Browne, at the Black Swan, W. Mears at the Lamb, without Temple Bar, and G. Strahan at the Golden Ball against the Exchange in Cornhill, 1720."

The repulse before Quebec, in 1690, of Sir William Phipps had not been forgotten in England. In 1708, an attempt had been made to obliterate the memory of this stinging disaster, but war breaking out in Europe, Gen. McCartney's troops were sent to Portugal instead of Quebec. Queen Anne revived the idea three years later, viz.: in 1711. England wished to crown by naval success the splendid victories achieved on land by the great captain of the age—Marlborough.

On the 11th April, 1711, about 7 p.m., Rear-Admiral of the White, Sir Hovenden Walker,* accompanied by Brigadier-General the Hon. John Hill, commander of the land forces, for the intended Canada expedition, waited on the Queen, at the Palace of St. James, to receive their instructions from Her Majesty.

Once in possession of his sealed orders, the Admiral hurried to Portsmouth, arrived next at Spithead, where a variety of delays, some caused by contrary winds, others by unforeseen

---

° Sir Hovenden Walker's squadron comprised the following : Flag ship the *Edgar*, 70 guns ; *Windsor*, 60 guns ; *Montague*, 60 guns ; *Swiftsure*, 70 guns ; *Sunderland*, 60 guns ; *Monmouth*, 70 guns ; *Dunkirk*, 60 guns ; *Humber*, 80 guns ; *Devonshire*, 80 guns.

Transports :—*Recovery, Delight, Eagle, Fortune, Reward, Success, Pink, Willing Mind, Rose, Life, Happy Union, Queen Anne, Resolution, Marlborough, Samuel, Pheasant, Three Martins, Smyrna Merchant, Globe, Colchester, Nathaniel and Elizabeth, Samuel and Anne, George, Isabella and Catherine, Blenheim, Chatham, Blessing, Rebecca, Samuel, Blessing, Goodwill, Anna, Marlborough, Dolphin, Two Sheriffs, Sarah, Rebecca Anne, Prince, Eugene, Dolphin, Mary, Herbin Galley, Friend's Increase, Anna, Susannah and Thomas, Barbadoes, Anchor and Hope, Adventure, Content, John and Mary, Speedwell, Baselisk, Granada (Bowles), John and Sarah, Margaret.*

New England Transports : *Dispatch, Four Friends, Francis, John and Hannah, Henrietta, Blessing, Antelope, Hannah and Elizabeth, Friend's Adventure, Rebecca, Martha and Hannah, Johannah, Unity, Newcastle.*

Enterprise, 40 guns ; *Sapphire*, 40 guns ; *Kingston*, 60 guns ; *Leopard*, 54 guns ; and *Chester*, 54 guns ; also a prize, the *Triton*, joined the Admiral in the Gulf of St. Lawrence. As to the *Leostoff* and the *Feversham*, both of 36 guns, who formed part of the fleet, no mention of them occurred thereafter.

casualties in the fleet, tried his patience and gave dissatisfaction to his royal mistress.   One day through an omission of the State Secretary, St. John, the captains refused to take orders from any one except from their superior officer, Sir Edward Whitaker, senior in rank to Admiral Walker.   The next, something was wrong in the outfits for the transport service ; at other times, high winds prevented the fleet from putting to sea ; a storm damaged the spars of the *Devonshire*, and the *Swiftsure* lost her topgallant masts.   During these *contretemps*, Secretary St. John, later on Lord Bolingbroke, was despatching to the worried Admiral letter on letter to hurry him on his expedition.   Finally, on the 29th April, 1711, the English fleet bade adieu to the white cliffs of England, and began its voyage towards the gulf of St. Lawrence.   Boston, visited by the Admiral twenty-five years previously, in 1686, was the port of rendezvous.   The object of the expedition was a dead secret for the twelve thousand men carried on the fleet—for all except the Admiral and the General.   At one hundred and fifty-three leagues from the Scilly Isles, the flag ship hove to, and the letter containing the sealed orders where every ship was to meet, was distributed to each commander.   Despite all that secrecy, the object of the expedition had leaked out.   On the 3rd of May, Sir H. Walker, having been compelled by stress of weather to anchor at Plymouth, whilst the transports sought protection at Catwater, a French sailor of the Medway, a renegade, who pretended to have made four trips to a Canada river, having learned in one of the city tap-rooms that an English fleet, destined for the capture of Canada, was now ready to sail, had his services offered to the Admiral to pilot the fleet to Quebec.   Walker, amazed at the discovery, tried to dissemble, pretending that he was bent merely on a cruise in the Bay of Biscay ; he had him, however, shipped on board of the *Humber*, with orders that he should be well treated.   The French renegade must have much relished his good fortune.   Later on in August, Col. Vetch, writing to the Admiral from Canso, states :

, AUGUST, 1711, at sea.

"SIR,—I could not but judge it my duty to give you a caution with regard to your French pilot, whom I would have you by no means depend upon, for I find him to be not only an ignorant, pretending, idle, drunken fellow, but fear he is come on no good design.

"Sir, yours devoted to serve you,

SAM. VETCH.

The admiral had much reliance on the experience of this Palinurus, to escape the dangers besetting the ascent of the St. Lawrence; some of these dangers appear to have been rather over-estimated. Col. Vetch's caution was no doubt timely. But trouble and vexation was besetting Walker on all sides. He was scarcely out at sea when it was discovered that the transport *Mary*, conveying a portion of Col. Desney's regiment, had been forgotten at Catwater. During a stormy night, the mizzen mast of the *Monmouth* broke like a reed. The frigates were constantly shortening sail to wait for the unwieldy transports; sometimes tow-ropes had to be thrown out to them; when it was indispensable to consult with Gen. Hill, who was on board the *Devonshire*, it was found that sea-sickness had so disordered the hero that he could not answer the letters with his own hand. Discipline itself was occasionally forgotten. In spite of the strict orders for the vessels of the fleet to remain together, one night, on nearing the Banks of Newfoundland, the *Dunkirk* and *Edgar* started in chase of a small vessel in the offing. An example was necessary. The Captain of the *Edgar*, Soams, and the Captain of the *Devonshire*, Butler, were both tried; one was condemned to lose three months' pay; the other, cashiered.

At last, on the 25th June, after a passage of fifty-eight days, Admiral Walker cast anchor in the harbour of Boston, where brilliant entertainments, as well as frequent annoyances, awaited him. On landing in New England, Sir Hovenden was the lion of the Colony: on the 4th July, he had to preside at the opening of the courses at Cambridge University ; on the 5th and 10th of the same month, he witnessed, on Noddles' Island, a grand review of the land and sea forces, which took place under Gen. Hill.

On the 24th, he hastened to Roxbury, to inspect a regiment destined for the Canada expedition. A series of dinners and balls took place on the 19th and 23rd July, on board of the *Humber*, in honour of the Indian Sachem of Connecticut, and also in honour of the Mohawk Indians admitted on board of the flag-ship, with a salvo of guns, music, cheers, and seamen's dances. The Mohawks treated the English to one of their peculiar dances, and this over, one of them, in the name of the Five Nations, says the Admiral, delivered a long harangue, which the interpreter told me was to this effect, " That they had long expected what they now saw, and were much rejoiced that the Queen had taken such care of them, of which they had almost despaired ; that at this time they would exert themselves in a most extraordinary manner, and hoped that the French in America would now be reduced. They pledged me, and drank the Queen's health, and when they went away I gave them cheers and guns." All these junkettings had an end. Sir Hovenden Walker set to work in earnest to ship stores and provisions to last four months, for 9,385 men, for the Canada expedition.

Walker's Journal contains the following entry under date of 25th July, 1711 : "This morning, a French prize called the *Neptune* was sent by Captain Matthews, which he had taken in his cruise. The mate of her gives an account that a man-of-war of 54 guns, and a store-ship of 30, was to follow them to Quebec in about a month's time. That in a fog they had lost company of two ships of 16 guns each, which came out with them from France. They had come above 100 leagues with Monsieur Duguay (Trouin ?), who had under his command a strong squadron of men-of-war and several transports with soldiers, but where designed for, was a secret. He said they had heard nothing in France of our expedition against Canada, nor thought any-

thing of it ; and that if I pretended to go up that river with this
fleet, I should lose all the ships. The master of the prize, who
was on board the *Chester*, it seems, told Capt. Matthews, as I
am informed, that last year the French lost eight ships out of
nine in that river, and that a great number of ships are cast
away there every year, for which reason the seamen of Rochelle
avoid the voyage as much as possible, and when shipped to Canada have double wages."

Various were the troubles occasioned to the English fleet
while at Boston, by the rapacity of the bakers and public contractors,—the desertion of some of the men,—the damage done
by storms or accidents to the ships, finally by the lukewarmness
of Governor Dudley. A final humiliation awaited the luckless
Admiral. The French pilots, enticed over and picked up all
through New England, refused to join, under frivolous pretexts ;
it required a Government warrant to compel them to do so.

At last, on the 30th July, 1711, the formidable squadron sent
out by England to humble France by the capture of its bulwark
across the Atlantic, left the pass of Nantasket, buoyant with hope.

It is curious to reconcile this hostile expedition with the fact
that England was not then at war with France. A proclamation was prepared ; it read well. We furnish some extracts of
this magniloquent document :

"The French have committed several hostilities against the
subjects of the Kings and Queens of Great Britain, therefore
those lands and territories so possessed by the French do, according to the laws of nature and nations, of right revert to the
Crown of Great Britain, where they originally were ; and it becomes lawful for Her Majesty of Great Britain, although there
were no actual war between Her Majesty and the Most Christian
King, to resume them. . . .

"Yet now, with a most pious intent for preserving for the
future a perpetual and lasting peace in North America . . .
Her Majesty has resolved (under the protection and assistance
of Almighty God), to recover all those said forfeited lands and

territories, and appoint her own Governors in all those several territories, cities, towns, castles and fortifications, where his most Christian Majesty has pretended to settle any.

"And because the French now inhabiting those parts may either out of ignorance or obstinacy, be induced by persons of malignant and turbulent spirits, to resist her Majesty's so good designs, she has thought fit, in reliance on the blessing of God upon her so pious and religious purposes and endeavors, to send such a strength as may by the Divine assistance be sufficient to force a compliance, and reduce all opposers to reason.

" And esteeming all the French who are settled in these said lands and territories, under the pretended title of His Most Christian Majesty, to be as much subjects of the Crown of Great Britain, as if born and settled there, or in Ireland, or in any other of Her Majesty's Colonies, more immediately under her protection, . . .

" It is hereby declared that after any hostilities shall be committed, then we think ourselves free from all these promises, and we shall then have no further regard than, by the assistance of God, to reduce all that resist by military force; trusting in the Almighty that He will favor and succeed her Majesty's arms, in so reasonable, just and religious a design."

This proclamation, duly approved of by Governor Dudley, was translated into French for the benefit of the Canadians.

When off the Coast of Cape Breton, the flagship *Edgar* was joined by the *Chester*, who conveyed to the Admiral what he much wanted—a French pilot for the St. Lawrence. This new Palinurus, by name Paradis,* had made forty voyages to Canada—his capture at this juncture was considered as a special interposition of Providence. Paradis was the master on board a Rochelle ship, the *Neptune*, ten guns, with a crew of seventy men,

---

° I am indebted to M. Faucher for the name of the French pilot; his summary of Walker's Journal in *De Tribord à Babord* I have also frequently used in this sketch, *à tout seigneur, tout honneur.*

thirty of whom were destined for the Garrison of Quebec. This French prize had been taken a few days previous by Captain Mathews, of the *Chester*. Paradis was offered 500 "pistoles" to pilot the English fleet to Quebec, and a provision promised for his declining years. Whether the temptation proved too great for the "ancient mariner?" history does not say. But what we do find recorded is a sombre picture of the dangers of the St. Lawrence drawn by the French pilot. Though the English Admiral at first strove to make light of the advice tendered, it seems to have much disturbed him, later on. In dismal array, like a hideous nightmare, stood before him: Canadian "seas and earth locked up by adamantine forests and swollen by high mountains of snow:" "Brave men famishing with hunger and drawing lots who should die first to feed the rest:" "Men left dead in the march and frozen into statues for their own monuments." (Walker's Journal, page 25.)

"This afternoon, (16th Aug., 1711)," says Walker, "I saw the land, being off Cape Gaspé, and upon sounding had ninety fathoms water.

"This day we saw the Island *Anticosti*. . . . . . That which now took up my thoughts chiefly was contriving how to secure the ships if we got up to Quebec; forseeing it to be impossible for them to leave that place before the winter should be too far advanced, and the only way I could think of was quite to unrig them, take out all their guns, stores, ballast, and even their masts, and with crabbs and machines contrived and made for that purpose, haul up the hulls on the dry ground, to lie shored up and secured in frames and cradles till the thaw ; for the ice in the river freezing to the bottom, would have utterly destroyed and bulged them, as much as if they had been squeezed between rocks." *

We next follow the Admiral up Gaspé Bay, within a harbor, where a French ship from Biscay lay unrigged, waiting to load

---

° Walker's Journal, page 121.

a cargo of fish for Europe. " I sent in," adds the Admiral, " and seized her, intending to rig her out."

On the 19th (August) the *Montague, Leopard* and *Sapphire* cruised off Gaspé; the two latter were to go to Bonaventure Island to destroy or bring away the fishing-boats of the place ; a calm prevented them—the work of devastation fell solely to the brigantines and sloops previously sent.

The French ship captured in the Gaspé harbor was fired, the channel (of the Basin ?) being too intricate to fetch her out. " I, therefore," says he, " ordered her to be burned, as well as the houses and stages ashore, and the men to be brought on board prisoners." This would have taken place, according to the entry in the Admiral's journal, on the 20th August. A Biscay fishing craft burnt—the ashes of a dozen of fishermen's huts—a few boats destroyed on the Gaspé shore ; such were the only trophies left at this spot by the great British Admiral of the White, Sir Hovenden Walker, Knight Commander-in-chief of Queen Anne's Armada.

A stiff breeze brought the fleet out of Gaspé Bay, but a calm and thick fog supervening, the Admiral issued strict orders to keep his vessels together in the fog and drizzly rain.* This weather lasted all that day, the 22nd August ; gusts of wind came on at night ; the fog grew thicker ; the lead gave no bottom, and, as no land had been seen for two days, it was thought that the north shore was far off. At ten that night " we found ourselves," says Admiral Walker, " upon the north shore, amongst rocks and islands, at least fifteen leagues farther than the log gave, when the whole fleet had like to have been lost. But by God's good providence all the men-of-war, though with extreme hazard and difficulty, escaped, eight transports were cast away, and almost

---

* " No commodore is to suffer any ship of his division to go ahead of him, and in case any do, to fire at them ; and the men-of-war in his division, or next to that ship that goes ahead, shall make up sail to get up with her and cause the shot to be paid for by the master."—*Additional Signals and Instructions*, given by Admiral Walker, p. 272.

900 men—officers, soldiers and seamen—lost; and had I not made the signals as I did, but continued sailing, it is a great question whether any ship or men had been saved." (Page 45.)

The *Edgar* had, indeed, a narrow escape. Captain Goddard, by his timely wearing, was mainly instrumental in saving the whole fleet. Paradis, the French pilot, who was asleep below, on reaching the deck, ordered every inch of canvas to be spread on the yards, and the *Edgar*, filling on the opposite tack, escaped the breakers by a few ship's lengths. The *Edgar* wore ship some time after and rejoined the squadron in the morning, meeting the *Swiftsure*. Soon Captain Alexander, of the *Chatham*, communicated the details of the disaster. Eight heavily laden transports, representing 2316 tons, the *Isabella and Catherine, Samuel and Anne, Nathaniel and Elizabeth, Marlborough, Chatham, Colchester, Content,* and the *Smyrna Merchant,* had been stranded during that night of the 22nd, on Egg Island. Captains Richard Bayly, Thomas Walkup and Henry Vernon were drowned. Eight hundred and eighty-four corpses strewed the beach of the Island and the Labrador shore. The *Windsor, Eagle* and *Montague* had escaped shipwreck by running into an anchorage near by. By that disaster the regiments of Cols. Windresse, Kane, Clayton, as well as that of General Seymour, entirely composed of the veteran troops of Marlborough, were nearly destroyed, and, says Charlevoix, two complete companies of the Royal Guards were identified amongst the dead on the beach by their scarlet coats. It is difficult to get at the real figure of the dead and missing. On the Admiral's arrival at Boston he had sent in requisitions to Governor Dudley for four months' rations for 9,385 men he had brought from England; and again, at the council of war, held after the wreck on Egg Island, when it was debated whether it would not be advisable to attack Placentia, he declared his frigates had but 3,802 and the transports 3,841—a total of 7,643 seamen and soldiers.

E

According to the official report of Admiral Walker * 320 men embarked on board of the *Isabella and Catherine;* 102 embarked on the *Chatham;* 150 on the *Marlborough;* 246 on the *Smyrna Merchant;* 354 on the *Colchester;* 188 on the *Nathaniel and Elizabeth,* and 150 on the *Samuel and Anne;* total, 1420. All these transports, together with the *Content,* not entered in his return, were stranded on Egg Island; and, with loss of men by death and by desertion, it does not seem unreasonable to fix at 1,100 the figure of those who failed to answer to their names when the roll was called the morning which dawned on the dreadful night of the 22nd August, 1711.

Twenty-one years previous, Admiral Phipps had lost over 1000 men and 38 vessels in an expedition against the same Quebec.

Dumbfounded by this fearful marine disaster, Admiral Walker instructed Captain Cook of the *Leopard,* to cruise round the Island to save life and property, himself doing the same in the *Edgar.*

Next day the *Monmouth* was sent to discover a safe anchorage for the fleet, but none having been found, and his pilots declaring their inability to take the fleet inside of the Bay of Seven Islands, the Admiral ordered that the survivors should be divided among the other ships of the fleet, and assembled his council of war on board of the *Windsor,* on which he hoisted temporarily his flag. The officers present were: Captain Soams, of the *Swiftsure,* Captain John Michel, of the *Monmouth,* Captain Robert Arris, of the *Windsor,* Captain George Watton, of the *Montague,* Captain Henry Gore, of the *Dunkirk,* Captain George Patton, of the *Edgar,* Captain John Cockburn, of the *Sunderland,* and Captain Augustin Rouse, of the *Sapphire.* Angry words were first exchanged; some of the commanders took occasion to remonstrate with the Admiral for his having failed to consult them prior to sailing from Boston. Captain Bonner, pilot on board the *Edgar,* and Mr. Miller, pilot on

---

° See page 190—Appendix to Walker's Journal.

beard the *Swiftsure*, urged the dangers which the narrow passage at *Isle aux Coudres* presented. The other pilots successively acknowledged their incompetency. It was then unanimously resolved to abandon the expedition against Quebec, and to steer for Spanish River, at Cape Breton, whilst the *Leopard*, in company of a brig, the *Four Friends*, and of the sloop *Blessing*, should continue to cruise in the vicinity of the spot where the transports had been stranded. At Cape Breton delays and hesitation recommenced. Walker was determined not to return to England without making an attempt on Placentia; this place being also mentioned in his instructions. Several of his captains sided with him, but General Hill opposed the project. A council of war was again resorted to, and as there were remaining provisions but for eleven weeks—the men being put on half rations—it was decided to return. But before leaving, the Admiral thought it his duty to take possession of the land, in the name of Queen Anne, and to replace the arms of France by a Latin inscription cut in the form of a cross.

Thus ended this formidable armada, equipped at such expense, and on which the Queen and Ministry had built such hopes. Desertion of the men—insubordination on behalf of the officers —incompetency of the pilots—the want of foresight on behalf of the Admiral—want of patriotism of the Boston people, always ready to instigate an attack on Quebec, but unwilling to submit to the smallest pecuniary sacrifice in order to help their Sovereign to prosecute such an undertaking—such were the leading causes of the disasters of a campaign which, far from weakening New France, rather contributed to enrich her.

" It was considered," says Mère Juchereau, " advisable to send persons to Egg Island to bring back what had been cast ashore there. Mr. Duplessis, receiver of the admiral's dues, and Monseignat, agent of the crown, freighted a vessel and engaged forty men, whom they provided with a pastor and provisions, to go and winter at Egg Island, so as to be able to save all the property possible by the spring. They left in 1711 and returned in June, 1712, with five vessels loaded. The spectacle which met their sight was awful to contemplate ; over 2,000 naked corpses, in every posture of anguish, strewed the shore; some appeared as if gnashing their teeth—others as if tearing out their hair; some were half covered with sand—others joined in a deadly embrace. One group was composed of seven women, holding one another by the hand—they had met death together. It may look strange that women should have been in this expedition, but the English seemed so sure of taking Quebec, that the offices, high and low, had been distributed beforehand ; the future incumbents had brought their children and wives, so as to be in readiness to settle. The French prisoners in the fleet saw many women and children following their husbands or fathers, and a number of families who had gone to reside in Canada.

The sight of so many dead bodies was awful, and the stench arising therefrom unbearable ; though the tide carried away each day many, there still remained enough to breed a pestilence. Some before death had secreted themselves in hollow trees, others had sought protection under high wild herbs. The footsteps of others could be followed for six to nine miles; it is thought some of the latter had walked to rejoin their ships lower down. There must have been old retired officers among them, as some commissions were found signed by James II., who had taken refuge in France in 1689. Some also were Roman Catholics, as images of the Virgin Mary were found on their clothes.

Heavy anchors, cannon, balls, iron chains, warm clothing, coverings, rich horse gear, silver swords, tents, numerous guns, plate, every kind of iron ware, bells, rigging for ships, and a multitude of other things were brought from Egg Island to Quebec—£5,000 worth was sold at auction ; every one rushed to the sale to obtain a souvenir of the English armada.

More goods were left behind than were taken away ; they were so deeply immersed in the sea that it was impossible to remove them.

Two years subsequently £12,000 worth, exclusive of what had been previously taken, was conveyed to Quebec. " It was enough to make us hope that our enemies would not again attack us, and to increase our confidence in God," adds the good nun who wrote the account.

In Quebec the feeling produced was intense. The news of the disaster had reached there on the 19th Oct., 1711. M. de la Valtrie, on his return from Labrador, had brought the first tidings; our forefathers, seeing that the colony had escaped from certain loss, were loud in exultation. The title of the small lower town church, *Notre Dame de la Victoire*, was altered to that of *Notre Dame des Victoires*.

Every one talked of the miraculous incident wrought to save us; the poets rhymed couplets in its honor. Grave historians narrated elaborately the English campaign; satirists pointed their envenomed shafts at the mode of death of the enemy. Mount Parnassus was climbed by all; even the ladies turned poetical; the gentlemen of course followed suit. The clergy and friars had their turn; each day a new piece of poetry on the shipwreck was indited.

We are told that the result "of the expedition to Canada has made a great noise in London, almost as if the fate of Britain had depended on it." (*Walker's Journal.*) Mourning in private families and at court ensued. Calamity followed the steps of the unfortunate Admiral. Scarcely had he arrived in London when a messenger brought him the terrible news that the *Edgar*, his flag ship, of seventy guns, with a crew of four hundred and seventy men, had blown up at Portsmouth. Not a marine—nor officer—nor document* had been saved; no vestige to indicate that the English navy once owned a magnificent line-of-battle ship, called the *Edgar*.

The luckless Admiral had not yet exhausted his cup of bitterness. Hunted out of London, ridiculed, maltreated by the

---

* Amongst the documents destroyed was the original of the Journal kept by Sir William Phipps, in the Quebec expedition of 1690, and presented Admiral Walker by the French Minister.

Lords of the Admiralty, some of whom had been his comrades when in the navy, we find him, on the 4th December, 1714, at his house at Somersham, in Huntingdonshire, explaining to Secretary Burchett the items of ship expenditure incurred for the Royal cause three years previously at Boston, in order to free himself from charges of extravagant expenditure brought against him by the Admiralty. His twenty-eight years' service in the navy, his captivity in France as a state prisoner, all seems forgotten. A London journal, the *St. James' Post*, announced that while at his London residence, Newington Stoak, the Admiral had been arrested by order of the Queen. Finally—though his services might have been readily accepted in the Venetian or Russian navy—he sought a refuge against malice and calumny on a plantation in South Carolina. All this time his colleague, General Hill, was enjoying the favor of the Court; he had one advantage, however, over Admiral Walker, he was the brother of Madame Masham, the favorite of Queen Anne.

Walker, on returning to Boston after the Canada expedition, was assailed, much to his surprise, by swarms of pamphlets and printed libels. He had expected some reward, some kind of acknowledgment for having saved the rest of the expedition. Governor Dudley and Col. Nicholson took a delight in attacking the unhappy Captain, even in his South Carolina home; and he, who at one time thought to eclipse in glory Admiral Drake, by the conquest he meditated of Quebec, was compelled to flee to Barbadoes. Finally, calm was restored to this perturbed soul. In 1720, Sir Hovendon Walker succeeded in having an account or journal of the expedition published, which placed the matter in a more favorable light. In close communion with the Muses, and especially so with his favorite author, Horace, from whom he had selected the motto for his defence,* Sir Hovendon Walker expired peaceably, in his American home, in the year 1725.

---

* " Rebus angustis animosus atque
Fortis appare : sapienter idem
Contrahes vento nimium secundo
Turgida vela."   *Hor., Lib.* 2, *Ode* 10.

CHAPTER X.

THE MAGDALEN ISLAND GROUP—ADMIRAL ISAAC COFFIN—
DEADMAN'S ISLAND—TOM MOORE, THE IRISH POET.

THE voyage to the Magdalen Islands is performed in a sailing packet which leaves Gaspé Basin the 5th, and Pictou the 25th of each month. This singular group of islands—thirteen in number—lies at the entrance of the Gulf. The chief ones are: Amherst, Entry, Grindstone, Allright, Coffin's, Grosse Isle, Bryon, Deadman's, and the Bird Rocks.

Amherst is called after the distinguished General Amherst, who, in 1759, took such an active part in dislodging the French from their colonial possessions. It is about eleven miles in length and four in breadth, contains excellent soil, and from its shores a most extensive cod, herring, seal, and mackerel fishery is carried on. The island is annually visited by hundreds of English, French, and American fishing vessels. The harbor, which is entered from Pleasant Bay, is capable of containing several hundred vessels (drawing not over twelve feet of water), and affords shelter from all winds. In the back-ground is seen the long sand beach, which divides Pleasant Bay from the waters of the Gulf, and extends to Sandy Hook Channel, which forms the entrance to Pleasant Bay. Amherst is a port of entry and a warehousing port. It is sixty miles direct from Cape North in Cape Breton, one hundred and fifty miles from Gaspé, in Lower Canada, one hundred and twenty miles from Cape Ray, Newfoundland, and fifty miles from the east point of Prince Edward Island.

They were granted on the 8th June, 1798, to Captain (afterwards Sir Isaac) Coffin. It is said he became possessed of them in the following manner: He was conveying out in his frigate the

Governor-General of Canada, Lord Dorchester; a furious gale of
north, north-west wind compelled him to seek shelter under the
lee of one of those islands, where the English man-of-war rode
another gale in safety.   Lord Dorchester, grateful for his escape,
and desirous of marking his gratitude, asked Captain Coffin
whether he would not like to possess these then insignificant
islands, to which he having assented, the patent was made out on
his arrival at Quebec. Admiral Coffin was born in Boston in 1760*,
entered the navy at the early age of thirteen, and passed
through the various grades of rank until the midshipman became
full admiral in 1814.   He died in 1839, and left the islands to
his nephew, Captain John Townsend Coffin, of Ryde in the Isle
of Wight, an officer in the British Navy, now an admiral.
They are an entailed estate in his possession.   Both the late
and the present possessor have in a variety of ways testified
their interest in the welfare of their tenants, the inhabitants of
the islands.   The income derived from them is merely nominal,
and is always expended in improvements designed to promote
the welfare of the inhabitants.

At the time the grant was made, the population was about
500 souls.   In 1861 the total population was found to be
2,651. Amherst Island contains about 1,000 inhabitants, and is
the most important of the Magdalen group. Let us mention the
island styled " Deadman's Island," which, on a dark September
evening, in the year 1804, when he passed it, inspired the poet
—Thomas Moore—with some harmonious verses, in connection

---

* In 1773 Isaac Coffin was taken to sea by Lieutenant Hunter of the
Gaspé, at the recommendation of Admiral John Montague.   His commanding officer said he never knew any young man to acquire so much nautical
knowledge in so short a time.   After reaching the grade of post captain,
Coffin, for a breach of the regulation of the service, was deprived of his
vessel, and Earl Howe struck his name from the list of post captains.   This
act being illegal, he was re-instated in 1790.   In 1804 he was made a
baronet, and in 1814 became a full admiral in the British Navy.

Nooks and Corners of New England Coast, DRAKE.

with the old superstition amongst sailors about the phantom
ship called the " Flying Dutchman."

DEADMAN'S ISLAND.

    o   o   o   o   o

" There lieth a wreck on the dismal shore
  Of cold and pitiless Labrador,
  Where, under the moon, upon mounts of frost,
  Full many a mariner's bones are tossed.

" Yon shadowy bark hath been to that wreck,
  And the dim blue fire that lights her deck
  Doth play on as pale and livid a crew
  As ever yet drank the churchyard dew.

" To Deadman's Isle in the eye of the blast,
  To Deadman's Isle she speeds her fast ;
  By skeleton shapes her sails are furl'd,
  And the hand that steers is not of this world ! "

Ours is, however, no supernatural craft, but a plain Gaspé
coaster, and that

" By skeleton shapes her sails are (not) furled,"

I can swear ; so I will look on without any superstitious awe
on the perpendicular rocks surrounded on all sides by deep
water. It is, however, well styled " Deadman's Monument."
It does point to the spot where many an English sailor found a
watery grave. Scarcely visible above the waves, the storm-
tossed bark which once strikes on its granite shores goes to
pieces instantly—a few spars, a shattered mast, possibly a solitary hencoop, with the return of day, indicate that during the
previous night, perhaps, a crowd of slumberers have been hurried
forever under the seething waters.

Bryon Island is an important one in the group; but to a
naturalist none are more interesting than the Bird Isles—" two
rocks, elevated above the water, upwards of one hundred feet.
Their flattened summits, whose circumference exceed not each
three hundred paces, exhibit a resplendent whiteness, produced

by the quantity of ordure, with which they are covered, from immense flocks of birds, which in summer take possession of the apertures in their perpendicular cliffs, where they form their nests and produce their young. When alarmed they hover above the rocks and overshadow their tops by their numbers. The abundance of their eggs affords to the inhabitants of the neighboring coast a material supply of food." So wrote Heriot in 1807. They had, however, been carefully noted and described by the Jesuits as far back as 1632. Father Paul Lejune calls these rocks *Les Colombiers* (dovecotes), from the myriads of waterfowl which resort to them in the summer months. At the period when he wrote, " birds were so plentiful there that a boat could be loaded with their eggs in a few hours, and persons ascending the rocks were liable to be prostrated to the ground by the clapping of the wings of these feathered denizens."

Dr. H. Bryant, of Boston, who visited these rocks on the 21st June, 1860, for ornithological purposes, thus describes them :—" They are two in number, called the Great Bird or Gannet Rock, and the Little or North Bird. They are about three-quarters of a mile apart, the water between them very shoal, showing that, at no very distant epoch, they formed a single island. They are composed entirely of a soft, reddish-brown sandstone, the strata of which are very regular and nearly horizontal, dipping very slightly to the S. W. The North Bird is much the smallest, and though the base is more accessible, the summit cannot, I believe, be reached—at least, I was unable to do so. It is the most irregular in its outline, presenting many enormous detached fragments, and is divided in one place into two separate islands at high water—the northerly one several times higher than broad, so as to present the appearance of a huge rocky pillar. Gannet Rock is a quarter of a mile in its longest diameter from S. W. to N. E. The highest point of the rock is at the northerly end, where, according to the chart, it is 140 feet high, and from which it gradually slopes to the southerly end, where it is from 80 to 100.

" The sides are nearly vertical—the summit in many places overhanging. There are two beaches at its base, on the southerly and westerly sides—the most westerly one comparatively smooth and composed of rounded stones. The easterly one, on the contrary, is very rough and covered by irregular blocks, many of large size and still angular, showing that they have but recently fallen from the cliffs above. This beach is very difficult to land on ; but the other presents no great difficulty in ordinary weather. The top of the rock cannot, however, be reached from either of them. The only spot from which at present the ascent can be made, is the rocky point between the two beaches. This has, probably, from the yielding nature of the rock, altered materially since Audubon's visit. At present it would be impossible to haul a boat up, from want of space. The landing is very difficult at all times, as it is necessary to jump from a boat, thrown about by the surf, on to the inclined surface of the ledge, rendered slippery by the fuci which cover it, and bounded towards the rock by a nearly vertical face. The landing once effected, the first part of the ascent is comparatively easy, being over large fragments and broad ledges; but the upper part is both difficult and dangerous, as in some places the face of the rock is vertical for eight or ten feet, and the projecting ledges very narrow, and the rock itself so soft that it cannot be trusted to, and in addition rendered slippery by the constant trickling from above, and the excrements of the birds that cover it in every direction.

" Since Audubon's time the fishery, which was carried on extensively in the neighborhood of Bryon Island, has failed—or at least is less productive than on the North shore; and I am inclined to think that at present the birds are but little disturbed, and that consequently their number, particularly of the Guillemots, has much increased. There was no appearance of any recent visit on the top of the rock, and though after making the ascent it was obvious that others had preceded us, still the traces were so faint that it was several hours before we succeeded in

finding the landing-place.   The birds breeding there, at the time
of our visit, were Gannets, Puffins, three species of Guillemots,
Razor-billed Auks, and Kittiwakes.   These birds are all mentioned by Audubon, with the exception of Brunnich's Guillemot,
confounded by him with the common species.   No other breed-
ing-place on our shore is so remarkable at once for the number
and variety of the species occupying it.

"Of the seven species mentioned, I am not aware that three,
namely, the Kittiwake and the Bridled and Brunnich's Guillemot, are known to breed at any other place south of the Straits
of Belle Isle ; of the remaining four, two, the Foolish Guillemot,
and Razor-billed Auk, are found at many other places and in
large numbers ; the Puffin in much greater abundance on the
North shore, particularly at the Perroquet Islands, near Mingan
and Bras d'Or ; the Gannet at only two other points in the Gulf
—at Percé Rock near Gaspé, which is perhaps even more
remarkable than Gannet Rock, but is at present inaccessible ;
and at Gannet Rock near Mingan, which will soon be deserted
by those birds in consequence of the depredations of the fisherman."

CHAPTER XI.

THE MAGDALEN ISLANDS VIEWED UNDER THEIR HISTORICAL, UTILITARIAN AND COMMERCIAL ASPECTS.

IN the preceding chapter this group of islands was viewed chiefly as a land-grant to Sir Isaac Coffin. "Deadman's Rock" —so called in consequence of its striking resemblance, when seen from a certain point, to a corpse covered by a shroud—came in for its share of notice, and also as mentioned by Tom Moore; the sketch was closed by Dr. Bryant's excellent ornithological report of the Bird Rocks, which however, possibly, will be relished by students of natural history alone. Let us portray these valuable islands under their most noticeable feature—a seal fishing-station of apparently inexhaustible wealth. I shall quote from Commander Fortin's excellent report for 1864 :—

" The Magdalen Islands are about forty-five miles in length; their greatest width is thirteen miles. They lie near the southern point of the Gulf of St. Lawrence, facing the principal entrance to that inland sea, between the 47th and 48th degrees of north latitude; their most southerly extremity being only twenty-five miles further north than the City of Quebec, and between the 61st and 62nd degrees of longitude west from Greenwich.

" Discovered by Jacques Cartier on his first voyage to the Gulf of St. Lawrence in 1534, these islands received the names of Ramées, Bryon and Alezay; and it was not until a later period that they acquired the names which they now bear.

" Situated as they are at the mouth of the Gulf of St. Lawrence, and in the sailing line of vessels on their way to Canada, they were frequently visited by the French trading and fishing vessels after the discovery of Canada. But it does not appear that at that time any considerable settlements were made upon them previous to their concession in 1663 by the company of New France to François Doublet, a ship captain of Honfleur, who in the following year associated with himself François Gon de Quimé and Claude de Landemarc, for the purpose of trading and fishing there. But there is reason to believe that in 1719 the islands again became the property of the French Government, as the latter, according to Charlevoix, conceded them to Lecompte de St. Pierre.

"In 1763, at the time of the cession of Canada and its dependencies to the British Government, they were only inhabited by some ten families of French and Acadian origin, who engaged in walrus and seal hunting, and to a small extent in the herring and cod fishery. Subsequently, an American shipper, Gridley by name, founded, on Amherst Island, near the entrance to the harbor of that name, a trading and fishing establishment, the ruins of which still exist. He took into his service families of French origin residing on the islands, in order specially to carry on, upon a large scale, the hunting of the walrus and the seal, the oil obtained from which brought a good price in the markets of the New England colonies, as did also the skins, which yielded a very thick leather, and the tusks which served as a substitute for ivory.

"The property of Mr. Gridley and his apparatus was partly destroyed during the American War by the privateers of the revolted colonies, but on the conclusion of peace he resumed his trade and his labors ; but the walruses, whose habits of coming in herds upon the beach had exposed them to the constant attacks of the hunters, to whom they had become a valuable prey, had already almost completely disappeared from the vicinity of the islands. On the other hand, the seals did not appear in as large numbers near the shore, and were not as easily captured as formerly, and in consequence the establishments of Mr. Gridley and of other shippers engaged more especially in the hunting of amphibious animals rapidly decreased in importance and prosperity.

"I must here observe that besides the fishermen of the Magdalen Islands, a large number had also come from the English Colonies since the conquest of Canada, to engage in walrus-hunting. They had carried it on with that perseverance and energy for which they are so celebrated, and to them, in great measure, is to be attributed the extinction in our waters of this amphibious animal, which is second in importance only to the whale.

"But the inhabitants settled on Amherst, Grindstone, and Allright Islands had already begun to engage in a more steady manner in the cod and herring fishery, the produce of which they bartered with the traders of the other British Provinces, and even of Jersey, for provisions and merchandise, and this yielded them undoubted benefit. Moreover, the cultivation of the soil which, however, they by far too much neglected, as their descendants do at the present day, yielded them some certain supplies, and at the time of the concession of all the Magdalen Islands by the British Government to Admiral Isaac Coffin in 1798, as a reward for the services which he had rendered to the English Crown during the American war, the population of the Islands was estimated at one hundred families; but from information I was enabled to obtain at Amherst, I believe this amount to be a little exaggerated. In 1821, according to Col. Bouchette, the number of families had increased to one hundred and thirty-three, and in 1831, to one hundred and fifty-three, the total population being about one thousand souls. The census of 1850 showed it to be two thousand two hundred and two, and that of 1860, two thousand six hundred and fifty-one. But it must not be forgotten that the Magdalen Islands had sent out three colonies to the north shore of the Gulf of St. Lawrence, the total population of which amounts to about five hundred souls.

"The fisheries of the Magdalen Islands in their order, from spring to autumn, are the seal fishery or rather seal hunting on the ice, the herring fishery, the spring mackerel fishery, the cod fishery, which lasts till autumn, and the summer mackerel fishery."

On these several pursuits I shall confine myself, borrowing the words of the portly ex-commander of the Canadian Navy,— Hon. P. Fortin—

SEAL HUNTING.

" Seal hunting is carried on upon the floating ice, in the Gulf of St. Lawrence, throughout nearly its whole extent, although it seldom happens that the schooners go higher up than Gaspé Cape to try their fortune in the River St. Lawrence. It is rather upon the North shore of the Gulf, near the Island of Anticosti, and at the entrance of the Straits of Belle Isle, that the fields of ice are met with upon which are generally found the greatest number of seals. It is hardly necessary for me to repeat that the female seals, which penetrate the Gulf of St. Lawrence in enormous herds in the month of December,* get up

---

° Is this a satisfactory reply to the question propounded by an American writer as to the hybernaculum of the Alaska seals, as follows :—

"The islands of Alaska are the summer resort of seals in immense numbers ; but where they spend their winters is an unsolved mystery. Sufficient search has been made for their winter abodes—with a view to taking their skins—to show that they do not land in any considerable numbers on any known ground. They begin to leave the islands early in October, and by the middle of December have all left, and none are seen again until April or May. A few hundred, mostly young pups, are taken by the Indians around Sitka, 1,200 miles east of the islands, during the month of December, again in March on their return to the islands, and in February off the coast of British Columbia ; but in such small numbers as to make no appreciable difference in the immense number that visit the islands annually. It is claimed by the natives that the seals return invariably the second year to their places of birth, and, when not too often disturbed by driving, continue to do so. In order to test the truth of this story, Mr. Byrant, Special Agent of the Treasury Department at St. Paul's Island, has instituted an experiment of an eminently practical character, although it might not command the entire approval of Mr. Bergh, whose jurisdiction, however, does not extend to Alaska. He had one hundred male pups selected before leaving, on a rookery one mile north of the village, and marked by cutting off the left ear, on a rookery to the south of the village. This has been done for two years, and next year the first will be old enough to be taken, when the result will be ascertained. It is evident that sharks or other voracious fish prey on the young pups while in the water, from the fact that of more than a million pups annually leaving the islands, not one-third return to them in the spring

on the floating ice about the middle or end of March to bring
forth their young, which they nurse with great tenderness and
suckle for the three or four weeks, or perhaps more, which time
they pass upon the ice without going into the water. It is during that period that our hunters have to use their endeavors to
get them into their possession by killing them either with clubs
or by shooting; for subsequently when they have attained sufficient strength, they take to the water and the hunters see them
no more. But the floating ice also serves for a habitation for
the adult seals—especially the females—while they are tending
their young, and our hunters pursue them eagerly where it is in
their power to do so—that is when they can approach them without being perceived, or else when these amphibious animals are
upon ice so closely packed together that they can find no open
place through which to plunge into the water, and so escape pursuit. Then our hunters make great slaughter among them, and
crews of seven men have been sometimes known to kill hundreds.

"Continuous high winds, blowing from the same quarter for
some length of time, drive the fields of ice covered with seals
towards the shores of the Islands, and keep them aground near
the coast until a change of wind supervenes, and at such times
great prizes fall to the Islanders. In an instant, the news is
spread through all the Islands by the ringing of bells and the
firing of guns, and soon the whole population rushes to the
shore, whence may easily be seen the seals scattered over the
ice as far as the eye can reach.

"Young and old men, each armed with a large knife, a rope
and a club, spring on to the fields of ice, while the women
remain on the shore within reach, to prepare their meals, and to
supply them with hot drinks in order to protect them from the
effects of the cold and damp, to which they are incessantly exposed. With their clubs they stun all the seals which they come
upon, and then use their knives to despatch them and remove the
skin and fat. When they think their harvest large enough, they tie

F

together with a rope, with which they are provided, as much of their spoils as will suffice to make a burthen of from three hundred to three hundred and fifty pounds, and they then drag this valuable load from one piece of ice to another to the shore, where they leave it in safety, and return to the same ground to gather a fresh harvest. This fatiguing and often dangerous labor continues throughout the whole day, and even the night in clear weather, so long as there are any seals on the ice near the shore, and the ice has not been driven away by the land breeze. I have been told that formerly, when the seals were more numerous than at present in the waters of the Gulf, the inhabitants of the Magdalen Islands had taken as many as from one thousand five hundred to two thousand seals, nearly all young, on the fields of ice aground near the shore. But since I have been visiting the islands, the results produced by seal-hunting have been less abundant, and have sometimes amounted to hardly anything. This year (1864) by a happy concurrence of circumstances, it was productive, having yielded at least six thousand seals, which cannot be valued at less than three dollars each, thus giving a total value of eighteen thousand dollars. This excellent hunting took place on the 27th, 28th, and part of the 29th April, having consequently lasted but two days and a half. The ice driven by a strong east wind drifted out to sea, carrying with it thousands of seals beyond the reach of the hunters, whose disappointment may be more easily imagined than described.

"This hunting is very often attended with danger, for the currents or the wind sometimes drive off the ice before the hunters can regain the shore, and if they are not taken off by boats, they are carried off to sea, there to perish inevitably from cold and hunger. Within some fifteen years several accidents of this nature have, to my knowledge, occurred. But every possible effort is made to prevent their occurrence by warning the hunters, who are busy on the ice, when the latter begins to move away from the shore by the firing of guns and by signals agreed on beforehand. The fat of the young seals is tender, and melts easily in the sun. It yields a very fine oil, which is white and almost devoid of unpleasant smell.

" The Magdalen Islands schooners fitted out for seal-hunting, amounted in number this year to 25."

The navigation of these crafts amongst the ice-floes, in early spring, amidst snow-storms and hurricanes, is attended with considerable danger. Thus perished the " Emma " and the " Breeze "—the crews leaving 13 widows and 45 orphans. Of the herring, mackerel and cod fisheries, etc., of these islands, important and remunerative pursuits though they be, I will, for want of space, merely give Commander Fortin's official returns for 1864 :—

Seal Hunting.

6,000 seals killed by the inhabitants on the ice, at $3.00 a seal,	$18,000 00
1,633 seals killed by the crews of schooners, at $6.00 a seal,	9,798 00

Herring Fishery.

1,500 barrels of herring, at $2.00 per barrel,	3,000 00

Spring Mackerel Fishery.

900 barrels of mackerel, at $6.00 a barrel,	5,400 00

Cod Fishery.

9,170 quintals of cod, at $3.60 a quintal,	32,944 00
5,811 gallons cod liver oil, at 55 cents a gallon,	3,196 05

Summer Mackerel Fishery.

1,400 barrels of mackerel, at $10.00 a barrel,	$14,000 00

Whale Oil.

360 of whale oil, at 70 cents a gallon,	252 00

$86,590 05

NOTE.—The seal fishery in the Lower St. Lawrence is becoming of importance. We read that (ST. JOHN'S, Nfld., Feb. 7th, 1872) a company has been formed in Montreal, part of the capital being subscribed here, for the prosecution of the seal fishery. Two fine new steamers, the " Iceland " and " Greenland," are now on the passage from Aberdeen, having been built by this Company. It is reported that Sir Hugh Allan has a considerable interest in this adventure. Another new steamer for the seal fishery, called the

" Wolf" has just arrived to W. Grieve & Co. The " Tigress," a fourth new steamer, owned by some of our own merchants, and built in Quebec, was unfortunately locked in the ice, in consequence of an " early closing movement " on the part of the St. Lawrence, last November. She is, of course, precluded from sharing in this year's fishery. (*So far, these bright expectations of profit for the Province of Quebec have not yet been fulfilled—1878*).

Allright Island lies to the north-east of Amherst Island, and forms the north-east boundary of Pleasant Bay, which has a width of about twelve miles. The island is about four miles long by two broad, and its surface is almost entirely a succession of small hills and valleys. Grindstone Island is so called from a lofty conical cape of sandstone on its south-east shore, called by the French Cap de Meule. This island forms the north-east boundary of Pleasant Bay, and is almost five miles in length. Its soil is rich, and agriculture is prosecuted with vigor. At its western limit is the thriving village of l'Etang du Nord. The Judge of Bonaventure District holds his court each year at the Magdalen Islands in September, and I had the pleasure of recognizing in this dignitary, a worthy Quebec Police Magistrate of ancient days—His Honor Mr. Justice Maguire.

From the Magdalen group, the sailing packet* takes you either to Gaspé Basin or to Pictou, and the Gulf Port steamers convey the traveller from the latter place to Paspebiac.

° Since these lines were written in 1871, a steamer, the "Albert," runs fortnightly from Pictou, N.S., to the Magdalen Islands.

CHAPTER XII.

New Richmond—Maria—Its Mysterious Light—Carleton—
The Abode of the Acadians.

THERE are several other points of interest in the Bay which
I had not an opportunity of visiting this trip, but which I hope
to visit hereafter. For the following notes on the same, I am
indebted to a well-informed official of Port Daniel :—

"On leaving Black Cape you travel over hills and valleys of
fertile, well-cultivated lands settled by Scotch and French
Canadians, until you arrive at the little river, the homestead of
the Pritchards on the flat lands.

"The first settlers of New Richmond were four French-
Canadian families—Burkets, Degousse, Sayer, Cormier—and in
1783 three families of Loyalists, viz., Pritchard, Willot, Duffey ;
—the head of one, Captain Pritchard, was rather more than a
Loyalist—being an officer in the American Army, he went over
to the British. He received half pay until his death in 1827,
and was to the last a stout, daring old man.

"On crossing the little river, fording at low water or by
scow at high, you arrive at the business part of it. There are
here two churches—a Presbyterian and a R. C. church within
half a mile of each other ; two mercantile establishments ; mills
where the business of the township is centered. Here Wm. Cuthbert, of Ayrshire, established himself in 1820. By dint of energy,
enterprise and honesty he accumulated a fortune of $400,000 as
partner of Robert Cuthbert, in Greenock, on the Clyde ; and
died recently, much respected. Robert Montgomery and Son
have succeeded him in New Richmond, and do a large business
in mills, timber, etc.

"The population is Scotch and French-Canadian intermixed. One mile and a half from Mrs. Cuthbert's brings you to the big river of New Richmond, in Indian language, Cascapediac, the division line of the township of Maria, on crossing the big river by scow, for it appears we are never destined to have bridges, (except on the·dawn of elections, they are never spoken off.) The east point of Maria is an Indian reserve of one thousand acres, where thirty families of Micmacs prolong a miserable and intemperate existence. They have a church, are visited by the priest of the mission, Point Restigouche, twice a year. These Indians are of the lowest *canaille* of the genus redskin. Leaving the Indians one mile, you get into a prosperous settlement of French-Canadians for one mile and a half, when you arrive at the snug residence of Harvey Manderson, Esq., J.P., a clever and original character. In rear of Mr. Manderson, there exists a prosperous settlement of Patlanders, formed twenty-five years ago. Two miles further brings you to the R. C. church, and to the residences of the numerous and patriarchal family of Audettes. One must not forget the hardy old Anticosti trapper, R. Campbell, Esq., now a successful merchant in Maria. On the Cape of Maria shines nightly the mysterious light which disappears when approached. Some say it indicates the presences of a treasure buried here in days of yore ; others, that it implies something much more dreadful—' But don't tell it to the Marines.' Five miles further is Carleton, the abode of the Acadians of old, the Landry, Allard, Allain, Le Blanc, Jacque, Caisy families. One of the former industries of the Bay, the smoking of herring, has quite disappeared, as it ceased to be remunerative. At the foot of the lofty mountain range known as the Tracadigetche Mountains, is clustered the romantic village of Carleton in a sheltered nook. In 1861, the population of the entire township was nine hundred and fifty-eight souls, of whom twenty-six were Protestants. This portion of the coast was first settled by Acadians, who, coming from Tracadie, named this spot Tracadigetche or little Tracadie.

" The Bay of Carleton is a fine sheet of water formed by Migouacha and Tracadigetche points. The river Nouvelle empties itself in this Bay. The anchorage is good, and the Bay affords a safe refuge for shipping from northerly and easterly gales. It is a favorite resort of the herring in spring as a spawning ground, and immense quantities are caught, which are used not only as food, but also as manure.

" Here resides the wealthy and respected member of the county, John Meagher, Esq.,* the father-in-law of our young friend at Quebec, P. Chauveau, Esq. Here our much-respected townsman, Dr. Landry (of Quebec), has built himself a snug villa, to spend thereat the summer months.

" New Richmond is a rich agricultural country for many years back, exporting largely to Halifax and Newfoundland, as well as several cargoes of timber and deals to Britain. Maria† and Bonaventure export agricultural produce to some extent. Carleton is a stirring place, with a bank agency and considerable business. A few years ago this place threatened to rival Rimouski as the seat of the Episcopacy for this district. There is a handsome convent at Carleton, founded mainly by the liberality of Mr. John Meagher. A few miles from Carleton the line of the Intercolonial Railroad comes out; the village of Matapedia will much benefit thereby."

° Mr. Meagher has since paid the debt of nature, and his son-in-law now owns and occupies his spacious and picturesque homestead.

† Maria, I have heard stated, was called after Lady Maria Dorchester, the daughter of the Earl of Effingham, when Lord Dorchester was Governor-General of Canada.

CHAPTER XIII.

ANTICOSTI—FLOTSAM AND JETSAM—THE PIRATE OF THE ST. LAWRENCE (GAMACHE), DELINEATED BY CHARLES LANMAN, A WASHINGTON LITTERATEUR.

"The dangerous, desolate shores of Anticosti, rich in wrecks, accursed in human suffering. This hideous wilderness has been the grave of hundreds, by the slowest and ghastliest of deaths—starvation. Washed ashore from maimed and sinking ships, saved to destruction, they drag their chilled and battered limbs up the rough rocks; for a moment, warm with hope, they look around with eager, straining eyes for shelter,—and there is none; the failing sight darkens on hill and forest, forest and hill, and black despair. Hours and days waste out the lamp of life, until, at length, the withered skeletons have only strength to die." (ELIOT WARBURTON).

I CAN recall Anticosti in its palmiest days for romance, and in its darkest era for seafaring men, before the epoch of fog-horns, lightships, and beacons. Fond memory takes me back to a well-remembered sea voyage, prescribed in 1843 by doctors to restore my health, and made by me in a well-known Gaspé whaler—the " Breeze," Captain Arbour. In that year I visited for the first time the desolate isle which Gamache—the legendary and dreaded wrecker—had selected as a secure retreat for his plunder, if not for a happy home. The redoubted pirate was then in the zenith of his fame, if fame means lawless deeds,—encounters with Her Majesty's Revenue officers—predatory attacks on the forlorn crews which the autumnal storms might, perchance, cast on the God-forsaken shores of Ellis Bay.

Louis Olivier Gamache, delineated by an adept of the new sensational school, would have exhibited in his person the imprint of a full-blown *héros de romans*. What rich vistas of feeling, bravado, and remorse, this master spirit of evil might have revealed under the magic wand of Alexander Dumas, Wilkie Collins, Eugene Sue, or Fenimore Cooper! It was, doubtless, from Gamache that Lever borrowed some of the dark traits of his " Black Boatswain " in " Con Cregan," selecting at the same time Anticosti as the landing-place on this side of the Atlantic for his adventurous " Gil Blas "—fresh from the groves of Blarney.

The historian Ferland has left us in one of his light, humorous papers a very good pen-and-ink photo of the pirate, whose den he visited in 1852. Amongst the implements of warfare which ornamented the walls, he noticed twelve fire-locks, chiefly double-barrel guns, and a small cannon in front of the house. The Abbé's sketch, no doubt, guided our friend, Charles Lanman, in his delineations of the celebrated sea rover, who was indeed

" A man of loneliness and mystery."

When I visited Anticosti for the first time, the particulars of the melancholy fate of the " Granicus " were still fresh in every mind.

The brig " Granicus " was stranded at Fox Bay, on the east end of the Island, in November, 1828. There are yet at the time I write, living witnesses amongst us of the " Granicus " tragedy ; amongst others, Captain Jesse Armstrong, our Harbor Master at Quebec, who having sailed from that port on the 24th October, 1828, for the West Indies, was in company with the " Granicus " and a dozen other craft, at Pointe de Monts a few days before the accident which befel those vessels. The greatest number were cast ashore ; some, never heard of afterwards. The passengers and crew of the " Granicus " safely arrived on land to meet a more hideous and lingering fate. All perished during the ensuing winter. When the Government schooner called at the Island in the spring following, to stock the light-house with provisions, etc., the decayed remains of these unfortunate men were discovered in a rude hut. They had literally starved to death. In a pot over a fire-place was human flesh, revealing the awful fact that in their last extremity they had resorted to cannibalism to prolong life. Amongst the passengers, there was a Montreal lady and her two children.

More than once the residents of Anticosti must have had duties to perform similar to those described by Thoreau, at Cap Cod :—

"Once," says he, "it was my business to go in search of the relics of a human body mangled by sharks, which had just been cast up a week after a wreck. Having got the direction from a lighthouse— I should find it a mile or two distant over the sand, a dozen rods from the water, covered with a cloth, by a stick stuck up—I expected that I must look very narrowly to find so small an object ; but the sandy beach, half a mile wide, and stretching farther than the eye could reach, was so perfectly smooth and bare, and the mirage towards the sea so magnifying, that when I was half a mile distant, the insignificant sliver which marked the spot looked like a bleached spear, and the relics were as conspicuous as if they lay in state on that sandy plain, or a generation had labored to pile up their cairn there. Close at hand there were simply some bones with a little flesh adhering to them; in fact, only a slight inequality in the sweep of the shore. There was nothing at all remarkable about them, and they were singularly inoffensive, both to the senses and the imagination; but as I stood there they grew more and more imposing. They were alone with the beach and the sea, whose hollow roar seemed addressed to them, and I was impressed as if there was an understanding between them and the ocean, which necessarily left me out with my snivelling sympathies. That dead body had taken possession of the shore, and reigned over it as no living one could, in the name of a certain majesty which belonged to it." (Cape Cod, *Thoreau*.)

Since the Department of Marine has lit up and buoyed the dangerous spots in our noble river, Anticosti, like Cape Rosier and

Manicouagan, have lost the greatest portion of their terrors.[*] As early as 1864, mariners have thanked the Canadian authorities, in prose and in verse too,[†] for their attention to navigation and commerce.

Directly in the path of inward and outward bound Quebec and Montreal traders, lies the extensive Island of Anticosti, which during the winter months is quite isolated from the rest of the Dominion.

Anticosti was first discovered by Cartier in 1534, and called by him in his second voyage " Assomption ; " by the pilot, Jean Alphonse, in 1542, " Ascension Isle ; " and by the Indians " Natiscotec," which the French transformed into " Anticosti." It was conceded in 1680 to Louis Jolliet. This island is 122 miles long, 30 broad, and 270 miles in circumference, and contains nearly 2,000,000 acres of land. Its nearest point is about 450 miles below Quebec.

The limestone rocks on the coast are covered with a thick

---

[*] In 1690 one of Sir William Phipps' troop ships, commanded by Captain Rainsford, was wrecked on Anticosti, during the retreat from Quebec, and but five of its people survived the winter on the Island. When the ice broke up these brave fellows started in a row-boat for Boston, nine hundred miles distant, and, after a passage of forty-four days, they reached their old home in safety. Anticosti was granted about 1680 to the Sieur Jolliet, who erected a fort there, but was soon plundered and ejected by the English. In 1814 H. B. M. frigate *Leopard*, 50, the same vessel which searched the U. S. frigate *Chesapeake*, in 1807, for deserters, was lost here.

[†] THE COMPLAINT OF THE " MARGARET."

On the 18th of November, 1864, the good ship " Margaret," of Aberdeen, Alexander Cruickshank, master, arrived in our port (Quebec) with a cargo of coals from Sunderland. Judging from the manner in which Captain Cruickshank has filled up his Report for the Custom House, we should say he is philosopher, wit, and poet combined. The intelligence he communicates respecting the weather he experienced is put in the following rhythmical style :—

" Breezy, Freezy ; Snowy, Blowy."

The Captain's muse is not of a melancholy turn. Instead of complaining of the breezy, freezy, snowy, blowy weather, he eulogizes in the subjoined

and often impenetrable forest of dwarf spruce, with gnarled branches so twisted and matted together that a man may walk for a considerable distance on their summits.

In the interior some fine timber exists. Pursh, who visited the Island in 1817, found the pond pine (*pinus sevotina*) there. This is a southern species, and it is a singular circumstance how it established itself on this northern island. The timber of the interior is birch, a little pine and spruce.

---

stanzas our lighthouses, and delicately points out in the two last verses a deficiency that exists at Manicouagan, which we hope, after Captain Cruick-shank's complaint, our Trinity House will see the necessity of remedying:—

> " I see ye hae been lanterns buyin',
>   An' they shine well ;
> Your river now, though dark's the night,
> Has many a beacon's cheerin' light ;
> From Quebec to Bic there's some in sight
>   Like guidin' star,
> On rock an' headlan', or in bight,
>   That shines afar.
>
> " Your pilots now may work for ever,
> The lights are placed for them so clever ;
> To keep them all their side the river,
>   Seems wide awake ;
> Saunt An-ton-ey bless the giver,
>   E'en for their sake !
>
> " But list ye, sirs, to a lady's prayer—
> Could you not your bounty share,
> And anither lantern spare
>   For Manicouagan ?
> A light is muckle wantit there
>   To save a flaggon.
>
> " For, sirs, I'll whisper in your ear,
> Its mony a bottom's scrubbed, I fear ;
> Even mine, alas ! it made feel queer
>   An' rumpled sairly ;
> Therefore I hope my words ye'll hear,
>   An' light it early."

The streams which descend to the coast abound with trout and salmon in the summer season. The chief ones are Jupiter River, Salmon River and Schallop Creek. Seals frequent the flat limestone rocks in vast numbers. Mackerel in immense shoals congregate around all parts of the coast. Bears are very numerous; foxes and martens abundant. Otters, and a few mice, complete the known list of quadrupeds. Neither snakes, toads nor frogs, are known to exist on this desolate island. There are no good natural harbors on Anticosti. Provision posts have been established by the Canadian Government, for the relief of crews wrecked on the Island, and four lighthouses are now maintained at the west, east, south and south-west points. When I visited the south-west point in 1843, the lighthouse was kept by an old Waterloo soldier of the name of McGilvray, so far as I can recollect.

Mr. Pope * was in charge of one of the chief lighthouses for many years. These lighthouses are about 100 feet high, most substantially built, and provided with revolving lights.

Mr. William Corbet, a most successful trapper, has been, for years, one of the chief inhabitants of the sea-girt isle.

In an account before us, we read that "an immense quantity of square timber and logs, ready cut for the saw mill, are scattered over the south coast, having drifted down the rivers of the main land, and particularly the St. Lawrence. Some of the squared timber may have been derived from wrecks. Anticosti from its position at the entrance of the Gulf, from its natural resources, and the teeming life of the sea which surrounds it, has attracted considerable notice of late years. Ellis Bay might become an important naval station. The island originally formed part of the country called Labrador. In 1825 it was reannexed to Lower Canada by an act of the Imperial Parliament. It is now in the hands of a considerable number of persons, some residing in England and some in Canada. Companies are now

---

* Since dead.

forming and applying * to Parliament for powers to open up and
turn to advantage the resources of the island, etc. I shall close
this notice of Anticosti with Mr. Lanman's sketch of its celebrated wrecker, Gamache, from the *New York Journal of Commerce* ; it was written several years ago :

" THE WIZARD OF ANTICOSTI.

 " Lonely and desolate are the shores of Anticosti. In winter
they are blocked up with ice and whitened with snow,—and in
summer almost continually enveloped in fogs. To all mariners
who have occasion to sail the Gulf of St. Lawrence, they are a
perpetual terror, and the many shipwrecks occurring there have
given to the Island a mournful celebrity. Two lighthouses,
lighted from March to December, and two provision depots are
the only localities on the Island where those who may have
escaped a watery grave can obtain succor from famine and cold,
and the most noted of them is the Bay of Gamache. It is about
five miles in circumference, the only really secure harbor in the
region, and derives its name from the strange man who there
first made himself a home. From Quebec to Gaspé,—from
Gaspé to Pictou, not a name was better known, and the manifold
stories picked up by the writer—during his Canadian and New
Brunswick wanderings—respecting him would fill a volume.
They were extravagant, made up of fact and fiction, representing
him as a kind of ancient mariner, a pirate, a being half savage
and half ogre, and enjoying the special protection of Satan himself. But the simple story of his actual life, well worth record-
ing, is as follows :—
 " Louis Olivier Gamache was born at Islet in Lower Canada
in 1784. When a mere boy he left his home and obtained a
sailor's berth on board an English frigate, in which capacity he

---

* Notice is hereby given, that application will be made to the Parliament
of the Dominion of Canada, at its next Session, for an Act to incorporate the
" Anticosti Company," for the purpose of colonizing, working and developing the resources of the Island of Anticosti ; and also for the purpose of
laying a submarine cable from South-West Point Lighthouse of Anticosti to
Cape Rosier, on the coast of Gaspé, to connect with the mainland telegraph
line ; and also for the purpose of running a line of steamers from Anticosti
to ports within the Dominion, and to foreign ports.

Montreal, 24th January, 1872.

spent about twenty years of his life, roaming over the entire world. On his return, he found his parents dead and himself friendless and poor. Having strayed into the little port of Rimouski, he tried his hand at business and failed. Disgusted with people generally, and somewhat so with life, he resolved to settle on the Island of Anticosti, whose lonely shores had taken his fancy captive when last returning from his ocean wanderings. Determined as he was to spend the balance of his days in the peaceful enjoyments of hunting, fishing, and sailing, his sagacity led him to the bay already mentioned. He built himself a rude cabin and then visited the main shore to obtain a good wife, in which effort he was successful. She was all he hoped for, but the loneliness and cold of Anticosti were more than she could bear, and she died during her first spring upon the Island.*

" Summer came and Gamache sought for peace of mind by sailing in his schooner among the icebergs of the north, and slaughtering the gray seal and walrus. With the money thus made he erected some new buildings, and gathered about his home a few of the comforts of an ordinary farm, such as horses, cows and sheep. He married a second wife, with whom he spent the seven happiest years of his life, but on returning from

---

* " THE LAMENT OF THE PIRATE'S BRIDE.

" By the sad sea waves
I listen while they moan
A lament o'er graves
Of hope and pleasure gone.
I was young, I was fair,
I had not a care
From the rising of the moon
To the setting of the sun ;
Yet I pine like a slave
By the sad sea wave.
Come again !
Bright days of hope
And pleasures gone
Come again !
Bright days—come again ! "

one of his winter hunts, he found her frozen * to death with his two children so nearly famished that they followed their mother and he was once more alone. A kind of gloom now settled upon his spirit, and though he led an active life, he became misanthropic. He cared not to have any intercourse with his fellow-men, and his only companion and confidante was a half-breed Frenchman ; but if a revenue officer, a professional fisherman, or a party of sporting characters happened to make him a visit, they were sure to be treated with kindness. He felt that death had robbed him of all that he most cherished, and how did he know, was his mode of reasoning, but some of his Indian neighbors would prove treacherous, and take his life without warning? Some band of pirates, moreover, might hear of his forlorn condition and sweep away his property and murder him in cold blood. These were impending calamities, and something must be done for protection. Hence it was that he resolved to adopt a series of measures that would inspire a dread of his person and name. He fully succeeded in all his romantic efforts, and the following are a few of the many with which his name is associated.

"On one occasion, having been windbound for several days, he anchored his vessel in one of the ports of Gaspé, and making his way to the village inn ordered a sumptuous supper for two persons. The truth was he was nearly famished, and having caused his man Friday to be on board the vessel, he had determined to have a good feast and any fun that might follow. Before sitting down to his repast he gave special directions to the effect that the door of the dining-room must be locked, and that it would be dangerous to have him disturbed. He devoured nearly everything on the table, and finally falling into a deep sleep did not wake till morning. The host and some of his inquisitive neighbors were moving about soon after daybreak, and a number of them declared that they had heard mysterious noises during the night, and when the unknown guest stepped out of the dining room into the sunshine, and while paying his bill with American gold, talked incoherently about the gentleman in black, the people who hung about the house were amazed, but when the landlord told them of the empty plates and platters, and

---

° Some curious story circulates on the coast about his second wife : less ethereal, and in order to escape the sad death by cold which befel her predecessor, she took to wearing bear-skin breeches.

they saw the stranger re-embark without saying a word, they were all confounded, and felt certain that the devil and an intimate friend had visited their town.

"On another occasion, while spending a day or two in Quebec, an officer of the law boarded the schooner of our hero, for the purpose of arresting him for debt. Gamache suspected what was in the wind, and as the autumn was far advanced, and he was prepared to leave for the Gulf, he told the officer that the captain should soon be on board, and suggested a glass of wine below by way of killing time. The wine was good, and the officer concluded that he would call again to see the Captain, as his business was of a private nature, but when he ascended to the deck he found himself a prisoner. He was compelled to visit the Island of Anticosti, where he spent the entire winter feasting on the fat of the land as well as of the sea. In the spring, with a good supply of wine and the money for his claim, he took passage in a fishing vessel, and returned a wiser and better man to Quebec, and to the bosom of his disconsolate family.

"Even the officers of the Hudson's Bay Company were compelled to measure their skill with the wit of our friend Gamache. He would barter with the Indians on the Labrador coast, although he knew that the consequence of being captured might be serious. Business had been brisk with him, and when on a quiet summer afternoon he was about leaving a little harbor on the forbidden coast, he was discovered by an armed vessel which immediately started in pursuit. Night came and Gamache found refuge in the harbor of Mingan. When the morning light appeared his enemy was in the offing. Another chase ensued, long and tedious, and night again settled on the waters. And then it was that a rude craft was made and launched, covered with a few tar-barrels, and the bright flame which soon illumined the ocean directly in the course of the frigate, convinced its officers that the runaway had, conscience-stricken, gone to the bottom of the sea. But a better fate awaited him, for he spent the subsequent night in his own bed on the Bay of Gamache.

"On another occasion when our hero happened to be left entirely alone at his house, he saw a stalwart Indian disembark from his canoe, and with a bottle in his hand, march directly for the dwelling. The movements of the savage, his fondness for liquor, and his well-known character for fighting, portended trouble. As he approached, Gamache planted himself at the

G

threshold of his castle, rifle in hand and exclaimed, 'One step further, and I will fire!' The step was taken, but it was the last, for a bullet shattered the thigh bone of the savage. Thus reduced to helplessness, he was gratified to find that Gamache carried him into the house, placed him on a bed, doctored his wound and took every care of him, until the damaged leg was restored; and then loading the Indian with provisions, escorted him to his canoe, with the parting benediction: 'When next you hear that Gamache is alone, and attempt to give him trouble, he will send the bullet through your head,—and now begone!' That lesson had its legitimate effect on the whole tribe of Anticosti Indians.

"One more incident touching the Wizard of Anticosti is to this effect: A young pilot had been driven by the stress of the weather into the Bay of Gamache. He had heard much of the supposed freebooter, and nothing but the dreadful state of things would have induced him to seek refuge in that particular Bay. A short time after he dropped anchor, Gamache came out in a small boat and asked the pilot to his house. Most reluctantly was the invitation accepted, but a manifestation of courage was deemed necessary. When the guest entered the dwelling and saw the walls of each room completely covered with guns, pistols, hatchets, cutlasses, and harpoons, his fears were excited to the highest pitch. Gamache observed this, but only enjoyed the stranger's consternation. A smoking supper was spread upon the table, but even the moofle and the beaver's tail were only tasted by one of the party—the eye of the other quivered, with excitement, and his thoughts were bent upon the tale that would circulate respecting his fate. He made a display of gayety; when the evening was waxing on, he rose to depart, and with many expressions of thankfulness he offered his hand to his host. 'No, no, my friend,' said Gamache, 'you must not leave here; the sea is rough, and the night is dark and wet, and you cannot leave the bay. I have a comfortable bed upstairs, and to-morrow you may leave if still alive.' These words sounded like a knell, and up to the chamber of death, as he supposed, ascended the pilot. 'You may sleep,' continued Gamache, as he handed his guest a lamp, 'as long and soundly as you can. Your bed is soft; it is made with the down of birds I myself have killed; for I am a good shot, and I never miss my game.' For a while the pilot had found it impossible to quiet his never certain sleep; but nature finally gave way, and he fell into a doze which was anything but refreshing. As the clock struck twelve he was startled by a noise, and opened his eyes. There stood Gamache by the bedside with a candle in one hand and a gun in the other. 'I see you are awaked,' said he, 'but why so very pale? You have heard, undoubtedly, that I am in the habit of murdering every one who tarries at my house, and—hanging the gun on the two wooden pegs— 'I have come to give you a settler for the night!' With this remark he displayed a bottle of brandy and tumbler, and after drinking the health of the pilot, handed him the glass, and continued—'There, take a good pull; it will make you sleep soundly, and if Gamache comes to attack you during the night, you can defend yourself with the loaded gun hanging over your head,' and thus the joke ended. When morning came, the storm had disappeared; and the pilot and his host were quite as happy as the day was bright.

"And thus was it as the mood came upon him, that Gamache endeavored to relieve the monotony of his self-inflicted exile. His afflictions seemed to have changed his character; though certainly without guile, a kind of passion for doing out-of-the-way things followed him to the close of his life, and gave him the unenviable reputation he possessed. He died in 1854 from the effects of exposure to cold, and the pleasant Bay with his name is about the only memorial he left behind.

"And now for a few authentic particulars respecting the general character of the Island of Anticosti, as developed by recent explorations. It is one hundred and thirty-six miles long, and thirty-six miles wide; a large part of the coast has a belt of limestone reels that are dry at low water; the south side of the Island is generally low, but on the northern coast there are hills and cliffs that attain an elevation of three, four and five hundred feet. The only attempts at cultivation that have been made are at Gamache Bay, South-West Point and Heath Point, and the chief agricultural productions are potatoes, barley and peas; the forest land is abundant, but the trees are commonly small, and even dwarfish, and peat or mossy bogs abound in every direction. Fruit-bearing trees and shrubs are quite plentiful, but one of the most valuable natural productions is a wild pea growing along the shore of the ocean. The two principal rivers are the Salmon and the Jupiter, and all the streams as well as the lakes, which are numerous, are said to swarm with salmon, salmon trout and trout; the wild animals are the bear, the black, red and silver fox, and the marten. In the bogs and more sheltered parts of the coast, seals are extremely abundant. Besides the harbor named after Gamache, but originally called Ellis Bay, there is a Harbor called Fox Bay, but neither of them would shelter vessels of more than **five** hundred tons burden. The Island is under the Jurisdiction of Lower Canada, but is the private property of a family residing at Quebec."

ANTICOSTI ISLAND.

By William Smith, Esq., Deputy Minister of Marine, Canada.

The island which bears the name of the heading of this article lies directly in the mouth of the St. Lawrence, between the 49th and 50th degrees of latitude, nearly the same as that of the north of France, and contains an area of 2,460,000 acres of land of the best quality, similar, says Sir William Logan, the eminent Canadian geologist, to the fine arable soil of Canada West, and the Genesee County, New York State; it is one-fourth larger in size than Prince Edward Island; it possesses over 300 miles of sea coast, is about 140 miles long, and 35 miles broad in the widest part, with an average breadth of $27\frac{1}{2}$ miles.

Anticosti is made mention of so long ago as 1660, in the geographical folio work of the celebrated loyalist, Dr. Peter Heylyn, known as "Cosmographia." He says that the proper name of the island is *Natiscotee*, which it is supposed was corrupted by the Spaniards, who fished in and off the St. Lawrence at that period, to its present appellation. He reports that the Island was then held by a tribe of Indians, who were exceedingly kind and friendly to such mariners as landed there. The fief of the island was granted by Louis XIV, about 1680, to Sieur Louis Joliet, as a recompense for his discovery of the mouths of the Mississippi and the Illinois, and other services rendered to his Government; and it seems to have been held of so little account in its primitive state that Père Charlevoix, writing about 1712, in his " Histoire du Canada," says that Joliet " would, perhaps, have preferred one of the smallest lordships in France." In La Hontan's " History of Canada," is a chart of the St. Lawrence, and a plan of the island, showing Joliet's Fort on the western flank. La Hontan was a French Marine officer, and he mentions that Joliet was captured in his boat off the island by the English expedition against Quebec, in 1690, under Admiral Phipps, but released after the failure of that expedition. Mr. T. Aubury, who sailed with General Burgoyne's army in 1766, devotes three pages of his work, " Interior Travels Through America," to the seal fisheries of Anticosti, and the method of catching these animals between the continent and the adjacent islands.

So much for the early records of Anticosti. When the feudal system became abolished, which had long prevailed under French domination of Canada, there being no tenants on the island, the seigneur, or lord of the manor, became possessed of the whole soil in fee simple, since which time it has been held jointly by a variety of persons, chief amongst whom are the Forsyth family. The title to this immense possession seems to have been fully acknowledged by the Parliament of Canada, as an act was passed during the last session (in the spring of 1873) incorporating a company to develop the resources of the island.

Anticosti slopes gradually from its elevated northern coast to the grassy savannahs which skirt the southern shore, and thus, in a great measure, the fertile portions of the country are protected from the severe winter winds. Its climate is very healthy, and it certainly is not severer than that of the other maritime provinces The atmosphere is pure and clear, and free from the fogs which are so frequent on and around Newfoundland. The winter's cold is considerably tempered by the waters of the Gulf and River St. Lawrence, and the heat of summer is, to a certain extent, moderated by the same influence. Vegetation progresses there very rapidly and crops come to perfection in good season.* The soil is of good quality, being a rich loam intermixed with limestone; valuable forests are to be found on the greater part of the island, and although the timber generally is not of the largest size, it is of a superior quality, and well adapted for ship-building.

The fisheries around the island, which have been hitherto comparatively neglected, are valuable and important. Speaking of them, Commander Lavoie, of *La Canadienne*, in his report, in 1870, to the Dominion Government, says : "This island is beginning to be frequented and settled by hardy fishermen, tempted by the desire of participating in its rich fisheries, which up to the last few years were, comparatively, unexplored. . . . The importance and value of its fisheries have increased along with the number of fishermen. The waters bordering on Anticosti are stocked with the same kinds as are to be met with on the south and north coast of the St. Lawrence."

In his report for last year (1872) Commander Lavoie says : " Large shoals of herrings visit its shores at about the same time they repair to Pleasant Bay, Magdalen Islands. A schooner, from Prince Edward Island, caught last spring with the seine 1,100 barrels of herrings in one day." He goes on to say : " The whole

---

* I cannot express so hopeful a view as Mr. Smith, from my experience of Anticosti.

1. Certainly, vegetables, such as potatoes, cabbages, turnips and other coarse products, thrive, but wheat, oats and corn will not ripen. Horned cattle will only live a short time.

2. The timber might do for spars.

3. The harbors are not safe.

Admiral Bayfield writes, p. 69 : " It is unusual to find an island so large as Anticosti without a good harbor. The reefs of flat limestone, extending in some parts to $1\frac{1}{4}$ miles from the shore, the want of anchorage off most parts of the coast, and, above all, the frequent fogs, justify this belief in part, but not in so great a degree as to render reasonable the dread with which they seem to have been occasionally regarded.

The loss, suffering, and memorable failure of the recent settlement is likely to make the Island shunned for many years to come."—*St. Lawrence Pilot.*

coast of Anticosti abounds with fish of all sorts, but harbors are scarce, even for fishing boats. Cod fish on this coast are all large, and no finer are seen even on the Miscou and Orphan Banks.' The number of fishermen frequenting its banks increases every year. Even when cod-fishing was a failure everywhere else in the Gulf, it did not fail at Anticosti. Halibut are so plentiful that 199 barrels were taken in one day.

The seal fishery, which could be carried on here as well in winter as in summer, might be turned to profitable account, large numbers of these animals being visible during the former season, and thousands of them being observed in the summer and autumn at the entrance of almost all the bays and rivers, where they remain comparatively unmolested.

Hunting on the island is of considerable value, though of far less importance than its fisheries. The animals whose skins are of marketable value which are found on the island, are black bears, which are very abundant, otters, martens, and silver grey, red, black, and, sometimes, the white fox. Great quantities of ducks, geese, and other wild fowl resort to the lakes and the bays of the island.

There are numerous natural harbors round the coast, which are comparatively safe in all winds—Ellis Bay and Fox Bay being especially so. The former is distant about eight miles from West End Lighthouse on the south side, the latter is fifteen miles from Heath Point Lighthouse on the north side. Ellis Bay is two miles in breadth, with deep water three-fourths of a mile from shore, but only with from three to four fathoms in shore. Fox Bay is smaller, the distance across its mouth is one mile and a half, with deep water in the centre, extending up the bay nine-tenths of a mile, but shoaling near the shores of it, the whole length of the bay being one mile and two-tenths. Mr. Gamache, who has resided at Ellis Bay for upwards of twenty-five years, states the harbor to be perfectly secure in all winds, and at all periods. A gentleman from England, in 1853, a member of Lloyd's who visited the island to inspect a vessel which had been wrecked on the coast, declared he considered the harbor "a most excellent one," so much so, that he should, on his return to England, make it specially known at Lloyd's, and added, further, that there are many places in England, and other countries, carrying on large maritime commerce, which have not got so deep, so spacious, or so safe a harbor as Ellis Bay. This gentleman had been three times round the world as captain of an East Indiaman.

The excellent position of Anticosti in regard to ships, commerce, etc., is easily seen, when we remember that every vessel must take one or other of the channels formed by the island, whether having passed from the Atlantic, or intending to pass to the ocean through the straits of Belle Isle, through the more frequented passage between Newfoundland and Cape Breton, or through the Gut of Canso, or whether running between Quebec and those portions of Canada and of the maritime provinces lying on the Gulf of St. Lawrence. Vessels taking either of the channels formed by the position of the island, must pass close to the island in consequence of the comparative narrowness of the northern one, and of the strong south-east current which always runs along the southern channel. To avoid this, and the risk of being driven on the rock-bound coast of the south shore of the Gulf and River, vessels generally stand out till they make the West Point of Anticosti, close to Ellis Bay. The inner anchorage of this has a depth of from three to four fathoms at low water, with excellent holding ground (gravel and mud); the outer portion of the anchorage could be materially improved at a trifling expense, so as to be able to contain in safety, during all winds, almost any number of vessels of the largest size. If docks were constructed at Ellis Bay, with a patent slip, it would be an admirable position for the repair of vessels stranded or damaged throughout the Lower St. Lawrence, many of which are now broken up by the sea, or dismantled by wreckers before assistance can be obtained from Quebec. For steam-tugs employed for the relief of vessels in distress, this might be made an excellent station; here, also, a few steamers or gunboats could command the two entrances to the river, or send out from this convenient and central spot cruisers to any part of the Gulf.

The establishment of depots of coal at Ellis Bay and Fox River would be an advantage, the importance of which it would be hard to estimate, coal being easily procurable from Nova Scotia, and laid down at either harbor, at a cost not exceeding from $3.50 to $4 per ton. Considering the fact that upwards of 2,000 vessels annually arrive from Europe in the season, besides a large fleet of coasting and fishing vessels, all of which must pass within sight of the island, some idea can be formed of the importance to be attached to the position and capabilities of these harbors for commercial purposes.

The company which has been formed for the purpose of colonizing the Island of Anticosti, and for working and developing its resources, propose to lay out town sites at Ellis Bay, Fox Bay, and at the South-west Point. The chief town will be at Ellis Bay, where the principal place of business will be established. The beautiful situation of the first of these places, with its bracing sea-air, must eventually make it a resort for thousands of pleasure-seekers, since sea-bathing could there be combined with many other summer sports and amusements. The capital of the company is $2,500,000, divided into 25,000 shares of $100 each. The island is to be divided into twenty counties, of about 120,000 acres each, subdivided into five townships. It is further proposed to lay a submarine telegraph cable to connect the island with the main-land ; to build saw-mills and grist-mills, establish a bank and a general hospital, churches and schools, and to establish, moreover, five fishing stations, in different parts of the island, where temporary buildings are to be erected for curing and drying fish.

Operations and improvements of such a kind have everywhere had the most beneficial result upon the industry, wealth, and general progress of the country in which they were attempted, and with the great resources and favorable geographical position of the Island of Anticosti, there is no reason to doubt that they will be attended there with similar results.

Sir William Logan, in his " Geographical Report of Canada," after referring to deposits of peat, or peat-bogs, in different parts of Canada, says, " the most extensive peat deposits in Canada are found in Anticosti, along the low land on the coast of the island, from Heath Point to within eight or nine miles of South-West Point. The thickness of the peat, as observed on the coast, was from three to ten feet, and it appears to be of an excellent quality. The height of this plain may be, on an average, fifteen feet above high-water mark, and it can be easily drained and worked. Between South-West Point and the west end of the island, there are many peat-bogs, varying in superficies from 100 to 1,000 acres."

Near South-West Point there are several large salt ponds, which, if labor was abundant, might be turned to a profitable account in the manufacture of salt ; a manufacture which would become of some value to a great part of our North American fisheries, which, as well as the greater part of Canada, are now supplied with salt from the Bahamas, and from England, or the United States ; and for curing fish and provisions, bay salt, formed from the sea and from salt ponds, is the most valuable.   In consequence of there not having being a sufficient supply of salt upon the island, an immense quantity of fish caught at Anticosti, a year or two ago, were rendered useless.   This was alluded to by Commander Lavoie, of " La Canadienne," in his report for 1871, where he says that " fishing was abundant this season, the yield being reckoned at 9,500 quintals of cod,   .   .   .   but the greatest drawback arose from the difficulty experienced in curing the fish, from the want of salt."   Some of the Bahama Islands are retained merely on account of the salt ponds which they contain, and in Ceylon a large revenue is derived from the salt works carried on in that island.

In Commander Lavoie's report for 1872, quoted from before, he says, that geologists and others, who have visited the interior of the island, agree in stating that its soil is rich, and that more than one million acres can be cultivated with advantage. Clearances have already been made at Gamache (Ellis Bay), at South West, and at West Point, where the vegetables and grains of the district of Montreal and Quebec flourish. Stories, however, of the numerous wrecks that have occurred on the shore of Anticosti have spread such terror that, up to 1861, nobody had thought of settling there. The reefs of flat limestone, extending in some parts to one mile and a quarter from the shore ; the want of anchorage of a great portion of the coast ; and, above all, the frequent fogs, justify this belief, in part ; but not in so great a degree as to render reasonable the dread with which they seem to have been regarded, and which can only have arisen from the natural tendency to magnify dangers, of which we have no precise knowledge.

Four lighthouses are erected on Anticosti ; one on Heath Point, at the east end of the island ; another at South-West Point, the third on West Point ; and the fourth at South Point, at Bagota Bluff. That on Heath Point is a round tower, built of a greyish white limestone, quarried on the island, and is ninety feet high. It shows, at an elevation of 110 feet above the level of high water, a fixed white light, which in clear weather should be visible from a distance of fifteen miles. The lighthouse on South-West Point is built of the same stone as the previous one, quarried on the spot, is seventy-five feet high, and of the usual conical form, exhibits a white light, which revolves every three minutes, and is visible at fifteen miles, with the eye ten feet above the sea ; with the eye at fifty feet, it can be seen nineteen and a-half miles, and with the eye at an elevation of 100 feet, it will be visible about twenty-three miles. The third lighthouse, erected on the West Point of Anticosti, is a circular stone tower, faced with white fire brick, 109 feet in height. It exhibits, at 112 feet above high-water mark, a fixed white light, visible from a distance of fifteen miles. A gun is fired every hour during fog and snow storms. The lighthouse at South Point is a comparatively new building, the light having been first exhibited in August, 1870. It is a hexagonal tower, painted white, seventy-five feet above high-water mark, with a revolving white flash light every twenty seconds. It should be seen at from fourteen to eighteen miles distance, and is visible from all points of approach. A powerful steam fog-whistle is also stationed there, about 300 feet east of the lighthouse. In foggy weather, and during snow storms, this is sounded ten seconds in every minute, thus making an interval of fifty seconds between each blast, which can be heard in calm weather, or with the wind from nine to fifteen miles distant, and in stormy weather, or against the wind, from three to eight miles. The lights are exhibited from the 1st of April to the 20th of December of each year.

Provision depots are also established on the island for the relief of wrecked crews. The first of those is at Ellis Bay, the second at the lighthouse at the South-West Point; the third which was formerly at Shallop Creek (Jupiter River), was this year removed to South Point, where the new lighthouse and steam fog-whistle have been located, and the fourth at the light-house on Heath Point. Direction boards are erected on the shore, or nailed to trees, from which the branches have been lopped off, near the beach, and on various points of the coast. These boards are intended to point out to shipwrecked persons the way to the provision posts.

Vessels are more frequently lost on Anticosti, in the bad weather, at the close of navigation, than at any other time, and their crews would perish from want, and the rigors of a Canadian winter, if it were not for this humane provision, made by Government, in the absence of settlements on the island. As, however, the population begins to increase, and dwellings become scattered about, there will be the less urgent need for these depots.

The currents around the Island of Anticosti are very variable and uncertain, and to this cause may be attributed many of the shipwrecks that have from time to time occurred there. At the north point of the island there is a current almost always setting over to the north-east, being turned in that direction by the west end of the island. Confined as it is, within a narrow channel, it is very strong. All along the south coast, between the south-west and west points, the swell and the current both set in shore, and the bottom being of clean flat limestone, will not hold an anchor. It is also by no means uncommon in summer for the breeze to die away suddenly to a calm.

The tide around the island only rises from four to seven feet.

It not unfrequently happens that when the current from the northward is running, another from W.N.W. comes along the south coast, in which case they meet at a reef off Heath Point, and cause a great ripple, or irregular breaking sea. This takes place when a fresh breeze is blowing along the land on either side of the island. A wind has been observed on the north side from N. or N.E., whilst that on the south side was W.N.W., and yet never meeting round the east end of the island. Between the two winds there is usually a triangular space of calm, and light baffling airs, extending from five to eight miles. In the space between the winds there is often observed a high cross sea, and constantly changing light airs, which would leave a vessel at the mercy of the current, and in great danger of being set on the Heath Point reef.

Streams of excellent water descend to the sea on every part of the coasts of Anticosti. They are, for the most part, too small to admit boats, becoming rapid immediately within their entrance, and even the largest of them are barred with sand, excepting for short intervals of time, after the spring floods, or after continued heavy rains.

There is no doubt that, in a very few years, there will be a numerous population on the island, as applications for land are being constantly received by the Anticosti Company, and the survey is being pressed forward with all practicable speed. Had the island been thrown open to settlement years ago, it would be in a very different position, commercially speaking, from what it now is ; but once opened, and found to be equally productive with the Maritime Provinces and Prince Edward Island, there is no reason why in a few decades it should not rival the latter. For long neglected and discarded, Anticosti now has a chance of prominence, and the Dominion will hail the advent of another link in her chain, which, though it may never assume the title now borne by Prince Edward Island, " The gem of the Gulf," may yet prove as valuable a jewel in the diadem of Confederation.

NOTE.—If the Anticosti Company turned out such an expensive failure, the efforts of individuals were more successful. We gather from different sources, and especially from a Gaspé communication in the *Morning Chronicle* of June, 1877, that after the collapse of the Company, in 1874, the aid extended by the Government, under the intelligent management of the Agent for the Marine Department at Quebec, T. U. Gregory, Esq., has resulted in most permanent and beneficial results. Mr. Gregory visited, in person, that fall, the forlorn settlers of Ellis Bay, and, instead of removing them to the main land, distributed biscuit, pork, flour, to last until the spring, impressing on them to cultivate the land, and not rely solely on the fisheries, and leaving them seed potatoes for the spring. The yield from these potatoes has been surprising—forty bushels to one—and, in 1877, whole cargoes of potatoes have been shipped to Quebec. We congratulate Mr. Gregory for his share in the beneficial results. The population, from 127 in 1871, reaches now some 300 souls.

CHAPTER XIV.

LOSS OF THE FRENCH FRIGATE " LA RENOMMÉE" ON ANTICOSTI,
14TH NOV., 1736—A WINTER OF HORRORS, STARVATION
AND DEATH—A MISSIONARY'S CAREER.

OF the many shipwrecks, which gave the lower St. Lawrence,
in former days, an unenviable notoriety, there were none, we
believe, more harrowing—none so fully described, though few as
little known, as that of His Most Christian Majesty's sloop-of-
war *La Renommée*, of which the full account in English is now
submitted. It is a translation from a narrative written by Father
Crespel,* one of the surviving passengers.

La Renommée, a French sloop-of-war, of 14 guns, com-
manded by Captain de Freneuse, was stranded on the 14th
Nov., 1736, on a ledge of flat rocks, scarcely a mile from shore,
about eight leagues from the south point of Anticosti, at the en-
trance of the Gulf of St. Lawrence. On the 3rd of Nov., 1736,
La Renommée, bound for Rochelle, France, and consigned to the
King's Treasurers, Messrs. Pacaud, sailed from the port of
Quebec, with a complement of 54 men. All went well until

---

* Father Emmanuel Crespel recounts this shipwreck, in a spirited letter
addressed by him to his brother.

This friar, according to Bibaud, seems to have landed in Canada in
October, 1724. Some time after he was sent to Sorel as a missionary ; there
he remained two years. We find him as almoner at Detroit, at Fort Frontenac, at Crown Point. . After his escape from death on Anticosti, he was sent to
Soulanges as pastor, where he remained two years. He was subsequently
sent to France, on the King's ship *Rubis*, to act as *vicaire* of the convent of
Anesnes in Hainault. Finally he returned to Canada, and died at Quebec,
28th April, 1775.

eleven days later, when the vessel, whilst standing over under a stiff breeze from the south, towards Anticosti, and in the act of wearing, suddenly touched ground and commenced to ship heavy seas. All was confusion on board. The gunner's mate, alone, had the presence of mind to rush below to the store-room and remove some biscuit and provisions, together with fire arms—a barrel of powder and cartridges ; these things were stowed in the jolly-boat. A heavy sea, having struck the vessel, wrenched off the rudder, when the commander ordered one of the masts to be cut, which, in its fall, made the ship careen over. Cool and collected, in the midst of danger, Captain de Freneuse quietly gave orders to have the long-boat hung to the davits. Twenty persons jumped in; as the last was entering, one of the blocks gave way. Half of the inmates were precipitated in the sea— the rest clung to the sides of the boat, dangling in mid air. Without moving a muscle the intrepid commander ordered the rear tackle to be let go, but as the boat straightened and touched the water, two seas struck her. At last she shoved off.

One of the officers steered with a broken oar, and with a drenching rain passengers and crew made for the shore, where the ominous roar of breakers fell dismally on their ears. Carried onward on the crest of a billow the boat was soon capsized and dashed on the iron-bound coast. The foresight of a sailor who jumped ashore, holding the painter, afforded the rest the means of dragging the craft out of the retreating billow. · The sea had disgorged its prey, but the position of the shipwrecked mariners was not much improved. They were huddled on a kind of small island, which the high tides evidently submerged. To reach the main island itself they had to cross the Pavillion stream ; this was nigh costing them their life.

Some hours later the jolly-boat, manned by six persons, rejoined them. The crew reported that Captain de Freneuse was still on board of *La Renommée*, with seventeen men, and that he refused to quit the ship.

One can imagine the prospect of those who had reached the

shore—on the dreary island of Anticosti without fire or shelter of any kind, whilst those that had persisted in remaining on the deck of the doomed ship expected her to break up every instant· At midnight, the storm was at its height; all hope of surviving had vanished. At dawn, it was found that *La Renom- mée*, being a new and staunch frigate, still held together. Not a moment was lost in making preparations to leave. Provisions, carpenters tools, tar, an axe, and some canvas were deposited in one of the remaining boats; and Captain de Freneuse, with a heavy heart, rolled up the Flag of his good ship, took it in the boat with him, and quitted, the last of all his companions, the quarter deck of the noble frigate.

The second night passed on the island was still more dread- ful than the first. Two feet of snow had fallen, and without the shelter of the canvas all would have succumbed to the in- clemency of the weather. There was no time, however, to de- spond. All set to work. The mizzen-mast of the ship had drifted on shore. It was cut up to make a keel for the boat; the latter was carefully caulked and made seaworthy. Whilst a supply of fuel was obtained by some of the crew, the others did their best to melt snow. Active occupation it was thought would deaden sorrow, but, on any interruption taking place, despair would again reappear. Six months' captivity awaited the ill-fated mariners on a dismal isle, until navigation should open in the ensuing spring. Their stores stood as follows :

Quebec ships homeward bound carried provisions for two months only. At the date of the shipwreck *La Renommée* had already been eleven days out. The salt water had destroyed a portion of her ships' stores, and even with the strictest economy in doling out a scanty, daily ration, there was barely enough for forty days' subsistence. With the arctic temperature of winter, the floating ice forming round the ship was rapidly cutting her out from intercourse with the shore. Snow was lying deep on the ground, and as a crowning evil, fever set in. • A final decision must be arrived at immediately. It was known that a party of

French, that winter, intended to pass the season at Mingan, on the north shore, in readiness for the spring seal-fishing. To meet it, it was necessary to travel forty leagues over the sea shore before the north-west point of the island was reached, and then twelve leagues of open sea had to be crossed. Would it be better to divide into two groups, one of which would winter at Pavillion river, whilst the other would push for Mingan to secure assistance? In theory, the proposition had much to recommend it. The trouble arose, when it came to a decision, as to who should go to Mingan, and who should remain behind. None would consent to remain. "In this emergency," says Father Crespel, "we resolved to seek counsel and succor from God."

On the 26th of Nov., he celebrated Mass. This over, twenty-four of the crew resigned themselves to the Divine Will to winter at Pavillion river, no matter what the consequences might be. Thus, was sundered the Gordian knot. All that night, the missionary was engaged in hearing confessions. Next day, after leaving provisions for their forlorn companions and swearing on the Holy Evangelists to return as soon as possible to take them away, Captain de Freneuse, Father Crespel, and M. de Senneville, with thirty-eight followers, set off for the unknown shores of Mingan. The sense of a common danger having obliterated all distinctions of rank, a hearty and solemn farewell was exchanged all round. Alas! to many it was to be a final one!

Two parties were formed by the commander.

The mode of travel was dreadful. By dint of tugging at the oars, six to nine miles per day was the most they could achieve. The snow was their couch at night. A diminutive quantity of dry codfish, a few teaspoonfuls of flour diluted with snow water: such was their evening meal.

Bright and balmy was the 2nd December; a gentle breeze springing up, hope revisited their emaciated countenances, when, on attempting to double the south-west point of the island, the long-boat, under sail, met with a heavy cross sea; and in wearing, the jolly-boat, next to them, was lost sight of. "Later on, we found out," says Father Crespel, "what had happened it: it was swamped." Being forced to run for shelter, we at last succeeded in landing after infinite trouble. A large fire was lit on the beach to indicate, if possible, to the missing boat the spot where Captain de Freneuse's party in the long-boat were located. After gulping down a little of the flour mixture, we sank down weary, to sleep amidst the snow. All slept until the roar of a terrible storm, which threw the long-boat on the shore, awoke us. We set to repairing the damage done to our craft; the delay had the good effect that we succeeded in capturing, in a trap set for the purpose, two foxes who were prowling in the neighborhood.

On the 7th December, Captain de Freneuse was able to set out again, but with a heavy heart, having, despite all his re_ searches, failed to obtain any tidings of the other boat. The craft had scarcely held her way for three hours, when another storm struck her. Not a harbor, not a creek to run into. This was one of our gloomiest nights—having to keep cruising, in the surf and floating ice, in a bay in which we could get no grapline to hold. A landing was effected at dawn. The cold got so intense that the bay froze over; the boat ceased to be of any use. Further, we could not go. The stores were landed; huts erected with spruce boughs, also a depot for provisions in such a position that none could have access to them without being seen by all. Rules were framed for their distribution. Four ounces of paste daily to each man, and two pounds of flour and two pounds of fox meat, constituted the daily allowance for seventeen men.

Once a week, a spoonful of peas varied the fare. "This,'' adds Father Crespel, " was our best meal." Bodily exercise became a necessity. Leger, Basile and Father Crespel used to go and cut branches for fuel; another party carried the wood to the huts, while the care of keeping the forest path beaten and open devolved on a third. In the midst of these associations, trials were not wanting. Having no change of clothing, vermin soon preyed on these unfortunates; the smoke in the huts and the whiteness of the snow brought on ophthalmia; while unwhole-

some food and snow water had engendered constipation and dia-
betes—but the energy of these hardy men failed them not.

On the 24th December, Father Crespel succeeded in thawing
some wine for sacred purposes. Christmas was at hand, and
midnight mass was to be solemnized. It was celebrated without
pomp—without church ornaments, in the largest of the huts.
A touching spectacle it must have presented: forlorn castaways,
amidst the solitude of Anticosti, wafting their tearful adoration
to the helpless babe in the stable of Bethlehem.

New Year's Day, 1737, was marked by a terrible reverse.
Foucault, sent at dawn to reconnoitre, came back with the appal-
ling news that the ice had carried away the long-boat. For five
days, nothing was heard but sobs and wailings. All, then, was
lost! The thought of death took possession of every mind;
the idea of suicide was rapidly invading these diseased brains.
Father Crespel, during these dark hours, unceasingly held forth
on the duties revealed religion imposed—on the sufferings undergone by the Son of God to save mankind, beseeching his
hearers to rely on Divine mercy. The mass *de Spiritu Sancto*
was again solemnized on Epiphany Day, to call down on the
deserted mariners, strength from above—courage to accept the
decrees of fate.

On the impulse of the moment, Foucault and Vaillant
consented to go and search for the lost boat.

Their generous zeal met with its reward. Two hours later,
they returned with the news that, whilst looking round, they
had come on an Indian wigwam and on two bark canoes, concealed under branches. They produced, in corroboration of
their statement, an axe and the fat of a seal, taken from the
wigwam.

This proved conclusively that the island was inhabited.
Noisy demonstrations of joy replaced the deep-set gloom.
Next day, another cheering incident was added. Two sailors,
who had wandered from the rest, discovered the long-boat,
stuck fast in a field of ice, and, in returning to camp, they had

the inexpressible satisfaction to find on the shore a chest, containing wearing apparel; it had floated there. Their joy, however, was of brief duration. On the 23rd January, the master carpenter died suddenly. Distressing symptoms were manifesting themselves among the crew; every seaman's legs began to swell.

On the 16th February, an astounding blow, like a bombshell, fell in their midst. Captain de Freneuse's brave spirit, borne on the wings of prayer, was wafted heavenwards. Next, expired Jerome Bosseman; next, Girard; lastly, died the master-gunner, a Calvinist, whose recantation, Father Crespel says, he received in due time. Religion claimed its rights, and dispensed around its soothing balm in those moments of anguish. Simple indeed was the burial. The dead were dragged out by their fellow sufferers; snow piled over the livid remains close to the entrance of the hut. This was all their physical exhaustion permitted them to do. Even the elements seemed leagued against them. On the sixth of March, a snow storm overwhelmed the hut of Father Crespel, who had to seek shelter in the sailors' hut. For three days, raged the blinding storm, keeping them prisoners in the hut, without fire, without provisions. They had snow water to drink. Five more of the party succumbed to cold and want. The snow had completely covered over their hut—to them a species of living tomb. By their united efforts, they forced open the door, emerged from the snow-drift and sought out provisions. The temperature outside was such, that half an hour of exposure sufficed to freeze the hands and feet of Basile and Foucault; their comrades carried them back in their arms. Their sally had resulted in procuring a little flour from the depot. After these three days of abstinence, it was so ravenously devoured that, at one time, death seemed likely to be the result for all.

Encouraged by the example of Basile and of Foucault, Leger, Furst and Father Crespel went to the woods to gather fuel. The scanty supply was exhausted before eight o'clock that night. The cold was so great that Vaillant, senior, was found next morning frozen stiff on his bed of spruce boughs. It was judged prudent to seek another shelter. Father Crespel's hut being smaller, might, when dug out of the deep snow, be more easily kept heated.

Nothing was more heart-rending to view than the dismal procession which took place on the removal to the small hut; the less broken-down of the seamen loading on their shoulders Messrs. de Senneville and Vaillant, jr., whose flesh was falling to pieces, whilst Le Vasseur, Basile and Foucault, whose limbs had been frozen, dragged themselves on their knees and elbows.

On the 17th March, their familiar, death, ended the sufferings of Basile; and on the 19th Foucault, who was youthful and athletic, closed his career after a frightful agony. The festering sores of the survivors were wrapped up and bandaged with the clothes taken from the dead bodies. Twelve days later, Messrs. de Senneville and Vaillant's feet dropped off, and their hands began to mortify; Christian resignation at times made room for despair.

On the 1st April, Leger, whilst reconnoitering in the direction where the bark canoe had been found concealed, captured an Indian and his squaw, whom he escorted to the camp. These were the first human faces seen since they had left Pavillion river, and Father Crespel, versed in Indian dialects, explained the state of affairs to the savages, urging them with tears to go and hunt for game for the party. The Indian solemnly promised. One, two, three days expired, and still no word of the Indians. Leger and Father Crespel dragged themselves as far as the wigwam, where they found to their utter consternation that one of the canoes had disappeared. Misfortune having sharpened their wits, the two walking skeletons yoked themselves to the remaining canoe, which they drew to their wigwam, fastening it securely to the door, so as to render the escape of the owner from the island, impossible without visiting the wigwam.

Alas! no visitor came to them, except the dreaded and

familiar visitor—death—which successively carried off Le Vasseur, Vaillant, jr., aged sixteen, and de Senneville, aged twenty
years, son of a King's Lieutenant, at Montreal—who had in his
youth been a page of Madame La Dauphine of France, and had
served in the *Mousquetaires*.

Having no more sick to look after, Father Crespel re-
assembled the survivors in council when it was resolved to quit
the funereal spot and to travel in a canoe. The frail craft in
custody was accordingly repaired—smeared with fat ; —rude
paddles were hewn in the woods, and the 21st of April fixed on,
as the day of departure.

Their commissariat consisted of the flesh of the hind leg of a
fox. It had been arranged that the juice alone of this meat, when
boiled, was to be served out that day to the famished mariners,
the flesh itself being reserved for the morrow ; but on the smell
of the cookery reaching their olfactory nerves, all ravenously
attacked and eat the meat, which disappeared in a trice. " Instead
of giving us strength, this surfeit weakened us. We awoke,"
says Father Crespel, " next morning more debilitated, and what
was worse, without any food to fall back on."

Two days thus elapsed in hunger and despair ; death was
waited for as a welcome deliverer ; the famished men were repeating on the sea shore, the Litanies for the dead ; all at once
was heard the report of fire-arms.

It was, adds Father Crespel, our friend, the Indian, who had
returned to ascertain what had become of his canoe. At this
juncture, the unfortunates dragged themselves towards the Indian, uttering pitiful cries, but the savage chose to consider himself deaf to all their entreaties, and shortly, took to his heels.
Father Crespel and Leger, though insufficiently shod, under the
sting of this new desertion, decided to give chase—crossed over
Bescie (Sheldrake) river, and managed to close on the fugitive,
whose flight was retarded by the weight of a seven-years child
slung to his shoulders. The savage, to make safe his escape,
pointed out to them a spot in the woods, where, he said, he had

stowed away a quarter of bear's meat, half cooked. All that
night was passed mutually watching one another. Next day
Father Crespel intimated to the Indian to conduct him to the
Indian encampment. The seven-years old Indian lad was
detained as a hostage, and placed on a sledge. Leger and
Father Crespel yoked themselves to it, whilst the big savage
walked before as their guide. After journeying on for three
miles, the party struck on the sea, and as this seemed the shortest route, it was decided to go by water. The canoe could only
contain three persons—Father Crespel, the Indian and his child.
Loud were the lamentations when the missionary got into the
canoe, after beseeching his companions to follow on foot along
the shore.

On the evening of that day, the savage induced Father
Crespel to land and make a fire, to which the Father acceded the
more readily that the wind was high, but having ascended a hum-
mock of ice to look round, the redskin took occasion of the coura-
geous father having his back turned, to fly into the woods with
his child. Nothing now remained for Father Crespel to complete
this chain of disaster, but death. Deserted by all around, the brave
missionary leaning on the barrel of his gun, poured out his sorrows
to God, and, as he says, recited the verses of the Book of Job.
Whilst thus engaged, he was joined by Leger, who, with eyes
swimming in tears, informed him that his comrade Furst had
fainted and fallen down on the snow some distance away, and
that he had been compelled to leave him to his fate. At that
instant, a gun-shot rent the air, in the direction of an opening in
the forest. Leger, still buoyed up with hope, pressed Father
Crespel to follow him. When in the act of entering the wood,
a second gun report was heard. Instead of firing off their own
muskets in reply, the Frenchmen advanced silently in the direction from whence came the sound, when soon they hit on a
clearing, in the centre of which stood the hut of an Indian chief,
with smoke issuing therefrom. The chief greeted them with
kind words, explaining to them that the singular conduct of the

Indian guide in running away from them was the effect of fear of the scurvy, small-pox, and " bad air."

But where was poor Furst ! The missionary tempted the Indian by an offer of his gun if he would go and fetch their missing comrade. It was all in vain. Furst spent the night lying on the snow, where God alone protected him from the intense cold ; " as for us," says Father Crespel, "though under the shelter of our hut, we suffered intolerably from the temperature, and it was only on the morrow, when we were starting to meet Furst, that he returned to us."

Two days more were allowed for recruiting, and mindful of the solemn pledge given to return with help from those who had remained at Pavillion River, they embarked on the 1st May for Mingan. Father Crespel reached there in advance of the others, having exchanged from the boat to a light canoe, which, alone, he paddled the space of six leagues. M. Volant, the head of the Mingan post, received his French compatriots with considerate kindness. Not a moment was lost to hurry on relief to the survivors of *La Renommée*. A large, well-equipped, and amply provisioned boat, under the guidance of Mr. Volant, shoved off, bearing also Father Crespel, Furst, and Leger.

On the craft nearing the Pavillion river, a volley was fired by the crew ; instantly from the woods emerged four men, in appearance more like savages; they knelt on the shore extending their suppliant hands towards the boat. The tenderest care was taken of these walking skeletons. During the absence of Father Crespel and party, these unfortunates had undergone incredible sufferings. Exposure, hunger, gangrene had successively decimated their numbers. Finally they had to face starvation, after every expedient had been resorted to. The shoes of the dead men were boiled in snow water and then roasted in embers for food ; last of all, the fur breeches they had worn were boiled and eaten ; a single pair remained when Mr. Volant arrived.

Thus reduced, the greatest caution was necessary to bring them round. Strictest orders were given to regulate the supply

of food for these exhausted stomachs. For all that, a native of
Brittany named Tenguy, died suddenly, whilst being helped to
a glass of brandy, and sudden joy produced insanity on another
named Tourillet. As for two of their comrades, Baudet and
Bonau, both natives of *Ile de Rhé*, their bodies began to smell.
Mr. Volant's boat was changed into an hospital, whilst those on
shore, set to digging graves for the twenty-one corpses, which
encircled the spot where the first detachment of the crew
of the French frigate had wintered. A modest cross was
raised to mark the place where these human beings had suffered
and resignedly closed their eyes in death. The boat then put
out to sea, hugging the shore and watching closely for any traces
of the small party who had entrusted their fortunes to the jolly-
boat. A few leagues from the spot where now stands the lighthouse, lately kept by Mr. Ed. Pope,* Mr. Volant now discovered
two dead bodies on the strand; close by, the fragments of a small
boat. These were the only remaining traces of the thirteen
men who had striven in the jolly-boat to keep company with
Captain de Freneuse and the long-boat, until they were lost
sight of on doubling, in a heavy sea, the south-west point of
Anticosti on the 2nd December, 1736.

---

* This respected gentleman died at Anticosti, aged 82 years, on the
2nd July, 1871.

CHAPTER XV.

"The Voices of the Sea"—A Storm Without Wind—Some
of Jacques Cartier's and Charlevoix's Tough Yarns—
The Legendary Lore of the St. Lawrence—Le Braillard de la Magdeleine.

My return trip from Anticosti, in 1843, was marked by a singular
incident—a heavy swell without a breath of wind. The "Breeze"
having no headway, would not steer, and rolled helplessly in the
trough of the sea ; so much at times, that one might have expected
her masts to snap like reeds—a most radiant sunshine during all
this while. No noise caught the ear except certain low mutter-
ings in the distance, which chimed in mournfully with the creak-
ing of the yards as the vessel rose and fell to the billows. A
school of whales, and some porpoises, disported themselves north
of us, the former spouting from their nostrils the briny surf. Did
these murmurings proceed from these leviathans of the deep? It
recalled those "mysterious noises of the ocean" so exquisitely
described by Chateaubriand, and likened by him to the voices of
birds :—" Ces oiseaux avaient des voix extraordinaires, comme
celles qui sortent de mers. Si l'ocean a sa Flore, il a aussi sa
Philomèle ; lorsqu'au coucher du soleil le courlis siffle sur la
pointe d'un rocher, et que le bruit des vagues l'accompagne, c'est
une des harmonies les plus plaintives que l'on puisse entendre."
It was not, however,

> o o o A wild, promiscuous sound,
> Like broken thunders that at distance roar,
> Or billows murmuring on the hollow shore.

The eccentric Thoreau depicts thus, those peculiar utterings of old Ocean which are at times heard in the midst of a calm or before a storm :—

" The sounds which the ocean makes must be very significant and interesting to those who live near it. When I was leaving the shore at this place (Cape Cod) the next summer, and had got a quarter of a mile distant, ascending a hill, I was startled by a certain loud sound from the sea, as if a large vessel were letting off steam by the shore, so that I caught my breath and felt my blood run cold for an instant, and I turned about expecting to see one of the Atlantic steamers thus far out of her course, but there was nothing unusual to be seen. There was a low bank at the entrance of the hollow, between me and the ocean, and suspecting that I might have risen into another stratum of air in ascending the hill, which had wafted to me only the ordinary roar of the sea, I immediately descended again, to see if I lost hearing of it ; but without regard to my ascending or descending, it died away in a minute or two, and yet there was scarcely any wind all the while. The old man said that this was what they called the 'rut,' a peculiar roar of the sea before the wind changes, which, however, he could not account for. He thought that he could tell all about the weather from the sounds which the sea made.

" Old Joselyn, who came to New England in 1638, has it among his weather signs that 'the resounding of the sea from the shore, and murmuring of winds in the woods, without apparent wind, sheweth wind to follow.'

" Being on another part of the coast one night since this, I heard the roar of the surf a mile distant, and the inhabitants said it was a sign that the wind would work round east, and we should have rainy weather. The ocean was heaped up somewhere at the eastward, and this roar was occasioned by its effort to preserve its equilibrium, the wave reaching the shore before the wind. Also the captain of a packet between this country and England told me that he sometimes met with a wave on the Atlantic coming

against the wind, perhaps in a calm sea, which indicated that at
a distance the wind was blowing from an opposite quarter, but
the undulation had travelled faster than it.   Sailors tell of 'tide-
rips' and 'ground-swells,' which they suppose to have been
occasioned by hurricanes and earthquakes, and to have travelled
many hundreds, and sometimes even two or three thousand miles."
(Cape Cod—Thoreau—p. 39.)

How many thousand miles away was brisk Eurus stirring up
his domain? and this inexplicable tide-rip, or ground-swell, from
whence had it travelled?

The caption to this chapter leads the reader to expect, *inter
alia*, some "tough yarns" from old travellers; the reader must
not be disappointed.

Charlevoix, the historian, relates that Jacques Cartier, on the
15th May, 1534, on visiting the Bird Rocks elsewhere described,
had an encounter with * "a white bear of the size of a cow, who
sprang into the sea on seeing Cartier's boats.   The day after, the
great discoverer captured Bruin whilst swimming near the coast
of Newfoundland—fourteen leagues distant!"   Heugh! what a
swim!   Leander's feat on the Hellespont was a mere joke to
this; the Arctic stranger may also have been swimming for love!
Who dares deny?   This seems tough, but what Charlevoix says
of the flesh and habits of the Canadian horned owl is even more
so.

"This bird," † says he, "is good eating, many prefer his flesh

---

°De là il (Cartier) remonta au nord, et gagna des iles qu'il appela dans
ses Mémoires, les Iles aux Oiseaux.   Elles sont éloignées de Terreneuve de
quatorze lieues, et il fut bien surpris d'y voir un ours blanc, de la grosseur
d'une vache, qui avait fait ce trajet à la nage.   Dès que cet animal eut
aperçu les chaloupes qui allaient à terre, il se jetta à la mer et le lendemain
Cartier l'ayant remontré assez près de Terreneuve, le tua et le prit." [Hist.
Nouvelle France, Vol. I, p. 8.)

† La chaire du Chat-Huant Canadien est bonne à manger, et bien des
gens la prefèrent à celle de la Poule . . . . Sa provision pour l'hyver sont
des Mulots, auxquels il casse les pattes, et qu'il engraiss et nourrit avec soin,
jusqu'à ce qu'il en ait besoin." (*Lettre de Charlevoix à la Duchesse de Les
Diguères*, 1721.)

to that of chickens. He lives in winter on ground-mice, which he has caught in the previous fall, breaking their legs first (a most useful precaution, to prevent their escape) and then fattens them up with care, for his daily use." This, no doubt, is pushing to its extreme limits, the privilege of great travellers.

I, for one, will unhesitatingly claim the right of accepting this "white bear story" and owl anecdote, as the Frenchman aptly says, *sous bénéfice d'inventaire.* At page 16 of Charlevoix's *Histoire de la Nouvelle France,* we find something else very spicy. Every one is aware of the popular tradition which goes to explain the ungainly appearance of the Esquimaux tribe, viz., that the Esquimaux are the offspring of two seals, who, having become tired of the liquid element, resolved, like Captain Cuttle, to spend the remainder of their lives on shore, and in their old age had several children who had lost all taste for the sea, and became the ancestors of the Esquimaux. This is startling enough with regard to our unctuous, oleaginous, and aromatic brethren of the far North, but the peculiar organization which Jacques Cartier lends them, is still more worthy of note. Cartier was told by Donacona that there existed in a distant land (nothing like distance to lend enchantment to objects), human beings who did not eat, but seemed to live by what they drank (Neal Dow has discovered many such, even in our own country); that in another place the men had but one leg, a very large one; one arm, with two hands on it—and a variety of other peculiarities of lively interest to Professor Owen and comparative anatomy. But *revenons à nos moutons:* the "storm of calm," as our captain called the troubled state of the waters without wind, lasted a few hours, during all which the brightest of noonday suns lit up the scene. The currents and winds wafted us then higher up than Little Fox River, and we anchored close to the River Magdeleine, so famous for its wild legends amongst the seafaring people at Gaspé.

The "Breeze" was riding at anchor in the vicinity of the spot where the famous *Braillard de la Magdeleine* was heard during the great storms which sweep the coast.

Before setting forth the version which an old dame—a second Bessie Millie,* and who also possibly "helped out her subsistence by selling favorable winds to mariners"—gave us, on landing, I shall quote from the *Soirées Canadiennes* for October, 1861, the humorous description of the Braillard, by our late and lamented friend, the historian of Canada, Abbé Ferland.

" We are opposite the River Magdeleine, famous in the chronicles of the country for ghost stories connected with it.

" Where is the Canadian sailor, familiar with this coast, who has not heard of the plaintive sounds and doleful cries uttered by the *Braillard de la Magdeleine?* Where would you find a native seaman who would consent to spend a few days by himself in this locality, wherein a troubled spirit seeks to make known the torments it endures ? Is it the soul of a shipwrecked mariner asking for Christian burial for its bones, or imploring the prayers of the Church for its repose ? Is it the voice of the murderer condemned to expiate his crime on the very spot which witnessed its commission? . . For it is well known that Gaspé wreckers have not always contented themselves with robbery and pillage, but have sometimes sought concealment and impunity by making away with victims,—convinced that the tomb is silent and reveals not its secrets. Or else, is this the celebrated Devil's Land mentioned by the cosmographer Thevet, where, according to him, Roberval (in 1542) abandoned his niece, la Demoyselle Marguerite with her lover and with her old Norman Duenna. The ancient chronicler places this land somewhere in the Gulf of St. Lawrence, and relates that after the death of her two companions, the Lady Marguerite had to contend with devils, who, under the disguise of white bears, tried to frighten her with their claws and their growls. On this legendary topic, Thevet might have found a match in one of our sailors, who certainly knew naught of the Lady Marguerite, but was particularly well posted in all matters referring to the *Braillard de la Magdeleine.* He felt ill at ease in this neighborhood, and

---

° Waverley Novels—*The Pirate.*

whistled for wind, were it even contrary : anything to him seemed preferable to remaining in the vicinity of the *Braillard.*" (*Log of the schooner Sarah, during her trip from Quebec to Gaspé in 1836.—Abbé Ferland.*)

On the other hand, the resident *cicerone* thus held forth : " An awful shipwreck once occurred at this place. A father and mother, amongst crowds of others, here found a watery grave. Their infant son, by some miraculous interposition of his guardian angel, was safely washed ashore." Whether in this case the guardian angel assumed the form of a Newfoundland dog, or the more orthodox appearance of a winged cherub, tradition has failed to say. " The darling boy was safely landed on the pebbly beach, and soon made it vocal with his grief and moans for the loss of his best friends. His infant wailings blended with the swelling storm, struck the ear of some belated fisherman whose boat was passing the entrance of the River Magdeleine. Hence the name 'Le Braillard Magdeleine.' The noise is still heard in stormy weather, and may be explained either by the action of the surf rolling into one of the many hollow caverns along the Gaspé coast, and which has astonished all observers, or by shelving rocks over which it moans, like an unquiet spirit. It would, however, be doing an injustice to my venerable and pious *cicerone* were I to conceal the fact that she admitted, albeit hesitatingly, that the moanings of the ' Braillard ' might be caused by the action of high winds on two large pines which overhang a neighboring cape, and whose trunks grate ominously on one another. Alas alas ! for the marvellous ! The Abbé Casgrain tells a tale about the *Braillard des Iles de la Magdeleine*, in which a bad priest became, through grief, reduced to a skeleton, for having refused to christen a child, who subsequently died unbaptized, and was heard to moan constantly afterwards." Gentle reader, you have your choice of these explanations.

[*Here closes our Nautical Journal for 1871. Two summers will elapse ere we resume our pleasant peregrinations in the kingdom of herring and cod.*]

CHAPTER XVI.

THE ISLE OF MISCOU—ITS EARLY HISTORY—FISHERIES—GAME —LIGHT HOUSES, &C.—ONE OF CHAMPLAIN'S FISHY STORIES—THE GOUGOU.

> " With deep affection,
> And recollection,
> I often think of the Chaleur Bay ;
> Whose river wild, would,
> In age or childhood,
> Cast round men's fancies, its magic sway."
> *(After Father Prout's Shandon Bells.)*   ARCHIE PELL.

" On board the G. P. S. " Secret—Sept. 1873."

BAIE DES CHALEURS has not only its teeming salmon rivers, Cacapedia, Bonaventure, Port Daniel, Restigouche, etc., many picturesque headlands, storm-beaten capes, enchanted islands sleep on the heaving bosom of its waters. Of the latter class, is the island of Miscou* at the entrance of the bay ; its early chronicles teem with the marvellous history of its fresh water spring, gushing amid ocean ; its land and sea monsters ; its well authenticated traditions of war, famine and human suffering. It also presents a most conspicuous landmark, and harbors of refuge for the bay fishermen, caught on the banks by a north-east storm. It lies contiguous to the dreaded Orphans' Bank, so famous under French domination for its codfish, in size ranking nearly as high as that of the great banks of Newfoundland. Miscou also has its record of wrecks ; a memorable marine disaster occurred here as early as the 31st Oct., 1685, the loss at *Pointe aux Bouleaux*, of the French ship carrying the Intendant de Meulles.

Here, at this point, our Government has constructed an octagonal wooden tower crowned by a red light ; three hundred and

---

* I am indebted to Mr. Faucher's work for several particulars concerning Miscou.

I

twenty-one feet to the east, may be seen a powerful steam fog-whistle which during thick weather and snow storms, sounds its note of alarm twice per minute at intervals of twenty-five seconds, with a duration of five seconds. On the western side of Miscou, blazes forth another beacon for mariners, a white light which takes two minutes to revolve. Frail fishing cobbles, unable to return through stress of weather to the north-eastern side of the bay, before losing hope, try to catch the point of Miscou; should they miss, a watery grave awaits the crew. Of late the island has been shorn of prestige, population and importance.

At present the finny tribes frequenting its shores hardly suffice to keep life and soul together in about a dozen of families located there, even with the adventitious profit accruing from the rich harvest of wild hay grown on its saline beaches. More than a century back, a Jesuit missionary wrote to his Superior : " The soil of Miscou is poor; its supply of fresh water is unwholesome; its trees are dwarfed—stunted * compared to those of the mainland, but it swarms with hares, grouse, and formerly it contained moosedeer (*élans*), but they have since all been destroyed. It is remarkable for its vast meadows which the tide daily overflows, and for its game." " The soil," adds Deny, " quakes under one's feet for fifty yards all round you; here sojourns cranes, white geese, thrushes (*grives*), like those of France; here the Canada goose (*outarde*) incubates and nestles in security during the mantling season of spring." The old Governor of the Maritime Provinces, it would seem, made a singular discovery here, in one of his exploring expeditions.

" A few hundred yards from the beach there spurts from the briny sea a gush of fresh water as big as your two fists, which

---

* In early times, a gunner who had charge of some powder accidentally set fire to it : the conflagration spread : the woods were soon in a blaze. The fishery failed the next year. (*Deny.*)

retains its freshness for a space of twenty yards without in any wise blending with the surrounding salt liquid, either at high or low tide. The fishermen come there in boats to fill their casks and draw it up as if it were from the reservoir of a fountain; at this singular spot, at low tide, the sea is but one fathom in depth; it is surrounded by water as salt as that of the rest of the ocean." The truthfulness of Governor Deny's narrative has been vouched for to me by seafaring people frequenting these shores; "and more than one," says Mr. Faucher, "has told me of his having drunk from Governor Deny's spring."

In early days Miscou was a post of importance, and gave its name to the surrounding districts of Miscou. It comprised all the Indian tribes of Gaspesia, of Miramichi, and of the Nipisiguit. De la Ralde in 1627, and Desdames had been in command, and Deny had erected here a habitation where he had planted "many peach and other stone-fruit trees, together with the grape vine; they all thrived." But the spirit of discord, rife among the Acadian magnates, reached even here; d'Aulnay de Charnisay destroyed this flourishing settlement in one day.

Labor and fishing establishments had made of Miscou a spot advantageously known all over New France. During the open season of summer, a regular packet, the ship *Ange Gardien*, plied between Miscou and Quebec. The summer months were spent in fishing and trading; each fall, the fishing crafts returned to France; in the spring, the catch of the autumn previous was sent from France to Quebec, the population of the city being too scanty to furnish men for this branch of commerce. Miscou, shorn of its inhabitants in the fall, assumed a solitary and sullen aspect with the approach of winter; a few fishermen remained in charge of the buildings, and during the cold and murky nights of December the sparse residents had to encounter foes more terrible yet than desertion. Champlain has traced the horrors of the winter of 1627, when from November to April following, more than eight feet of snow fell, at Miscou. De la Ralde that year had left behind a few Frenchmen to trade off some goods he was unwilling to bring back to France; these unfortunates nearly all died of scurvy. The next year was not more auspicious for the settlement. One morning David Kertk's ship of war, the *Vicaille*, anchored near the island, and took possession of the house, coasting craft and small boats of the place. On the return of Miscou with Quebec, by the English to France, in 1632, the banner of the "Hundred Partners," whose fleet fished or traded from Cape Breton to Tadousac, again floated over the lonely, but prolific, shores of Miscou.

This branch of commerce and brisk business had induced the Jesuits to found, in 1635, the mission of Saint Charles, in the island *Saint Louis de Miscou.* Innumerable savage hordes brought here, each spring, for barter, their packages of furs; here these fleets of light canoes *rendezvoused* previous to levying war against the Birsimis Indians of the North Shore; here, they sought shelter from the deadly and ubiquitous Iroquois; here, indeed, existed the seed for an abundant harvest of souls, which was reaped by zealous missionaries. Fathers Charles Turgis and Charles du Marché were sent to look after the spiritual welfare of twenty-three Frenchmen, the nucleus of a missionary settlement; but physical suffering was about the only occupation of these poor people, says the *Relations* of 1647. Disease and famine decimated the settlement. Father du Marché was obliged to return to France. Father Turgis, for some time, fought the unequal contest, consoling some, administering the last rites of the Church to others, before committing them to the earth, after death. He too, at last, had to give in; fatigue and malaria brought him low. Before expiring, he buried the captain, the clerk, the surgeon of the settlement, together with all the officers and some nine laboring hands. Having prepared for death the only sick man surviving, he yielded up in peace his own brave spirit. (*Relations of* 1637.)

On the sad news of his end reaching Quebec, Fathers Jacques de la Place and Nicholas Gondoin were sent to continue the missionary labors of Father Turgis. They found the habitation desolate ; the duty of removing the dead bodies from their couches to their newly made graves devolved on the Indians ; the French being too emaciated to do so.   Some, of a more barbarous turn of mind, seeing the universal ruin of all their hopes, wished to pillage the store-houses, but the survivors, putting a good face on things, arrested them in their evil designs.   According to the *Relations*, the Miscou mission was terrible to encounter. Father Goudoin had to quit it, and Father Claude Quentin had recovered his health there, after having to bury his assistant, a lad he had with him.   Father Jean Dolbeau lost there the use of his limbs, and on his way to France in quest of more genial air, the powder magazine of the ship which conveyed him having ignited, " he was blown into heaven," quaintly says the *Relations*. Father André Richard and Father de Lyonne could alone withstand the severity of the climate ; they succeeded in getting up a small church, which for a time seemed to prosper, but which disappeared when the island was abandoned.

Miscou of old, we think ourselves safe in considering anything but a genial place of abode ; not even to the most sanguine fisher, was it an earthly paradise.   In addition to its traditions of sickness, desolation, death, war, and piracy, Champlain, the great historiographer, peoples it with forms uncanny and unlovely, calculated, if possible, to enhance the weird interest the spot already possesses.*

---

* " Il y a, disait-il, une chose étrange, digne de réciter, que plusieurs sauvages m'ont accusé d'être vraie ; c'est que proche de la Baie des Chaleurs, tirant au Sud, est une île où fait résidence un monstre qui avait la forme d'une femme mais fort effroyable, et d'une telle grandeur qu'ils me disaient que le bout des mâts de notre vaisseau ne lui fût pas venu jusqu'a la ceinture.   Ils le peignent grand : il a dévoré et dévore beaucoup de sauvages lesquels il met dedans une grande poche, quand il peut les attraper, puis les mange, et disaient ceux qui avaient évité le péril de cette malheureuse bête, que sa poche était tellement grande qu'il y eût pu mettre notre vaisseau. Ce monstre fait des bruits horribles devant cette île, que les sauvages appellent le Gougou et quand ils en parlent ce n'est qu'avec une peur si étrange qu'il ne se peut dire de plus et m'ont assuré plusieurs l'avoir vû.   Même le

In sketching it, he winds up rather jocosely, we are inclined to think, by marking it out as the headquarters of a Satanic fiend—a female devil, who delighted in torturing the sons of men.

What was the female devil like?

"Old Harry" has ever, from our tenderest years, to our susceptible mind, typified a male devil; that is admitted on all hands to be bad enough, but what his lady, or any female member of the brood might be, this we unhesitatingly admit to be beyond our ken. According to the text of the illustrious discoverer, a fearful monster, in shape and size like a female giant, without, seemingly, the least affinity to fish, flesh, or fowl, haunted the humid margin of Miscou. The terror-stricken Indians knew it as the "Gougou." Of its sex, in their minds, no uncertainty existed—it ranked under the feminine gender. Had it the trademark of a Syren? Nothing indicates it had a tail, with those womanly attractions sung by poets:

"Desinit in piscem, mulier formosa superne."

It was certainly amphibious; sometimes, like that famed Syren, the Goddess Calypso, it inhabited an island. Like Ulysses's charmer, it was keen after men, red Indians especially; not to enlist them, however, as lovers, but merely as tit-bits for its morning meal—a *bonne bouche* previous, probably, to retiring to the "Orphans' Bank," where a few porpoises, or an adult whale, would constitute its dinner. From Champlain's testimony, plainly it was an uncomely, nay, a repulsive monster—

Sieur Prevert de Saint Malo, en allant à la découverte des Mines, m'a dit avoir passé si proche de la demeure de cette effroyable bête que lui et tout ceux de son vaisseau, entendaient les sifflements étranges des bruits qu'elle faisait et que les sauvages qu'il avait avec lui, lui dire que c'était la même bête et avaient une telle peur qu'ils se cachaient de toute part, craignant qu'elle fut venu à eux pour les emporter." Je tiens, disait Champlain, en terminant cette description du Gougou par cette réflexion pleine de logique, "que l'île soit la résidence de quelque diable qui les tourmente de cette facon."— (*Voyages de Champlain.*)

un monstre effroyable—and the founder of Quebec, the happy spouse of the blooming Hélène Boulé, the prettiest woman in New France, was of an appreciative turn of mind. The " Gougou," for all that, in shape resembled a woman — " *un monstre qui avait la forme d'une femme, mais fort effroyable.*" Had any one except those devoured ever been close enough to the giantess to form a correct opinion ? We are again left in the dark. A St. Malo miner, it is true, le Sieur Prevert, while " prospecting for a pocket," had passed so close to the abode of the *monstre effroyable* that he heard the extraordinary hissing, *sifflements étranges*, of the fiend. However, whilst thus in quest of a " Big Bonanza," whether a pocket or a vein, le Sieur Prevert, together with his ship's crew and some Indians, was fortunate enough to escape a pocket he was not looking for, the *grande poche*, great pocket, described by Champlain as the receptacle of Madame Gougou's booty. Sieur Prevert, be it remembered, was a miner, and unless his story had been corroborated to Champlain previously by Indians, we confess we would be inclined, like the stories of other miners, to accept it, *cum grano.* There is a fishy flavor about it, requiring many " grains of salt " to render it palatable.

But again this Gougou haunts us. Where, then, was the alleged resemblance to one of the softer sex ? The Gougou, we are told, when seen by men, uttered "extraordinary hissings," *sifflements étranges.* Will any one dare pretend it might not have been a fashionable Syren—Syrens, it is well known, are most common on the sea shore—showing off, before so many Ulysses, her powerful *staccato trills*, like a Calypso, a fast girl of that period, might be expected to do ? What, in verity, constitutes a female " *monstre effroyable* " ? Did Madame Gougou, out of her teens, sport high-heel shoes, a Grecian bend, a crinoline like Mont Blanc, a chignon Alpine in its dimensions ? Here again Plutonian darkness awaits us.

Still, in this age of inquiry and intellectual development, shall we throw up the sponge and proclaim our inability to

explain what sort of creature might be the Miscou Giantess, who
could swallow red Indians like shrimps or doughnuts ?   Which
" missing link " would the venerable Darwin assign to it ?   If it
was not a " mermaid fair," could it be

> That great sea-snake under the sea,

who,

> From his coiled sleeps in the central deeps,
> Would slowly trail himself sevenfold ?

Or else, would it be a gigantic specimen of Victor Hugo's Devil
Fish (like the one recently found at Newfoundland) who still
lived in the popular mind, from the terror he had caused by
having drawn beneath the seething sea, to his slimy and deadly
embrace, some noted Indian warrior, whilst bathing, etc. ?

Or else, again, shall we adopt the more probable theory, that
in Champlain's day a morose old sea-cow—(the Morse)—had
elected a domicile at Miscou ?   It is well known that the Morse
inhabited the Magdalen Islands, close by, and other isles in the
St. Lawrence, until the end of the last century ; that their beaten
paths are visible to this day on the shores of the Magdalen Group.
Who will unravel the mystery ?   Is it, therefore, a subject of
surprise that Miscou, with its far-reaching memories of scurvy,
suffering and death, its solitary, woodless marshes, for six months
in the year swept by the wintry blast, at all times fruitful in
malaria, with its Avernian, boiling spring, should have seemed
to the father of New France, a fitting symposium for a dreaded
giantess—the Gougou ?   For us, scudding past its shores, under
a lowering sky, with the equinoctial gale howling over our frail
steamer, which also carried to the God-forsaken land of Tracadie
a squad of close-shorn, devoted Trappist Monks, to take charge
of the Lazaretto, the island did appear as a not uncongenial trysting place, where the last of the order, an ascetic anchorite, made
holy by orisons, a long fast and fish diet, might, on one of those
" starless December nights " described by Champlain, have closed
creditably his Lenten tenure of life.   Could not Campbell's
" Last Man " find on this forlorn isle many subjects of reflection
before bidding adieu to the sorrows of this sorrowful planet ?

CHAPTER XVII.

St. Joseph of Tracadie in New Brunswick—Its Lazaretto —Its Lepers—Is it the Eastern Plague? The Kingdom of Death's Eldest Daughter "—Diagnosis of the Disease.

On the marshy shores of the county of Gloucester, in New Brunswick, fifty miles from Miramichi, twenty-five miles south of Caraquet, there stands, close to a small stream, a village bearing the name of the latter. Its aspect is sullen, lonely, desolate in the extreme. On one side, the seething waters of the Gulf of St. Lawrence, rarely enlivened by a sail; on the other, a low, naked, monotonous sea-shore, dotted here and there with a few fishermen's huts. Even old Ocean, so grand at times, seems here to have doffed some of her wonted majesty of mien. Nakedness is the prevailing feature of the landscape : one would fancy the hand of man, in general ready to adorn, has drawn back in despair or disgust. The houses are poverty stricken ; their roofs, dark, rude, thatched. Close by, the parish church —small—inornate—unassuming. Further on, a large, sombre edifice, hideous to the eye, surrounded by a lofty fence of cedar pickets. The uses to which the building is destined, we will shortly explain. There is, in fact, about the whole landscape— the dwellings—their inmates—their surroundings, such a cold, hopeless, all-pervading sense of dejectedness, that a traveller journeying through this dismal country might be tempted to exclaim : " Is not this place accursed ? "

Rightly so ; there is a curse on this spot : the " eldest daughter of death," she of Holy Writ, has made it her sanctuary : this is her undisputed kingdom—the Kingdom of Death. Ask the frenzied inmates of yonder gloomy dungeon, if they do not think so.

Reader, the funereal village we have just sketched is that of Tracadie, and the lofty, gloom-pervading structure, with iron bars* in the windows, like a prison, is the State Lazaretto, built in 1847: its inmates, the plague-stricken, incurable, doomed lepers.

The Tracadie Lazaretto succeeded to that of Sheldrake—was an improvement on it—such as it is.

Why such a structure?

Public opinion in New Brunswick had been much agitated —painfully disturbed at the increasing, though concealed ravages of a mysterious contagion, tracing not only to 1817, but much beyond. In 1844, a medical commission recommended the opening of a close hospital, on an island called Sheldrake, in the River Miramichi. Here, the victims of the terrible malady were gathered together, sometimes by force, and rigidly sequestrated from all intercourse with the rest of human kind. Discipline as well as religion, seem to have been strangers to this foul receptacle of human misery. Every species of crime except murder,—blasphemy and despair were the familiars of the hopeless captives, until some devoted nuns and fearless missionaries were allowed to comprise these loathsome victims within the scope of their ministrations. Female heroism, whether it comes before us under the guise of Florence Nightingale in the fever-stricken hospitals of Scutari, or as a Hotel Dieu Nun* amidst the incurable lepers of Tracadie, is equally welcome, equally blessed.

Of all the hateful emanations from the bottomless pit, to afflict poor mortality, leprosy seems to have been reckoned one of the direst, the most insidious, the most inexorable. It

---

°They have since been removed and a green lawn added round the building.

° The Hotel Dieu Nuns of Montreal, in 1868-9, accepted the charge of nursing the Tracadie lepers, and we recollect, about 1875, meeting on the Gulf Port steamers, three Trappists, from the Trappist settlement in Dorchester, bound on the same pious errand.

would furnish a curious and not uninstructive study to follow the march of the ancient and modern legislator intent on facing the cruel malady.

In the middle ages, the leper was counted as dead, long before the period of dissolution : he was even compelled to march to the church, and in order to mark more unmistakably his isolation from mankind, the church service for the dead was publicly read, masses were said for the repose of his soul; and so that the ceremony should be more impressive, a shovelful of earth was scattered over his body. In France, under Louis VII., a gallows stood in front of the Lepers' Lazarettos, which went by the name of Leproseries.

The hangman's assistant was constantly on the spot to "tuck up" any leper hardy enough to venture beyond the portals of these accursed abodes. The Church, too, struck them off from the communion of the faithful, so that they escaped the hangman's hempen halter to prepare for the torments of the damned. The prospect, it will be admitted, was not cheering.

Thanks to the writings and reports of Sir Arthur Hamilton Gordon, (1) Lieut.-Governor of New Brunswick ; of the Rev. Abbé Ferdinand Gauvreau, (2) for eighteen years *Curé* of Tracadie and Chaplain of the Lazaretto; of M. de Bellefeuille, (3) of several eminent medical men charged by Government to investigate and report on the origin, nature and cure of the mysterious plague of Tracadie, there are at command, for those who choose to investigate the subject, ample sources of information.

---

(1). *Wilderness Journeys in New Brunswick in* 1862-3, by His Excellency the Honorable Arthur Hamilton Gordon.

(2). *Letters in* 1859, par le Rev. Ferdinand Gauvreau, Chaplain du Lazaret, a un ami.

(3). *Les Lepreux de Tracadie*, par E. Lef. de Bellefeuille, *Revue Canadienne*, 1870.

(4). *Dr. Benson's Report, to Lieutenant-Governor of New Brunswick.*

(5). *Report on Leprosy*, by the Royal College of Physicians, prepared by Her Majesty's Secretary of State for the Colonies, with an Appendix, London, 1867.

(6). *Lieutenant-Governor Gordon's Letter to the Duke of Newcastle*, 1867.

What is the origin and nature of the formidable disease existing at Tracadie, for more than a century? Is it really leprosy, such as we read of in ancient days? the unclean disease of the Mosaic record? Is it the elephantiasis of the Greeks? the elephantiasis of the Arabs? asks Mr. de Bellefeuille, from whom we have borrowed so much information. Is it the *leucea vitiligo* of the Latins? the leprosy of the middle ages? *psoriasis*? or is it merely an aggravated form of syphilis, intensified by bad treatment, or by external circumstances? Such questions are of the province of the Faculty. We do not belong to the Faculty, and have but a qualified belief in all its *dicta*. The greater number of medical men, we have been told, favor the idea that the Tracadie plague is the elephantiasis of the Greeks.

Mr. de Bellefeuille, amongst others, furnishes some general information on leprosy which, we think, is not inopportune.

Leprosy dates from the dawn of history. In the early ages, it caused more stir than at present. We find it classed among the punishments inflicted by God on erring men. Its external manifestations were at all times so dreadful, so unmistakable that several learned commentators on the sacred volume, have striven to identify with leprosy, the indelible mark set by Omnipotence on the brow of the first murderer. The terror it spread among nations is ascribable less to its hideous and debasing characteristics than to the general conviction that it was incurable. Hence the wide spread idea that leprosy was a visitation from the Divinity to chasten the wicked and try the righteous.

This scourge appears to have been known long before the Mosaic era : we find it first mentioned in the fourth Chapter of EXODUS. God tells man to put his hand in his bosom, and when he pulls it out, it is " leprous like snow "--*leprosus instar nivis.* This naturally supposes the characteristic symptoms of leprosy must have been previously known. Moses might have seen it in the country of Midian, where resided his father-in-law, Jethro. Several able writers, Don Calmet, Marathon, Lysimacchus,

Molon, Appianus, Tacitus, Justinius, have stated, with various circumstances, that the Jews came out of Egypt on account of leprosy. What a terrifying visitation it must then have been ! and it was to become still more virulent forty years later on, in the land of Canaan. Chapter XII. of LEVITICUS discloses the aggravated malignity the disease was destined to attain forty years later among the descendants of the Israelites, in the promised land. Several kinds are indicated. We have leprosy in clothes, and the purifications attending it ; leprosy in the walls of houses—the fatal " red spots" ; and the interference of the priests. The dwelling radically unclean was doomed to destruction, and the materials to be cast out of the city.

Don Calmet, in commenting on the Scriptures, prefaces LEVITICUS with his explanatory notes. He assigns, as the agency of disease and death, a multitude of small worms, located between the skin and eating away the flesh, tendons, nerves, so as to produce the symptoms observable in leprosy, closing his remarks by stating that the venereal disease is a species of leprosy well known to antiquity. At present, leprosy exists in Italy ; in Norway ; in Turkey, in a village on the Ægean Sea ; in the East Indies ; it is found, as formerly, on the coast of Africa ; in the Indian Archipelago.

Mr. de Bellefeuille noticed it in Jerusalem ;—at Naplouse (the ancient Samaria), at Damascus, where exists a Lepers' Lazaretto, very badly kept— supported by public contributions. Charles Dana, in his *New American Cyclopedia*, notices its presence in Tracadie and other points in America.

Leprosy, as we all know, was one of the trials sent to Job, much to the scandal of the good man's wife, who thought that it proved he had committed some great crime. Christ more than once, in His mission of Mercy, heals lepers.

Herodotus, Eschines, Pliny, allude to leprosy amongst the Persians, Greeks and Egyptians. Our space precludes us from enlarging on this branch of the subject.

The first settlements on the Miramichi River, in New

Brunswick, took place shortly after the treaty of Utrecht in 1713, by the French, chiefly Basque, Norman or Breton colonists. Under the administration of Cardinal Fleury, strenuous efforts were made to promote this enterprise, to that degree that a French gentleman, Mr. de Beaubair, was sent out as Intendant by France. He founded at the north-west entrance of the Miramichi river a small town which still bears his name : the island facing the town, also known as Beaubair Island, was strongly fortified : old residents still talk of a foundry thereat, for pieces of artillery—workshops and shot, and shell factories.

During the year 1757, the Miramichi settlements were sorely afflicted in consequence of the war raging between England and France, which quite paralyzed their fish and fur trade: the ensuing winter, a famine carried off a number of the inhabitants.

Two transports loaded with supplies were sent to their relief ; they fell in the clutches of the English cruizers round Louisbourg.

When matters were at their lowest ebb for the French settlers, a French vessel from Morlaix, the *Indienne*, was stranded at the entrance of the Miramichi river close to the little stream of Wind Bay, corrupted into Wine Bay ; this was during the fall of 1758. Tradition adds, that, previous to entering American waters, the *Indienne* had been engaged in the Levant trade, and had on board some packages of old clothes, shipped at Smyrna. On the vessel breaking up, these old garments floated ashore ; the poor fishermen thanked Providence for this windfall, alas ! and therewith, clad their nakedness. Other accounts connect the breaking out of the plague with the intercourse of the *Indienne's* crew with the natives, whose hospitality is well known, and who thus unwittingly received in exchange for their generous relief, the direst of diseases as an inmate of their homes. Be this as it may, it is certain that about this time, first broke out the awful malady amongst the half-starved fishermen. The contagion especially preyed on the town of Beaubair ; the Intendant, Mr. Beaubair, falling one of the first victims; so that between famine and sickness no less than eight hundred inhabitants died and were buried at Pointe Beaubair. The survivors fled from Miramichi: some went to Prince Edward Island ; the greater number sought an asylum on the western coast of the gulf, and founded new settlements, such as that of Niguamech, Tracadie, Pockmouche ; they also swelled the population of Caraquet. For more than eighty years after, though leprosy was known to exist in these obscure and distant localities, it caused little alarm. In 1817, the death of an unfortunate, Marie Ursule Landry, drew attention to the ravages of the fell destroyer. How was the disease propagated ? No one can tell, replies Lieut.-Governor Gordon. 1st. It can scarcely be considered as hereditary, since in the same family, father and mother may be lepers and their children, clean, whilst in others, the contagion attacks the children and spares the parents; such was the case in 1856-7. A woman named Domitilde Brideau, wife of François Robichaud, was so foul with leprosy that her whole person seemed a mass of corruption. She gave birth to a daughter, whom she suckled; death shortly after closed the career of the mother in the hospital. The daughter remained free of any taint, resided three years at the hospital, from whence she was removed. She has since grown to womanhood,—got married, —has become a mother ; her children are hale and well. Many such instances might be adduced. 2nd. Is the disease contagious ? What is witnessed does not seem to favor that view. In some families the husband is a leper; his wife is free from the taint, and *vice versa* in others.

There is now living in Tracadie a man named François Robichaud, who was thrice married; his two first wives died of leprosy ; the third is now in hospital. He himself is in perfect health and free from the disease. In some families one or two of the children are lepers the rest are clean. A woman employed to wait on the lepers, remained in the hospital eight years, eating and drinking with them, and she escaped the contagion. We have seen her several times ; she is free from leprosy.

The laundress who washes the clothes of the sick has been living in the hospital the two last years, and has not caught the infection. It has happened in several cases that persons suspected wrongly of being lepers had been forcibly retained in the Lazaretto several years; when let out, they never afterwards exhibited any symptoms of leprosy.

The lepers now in the Lazaretto are unanimous in asserting they caught the disease by sleeping in the same bed in which lepers had slept, or eating and drinking with them.

Shall we then conclude that God scourges with leprosy those whom it pleases Him to afflict ?

I am strongly inclined to believe that food and improper diet have much to do with leprosy. The poverty amongst the Tracadie fishermen is extreme : there are scarcely amongst them ten families who can afford to procure bread : they are all seafaring or fishermen, and subsist entirely on fish, herrings, potatoes and turnips. Vapour baths, arsenical preparations, in many instances have mitigated the violence of the disease, and afforded temporary relief.

In 1849–50, a celebrated French physician established at Dalhousie, Dr. LaBillois, treated the Tracadie lepers for sixteen months, and pretended to have cured ten of them, viz., J. Gouthiau, Chs. Comeau, T. Brideau, A. Benoit, L. Sonier, Ed. Vienneau, Madame A. Sonnier, M. Sonnier, Madame Ferguson, Melina Lavoie. "The entire of the above cases," adds Dr. LaBillois, "are now quite well, and the treatment I adopted was entirely for syphilitic disease, thus establishing without any doubt the true nature of the disease." (Dr. LaBillois's Report, 1850.)

However, on glancing over the Report of the Health Committee, of which Hon. James Davidson was secretary, one notices that all these patients re-entered the hospital and died there, with the exception of two, who died in their own dwellings. Of the third, Dr. Gordon, of Bathurst, wrote: "The disease is making slow progress, but it is still going on to a fatal termination. We do not believe that the lepers in the Lazaretto either exceed sixty in number at any one time."

His Excellency Governor Gordon most graphically describes the heart-rending scenes which took place occasionally, when the individuals bearing the symptoms of leprosy were forcibly marked out for the Lazaretto, and ejected forever from the family circle : one day it was a mother rudely torn from the uplifted arms of her tender, unresisting offspring ; the next, it was a wife or husband, apparently in health and full of vigor, but plague-stricken, in reality bidding one another an eternal adieu. You might also see helpless childhood violently and remorse-lessly thrust in the living tomb, known as the Lazaretto,—that inexorable prison, on whose cold portals ought to have been inscribed the words of Dante's *Inferno :* " He who once enters here, leaves hope outside."

When the victim was refractory, he was mercilessly struck with sticks, felled like a wild beast, bound with cords, and dragged to the Lazaretto, for who would dare touch a leper !

In a letter addressed to a friend, and re-published by Mr. E. Lef. de Bellefeuille in the *Revue Canadienne,* for 1870, the respected almoner of the *Tracadie* Lazaretto, Rev. Ferdinand Gauvreau, thus describes leprosy as he had seen it in over one hundred cases during his ministrations, that is above eighteen years : " Once the disease has laid hold of a new subject, its action is so insidious, so underhand, that for a long time, perhaps two, four or more years, the doomed man notices no change either in his daily wants or bodily habits ; slumber to him is just as balmy, as sweet ; digestion goes on regularly ; breathing, as freely as heretofore. But, alas ! and may Almighty God have mercy on him ! he is but a leper ! the deadly virus is in him ! There it lies in wait, ready to spring forth at any moment. The fiend, like a venomous adder, will be on him as soon as it will awake. At the beginning of the malady, the skin soon loses its healthy and natural color, the complexion, its freshness and brilliancy ; a death-like, morbid white color covers the victim from head to

K

foot.   One would imagine the relentless malady had got hold of
the mucous membranes and taken the place of the fluids necessary
to the vital functions.

Without going so far as to assert whether eastern leprosy
has ever manifested other outward symptoms, it is undeniable
that the Tracadie disease, at least in its rudimentary stage,
assumes all the external marks of the eastern leprosy,—I mean
the unnatural whiteness of the skin. This, in the second stage,
turns to a faint yellow ; in the third or last stage, it changes
to a dark violet-red, or deepens even sometimes into a greenish
hue. The disease cannot then be mistaken.

Nay, the inhabitants of Tracadie, as well as myself, have
become so familiarized with this precursory symptom of leprosy
that, on the sole appearance of the whiteness of the skin, we
make sure of the presence of the scourge : seldom are we wrong.
One case of death only—that of Cyrille Austin, occurred in
what I term the first stage. All the other cases before ending
fatally, went through the second and third stages. Let us now
follow, if possible, step by step, the dire infection.

At first, the poor victim is a prey to a devouring fever, with
trembling all over—a rigidness and weakness in every joint—a
weight on the chest as if oppressed by a violent sorrow—a rush
of blood to the head—lassitude—drowsiness—a sense of loneliness, and other very disagreeable sensations, which lepers
have often described to me, but some of which have escaped
from my memory. The whole nervous system is thus affected
with a complete insensibility to pain, to that degree, that a sharp
instrument, like a needle or the blade of a knife, stuck in the
fleshy parts, or even through the cartilages and tendons of the unfortunate leper, cause him no pain whatever. What is more, the
leper could calmly place his arm or his leg in a blazing pitch or
wood fire without enduring any pain whatever, even after the
member was entirely consumed. He might even in that state
doze off, and sleep as placidly as if he were on a comfortable bed.
Gradually, however, says Mr. Gauvreau, this unnatural white-

ness of the skin wears off to make room for spots more or less large, of a light yellowish hue ; in some individuals, these spots are not broader than a dollar. When of that size, they come out symmetrically and at intervals corresponding between each other, either on the arms, on the shoulders, or on the limbs,— more often on the chest. These spots at first are more or less distant from one another, but, as the virus permeates the vital parts, they get contiguous to one another, and, when all united, they end by converting the body of the leper into a mass of corruption. Then follows the swelling of all the limbs—the tumefaction of every part of the body from head to foot ; and when these swellings have attained their maximum, the skin bursts, to allow the escape of purulent ulcers, disgusting and repulsive to the last degree. The whole skin gets stretched, and emits a slimy perspiration something like varnish. The skin between the index and thumb, withdraws ; the extreme points of the fingers and toes get very diminutive, and occasionally some joints fall off unawares, and painless to the victim. The noblest portion of the human body—that created to the image of God—the face equally with other parts suffers. The features swell and bulge out. The chin, the cheeks and the ears are covered with tubercles hard and red, as large as a large pea ; the eyes, half protruded from their sockets, get covered with a species of cataract, which, in some subjects, end in total blindness. Such is the condition of one of the patients at the present moment. The skin of the forehead swells and thickens, and in some instances assumes a leaden hue, which occasionally pervades the whole face ; in some cases, it turns to red, possibly as the bilious, the sanguine or the lymphatic temperament, predominates. A face previously remarkable for its comeliness and dignity will get full of gashes—deep ridges ; the lips form two purulent ulcers, the upper one swollen and upturned towards the nose, which has disappeared, and the lower lip hanging on the chin, shiny and lustred by swelling. Can anything be imagined more hideous ?

In some subjects, the lips are contracted and turned up like the mouth of a purse drawn together with a string. This deformity, adds the Rev. Mr. Guillemin, is the worst of all, since it precludes the victim from receiving Holy Communion, which many long for. The malady runs its course of destruction in the interior of the victim. At last, it settles in the larynx and all its bronchial ramifications. So great is the disturbance caused here, that the miserable patient can find no rest in any position he dares assume. His breathing resembles a sharp wheezing; it becomes so laborious that he fears to choke at every moment; death by strangulation would be welcome. Having myself witnessed some of these death-bed scenes, I should not like to see any more. Spare me a detailed account of this insuperable agony; my courage would fail me. Just imagine you see the expiring leper making spasmodic movements—horrible contortions—rushing anon to an open door for more air, and then throwing himself on his couch. Hark to his furious yells—his lamentations, which would move the most savage heart—his frenzy—his tears—his despair, amidst exclamations "Oh God! have mercy on me! mercy! oh, mercy!"

At last, exhausted, worn out by the protracted struggle, he chokes. All is over! another Lazarus may have been taken to the bosom of Abraham!"

CHAPTER XVIII.

DALHOUSIE ON A CIRCUS DAY—CAMPBELLTON—THE MICMACS
OF CROSS POINT.

DALHOUSIE, *Aug.* 14, 1873.

IT was our fate to see this little town rather under a cloud.
The railway navvies were thronging every hotel: a circus was
momently expected: everywhere reigned noise—bustle, discord
though a man in authority has told us, that at times the place is
quiet, even to dulness: he ought to know.

Dalhousie, N B., with broad streets laid out at right angles,
is tastefully built on the slope of a fertile ridge. It seemingly
dates about half a century back to those peaceful, halcyon days
of the good Earl of Dalhousie, at one time Governor of Nova
Scotia—on the 16th June, 1820, Governor General of Canada.
From him, it borrowed its name. During this half century,
striking changes have taken place. Where you might have seen,
fifty years ago, an Indian encampment on the green banks of the
Restigouche, now stands a growing town of 110 families; where
now flourish clustered birch bark wigwams, churches, bar-rooms,
piety and whiskey. Yes, bars and bar-rooms—and many could you
count in 1873, from the timber cribs and piles of sawn lumber, on
the beach towards the heights, raising their blitheing heads
amongst the houses of the laboring class and the stores of the traders. I found it a pandemonium of tumult and noise. The railway
navvies shouted—the boys shouted—the bar-keeper shouted,
and louder than others—Charley, the Ethiopean, shouted;
amidst these shoutings, barking of curs and cracking of whips
by owners of trotting horses, I realized what glorious times king
alcohol can establish when nothing, not even the municipality,

nor a female temperance crusade, arrests his sway, on a circus day.

As a sunbeam amidst this gloom, the eye gathers in the contour of comely dwellings and churches lining the tops of the hill, without forgetting a spacious public hall in course of erection, destined to become quite an ornament. The houses themselves are what we could call in Quebec, paste-board shells— some totally unfit to keep out January frosts. Their design, though, pleases the eye. If the number of churches be taken as a criterion, the Dalhousieites make up a good show in the spiritual line. At, one end of the town, embosomed in green foliage, like a bird's nest, is perceptible the dwelling of a mill owner ; a few roods up the hill peers out, from under the trees, the homestead of Hon. Mr. Hamilton ; higher up still, a monument erected to his sire, one of the founders of the settlement—it also serves as a landmark to seamen.* Formerly, the leading industry here was lumbering and the Restigouche salmon fishery ; the Intercolonial has of late shaken its golden fleece amongst the laboring class. Railways are great civilizers—granted. Railway laborers, navvies and whisky are not. Inflated wages ; that pink of modern institutions —the strike ; bar-room rows : such are some of the evils which the construction of a railway line occasionally brings in a heretofore quiet locality, on pay day.

The scenery at Dalhousie is very beautiful in summer : the salmon and trout fishery of the Restigouche, together with the

—→

° HAMILTON'S MONUMENT

Is of freestone. It was cut in Glasgow, Scotland, and erected in 1851. It stands twenty feet high, and bears the following inscription :

"In Memory of

CAPTAIN JOHN HAMILTON,

A native of King's Cross, Arran, Scotland. He was the first merchant who settled at Dalhousie, and along with many benevolent actions built St· John's Presbyterian Church, for which his friends and countrymen here thus record their gratitude.

He passed the last ten years of his life in his native land, and died at Irvine, 24th August, 1868, aged 80 years."

cod and mackerel fishery beyond, and the sea bathing, is likely to attract many tourists and sportsmen. Health, wealth and morals will increase, no doubt, as M. W. W. Ross, a recent tourist, well observes, when gin cock-tails decrease, on the departure of the transient population of laborers, etc., which the construction of the Intercolonial gathered at this spot.

Our popular Viceroy once honored Dalhousie with a morning call, at a very short notice. This naturally elicited an outburst of loyalty; the local celebrities came to the front.

Dalhousie then rejoiced in an unusually big black Ethiopian of the name of Charley; many and curious were the privileges daft Charley enjoyed in the commonwealth. Charley, a black prince of blood royal, was bent on asserting his right to meet familiarly white Princes, no matter how long their pedigree might be. Charley withal is loyal to the back-bone, and in order that no misconception might arise on this point, he, on hearing of the coming visit of the great earl hurried home, decked himself in his Sunday's best, added a waving plume to his bonnet, and with much dignity of mien, rushed down to the beach, in advance of the deputation. As this humorous incident may yet, for aught we know, find its place in some future chapter on the "Lights and Shadows of Colonial Life," if sketched by the magic pen to which we owe the photo of "Dismal Wilson" of the *Foam*, we shall not enlarge. Sixteen miles of pleasant travel takes you from Dalhousie to the next settlement on the Restigouche, Campbellton, a thriving village, with three churches, Presbyterian, Methodist and Roman Catholic,—the last a new structure prettily located on a hill. It contains an office for the Intercolonial Railway, presided over by an official, in whom we recognised with pleasure an old Quebecer, as polite and obliging as if he still was one of the denizens of the ancient capital: D. Busteed, Esq. The general features of Campbellton reminded one of Dalhousie; abundance of bar-rooms, with occasionally a few sons and daughters of the forest, perambulating the streets; the placid waters of the Restigouche in full view of the village and serving as a line of demarcation between the Campbelltonites and the Micmac Indian mission at Cross Point, opposite.

"The name Restigouche, meaning 'river that divides like a hand,' is of Indian origin, and is derived from the fact that it has five leading tributaries. It is about two hundred miles long, and has its source near Lake Temiscouata. Between Campbellton and the village of Cross Point, on the opposite side, it is only 3,100 feet wide, but its average width in the estuary is about two miles. The depth of the river opposite Campbellton, at low tide, is twenty feet, and the harbor is safe and commodious."

It would be wrong to imagine that Campbellton, in Canada, means prime whisky. That ambrosial usquebaugh, known in the land o'cakes as Campbellton whisky, had neither a habitation nor a name in these localities. "Forty Rod" was the name of the wine of the country—the balm of Gilead of the railway navvy on a Saturday night.

Campbellton is called after Major General Sir Arch. Campbell, at one time Governor of New Brunswick. 'Tis a pretty village, laid off in streets in 1833, by the late Robert Ferguson, Esq., of Athol House, with nothing Indian about it, save the occasional presence in its precincts of a couple of tawny warriors and some smoke-dried Pocahontas from the Micmac reserve across the river, at Cross Point, on the Canada side of the Restigouche. At Cross Point, the Government has allotted 1000 acres of land, on the lovely banks of the Restigouche, for what now survives of the once powerful tribe of Micmac or Souriquois Indians, an offshoot of the Algonquins, once the masters of the country. They number eighty-six families. Each family owns a small wooden house 20 x 20 feet, to which are attached a few acres of arable land. Their chief business seems to be to hoe potatoes,—build birch bark canoes—eat, smoke and sleep. A resident missionary christens, marries and buries them. The redskin, withdrawn from his former modes of subsistence—spiced and served up into a civilized being—

does not appear to flourish better at Mission Point than elsewhere.
The R. C. clergyman,* who manages the temporal and spiritual
concerns of his Indian flock, appeared to be both beloved by his
parishioners, as well as much attached to them. His church
register showed for the year ending 31st December, 1872, forty-
one births and forty-six deaths ; with this melancholy result the
ultimate fate of the mission cannot long be uncertain.

Whilst death had knocked at nearly every second door, the
angel of fecundity had passed by more than the half without
entering. We were invited to pay our respects to the chief
and interpreter of the mission—old Sam Suke. Sam, with
his piercing black eyes, intelligent face, and fluent discourse,
makes a very respectable chief; he speaks Micmac, French and
English. Old Sam, with your kind Micmac wife, keep up your
spirits, there will yet be a cosy spot for you in the happy hunting grounds, towards which old age is hurrying you !

In the neighborhood of the mission, there is a very rich
quarry of sandstone, which the contractors for the Intercolonial
have opened up ; from it magnificent blocks for the culverts
have been shaped. Mr. Busteed's house close by contains several
interesting relics of former times—substantial mementoes of the
strife which in 1690 and 1758-60 raged between the navies of
France and England. At the entrance of the Restigouche,
Admiral Byron sunk a French frigate close to Cross Point ; a
few miles lower down, Percé and Bonaventure had been mercilessly pillaged in 1690. The hulls of the French vessels can
yet be seen in very low tides, from one of which a massive cannon was procured some years back, and now ornaments the fire-
place of Mr. Busteed's dwelling ; it was shown to us. A piece
of oak in excellent preservation was presented to us as having
been cut from the timbers of the vessel sunk by the fiery admiral. This prized trophy we intend to convert into a walking
stick.

----

* Rev. Mr. Leonhard.

NAVAL OPERATIONS ON THE RESTIGOUCHE, 1760.

Methinks the spirits of the brave,
Who on thy banks have found a grave,
      Still linger, loath to fly ;
And on the moanings of the gale,
Strange shapes ride forth, all cold and pale,
      Unseen by heedless eye.

Oft in mine ears hath darkly rung
Their solemn requiem, softly sung,
      Mysterious, deep and chill ;
And, dying oft, come back again
In sweet, unearthly, ghostly strain,
      The mournful night winds o'er the hill,
                                    K. K. K.

The historian, Ferland, in his interesting narrative of a trip to the Lower St. Lawrence, in 1836, whilst describing Campbellton and Cross Point, thus recalls some of the warlike memories of the past, in connection with the River Restigouche :—   .

> *Bella horrida bella*
> *Et Tyberim multo spumantem sanguine cerno.*

"The horrors of war in days of yore disturbed those waters which at present flow in such placid silence over the bones of warriors of another era.   Here, pride, hatred, love of glory, love of country, warmly disputed the laurels of victory.   It was in the spring of 1760, Quebec had fallen the preceding autumn. Urged on by the Marquis of Vaudreuil, the French Court had sent tardy and weak succor to the Chevalier de Levis, who was bent on attacking Quebec.   The French fleet had on its way to Canada wasted its time in giving chase to some of the enemy's ships : the English arrived first on the coast, to dispute the entry of the St. Lawrence.   The French squadron then took refuge in *Baie des Chaleurs*, and ascended the Restigouche, where the Admiral, M. de Danjac, found fifteen hundred persons who had sought a refuge on its banks, where they lived in the greatest misery.   Captain Byron, probably the celebrated navigator, the grandfather of the poet Byron, at the head of the men-of-war, 'Fame,' 'Dorsetshire,' 'Achilles,' 'Scarborough,' and 'Repulse,' (with the 'Prince of Orange,' 'Rochester' and 'Eurus,' and three armed vessels from Quebec) set to attack the French fleet, which he met on the 8th July, about this point of the Restigouche. The French ships of war, were the 'Machault', 32 guns ; the 'Espérance,' 20 guns ; the 'Bienfaisant,' 22 guns; the 'Marquis de Marloze,' 18 guns. The French had made preparations to meet the enemy ; several cannon had been placed on Battery Point. Lower down, at *Pointe à la Garde*, from whence the eye reaches as far as the entry of the Restigouche, there was a detachment of soldiers who were charged with keeping guard over the course of the river and give notice of the advance of the English fleet.

The wind being fair, Byron's ships ascended the stream without hindrance, until they reached Battery Point, where they experienced a brisk fire from the guns.

" Two French ships were disabled and the guns of the battery silenced ; the 'Bienfaisant' and the 'Marquis de Marloze' were compelled to withdraw towards the Indian village, whilst the English pushed forward to Pointe à Martin (now Campbellton), on the opposite side, where they suffered much from the fire of some guns placed flush with the water. However, their superior artillery riddled the French ships. One of these was run ashore close to the Restigouche Chapel, whilst the commander of the other fired its magazine to prevent it from falling into the hands of the English. The destruction of the French fleet having left Commodore Byron master of the field, he gave orders that an assemblage of huts, which had been honored by the name of Nouvelle Rochelle, and were built on Pointe a Bourdon, three miles higher than the Restigouche village, should be razed. During the engagement, the French and the Micmacs had retreated to the woods, where they awaited in safety the departure of the English fleet.

" The imagination of the visitor who contemplates the *locale*, vividly brings to mind those stirring and terrible scenes. The ships of both nations, then at war, closing, or fleeing, or grappling one another, their long pennants streaming to the breeze defiantly and proudly ; amidst the thickets on the shore, groups of Indians curiously decked out or grotesquely clad; those sterile capes crowned with grim cannon scattering death and surmounted with the white flag of France ; the clouds of smoke hanging over the river and hiding the shores from the eye of the fierce combatants ; the crashing of spars and masts, and the stern voice of command ; the popping of musketry and roar of artillery ; the shouts of victory, mixed with the groans of death or rage ; such were some of the incidents of the drama, which some seventy-five years ago were enacted, on the narrow theatre where we now stand. It was but one of the episodes of the long rivalry between France and England,"—(*Les Cotes de la Gaspésie*, 1836.)

CHAPTER XIX.

St. John, N. B.—Its Scenery—Suspension Bridge—Victoria Hotel.

My knowledge of this thriving town dates to a few years later than my summer trip to the Lower St. Lawrence in 1875. I left Quebec per Grand Trunk Railway in January, 1874, to spend a few days at St. John and Halifax : it is unnecessary to remind the reader the Intercolonial Railway was not then in operation. The Quebec traveller had to stop over night at Bangor, in Maine, arriving at St. John the next night.

I shall first describe St. John, the chief shipping port of New Brunswick. Doubtless you will ask me why it is called St. John, there being a St. John's in the neighboring province of Newfoundland ? When I put that question myself, the only reply vouchsafed was that it had changed its old name, some generations back, from Parr's City to that of St. John, on account of the noble river on which it is built, and which opens out for it such untold vistas of wealth. Why called Parr's City ? This appellation was bestowed on it by one of its former Governors. Had it been preserved, there would have been but one St. John in the Maritime Provinces—a circumstance which no doubt would have saved many letters from going astray. Railway travel has made the Lower Provinces very accessible to the Ontario and Quebec folks ; you quietly retire to rest at 8 p. m., in a gorgeous Pullman car, at the Levis station, and in forty-seven hours,* after enjoying a comfortable night's rest at the Bangor House, in Bangor, Maine, you are safely landed at 6 p.m.,

---

*. Fifteen hours now suffice, since the opening of the Intercolonial Railway.

at the Carleton ferry, opposite St. John, whence a steamer, more remarkable for adaptability than beauty, at 7 p.m., takes you across the St. John river, and curiously poised, covered vehicles deposit you in the handsome hall of the Victoria Hotel—the prince of hotels, not only in the Maritime Provinces, but in the Dominion, Toronto alone excepted—of this hereafter.

St. John is a city of 29,000 souls,—with a port open the whole year round, and which, were it not for the tumultuous tide of the Bay of Fundy, which rushes over the flats with race-horse speed—in some instances, would compare even to our port, for commerce, depth of water, and safety. On one side are the ship-yards, at a place called Courtney Bay. St. John has ever been celebrated for her ships; her clipper, the Marco Puolo, for instance, has a European fame. The draftsman who furnished the specifications of this splendid craft has since accepted an appointment in the Revenue Department of his native city. St. John is the fourth shipping port in the world ; Quebec the third, we think ; so much for the Dominion. The city is a curious combination of commercial interests, wooden houses and piety, judging from the number of churches, many of consider-able beauty. I would be inclined to fix the proportion at one church for every 1,000 souls. Taking temples of worship as an exponent, St. John is decidedly pious.—It is more than pious ; and, bearing in account the eagerness of all classes for intellectual pursuits by means of Institutes—reading rooms—natural history societies, especially by lectures from celebrated *littérateurs*, who receive from $50 to $200 for a lecture, the people, I opine, are of a progressive and enlightened tendency. True, it has not the time-honored seats of learning of Ontario and Quebec, first-class Universities, nor does there appear to be a very high classical standard in the sciences;—it has, what is of more moment for a shipping port, a sound system of commercial education ; the Tilleys and Tuppers, and Mitchells and Howes have shown in the great council of the nation of what stuff they were made ; their successors have now a fair field before them, and are certain of one thing, a fair trial.

Ontario and Quebec for years had their running sores—which, under the treatment of political quacks, used periodically to fester and produce much proud flesh, the Clergy Reserves, in Western, the Seigniorial Tenure, in Eastern Canada; able practitioners at last came forth, cut and carved, the patients rallied and grew strong and healthy. It will yet be so, let us hope, for New Brunswick; some daring operator will plunge the scalpel in a very bad ulcer, which has bothered her for years,—the School question. Let us hope this may soon be.

Compared with Montreal, with its 120,000 souls, and exquisite style of architecture, St. John appears small indeed, but in breadth of views on many topics, in a certain geniality of manners, in that cosmopolitan feeling of interest towards strangers, one of the results no doubt of the geographical position which brings in foreigners in crowds at all times of the year, St. John is entitled to a high mead of praise. Next to travelling itself, there is no surer method of getting rid of local prejudices, scraping off exclusiveness, than holding converse and comparing notes with men educated, or even practical, who belong to other climes.

St. John is not a well-built city by any means, and barring its magnificent hostelry, the Victoria Hotel, few edifices by chasteness of design or richness of material will attract the eye of the stranger. It may be called a wooden city; here and there a granite, free-stone or brick building varies the landscape. There are ugly traces of excavations in the streets, which no doubt after a few years will be removed. The footpaths are like those of Quebec—no credit to the municipality. Of their system of taxation, I cannot say a great deal. One feature about it, the income tax, will cause moneyed strangers seeking a home to give it the cold shoulder. Capital ought to be coaxed and invited to stop in places; the inquisitorial system of legalized perjury, called the income tax, confided to the tender mercies of city councillors for its execution, may flourish in the realms rendered memorable by the peculations of a Tweed, a Connolly, a Field, but true-born Canadians abhor it, and have found means of building up the most gorgeous of Canadian cities—Montreal—without an income tax.

The Skating Rink of St. John, 'tis admitted, is the finest in the Dominion;* it cost $14,500, and can accommodate 3,000 or 4,000 people. The form is circular—well lit up at night, and the directors, energetic men.

Curling is a great institution in St. John, Halifax, and Pictou —the dining room of our hotel is now ringing with the songs and toasts of the Pictou curlers on a visit to the St. John curlers. They have achieved a glorious triumph over their rivals.

Of Fredericton, the capital of New Brunswick, with its 6,000 souls, parliamentary honors and high aristocracy, I am not in a position to say anything, time to visit it having been denied me

During my stay in St. John I was struck with the uniform loyal feeling towards the mother country, combined with a manly reliance on self, should the day ever come for a separation. This noble sentiment I found vigorously set forth in a most practical lecture delivered by the Rev. Mr. Graetz, under the auspices of the Mechanics' Institute, now presided over by Gilbert Murdock, Esq., Superintendent of the City Water Works, etc.,—a practical, scientific engineer, much in the style of our City Surveyor, Chas. Baillargé. To him I am indebted for a deal of information on New Brunswick. In addition to a flourishing Institute for Mechanics, St. John boasts a Natural History Society. It is not difficult to imagine that such a specialty, left to itself, can scarcely be expected to strike forth very deep roots in a seaport famous chiefly for pine deals, square timber and sailing ships. The two societies, however, *might be* combined in one, and an object involving original research in history, arts and literature introduced. The society with a new charter from the Provincial Legislature, headed by the first New Brunswicker, Lieutenant-Governor Tilley, helped by Legislative endowment, and perpetuating its usefulness in a

---

° Since this was written, the citizens of Quebec have erected, at a cost of $32,000, a splendid structure for a Skating Rink.

series of "Transactions" published annually, in my opinion, would in a few years become for New Brunswickers what the Earl of Dalhousie's old foundation, the Literary and Historical Society of Quebec, is to Quebecers generally—a household-word and an honor.

In more respects than one, Quebec might with advantage take pattern from this maritime city—in none more than in hotel accommodation. Quebec has had for years one of the most popular of hotel-keepers—Willis Russell—a name known with advantage from Halifax to New Orleans. Why cannot a first-class hotel be started in a city of 60,000 souls, like Quebec, when St. John with its 29,000 has built a most princely one, and has also five or six hotels as large as the St. Louis, without counting minor ones ?

The Victoria Hotel * was built by a joint stock company in 1870, at a cost of £50,000. It is a six story, handsome, stone edifice, with a very ornate front, at the corner of Germain street —one of the highest points in St. John. It looms out grandly ; in bright weather during summer, a magnificent view is obtainable from its lofty roof. The dining-room and entrance hall are paved with red and white marble tiles. The contrast pleases the eye. The bed-rooms contain fireplaces, and the arrangements for hot or cold water baths and patent water-closets on the latest American principle, are all that can be desired. Like first-class American hotels, there is a profusion of pier glasses, mirrors, etc. The bed-room furniture is of black walnut, neatly carved; the washstands, decked with white marble slabs.

In the hall, there is a solid elevator, which is worked by a small boy who stands inside; it takes up boarders to the fifth

---

° " The ' Victoria,' that grand hotel which was St. John to every traveller that came here, was opened for business, July, 1871, under the following board of Directors : Otis Small, Esq., President ; John Magee, A. Chipman,—Smith, John McMillan and William F. Harrison, Esq. Like dozens of other public edifices it was destroyed by the awful fire of 20th June, 1877 "—GEO. STEWART, JR.

story in one minute and a half. It can lift fifteen persons at a
time, and cannot by any chance cause an accident, as the slides
run on ratchets; so that if any of the gear gave way, the highest
it could fall would be six inches. It is set in motion by a small
steam engine in the basement, and cost altogether $10,000.

The Victoria Hotel was started by a company of wealthy
merchants, and by some seeking to become so, as a hostelry
which by its comfort and luxury might attract the most luxuri-
ous and wealthiest of the American travelling public, in quest of
a cool atmosphere and sea breezes in the dog days. The Bay of
Fundy is lavish to St. John, of moisture in winter, and of coolness
in the summer months.

The city, unlike London or New York, has none of that
sultry, suffocating heat in which raiment of any kind is a
weight and torment—in which man longs for breathing air,
and would fain, as Sidney Smith quaintly puts it, rid himself
of his flesh and "sit in his bones only." The building is
heated by steam pipes, such as the Quebec and Union Banks—
from a boiler and engine of fifty-horse power in the basement.
It uses about one ton of coal per day in winter, the steam also
serves for all household purposes, washing, cooking, etc. The
Victoria Hotel, from the crowd of wealthy Americans it has
attracted, is considered one of the best investments for the city,
a veritable Pactolus for dry goods merchants, fur stores, glove
and tailoring establishments, and fancy stores generally, etc. It
will contain from 300 to 400 guests; its staff of employees is
about 80 in number.

There is no reason why Quebec should not have a Victoria
Hotel; such an establishment built by a company and super-
intended by a Willis Russell, would roll wealth in the coffers
of our dry goods retailers, fur dealers, railway companies and
river steamers etc. If a suitable site could not be procured
near the Government Garden facing the river, I know of but
one other, which, by the airiness of the situation and beauty of
surrounding landscape, seems well adapted, if money could

procure it; that is the lot on Perrault's Hill—the old *Asyle Champêtre*, now owned by Hy. Dinning, Esq.

The city has two squares ornamented with trees, of rather a sickly constitution, one might think, judging from their size. The mists and fogs of the Bay of Fundy are anything but favorable to this style of ornamentation.

Now, let us have a drive and see the country seats and lovely views round St. John.*

A suburb, adjoining the city, and merely divided by the railway bridge, called Portland, contains on a high ridge dotted with spruce and cedar plantations many of the residences of the wealthy merchants. High over the rest, looms out Reed's Castle; lower down the homesteads of the two Burpees—one of whom, Isaac, is our present Minister of Customs. Further on, is the magnificent suspension bridge, built by W. K. Reynolds in 1852. Its span is 640 feet and cost about $100,000. The bridge is suspended 100 feet above low water, by wire cables which pass over massive granite towers. From the bridge, a grand view of the St. John Falls may be had; at low water the river rushes through a narrow gorge, 450 feet wide, with tremendous velocity; and at high water, the tide which rises above the level of the rapid in the harbor below, forces the water back and causes the same rush in the opposite direction. For some time every tide, vessels may pass up and down with perfect safety : thence, the road leads to Carleton, called after General Carleton, first Governor of New Brunswick, in 1785, under whom Fredericton was selected as the capital. Carleton is a thriving suburb of St. John, connected to the city also by a ferry—there the St. John's train has its terminus.

° What a sombre pall now hangs over the city we found so brilliant— so prosperous—so enterprising—so hospitable in 1874. St. John seems to have suffered as much as any other Canadian city from the fire-fiend. The years, 1784, 1788, 1816, 1823, 1837, 1839, 1841, 1845, were marked by great conflagrations—that of 1837, though a crushing blow, was nothing compared to the terrible scourge which, during a few hours on the 20th

I noticed here several ornate dwellings, some owned by wealthy Americans engaged in the lumber trade. But to a Quebecer, accustomed to our picturesque scenery, nothing is more attractive than the green banks of the Kenebeccasis * about eight miles from the city, at a settlement called Rothesay. The railway has here a station, and takes in each morning to the city the owners of the country seats of Rothesay. These dwellings line the river or lake bank, and seem much and deservedly sought after. Here took place the celebrated regatta which ended in such a melancholy manner for England's champion. I was shown the wharf where poor Renforth landed and shortly after expired.

St. John, until 1785 a portion of Nova Scotia, the first European settlement on the continent of North America, has been sketched, under its social, commercial, and educational aspect, let us now see New Brunswick in a historical point of view. †

" Although settlements have been made in Acadia for many years, no mention is made of St. John until 1604, when the

———

June, 1877, reduced to ashes two-fifths of the city, destroying 1612 houses and public buildings. This dire calamity has found an able annalist in one of St. John's most brilliant *littérateurs*, George Stewart, jun., the founder of *Stewart's Literary Quarterly*, and present Editor of *Belford's Magazine*.

° Nearly all the rivers in New Brunswick are designated by Indian names, either significant of a personal right, or expressive of some prominent locality. Thus the Etienne, the Burnaby, the Bartholomew and others are called after the respective chiefs to whom they originally belonged ; whilst the *Looshtork* (now Saint John) signifies Long River ; the *Restigouche*, Broad River ; the *Miramichi*, Happy Retreat ; the *Nipisiguit*, Noisy or Foaming River ; the *Tootooguse*, Fairy River ; the *Tabusintac*, the Place Where Two Reside ; the *Magaguadavic*, the River of Hills ; the *Richibucto*, the River of Fire.

† The first grant of land in it was given by King James I., in 1621, to his secretary, Sir William Alexander, who called it Nova Scotia, or New England. It was then considered by the English, as a part of Cabot's discovery of *Terra Nova*......Sir William being unable to colonize his grant, sold it to Claude De la Tour.....And the treaty of St. Germain ratified in 1632, ceding Acadia to France, the French became possessors of it, by both possession and purchase.

great founder of Quebec (Champlain), pilot of an expedition, commanded by M. de Monts, after coasting along the shores of Nova Scotia, crossed the Bay of Fundy and discovered the magnificent river which he named St. John. At that time it was called by the aborigines, *Ouangondy.* The river runs five hundred miles through the finest lumber districts of the Province ; its head waters being within fifteen miles of the River St. Lawrence. No settlement was made until 1635, when a French nobleman named Claude De la Tour commenced the erection of a palisade fort opposite Navy Island, in the harbor of St. John. De la Tour, having been appointed Lieutenant-General, lived here for a long time, with a large number of retainers and soldiers, and traded in furs with the Indians. But, having fallen into disfavor with the French King, was ordered to surrender his fort and commission ; this he refused to do, and an expedition under the command of D'Aulnay Charnisay, was sent out in 1643, to eject him. D'Aulnay blockaded the fort, but De la Tour, having got assistance of men and ships from Governor Winthrop, of Boston, drove his fleet back to Port Royal, (now Annapolis, N. S.) where a number of his vessels were driven ashore and destroyed. Again, in 1645, D'Aulnay attacked the fort, and De la Tour being absent with a number of his men, his lady took command, and defended it with so much skill and perseverance that the fleet was compelled to withdraw. Having received reinforcements, D'Aulnay shortly after returned, and again attacked the fort by land ; after three days spent in un-successful attacks, a Swiss sentry, who had been bribed, betrayed the garrison, and allowed the enemy to scale the walls. Madame De la Tour personally headed her little band of fifty men, and heroically attacked the invaders ; but, seeing how hopeless was success, she consented to terms of peace offered by D'Aulnay, if she would surrender the fort. He immediately, upon getting possession, disregarded all the conditions agreed to, hung the whole garrison, compelled this noble woman, with a rope round her neck, to witness the execution ; she, a few days afterwards,

died, of a broken heart.   In 1650, De la Tour returned to St.
John, and received from the widow of D'Aulnay, who had died
in the meantime, the possession of his old fort.

In 1653, they were married, and he once more held peaceable control of his former lands, as well as those of his deceased
rival.   In 1654, an expedition was sent by Oliver Cromwell, from
England, which captured Acadia from the French, and De la Tour
was once more deprived of his property and possession.   In 1667,
Acadia was ceded to France, at the treaty of Breda, but, in consequence of the violation of this compact by the French, it was
re-taken by Sir William Phipps, in 1690.   The British remained
sole masters of Acadia until in 1697; the Treaty of Ryswick
in Holland restored it to France.   It was given back to England
by the Treaty of Utrecht, in 1713, and retained ever since.   No
settlement of importance, was made until the year 1749, when a
fort was built at the mouth of the Nerepis River, about ten miles
from the City of St. John.   In 1745, the French were again
driven out by the English; and, in 1758, a garrison was established
at St. John, under the command of Colonel Monckton.   In 1764,
the first English settlers came to New Brunswick, but no permanent settlement was made until 1783, when the U. E.
Loyalists arrived and founded the present city."   I cannot close
this short historical sketch, which the guide books are safe in
crediting to Abbé Ferland's " Cours d'Histoire du Canada," and
a few other historians, without adding that De la Tour's heroism
did not only find a suitable niche in history, but that poetry also
lent to it, a lasting consecration.   Under the title of " Le Jeune
De la Tour," Mr. Gerin Lajoie, now of Ottawa, has written a brilliant drama, admired by every friend of Canadian literature.

I should have much liked to visit what are called, the French
Counties in the Upper Provinces, in order to see how the descendants of those men so sweetly sung by Longfellow still fared in
this vale of sorrow, where suffering was their lot at the beginning, and, possibly, indifference and oppression afterwards.   As
we approached Halifax, the country became more mountainous;

deep cuts in the rocks for the rail, were covered over with a plank roof, to exclude snow drifts ; the old pines looked down mournfully, snow-crowned and bending from the distant hills ; a small brook wound its tortuous course, in the depth of a ravine over which our iron horse sprang with one bound; old ocean was misty, as of yore.   How true are your words, sweet singer :

" Still stands the forest primeval, but under the shade of its branches
   Dwells another race, with other customs and language.
   Only along the shores of the mournful and misty Atlantic
   Lingers a few Acadian peasants, whose fathers from exile
   Wandered back to their native land, to die in its bosom.

PRIVATEERING IN THE BAY OF FUNDY, A. D. 1776.

The following interesting account of the Yankee privateer *Defence*, in her vain endeavors to sail up the Avon river, for the purpose of plundering the town of Windsor, is from an old paper supposed to be written by one of the mariners taken from the British sloop *Dover*, by the Yankee privateer :

His declaration is, " that on Tuesday, the 21st day of August, 1776, the schooner *Dover* was taken between the Isle of Haute and Cape Dorée, by the sloop of war *Defence*, belonging to the State of Massachusetts Bay, Capt. Evans, master, mounting six double fortified cannon, six pounders, and six double fortified four pounders, with a number of swivels and 58 men. This sloop was completely equipped as a privateer ; that soon after the capture of the schooner *Dover*, they communicated to Marsters their design of going to Windsor to take Fort Edward, plunder the stores and capture an armed British schooner anchored in the river. Pretending to be unacquainted with the river, they told Marsters he must pilot them up ; as he refused, he was put in irons. Their intention was to anchor the sloop at Mount Denson, arm the schooner *Dover* and a whale boat with thirty-five men, which were to proceed to Windsor by night ; but by some mistake they got into the current which made up Cobequid river, and it being high tides they could not get out of it until it was too late to carry their purpose into execution. On Wednesday morning, the sloop took the schooner *Three Friends*, Farnam, Master, and a large shallop bound to Cornwallis ; that night they again endeavored to sail up to Windsor, but the current prevailed against them so much, they could not accomplish their purpose.

" Some of the officers and men of the privateer landed at Partridge Island, and found a soldier who had been sent from Fort Cumberland with despatches on the King's service; after threatening him, he acknowledged the package was left at the house of a Mr. Pettis, of Parrsboro, and also, Mr. Pettis had sent back a drove of cattle belonging to Col. Franklyn. This so exasperated the Yankees, that they went ashore, plundered Pettis' house and set fire to it.

" On Saturday, the 25th, in the morning, some conversation occurred between the privateer men and the prisoners concerning the Charlestown Frigate being expected in the Bay, and that then they proceeded down the Bay, taking with them the several vessels captured, having first set ashore the prisoners. That during the stay of the privateer in the Basin, a certain party landed and plundered the people of Cornwallis."

The great object of the privateer was the plundering of the large amount of stores in Windsor, but, owing to the swift current of the river and the knowledge that a British Cruiser was expected up the Bay, prevented the successful carrying out of the enterprise.

CHAPTER XX.

Halifax—its Citadel—its Port—its Wealth—its History.

Halifax, Feb. 25, 1874.

We have left far behind us St. John, the genial, thriving head-quarters of the " Blue Noses "; thirteen hours of railroad travel will land us at the north end of Halifax, at Richmond Depot. A few miles beyond, on a ridge facing a lovely sheet of water, still stands, but renovated, Prince Edward's Lodge, dating from 1795. It is masterly described by Haliburton. Here Farmer George's big, burly, jovial, though persecuted son, of Quebec notoriety, spent some of the best days of his youth, with his fair charmer *Madame de St. Laurent.** Alphonsine Thérèse Bernadine Julie de Montgenet de St. Laurent. Her late husband appears to have been a colonel in the French army.

We are now snugly housed in Mynheer Von Hesslein's com-fortable hotel, on Hollis street. An antiquary would ask. " Who was Mynheer's grandfather? Was he coëval with the great Diedrich Knickerbocker, who flourished in Manhattan, at the dawn of Yankeedom? Was his progenitor one of those hospitable Brunswickers who, in 1757, settled at the north end of the city, since known as Dutch Town? Or else, are we to pin our faith to the ancient traditions (for I love popular tradi-tions : they dress up fiction so much like fact) according to

---

° This elegant French lady, widow of Baron Fortisson, lived twenty-eight years in the intimacy of the Prince ; as his lawful wife, many thought. In 1818 we find her leaving her protector and entering into a convent in France ; that year the Duke was married.

which his worthy sire was a much respected gun-room officer
on board the sloop-of-war *Sphinx*, which arrived on 14th July,
1749, in Chedabucto Bay, bearing Hon Ed. Cornwallis, the
first Nova Scotian Governor and his fortunes.   For subsequent
travellers, let this remain an open question.   Mynheer Hesslein,
our contemporary and host, is an excellent type of the prosperous *pater familias*, happy as the day is long, with or without
the soothing fumes of a meerschaum or the soul-inspiring aroma
of that divine nectar, lager beer.

> "When you're weary
>   Night or day
> Smoke a cheery yard of clay ;
>   When I'm smoking,
> Musing, joking,
>   There is no King
> Half as gay."

I hail thee, Halifax, England's last bulwark across the sea !
land, watched over by the " brave and the free " in the midst
of thy fogs, warmly wrapped in the folds of that glorious old flag
which for " a thousand years has braved the battle and the
breeze."

From the frowning battlements of thy airy citadel, you can
well afford to look down complacently on the ships of all nations,
which deck your incomparable harbor ! Shall we then view you,
as Britannia's supreme hope—her last standpoint in this land of
the West, in the long run, so uncongenial to European poten-
tates and European dynasties ? Yes, joyfully did the Great Napoleon, in 1804, sell out his interest in the territory called after
the Great Louis, his predecessor—Louisiana.   Joyfully did the
Russian autocrat, barter away Alaska and *all* its wealth of fog.
Not more so, however, some say, than Manchester and Sheffield
would feel were Queen Victoria to sell out or give away her interest in these, our fair realms of Canada.   Did George III. really
offer to return Canada, bought with the blood of Wolfe—to
France, if the latter would only promise to keep out of the quar-

rel with her American provinces in 1775? but, fate had decreed Lafayette should go.

Have kings then, like other men, their price?—is that price summed up in the one word expediency? No, England can never apply to the metropolis of Nova Scotia, Walpole's withering doctrine never, except on the day, distant we hope, when the cutlers of Sheffield and the weavers of Manchester will have pushed the Sovereign of the sea, down amongst nations, to the level of Holland.

What, then, are we to admire the most at Halifax, her spacious port or her picturesque citadel? Of the spirit of enterprise amongst her many wealthy citizens, we are inclined to think soberly. Her money grubbers remind us too much of the similar class, in our own Canadian cities—a sleek—fat—unctuous race, doting on shipping news—well versed in ocean freights—rates of exchange—dry, very dry Sherry and Newfoundland old Port. Rather unbelievers in schools of design—history—lyric poetry or the like. Catch them building a "Crystal block"—a Victoria hotel—a university—not they—they have something better to do—so long as the coal fields, mineral deposits, coast fisheries hold out. They do not lack hospitality, nor generosity, but love routine too much. See how they carefully button up in winter in their well padded coats—happy in their truly British reserve, which makes them look on people of other climes as outside barbarians. I like Halifax folks as specimens of comfort, in a garrison town.

They are keen at discounts, but do not talk to them of building up a handsome city; they have not too much time to watch the rates of exchange in New York, or the returns of the sugar crop in Cuba. Are they then wrong? Certainly not, if life's sole aim at Halifax or at Quebec, is good markets for timber, coal, fish, oil. In a thousand ways does Halifax resemble our old Quebec. Her port, her commanding citadel, her fortifications, her commerce, her shipping, and her garrison of British troops, all remind us of her dear sister city. I mean fortified

Quebec—before the City Council had laid violent hands on all that which distinguished her from the mushroom third class cities in Yankee Land. The sea fogs and coal smoke give a dingy appearance to the buildings, many of which owned by the wealthy are built of wood—something like the third-class tenements, visible at Montreal, some thirty years ago. The tone of society in Halifax is English, with all its national reserve. The names of her streets are English; you have Granville, Hollis, Sussex, Richmond, Kent, Albermarle, Grafton, Russell, Seymour, Wellington, Bedford, Birmingham streets. Granville street is the chief commercial street.

As many as fourteen men-of-war have been moored at once in her spacious bay; the English flag, close to the French—the American, all amicably, within hailing distance. Imagine the deviltry and frolic of eight or ten thousand jolly tars, let loose in a sea port town, with plenty of solid gold guineas!

The Halifax Club appears well patronized—well kept.

The western part of the city and environs contain many substantial and some ornate villas and old homesteads; the northern part is populated by the poorer class—with a sprinkling of colored people.

The Skating Rink of Halifax is situated in rear of the Citadel, on South Park street. It is a roomy building much less ambitious in appearance than the St. John's Rink; a place well adapted where the youth and beauty of the city can learn the "poetry of motion." Once or twice a week, the martial strains of one of the city bands enliven it, when the *beau monde*, of course, turns out *en masse*. Halifax, though essentially a military and naval station, does not appear to me as genial a soil for the Lotharios sporting epaulettes as Toronto, Montreal and Quebec used to be in days of yore. Many sons of Mars are still perversely holding out against the melting glances of the Nova Scotian *belles*. Benedicts they wont be ! What a bug-bear those North American colonies have been, in the past, to Belgravian Mammas having "hopefuls" serving there, ever since the fatal day when brave Wolfe met death for an idea! Whether the style of beauty prevailing in the city, is of the Grecian or Roman type, want of time prevented any investigation such an interesting subject might warrant. Ever since the days of Governor Cornwallis, Halifax has passed for a kind of emporium, where British officers are "provided with wives."

Club life, an occasional tandem drive, a skate in winter, a dash of yachting or a cast with the salmon fly, bobbing for mackerel in summer : such, the chief programme of amusement for the military. Bedford Basin and the bay present rare facilities for yachting and boating. More than likely, our sea-loving Viceroy will be next summer dipping his colors in Nova Scotian waters, to the Commodore of the " Royal Halifax Yacht Club."

There are two men, above others, of whom the citizens seem proud—their energetic, liberal minded Archbishop, *Monseigneur* Connolly,* and the popular Lieutenant-Governor, Adams G. Archibald.

The sea-going merchant craft of Halifax differ materially in size from that of St. John, whose sixty-four shares may represent the interest of as many individuals in the city, man, woman and child. In the latter, large waisted timber ships are required to convey to other lands the wealth of New Brunswick forests. In Halifax, snug, fast sailing brigantines, from 100 to 250 tons, suit better for an expensive cargo of fish, for Cuba, the Brazils, etc., and to bring back rum, sugar, and molasses. The number of arrivals from sea for 1873 being 1,384 ships, representing 372,985 tons ; departures—1,012 ships, representing 313,240 tons. This lucrative business was formerly colossal in its proportion ; it is still very large, and suffices to keep busy the whole year round the Collector of the port, Mr. McDonald.

The new Provincial buildings, a massive granite block, contain the Inland Revenue Department, the Customs, Post Office, and in its upper story the Museum, particularly rich in mineral

---

* He died in 1876.

specimens, fossils, Indian curiosities, native marbles ; birds, reptiles and fishes preserved by the art of the taxidermist ; this collection is mainly due to the unceasing efforts of Professor Honeyman, who may daily be seen at the rooms, when not attending his classes. The Doctor is versed in mineralogy, and takes pleasure to show his treasures and furnish explanations about the fossil remains and other curiosities committed to his care. I was happy to notice amongst the daily attendants several young ladies, taking nearly as lively an interest in a trilobite or a saurian, twenty thousand years old, more or less, as a Lyell, a Murchison, or a Dawson would have done. Dr. Gilpin and Mr. Morrow, two scientific citizens versed in natural history, I regretted not having met. I found the Halifax Museum far ahead of that of our Literary and Historical Society in minerals, but its Ornithological Department was far behind. This scientific *corps* publishes annually a volume of its Transactions, which it exchanges with similar institutions in the American Republic and several European associations. The School question occasionally crops out in Halifax, but under a different aspect from that of New Brunswick; there seems a tendency at present towards associating the rate payers more intimately with the direction of the schools, by obtaining for them the selection of trustees, instead of leaving it to Government to do so.

Protestant supremacy seems the order of the day in the Maritime Provinces. Bismarck must be a saint of high degree amongst them. A charter to an Orange Society has been recently granted ; it only remains for the Ribbonmen to seek and obtain one, to meet their opponents on equal grounds, when both will "fight like devils, for conciliation, and cut each other's throats for the love of God."

Halifax, the capital of the Province of Nova Scotia, was founded in 1749 by the Lords of the Board of Trade, and named after the President, Geo. Montague, Earl of Halifax. The sum of £40,000 was granted by the Government, and a fleet of

thirteen transports, with 2,576 emigrants left England, con-
voyed by the sloop of war "Sphinx"—on board of which was
Colonel the Honorable Edward Cornwallis, as Captain-General
and Governor of Nova Scotia. They arrived in Chedabucto
Bay on the 21st June, 1749, and the civil government was
organized on board the "Beauport" transport, on the 14th July.
The same month the town was laid out in squares, the streets
being from fifty-five to sixty feet wide.

On clearing away the ground for settlement, a number of
dead bodies were found, supposed to have been the remains of
the soldiers of the Duke d'Anville's expedition which wintered
there in 1740. The town of Dartmouth opposite was commenced
in 1750. The settlement suffered continually from attacks by
the French Indians, and a fearful disease carried off one thousand
souls. For a protection, a fence was built, consisting of upright
pickets or palisades, with block houses situated at a short distance
apart; this fence ran from the water up to where St. Mary's
(Roman Catholic) Cathedral now stands, from there to Jacob
street, and down to the Harbor again. A Government House
was built where the Parliament building now stands; it was a
low, one-story building, and was surrounded by hogsheads filled
with gravel and sand, upon which small pieces of ordnance were
mounted for its defence.

Between the years 1751 and 1758 a number of German
settlers arrived at the colony, and settled at the north end, now
called Dutch Town. In 1780, the streets of the town were in a
very rough condition, and, from stumps of trees and rocks, were
unpassable for carriages. St. Paul's Church—now standing,
although much improved and enlarged—was built by the Government in 1750; and the old German Church in 1761, on
Brunswick street, where it still stands as a relic of the old German settlement.

The city is built on the side of a hill, sloping gradually up
from the water some distance, when it suddenly becomes steep
and high. Upon the summit is built the Citadel, covering the

top with its fortifications. This immense fortress, 260 feet above the sea level, was commenced by Edward, Duke of Kent, when commander-in-chief of the garrison, and also the towers of Point Pleasant, George's Island, Eastern Battery, Meagher's Beach, and York Redoubt, were built about the same time. From the Citadel a most extending and interesting view may be enjoyed. The city at our feet, extending some four miles along the shore of the harbor, with its wharves crowded with shipping, and the town of Dartmouth on the other side; on our left, the British squadron at anchor off the dockyard,—the narrows and Bedford Basin, beyond; on our right, George's Island commanding the harbor with its fortifications, McNab's Island, the Light-house, and the Atlantic Ocean in the distance,—the magnificent harbor, with ports and batteries everywhere, and the north-west arm and mountains in our rear. Passes can be procured from the Town Major, at the Brigade office, to visit the Citadel or any of the other forts.

The dockyard was first established in 1748; was extended and improved in 1749 and the present wall built in 1770. It contains stores, workshops, warehouses, naval hospital, residences for the officers, and extends about half-a-mile along the shore of the harbor. In it, are many war trophies taken by English cruisers in 1812; among others the head-figure of the Chesapeake, placed there by the officers of the Shannon.

The Parliament buildings, situated in the centre of a large square, between Hollis and Granville streets, are built of grey free-stone, and contain the House of Assembly Rooms, Legislative Council Chamber, Library, and Public Offices of the Local Government.

I had not leisure to visit the magnificent room of the Legislative Council, which contains a painting of one of Nova Scotia's most illustrious sons, Sir Fenwick Williams, the heroic defender of Kars, of whom the city is as proud as of her Haliburtons and Howes.

The new Provincial Building is a handsome edifice, costing

about $120,000. It contains the Provincial Museum, Custom House, and other offices of the Dominion Government.

There is a Citizens' Free Library at the City Court House, in which building are held the meetings of the Mayor and Corporation, and the Stipendary Magistrate's Court. The other principal buildings are the Government House, St. Mary's Cathedral, Dalhousie College, the Asylum for the Insane (on the Dartmouth side,) Admiralty House, Halifax Club House, Supreme Court House, Gaol, Wellington Barracks, City Hospital, Penitentiary, City Marble House. The "Royal Halifax Yacht Club" have recently erected a commodious club house, with the necessary accessories of piers, slips, boat houses, etc., at Richmond, in the north suburb of the city. The building is large and well arranged, and does great credit to the members. It is provided with refreshment, reading, billiard rooms, etc., and all the necessaries of nautical enjoyment.

The Poor Asylum is a large building of brick and granite, put up at the cost of about $260,000. It is one of the finest edifices in the city.

The Blind Asylum is a brick and stone building only lately completed through the philanthropy of the late William Murdoch, Esq., who left $25,000 towards educating the blind in Nova Scotia.

The Imperial Government has finished recently a Military Hospital, at a cost of about $150,000. The Free School system in Nova Scotia has caused the erection of several handsome stone buildings in the city, to be used as school houses.

Halifax is well supplied in Banks of a most solid and substantial character,—the Halifax Bank, Bank of Nova Scotia, People's Bank, Union Bank, Merchants' Bank, Bank of British North America, Bank of Montreal, and two Savings Banks. Two Building Societies, four Public Libraries, one Free Library, and several reading and other recreation rooms are established. There are nineteen newspapers published in this city—three daily, and the remainder tri-weekly and monthly journals.

M

Twenty-four places of worship, composed of Church of England, 7 ; Roman Catholic, 3 ; Presbyterian, 5 ; Wesleyan, 3 ; Baptist, 3 ; Congregational, 1 ; and two belonging to the colored population.

Halifax is famous for its beautiful drives and walks ; the fine cool temperature enjoyed in the hot season, owing to its proximity to the ocean, will make it a foremost place of resort for tourists.   It has one of the finest harbors in the world, and with Bedford Basin at its head, affords opportunity for sea-bathing, yachting, and other water amusements seldom offered elsewhere.   The Horticultural Gardens, situated in Spring Gardens, are very tastily and prettily arranged and laid out, so are the public gardens in the rear.   The military and city bands frequently give concerts here, and afford recreation and amusement to thousands.

Steamers leave Halifax for Portland, Boston and New York, also for ports along the western shore of the Provinces, Prince Edward Island, Newfoundland, Bermuda, and the West Indies. The Allan line call there going and returning.   Nova Scotia with Prince Edward Island, Newfoundland, and a large part of the State of Maine, was called by the French in the seventeenth century, Acadia.   Subsequently, when conquered by the English, the whole country was called Nova Scotia, and afterwards divided into provinces and named as at present.   England, though claiming Acadia from its discovery by Cabot, in 1497, had maintained no permanent hold, and for upwards of a century there was constant change of ownership between England and France, and the inhabitants, or Acadians, had no sooner acknowledged themselves the subjects of the Crown, when, without the slightest regard to their feelings, interests, or wishes, they were transferred to the other.   Discovered in 1497, by English navigators ; in 1604, in possession of the French.   In 1613, the English under Argal, drove the French away and Sir William Alexander is appointed Governor by James I.   In 1632, it is again restored to France by the Treaty of St. Germain ; and in 1654, it is captured by the English, and Cromwell appoints Sir Thomas Temple,

Governor. By the treaty of Breda, it once more comes under the crown of France, in 1667.

In 1680, we find the English again in possession, having captured Port Royal and all the principal settlements. In 1682, the French are once more masters; and finally the English in 1710, besiege Port Royal, compel the French to surrender, and name it Annapolis Royal, in honor of Queen Ann, then on the throne of England.

In Nova Scotia, there is an abundance of mineral wealth. Coal is found in Pictou, Cumberland and Cape Breton; gold, all along the Atlantic coast; iron ore, in Colchester and Annapolis Counties; gypsum, in Hants; marble and limestone, in many different localities; freestone, in Pictou; amethyst, at Parrsborough; copper ore and silver mines have been discovered in many places; manganese, at Tennicape; oil, in Cape Breton, and an immense marble mountain of the finest description. The forests abounds in lumber. The fisheries on the coast are abundant, and the harbors excellent. The fishing grounds are notorious, the forests are supplied with game, and wild animals are plentiful.

The wealth of the Maritime Provinces must be very large, judging from the amount appropriated each year to carry on the civil government in the four neighboring provinces. A legislative union of all the provinces included in the Dominion would be an immense saving in the long run, now that all the great political questions are settled; legislation ought to be limited to charters of companies and a few minor points. Could this not be managed well and cheaply, in the different Parliamentary Committees at Ottawa?

I have heard it stated that the interest of the Maritime Provinces was not identical with that of Ontario and Quebec; this may be the case to a certain extent; still, if the four lower provinces were grouped under one Parliament,* instead of each having

---

* Since these lines were written the question of uniting together the Maritime Provinces is assuming a more tangible form.

its Legislature, which much resembles a large municipality, how many additional thousands of pounds could then be appropriated to educational and municipal purposes. These four provinces each year must increase in importance ; even Prince Edward Island, the youngest daughter of Confederation, is waking up, and will be in the spring traversed from end to end by a railroad. The railway facilities, and the Gulf Ports Line of steamers, will, during the summer season, continue to bring from abroad myriads of American tourists, eager to enjoy the exquisite scenery of Nova Scotia, Cape Breton, and Newfoundland.

CHAPTER XXI.

PRINCE EDWARD ISLAND—ITS EARLY HISTORY—POPULATION—
RESOURCES—ADMIRAL BAYFIELD—CHARLOTTETOWN—SUM-
MERSIDE—A WINTER STEAM FERRY.

OF late years the Gulf Port Steamship Company has wisely
decided to enlarge the area comprised in the weekly round trip of its
steamers, so as to include a call at the Island of Prince Edward,
the lovely isle, the gem of the Gulf, which stands like a
vase of greenery, at the entrance of the St. Lawrence, not
inappropriately called "the Garden of the St. Lawrence.'
Until 1758, it was French territory, but that year it was ceded
to Great Britain.   In 1763, the island was annexed to Nova
Scotia (or Acadia); in 1771, it was erected into a separate
government, and in 1851, responsible government was declared.
Under French domination, it bore the name of *Isle Saint-Jean*,
and was granted by letters patent, bearing date August, 1719, to
the *Compagnie de l'Isle Saint-Jean.*

Prince Edward Island was sighted by Sebastian Cabot, in
1497 ; three centuries later, it received its present name, in
honor of the father of our gentle Queen, Edward, Duke of Kent,
then commander of the forces in Nova Scotia, Cape Breton, and
Newfoundland. A year later on, in 1798, an Act of the Colonial
Parliament ratified the name.

It is one hundred and thirty-four miles long, and varies in
breadth, by the indentations of its shores, from five to thirty-four
miles. In former times, Prince Edward Island numbered a population of 7,000 Acadians ; peaceable and thriving tillers of a generous soil, some of whom would export as many as 1,200 bushels

of oats to the Quebec market, in a season. The hand of fate was
on the Acadian here, as formerly amidst the valleys and fertile
plains of Grand Pré. National antipathy suggested to the British,
another raid on this helpless people. The compatriots of
Evangeline were forcibly deported in ships ; barely one hundred
and fifty families evaded the stern decree, by hiding in the
woods or near the sea, or by leading in their boats, a roving, seafaring life.* Now came to the victors, the spoils. The island
was divided into three counties, the lands of the proscribed race
formed sixty-seven lots or townships of 20,000 acres each. The
total, 1,300,000 acres, was divided by lottery, among Imperial
servants and favorites, who, rightly or wrongly, claimed to have
served the British crown. These new land-owners, who owed to
chance their title-deeds, were compelled by the terms of the
patent either to reside themselves on the island or to provide
occupants within ten years. Some fulfilled the terms of the
grant, others did not. It mattered little ; the hated Acadians were
expelled !

Change of owners gradually took place : this land was soon
groaning under the curse of leaseholds of a *quasi* indefinite duration. Some leases ran for twenty-one years, others were worded
for nine hundred and ninety-nine years. A settler under one of the
latter leases, occupied the land rent-free the first two years ; at
the annual rate of threepence an acre, for the next three years ;
at six-pence per acre, for the fifth and sixth year ; at nine-pence
per acre, for the seventh and eighth year ; for the remainder of the
term, he was held to pay a shilling per acre and taxes. This
cumbersome land tenure caused incredible trouble and parliamentary agitation ever since its inception in 1773 ; but of late,
the Government,† by compensating the extensive land owners

° *De Tribord à Babord.*

† A Bill was introduced in the P. E. I. Parliament in 1852, by the Hon.
George Coles, called the Land Purchase Bill, placing in the hands of the Government £100,000, with which they were authorized to purchase the claims
of proprietors willing to sell.

of the island, have much improved the condition of the settlers, enabling them to become proprietors. Governor Denys, who explored the island in 1672, and Admiral Bayfield, who in his hydrographical reports, described it in 1860, both assign to it, the form of a crescent. At its highest points, it does not exceed from four to five hundred feet. The census of 1871 fixes its population at 94,021 souls. Its chief sources of wealth up to this time, are its deep-sea fisheries, agriculture and ship-building ; though, according to Professor Dawson, vast coal formations underlie the whole island.

Its healthiness is unquestionable ; the Asiatic scourge, cholera, has never yet penetrated there. The summer heat and winter cold is less than that of Quebec, though, according to Bayfield, the spring would be retarded, by the icy breath of the north wind blowing from the Gulf. This scientific naval officer sets forth that the south-west breezes, which, in June, July and August, veil in murky fog, the Bay of Fundy, changes to tepid and delightful emanations, in their passage through the Strait of Northumberland and over the island, and then again turn to dank, penetrating mist, as they career seaward towards Labrador.

Charlottetown, the capital, sits gracefully on a short neck of land between the North and Hillsboro rivers, on a safe, capacious harbor, called by the French *Port de la Joye.* Its quays, however, are not very commodious. The town is lighted by gas and well laid out ; the streets, crossing each other at right angles and several of them one hundred feet wide. Here and there, hedges and shade trees in front of private residences, with tiny gardenplots ; fountains gushing amidst moss, ferns, and rockeries. Every wealthy citizen seems to think himself in duty bound to adorn his home and its approaches. On all sides, indications of refinement, affluence, public order : one feature, above others, welcome—no beggars, cripples, public mendicants soliciting alms. Alas ! when will old Quebec borrow a leaf from the book of her young sister ? The colonial building is the handsomest edifice in the place. It is built of Nova Scotia freestone. The other principal build-

ings are the post office, market house, public hall, exchange, drill
shed, Prince of Wales, St. Dunstan's, and Methodist colleges,
Normal school, convent, lunatic asylum, gaol and government
house. The fourth estate is well represented at Prince Edward
Island.

The environs of the city teem with beautiful drives ; wide,
well-kept public roads intersecting the island in all directions
and running under the shade of spruce, fir and maple trees, occasionally skirted by a thorn hedge or rose bushes.

From the dome of the colonial building, a commanding
view of Charlottetown is enjoyed.

In addition to many beautiful drives round the city, visitors
of a piscatorial and meditative turn of mind, have close at hand
several streams and rivers, in which the finny tribe gambol
the live-long day.

There is also a charming trip by steamer to be taken to
Mount Stewart, eighteen miles distant.

At Charlottetown, is the residence of Admiral Bayfield,*
whose name, as commander of the exploring Government vessel,
" Gulnare, " for years, was a household word to every Quebecer.

The hydrographical labors of this able naval officer comprise, not only the boundless shores of our St. Lawrence,
but also many of the western lakes and inland seas of Ontario : he

---

° Henry Wolsey Bayfield is descended from a very ancient English
family, the Bayfields, formerly of Bayfield Hall, County of Norfolk, England. He entered the royal navy on the 6th January, 1806, as a supernu-
merary volunteer, on board H. M. ship *Pompey*, bearing the flag of Sir William
Sidney Smith ; we find him subsequently in the *Queen*, 98 guns, the flag
ship of Admiral Lord Collingwood, next in the *Duchess of Bedford*. After
brilliant service in the *Beagle*, and *Wanderer*, we find him commanding a
gun-boat, on the lakes in Canada in 1814, and, in 1815, assisting captain
Owen in the survey of Lake Ontario ; the St. Lawrence, from Kingston to
Prescott, and the Niagara river. In 1827, the Lord High Admiral, the Duke
of Clarence, appointed him to the survey of the St. Lawrence. This laborious
and very important service lasted until 1856, when he attained the rank of
rear-admiral. His connection with Canada began in 1814 ; he was a resident
of Quebec from 1827 to 1841.

holds his place amongst the band of indefatigable explorers and hydrographers, famous amongst Canadians : Jacques Cartier, Champlain, Nicholas Denys, La Verendrye, Joliet, Belin, &c.

Charlottetown, at five hours run, has a commercial rival— SUMMERSIDE, on the Strait of Northumberland, provided with a spacious harbor. Summerside is noted for its commerce, ship-building, and especially, for its delicious oysters.

Prince Edward Island, since the new arrangement of our steamers, the opening of the railway through the Island, and the efforts made by the Dominion Government to connect it during the winter months with the main land by a regular winter steam ferry, * is getting widely known, appreciated and admired by every denizen of Canada.

Until recently, the connection between the Island and main land, was kept up in winter, by experienced canoe men.

° It is a pleasing incident for us to connect the name of a talented Quebec shipbuilder with the winter navigation of the strait dividing the Island, from *terra firma*. Though the *Northern Light Steamer* may not entirely overcome the obstacles created by nature, under good management and in favorable seasons, she will certainly shorten the period of isolation for the islanders, and the name of Edward Sewell, Esq., of Levi, will yet, we hope, be remembered as that of one of the benefactors of Prince Edward Island.

THE ROUND TRIP

TO

MURRAY BAY—CACOUNA—TADOUSAC—CHICOUTIMI AND INTERVENING PLACES.

THREE decades have not yet elapsed since the Saguenay and "its terrors," Murray Bay, Cacouna, Tadousac, with their hotels and lovely beaches, have been thrown open to Canadian, American and European travel. The time was—well do we remember it—when each summer a few of the venturesome spirits among us, at the approach of the dog days, tearing themselves away from business, gave a few weeks to recreation and health. It was customary then to walk to the *Cul-de-Sac* * or *Palais* harbor and select a berth in one of the many coasters bringing to market hay, deals, cord-wood, oats or other produce from the lower parishes ; a trip to Murray Bay in those days was styled a sea voyage ; it was also supposed to include salt water baths. The coasting craft, who could rejoice in a sober skipper—sails with few rents—decks tolerably tidy—a clean cabin—spacious enough for a man "to fling round a cat by the tail," with security to the cat, rightfully commanded a preference. The schooner's provisions for the trip (which often in duration exceeded the time our Atlantic steamships now take to reach England) were next examined. Black bread, junk pork, onions and Molson's "forty rods" being generally pronounced insufficient fare ; by some, even unwholesome, the tourist was told to provide his own ship's stores.

---

* The erecting of the Champlain market and wharves in 1854, and of the new wharves at the *Palais*, has done away with both these valued harbors for small river craft.

A prime Westphalia ham, from Robertson's—a loaf of Clearihue's white bread—some of Glass's wine-biscuits and crackers—a case of Teneriffe or good Benecarlo wine from Shaw and Torrance's— (alas! how our respected ancestors used to vaunt these beverages, which money now can scarcely purchase)—a few dozen of McCallum or Racey's pale ale—a bottle of Scheidam or St. Croix old white rum, to restore the circulation after bathing and prevent cramps : such then, was the indispensable commissariat of the wealthy traveller. Occasionally, a rheumatic or dyspeptic subject was ordered, as a *dernier resort*, to try sea baths, by those eminent members of the faculty, Fargues, Blanchet, Fremont, Morrin, Marsden, Sewell.

The "sea voyage," to the invalid, was not always an unalloyed delight.   Should he, for instance, not have owned such a thing as a pair of "sea legs" the major part of the trip, especially when the Murray Bay "Argo," close-hauled, was caught tacking, in a stiff south-easter, was spent in making a prolonged, but not interesting, experimental study of what *Monsieur le Capitaine* styled "mal de mer;" the skipper, however, generally a humane and prudent commander, scarcely ever failed to notify the passengers in time to prepare and requested them as a specific against nausea, to remain on deck, when they neared the chopping seas of the *Gouffre,* the dreaded maelstrom between *Ile aux Coudres* and *Cap au Corbeau,* famous for its dangers even in the days of the historian Charlevoix. This perilous eddy once passed, a few hours of fair wind brought the schooner to the sand-obstructed mouth of the river Malbaie ; this could only be made with a high or rising tide.   The coaster then hoisting sail, entered, dipping perhaps her *tricolor* flag either to the popular and well remembered seigneur, John Nairn, whose little *chateau* stood and still stands on the western point, or else to the esteemed Scotch merchant, Hon. John Malcolm Fraser, whose cosy old stone manor, redolent of Highland memoirs of 1782, looms out on a high bank at *Pointe à Gaze,* to the east of river Murray.   There would take place the disembarking in the schooner's jolly-boat, amidst the unharmonious dialect of the Warrens, Blackburns, Harveys and McNeills, and other French-ified Scotch of the Bay, greeting the captain on his safe return, and amidst the suppressed oaths of the sailors, having to wade from the jolly-boat to the rocks or sandy shore, carrying on their backs the invalid tourist or adventurous Quebec traveller, there being no wharves. In a trice, a sitting-room and *cabinet* or sleeping apartment was rented in one of the white-roofed cottages lining the shore, at the rate of $10 per month, including board.

It was etiquette to go the next day and make a call on the genial *seigneur* of Murray Bay, as well as on the *curé*, the post-master and other howling swells of the place. Amidst excellent cheer, good salmon fishing in the river Murray, and trout fly fishing at the *Chute*, at *Grand Lac* and *Lac Gravel*, July and August flew over like the vistas of an enchanted dream. After luxuriating on fresh herring, fresh salmon, luscious sardines, new potatoes, French cherries, raspberries, plums and blueberries, the quandam invalid or adventurous traveller, as the case might be, would, by the 1st September, re-land at the *Palais* market pier or Cul-de-sac—as to the coats of his stomach,—a new, a better man.

This quasi-pastoral era closed in 1853, when the staunch steamer "Saguenay," Capt. René Simard, built by an enterpris-ing company,* was put on the Murray Bay and Saguenay route. John Laird, Esquire, was the esteemed agent of this company, from 1852 until the sale of the " Saguenay."

The " Saguenay " steamer was succeeded by the " May Flower, " the " Comet, " the " Lord Elgin, " &c., until the es-tablishment of the *St. Lawrence Steam Navigation Co.*, which put on this route, the first-class steamers "St. Lawrence, " "Saguenay, " "Union " and " Clyde."

---

* Incorporated by 16 Vict. cap. 247, as "The Quebec and Trois Pistoles Steam Navigation Company ;" composed as follows : William Price, C. H. Tetu, (Trois Pistoles), Henry John Noad, James Gibb, Gibb & Ross, Louis Renaud & Brothers, Julien Chouinard, L. & C .Tetu, F. X. Paradis, Archibald Campbell, sen., and François De Foy. Act assented to, 14th June, 1853.

POINT LEVI.

On casting off from the wharf of the Richelieu Company, the
steamer runs east, giving a wide berth to that shallow, dangerous
far-reaching point to which a Levi,* more than two centuries
back, lent his name—Pointe Levi, previously known as Cape
Levi. This Levi was one of the first Viceroys of Canada.
Pointe Levi—St. Joseph de Levi, as it was styled until 1850—
has undergone many subdivisions. It comprises now, a town,—
Levi; two flourishing villages,—Lauzon and Bienville, both incorporated under the municipal act, a few years after, 1860; the new
Parish of St. David de l'Aube Rivière, erected in 1876, and the
adjoining parish of St. Romuald to the west, created a separate
parish about 1854. The only part which has retained its old
name is the eastern portion. The Town of Levi, incorporated
in 1861,† is, of course, by its growing wealth, population (13,464
souls) and commanding position, the most noticeable. Perched
high on the hill, she seems to eye defiantly her big and elder
sister on the west shore of the great stream,—old Quebec. The
stately churches of Levi, her colleges, convents, hospices, glistening white-roofed dwellings loom out imposingly from the river.
At the foot of the precipice on a spare strip of land, oversha-
dowed by pine-crowned cliffs, and skirted by the murmuring St.
Lawrence, you see from the deck of the passing steamer, crowded
thoroughfares, tortuously creeping through two rows of
houses, a vast brick-built market hall, shops, foundries, hotels,

---

* "The family of Levi," says the historian Ferland, "was of ancient and
biblical origin, and laid claim to important prerogatives; it traced back to
the patriarch Jacob, by his son Levi. This reminds one that in a chapel,
owned by the family, might be seen a painting, depicting the Holy Virgin,
and a member of the house of Levi, with his hat in his hand. Two inscrip-
tions explained the scene, 'Keep your hat on, Cousin,' says the Virgin; 'It
is my pleasure to do so, Cousin,' replies the descendant of Levi."—(Cour
d'Histoire du Canada, Ferland, Vol. I., p. 214.

† The Act of Incorporation, the 24 Vic., cap. 70, was sanctioned 16th
January, 1861.

steamers, ship-yards lining the numerous piers, from Chabot's hill to the sheds, offices and terminus of the Grand Trunk Railway, up to Hadlow Cove; everywhere, the hum and bustle of commerce.

Up to 1850, the eastern portion of the point, used every summer to be thickly studded with the bark wigwams of the Micmac Indians from Baie des Chaleurs, or the North Shore Montagnais—the presumed descendants of the warriors who in 1775 or 1812 (without the privilege of scalping) had helped Old England to keep out the irrepressible Yankees. The city precincts being closed to these lawless and rum-loving worthies, each summer they paddled their canoes to the historic point of Levi, erected bark huts, awaiting patiently until the English Commissariat handed them their annual presents for services rendered in time of need ; blankets, clothing, beads, trinkets for the Indian princesses ;—red cloth, feathers, axes, ammunition for the Indian princes.

Hence the origin of the name of the adjoining indention in the shore—Indian Cove—*Anse aux Sauvages*. It now comprises even the site lower down, selected about twenty years back by the wealthy Quebec firm, Allan, Gilmour & Co., for a lumber cove, conspicuous from afar, by its forest of masts, its extensive deal wharves and booms for square timber. On a declivity, shaded by a hill in rear, to the west, were begun in 1867 the earthworks of Fort No. 3, a splendid piece of military engineering. It was in the adjoining cemetery of St. Joseph that was found underground, in 1850, the rusty old cage, in which the fiend La Corriveau, court-martialed in 1764, was hung, to starve and die—(See *Maple Leaves*, 1st series, for particulars.)

On the Levi heights, were encamped the invading hosts, in June, 1759, and in November, 1775, under Wolfe and Arnold. "It was," says the annalist, Jean Claude Panet, himself an inmate of Quebec in 1759, "on the 24th June (1759), we first noticed from the city the English fleet, anchored along the Levis shore near Beaumont."

" Brigadier-General Monckton, in June, 1759, with the fighting Highlanders (78th Frasers), the 15th Foot and the ferocious Rangers, had some lively encounters with the French, round the old church of St. Joseph. On the 4th July of that year, Wolfe was supposed to be evacuating his Levis camp to take up position on the Island of Orleans." Again we read in old John Thompson's MS. journal of the siege, some graphic particulars, describing how several of the unfortunate wounded (English and French) at the battle of the 13th September, 1759, were crossed over from Wolfe's Cove, Quebec, in boats to Levi, carried on litters from the ferry all the way to the church of St. Joseph, temporarily converted into an hospital; how the stalwart Highlander, in carrying in his arms a wounded French prisoner some three miles, ruined his uniform: old Thompson must have been something of a Hercules to attempt such a feat.

This Church of St. Joseph was again in the ensuing winter, when British colors floated on Cape Diamond, the scene of active military operations. On the 13th February, 1760, (the ice-bridge having formed about the 5th,) General Murray sent over detachments of the 78th, under Lieut. McNeil, to pursue a French force hovering in the neighborhood. On the 24th February, 1760, Capt. Saint Martin, having returned with a body of 800 French troops to attack the English detachment posted at the church, General Murray, in person, crossed over on the ice with the 15th, 28th, 78th and some light infantry, supported by two field pieces; Saint Martin escaped, and the General recrossed that night, bringing over with him fifteen prisoners, but without losing a single one of his men.

On the 4th Nov., 1775, Arnold's indomitable New Englanders, reduced in numbers by hunger, illness, desertion,—exhausted by their three months' trudge through the then trackless forest of Maine, wading through streams thick with ice and snow, debouched on the Pointe Levi heights, from the St. Henri wood, somewhere near the Kennebec Railway terminus; after feeling slightly put out—Lieutenant-Governor Cramahe having had all the water craft crossed over to Quebec—they induced the Indians they had met on the Kennebec and Chaudière rivers, to ferry them over in their canoes during a dark night, (on the 14th November,) to Wolfe's Cove and Spencer Cove at Sillery, in order to elude the *Hunter* and other English frigates anchored abreast of the city. The whole ground is alive with the warlike memories of the historic past. The parishes adjoining St. Joseph to the east, though overrun, in 1759, by the English forces: Beaumont, St. Michel, St. Valier, Berthier, St. Thomas, have little in their history to attract the tourist, but opposite Levi begins the fertile and verdant

ISLE OF ORLEANS,

full of *souvenirs* for the beholder. It lies on the placid bosom of the great river, amphitheatre like, with a southern exposure, four miles lower down than Quebec, in length about twenty miles, and five and a half miles broad; being seventy miles in area, and divided into six parishes, viz. :—

ST. PETRONILE DE BEAULIEU,

on the western extremity, St. Pierre, Ste. Famille, St. François, St. Jean, St. Laurent. "The beautiful situation of the island, in the broad St. Lawrence, its picturesque heights and umbrageous groves, its quaint little hamlets and peaceful and primitive people, render Orleans one of the most attractive districts of the Lower St. Lawrence." The late N. H. Bowen, Esq., of Quebec, whose villa adorns the western point, published, in 1866, a short but excellent sketch of the place; in 1867, Mr. L. P. Turcotte, aided by the notes of the Abbé Bois of Maskinongé, gave a complete history of his native island, from which the following particulars are mainly condensed. One of the most noticeable edifices on the island, is the new and tasty temple of Roman Catholic worship erected by the denizens of the new parish of St. Petronile de Beaulieu, amidst graceful cottages, on a high bluff in full view of Quebec. It is connected with the city by a regular ferry during the summer months and an ice-bridge in winter.

"The island was called Minigo by the Indians, a large tribe of whom lived here and carried on the fisheries, providing also a place of retreat for the mainland tribes in case of invasion.   In 1535, Jacques Cartier explored these shores and the hills and forests beyond, being warmly welcomed by the resident Indians, and feasted with fish, honey and melons."   He speaks of the noble forests, and adds : "We found there grape-vines, such as we had not seen before in all the world ; and for that, we named it the Isle of Bacchus."   A year later, it received the name of the Isle of Orleans, in honor of De Valois, Duke of Orleans, the son of Francis I., of France.   The popular name, *L'Isle des Sorciers* (*Wizard's Island*), originated either on account of the marvellous skill of the natives in foretelling future storms and nautical events, or else because the superstitious colonists on the mainland were alarmed at the nightly movements of lights along the insular shores, and attributed to demons and wizards the dancing fires which were carried by the Indians in visiting their fish nets during the night tides.

The island was granted in 1620, to the Sieur de Caen, by the Duke de Montmorency, Viceroy of New France.   In 1675, this district was formed into the Earldom of St. Laurent, and was conferred on M. François Berthelot, who assumed the title of the Count of St. Laurent.   In 1657, part of it was occupied by six hundred Christian Huron Indians, who had taken refuge under the walls of Quebec from the exterminating Iroquois.   In 1656, the Iroquois demanded that they should come and dwell in their country, and upon their refusal fell upon the Hurons with a force of 300 warriors, devastated the island and killed seventy-two of the unfortunate Christians.   Two tribes[*] were compelled soon after to surrender and held as captives into the Iroquois' country, while the tribe of the Corde left the island

---

[*] The Hurons were divided into three tribes : the tribe of the *Rock*, of the *Bear*, and of the *Corde*.

and settled at Lorette. The isle was over-run by the Iroquois on the 18th June, 1661; they massacred indiscriminately, there and on the *Côte de Beaupré* opposite, the helpless French settlers. A Quebec sportsman, Couillard de L'Epinay, was at that time on the island, on a shooting excursion; Jean de Lauzon, son of the Governor of the Colony and brother-in-law to Couillard de L'Epinay, also Seneschal of New France, made up a party of seven spirited Quebecers, and sailed down in a boat to warn his brother-in-law of his danger. They landed near *Rivière Maheu*, where their boat grounded. De Lauzon sent two of his followers to see whether there were any one in a neighboring house belonging to René Maheu, pilot; on opening the door, they found themselves confronted by eighty Iroquois, who raising the warwhoop surrounded the seven Frenchmen, unable to put to sea, as their boat was aground; they summoned the French to surrender, promising to spare their lives, but De Lauzon, who knew too well the ferocity and perfidy of the foe, refused, firing away at them until the savages had to cut off his arms; they then cut off the Seneschal's head. The brave seven were all slaughtered, one excepted, who though grievously wounded was carried away to be tortured; before leaving, they burnt the bodies of their own dead warriors. The great cross of Argentenay was carried away and raised in triumph at the Iroquois' village, on Lake Onondaga, (New York.)

For nearly a century, the isle enjoyed peace and prosperity, until it had 2,000 inhabitants with 5,000 cattle and rich and productive farms. Then, came the advance of Wolfe's fleet in June, 1759; the inhabitants all fled to Charlesbourg; the unavailing French troops and artillery left these shores; Wolfe's soldiers landed at St. Laurent, and erected camps, forts and hospitals on the south-east point; and soon afterwards, the British forces systematically ravaged the deserted country, burning many houses on the Isle.

Orleans is now divided into two seigniories, or lordships, whose revenues and titles are vested in ancient French families

of Quebec, the Poulin, Gourdeau, Drapeau, etc.   The soil is rich
and diversified, and its pretty vistas justify Charlevoix's sketch
(of 1720) :   " We took a stroll on the Island of Orleans, whose
cultivated fields extend around, like a broad amphitheatre, and
gracefully end the view on either side.   I have found this country beautiful, the soil good, and the inhabitants very much at
their ease."   The farms are celebrated for their excellent potatoes,
prunes and apples and for their high flavored cheese (*fromage
rafiné*).   The people by their insular position still preserve
many of their early Norman customs ; the island is the residence
of many river pilots.

ST. PIERRE

occupies the southwest end of the island, where Capt. Hardy, one
of Wolfe's officers, had a post.   It has a population of 700 inhabitants, and runs eastward about seven miles, until it reaches *Ste.
Famille*, with the river *Pot-au-Beurre*, as the boundary.   The
first chapel, for the French and Indians, erected there in 1651,
was consecrated on the 2nd July, 1653, by the Jesuit Father
Lallemand.   It stood near *Anse du Fort*, where the " Columbus,"
3,700 tons, and the " Baron Renfrew," 3,000 tons, were built in
1824 and 1825, the largest vessels that the world had seen up to
that time.   The next parish,

STE. FAMILLE,

facing Ange Gardien and Chateau Richer, is six miles in length,
and is bounded to the east by *St. François Bout de l'Isle ;* in
1671, it had a stone R. C. church more than eighty feet long, by
thirty-six feet broad.

   " The convent of Ste. Famille was founded in 1685, by the
Sisters of the Congregation, and since that time the good nuns
have educated the girls of the village, having generally about
seventy, in the institution. The nunnery is seen near the church,
and was built in 1699, having received additions, from time to
time, as the village increased.   Its cellar is divided into narrow

and contracted cells, whose design has been long forgotten. The woodwork of the convent was burned by Wolfe's foragers in 1759, but was restored in 1761, after the conquest of Canada by the English. The first church of Ste. Famille was built in 1671, and the present church dates from 1745; the village is nearly opposite to Chateau Richer, and commands fine views of the Laurentian Mountains.

ST. FRANÇOIS.

This parish includes the domain of the ancient fief of Argentenay, and was formed in 1678. In 1683, the first church was built; the present church dates from 1736, and was plundered by Wolfe's troops in 1759. The view from the church is very beautiful, and includes the St. Lawrence to the horizon, the white villages of the south coast, the *Isle Madame, Grosse Isle* and *Isle aux Reaux*. On the north shore, at the end of the island, are the broad meadows of Argentenay, where wild fowl and other game are sought by the sportsmen of Quebec. This district looks across the north channel upon the dark and imposing ridges of the Ste. Anne mountains and the peaks of St. Fereol; and the view from the church is yet more extensive and beautiful.

ST. JEAN.

The church of St. John was built in 1735, near the site of a chapel dating from 1675, and contemporary with the hamlet. This parish is famous for the number of skillful river pilots which it has furnished. It has about 1,300 inhabitants, and is the most important parish on the island. It is nearly opposite the south shore village of St. Michel.

ST. LAURENT,

facing the south shore, is seven miles from St. Jean, upon the well settled royal road. The parish is entered after crossing the river Maheu, where the Seneschal of New France fell in battle. It was originally erected under the name of St. Paul, which

name it kept until 1698. It was, it is said, at the request of Mr.
Berthelot, Seignior of the Island and County of St. Laurent, that
its first name was changed into that of St. Laurent. A first early
church, dedicated to St. Paul, was built about 1675, at a spot
called *L'Arbre Sec* (the Dry Tree), several arpents west of the
Jesuit Church, where the hills begin. The R. C. church of St.
Laurent is a stately edifice of cut stone, with a shining tin roof,
and is 113 feet in length. It replaced the churches of 1675 and
1697, and was begun in 1860, and consecrated in 1861. The
Route des Pretres runs north from St. Laurent to St. Pierre, and
was so named fifty years ago, when this church had a piece of
St. Paul's arm-bone, which was taken away to St. Pierre, and
thence was stolen at night by the St. Laurent people. After a
long controversy, the Bishop of Quebec ordered that each church
should restore to the other its own relics, which was done along
this road by large processions, the relics being exchanged at the
great black cross, midway on the road. One and a half miles
west of St. Laurent, is the celebrated haven called *Trou St. Pat-*
rice (as early as 1689), or *Patrick's Hole*, where vessels, especially coasting crafts, seek shelter in a storm, or outward-
bound ships, await orders to sail.

We have still a vivid recollection of a cosy wayside inn, kept
by a bustling and hospitable landlady, Madame Cookson, who was
reckoned, as the Canadian *caboteurs* used to style her, *La Provi-*
dence des Marins. Here anchored, it would seem, Nelson's
sloop of war the " Albermarle," in 1782, when the love-sick
Horatio* returned to Quebec for a last farewell from the blooming
Miss Simpson, a daughter of Sandy Simpson, one of Wolfe's
Prevost-Marshals. Miss Simpson afterwards married Col.
Mathews, Governor of Chelsea pensioners, and died in 1830,
speaking tenderly of her first love, the hero of Trafalgar.

The river is a mile and a quarter wide here, and there are ten
or twelve fathoms of water in the cove.

---

* Southey in his LIFE OF NELSON, alludes to this youthful passion, and
letters recently discovered throw new light on it.

Two miles west of this point is the curious *Caverne de Bon-temps*, a grotto about twenty feet deep, cut in the solid rock, near the level of the river. It lies on the land of one François Mar-anda, and was called after one Bontemps, who sought refuge there. The people of St. Laurent are noted as skillful boat builders. In 1865, close to the church to the east, was erected a tower or lighthouse, to guide inward-bound ships.

ILE MADAME AND ILE AUX REAUX.

These two islands, one league to the south of St. François, are under the spiritual charge of the pastor of St. François. *Ile aux Reaux* was granted to the Jesuits, in 1638, by Governor de Montmagny ; for many years the late Dr. Geo. Mellous Douglas owned it, and had it in a high state of culture.

GROSSE ISLE—THE QUARANTINE STATION.

This island, about two and a half miles long, was purchased in 1832, by the Provincial Government from the Ursuline Nuns of Quebec. It was considered necessary to have a quarantine station, on the appearance of the Asiatic scourge in 1832, where all foreign ships bound for Quebec should stop to undergo a medical exam-ination and purification in case of contagion amongst the crew and passengers : all invalids were immediately sent to hospital, and the vessels fumigated and disinfected, under the personal superintendence of a medical man and staff, stationed there from 15th April to 10th December, each year. Dr. Charles Poole, a London surgeon, was the first, appointed to this charge : he was succeeded, in 1836, by Dr. George Mellous Douglass, who held the appointment for many years, and during the trying season of 1847. At his death, in 1864, he was succeeded by young Dr. Charles Montizambert, the present incumbent.

No one is allowed to live on the island without the permis-sion of the medical man in charge. Until 1864, in order to en-force sanitary regulations and compel ships to stop, a company of British soldiers, under a military head, vested with supreme authority over the island and its inhabitants, was stationed there every summer: they were furnished with heavy guns, and no passing ship felt inclined to disregard the shot fired across her bows. The blue coat of the policeman has since replaced the scarlet uniform. Though cholera, in 1834 and 1849, gave the authorities busy times, the deadly ship fever of 1847 amongst the Irish emigrants, who landed by thousands on our shores, rendered that year a painfully memorable one : ships, in order to escape quarantine, sometimes concealed all trace of disease, by throwing over board the dead before hearing the *boom* of the Grosse Isle cannon : the flow and ebb of the tide would float ashore those bloated corpses, a ghastly sight. Instead of a short and pleasant ten days' trip in the splendid Allan steamers, as at present, the emigration in former times, to the extent of 40,000 to 50,000, took place in ill-provided sailing ships ; the voyage being frequently protracted to fourteen weeks, and six or seven hundred emigrants huddled together in one small vessel. The mortality and human suffering was incredible : still hover over the island as a hideous nightmare the memories of 1847. In one grave alone, 7,000 victims of ship-fever lie buried. There is a good wharf for landing, and the long white sheds and buildings seen from the passing steamer, are the hospitals for the sick and the quarters of the medical man.

STE. MARGUERITE ISLAND AND ITS GROUP.

This island, about five miles in length, is not inhabited : owned by residents of St. Thomas, Crane Island, etc., it is of value merely on account of the fuel it yields. The beaches in summer, are used to pasture young cattle belonging to the south shore of the St. Lawrence, and which, from rarely seeing man, become perfectly wild when the owners cross over at the approach of winter, to convey these *mustangs* and bullocks home. A hut and a barn have been built here. The shallows near the island used to be a favorite fishing ground for *bass :* the fishing is done in boats. To the north and east of St. Marguerite Island the map shows a group of bare, uninhabited islets, some with scarce any trace of vegetation, and whose barren, reddish rocks are visible from afar : several generate in storms, eddies and tide-rips dangerous to boats and small craft. The principal ones are Patience I., Two Head I., Heron I., Canoe I., Race I., Mile I., Onion I. One, Canoe Island, the largest, is inhabited and fit for culture ; it exhibits one solitary dwelling : here, however, a re-spected R. C. prelate, the late Archbishop Baillargeon, was born in 1809. The eye next embraces a fertile island six miles in length, by one mile broad, or so ; it is connected by a vast, verdurous meadow, submerged by every spring tide, with the adjoining isle, Goose Island—so named nearly three centuries ago on account of the myriads of geese, ducks, etc., seeking their subsistence on its muddy flats.

CRANE ISLAND.

In 1646, one of the most picturesque islands of the St. Lawrence, thirty-six miles lower down than Quebec, from the incredible number of sea fowl and game it harbored, had attracted the attention of a *Grand Seigneur*, sent out by the *Grand Monarque, Louis XIV.* to administer New France. He obtained a land-patent, and found here ample scope for his sporting tastes. Charles Huault de Montmagny, Knight Grand Cross of Jerusalem and Governor of Quebec, was *Seigneur*, the first *Seigneur* of Crane Island.

Of the bags of game he annually made up on the verdant and swampy beaches of his lovely isle ; of the roasted duck, teal or snipe he served up to his little court, within the precincts of the Castle of St. Louis, we have no record, save the faint tracings of tradition.

That erratic wanderer, sung by Horace *Gruem advenam*, the wary crane, having also sought the island as a trysting place, during its spring and fall migrations from Florida to the fur countries and Hudson Bay, the place was called after it Crane Island. Under French rule, the law lent its protection to the game it contained. Special *ordonnances de chasse* were passed to that effect; and some legislation to protect the ducks, etc., at the period of incubation, also took place under the early English Governors; at one time, several varieties of aquatic fowl resorted to its vast meadows. Pot hunters having undertaken to hunt with dogs the fledglings, in July, before they could fly, the parent birds resented such unsportsmanlike practices, and sought new breeding places in the more secluded isles, on the Labrador coast or in the neighborhood of Lake St. John.

Amongst the early proprietors, figure the names of some of the Carignan-Salières Regiment, subsequently to whom we find the name of a descendant of Charles LeMoyne de Longueuil. In 1775, the *Seigneur* was M. de Beaujeu, brother of the famous de Beaujeu, who, in 1755, won from the English the memorable battle of Monangahela.* In 1759, he had been intrusted with the command of an important post, that of Michillimakinac in the west; for his services and devotion to the cause of His Most Christian Majesty, he was decorated. De Beaujeu, at the head of his *censitaires*, was a sturdy chieftain; nor did he hesitate during the winter of 1775-6, to cross over and join the succor, which De Gaspé, *Seigneur* of St. Jean Port Joly, Couillard, *Seigneur* of St. Thomas, and an old Highland officer, Thos. Ross, of Beaumont, made a noble effort to pour into Quebec.

It is curious to follow the warlike *Seigneur* de Beaujeu, up-

---

* " Louis Lienard Villemonde de Beaujeu was the brother of the hero of the Monangahela and his worthy emulator. Ensign from 1731 to 1738 ; lieutenant in 1744 ; he was appointed in 1751 captain of the company of Soldiers of the Marine, in place of M. de la Verendrye, and, by his honorable conduct, in January, 1754, obtained the cross of St. Louis. The authorities granted him that year a concession of land, four leagues in depth by four front, on the border of Lake Champlain, and he applied himself to the work of clearing it. Sometime afterwards he was appointed commander of the post of Michillimakinac, and he served in this position during many years. Later, he took an active part in the defence of the country during the American war. M. de Beaujeu died on the fifth of June, 1802, at his manor, at Crane Island, at the advanced age of eighty-five years and five months." *Collections of the State Historical Society of Wisconsin, Vol. VII., page* 138.

holding the standard of England in 1775-6—the same standard he had so successfully opposed, before the desertion of the colony by France—De Beaujeu, whose name still survives in that of the sand-bank in the St. Lawrence, opposite the manor house—as laid down in Bayfield's Chart. It is proper to state that his winter expedition of 1775-6 to relieve His Excellency, Guy Carleton, blockaded in Quebec, ended in a disaster, nearly costing him and his followers their lives. Capt. DeBeaujeu expired at Crane Island in 1802. In our early sporting days, we recollect hearing from the *anciens* of the Island, quaint anecdotes relating to their aged and warlike seigneur, Capt. DeBeaujeu. It would seem that on great holy days, the Chevalier de St. Louis took particular pride in wearing in his button-hole the red ribbon of the order sent out to him by the King of France, Louis XV. Age and infirmities creeping on, the old lion used to remain in his den the greater part of the day, and, when the *censitaires* came to fetch the rents and seigniorial capon, at Michaelmas, more than once they had to light the fire on the very spacious hearth, enclosed by an antique, " wide-throated " chimney,—which, to this day, is a subject of curiosity to all visitors,—so as to render the hall tenantable. Recently, two antiquated rusty cannon were shown to us lying on the shore at Crane Island near the Church; in our opinion they must have belonged to the French man-of-war *l'Eléphant*, stranded on the 1st September, 1729, on the shoal of *Cap Brûlé*, opposite to Crane Island, on the north side, whence they were brought.

In 1859, a similar cannon, measuring in length five feet eight inches, and twelve inches in diameter, was presented by a resident of Crane island, Capt. Lavoie, to the Quebec Seminary : at that period, some of the timber of this old wreck was still visible.

History furnishes the following, anent this memorable shipwreck, by which the Bishop of Canada (Monseigneur Dosquet) and its Intendant Hocquart, with several other men of note, were near losing their lives.

Bishop Dosquet obtained one thousand half-crowns (écus)

from the French Government for his losses, and described in a letter still extant, the manner in which the *Elephant* was wrecked.

We have also a very detailed *procès verbal* of the accident, from the pen of M. Hocquart, the Intendant who was a passenger

The *Elephant*, commanded by Monsieur Le Comte de Vaudreuil, "lieutenant de vaisseau," was at the time in charge of a river pilot, by name Chariteau. M. Hocquart relates how the frigate, at the request of the pilot, got under way at 3 p.m., with a fresh north-easter and rising tide, and how at 12 midnight, being deceived by a fire on the beach, it struck heavily three times on the ledge. An attempt was made to carry out in a boat a kedge anchor, but the boat was swamped.

For two hours, the ship made no water; with the ebb, she keeled over and broke her back; on the 2nd September, it was decided, the pumps being insufficient, to cut her masts, in order to save the very valuable cargo the frigate contained.

The Quebec harbor master, M. de la Richaudière, had got on board at ten o'clock the following morning, and was present at the consultation, which resulted in the cutting of the vessel's masts; a number of small craft were sent from Quebec to unload the stranded ship, which was effected by the 12th October. In the meantime, a violent storm came on, causing great damage to the small craft thus employed, and resulting in the death of a young carpenter, of the name of Prenouveau; the king granted his mother a pension of 150 *livres*. The frame of the *Elephant* was broken up—the timbers having been found much decayed.

The *procès verbal* is signed by the officers of the ship; Serigny de Loire, and Duquesne Meneville, le Chevalier de Bretonville, Duperat de la Bernandaye; Blanchard, maître; Chariteau, maître-pilote; Testu, Vaudreuil and Rivière.

(Signed,)   HOCQUART.

The population of Crane and Goose Islands may reach 800 souls.

With the exception of the seigniorial manor, on the lower end of Crane Island, rebuilt and enlarged by McPherson Le

Moyne, Esquire, the new seigneur, who occupies it during the summer months, all the dwellings stand on the northern side of the island. A thick belt of forest trees hides them from view, except when the steamer takes the north channel, when they are faintly seen in the distance.

The locality ranked as a parish, under the name of *St. Antoine de l'Ile aux Grues*, as early as 1683, when it comprised but three families, in all fifteen souls. In 1678, Pierre de Becart, Sieur de Granville, was the seigneur. It was the birthplace of a public-spirited and talented ecclesiastic, the Rev. Messire Painchaud, who in 1827 founded the College of *Ste. Anne des Aulnets*, county of Kamouraska. A marble slab now marks the spot in the island cemetery where repose the remains of this warm friend of education, deceased in 1839.

Crane Island during the "leafy months" is noted for its salubrity and attractiveness. A highway for carriages runs from one end to the other, and dense woods, descending to the shores, intersect the portion of the island which is not under culture. A grove of young maple and oak, some thirty acres long, fringes the crest of this *plateau*, at the west point facing the anchorage, so well known to every river pilot, *La Pointe aux Pins*.

Twelve years ago, the Marine and Fishery Department erected here a *lighthouse* on a detached pier : also several upright beacons along the shore, to mark out the course of ships steering inside of *Beaujeu's* bank, opposite the manor house. In rear the ground rises in successive terraces studded with dwarf, parasol pines of singular beauty, and leads through natural avenues to the wooded and umbrageous *plateau* above, known as " Le Domaine du Seigneur," a cool, delightful spot for a picnic or *fête champêtre*, if ever there was one. These picturesque highlands have also their heather : a fuzzy graceful carpet of juniper bushes weighted down each fall with fruit. When September crimsons the adjoining maple groves, a visit to this elysium is a thing to be remembered ; few sites in our gorgeous Canadian scenery can surpass its river views, extending to Cape Tourmente, Cape Maillard and over the innumerable islets basking in sunshine at your feet.

The old manor, with its gay *parterres*, *orchard*, ample verandah, flag staff and numerous outhouses, is in full view from the steamer ascending the south channel : it stands on the spot where dwelt the warlike Seigneur de Beaujeu. Some distance in rear, is visible an old windmill, beyond which may be seen a string of pretty white cottages extending to the extreme west end of the island ; the parish church, of course, as in all Canadian scenery, looms out in the centre—*the parent watching over the welfare of her offspring.* As a river view, nothing can surpass in grandeur the panorama which the broad St. Lawrence here unfolds on a radiant summer morning, when, with the rising tide, a fleet of swan-winged merchantmen emerge from the *Traverse*, far below, in the direction of the church of *St. Roch des Aulnets :* at first imperceptible white specks on the horizon, gradually growing larger and larger, on the bosom of the glad waters, until they each in succession crowd on you, top sails, top gallant-sails and royals all set ; a moving tower of canvas advancing straight to where you stand—so close, when an island pilot, perchance, is in charge, and takes the inshore channel, the deepest though the narrowest, that you can distinctly hear the voices of all on board.

The high tides of spring and fall wash the foot of the rising ground on which the manor stands ; the game, such as ring-plovers, curlews, sea-snipe, sand-pipers, then light within a few rods of the house. To the north of Crane Island, and separated by a narrow pass, you notice a small island, which the tide covers each day ; that is the celebrated *Dune* well known to Canadian sportsmen as abounding with Canada geese (outardes), snow-geese, ducks and small game. In May and September, you may daily see a flock of snow-geese and *outardes* feeding there, some three thousand, beyond a rifle's range, or winging their rapid, noisy, wedge-like flight towards the muddy St. Joachim flats opposite.

Home of our boyhood, thrice blessed isle, the congenial abode of many feathered denizens, the seat of plenty and of domestic peace, how oft, a youthful fowler, have we, gun in hand, trudged knee-deep through thy reedy, boundless marshes! Fatigue! pooh! there was in those days no such word in our vocabulary. How many sunny, blissful hours, during the long mid-summer vacation, have we not beguiled away on thy grassy lawn or in thy well-stocked orchard, dreaming away life's day dreams, or waiting impatiently until the increasing murmur of the swelling, bursting tide should indicate high water, the auspicious moment when we sallied forth to pour destruction among the serried flocks of beach-birds cooped up on thy pebbly shores! Haunts of our early days, can we ever forget you?

> "Sweet memory, wafted by thy gentle gale,
> Oft up the stream of time I turn my sail,
> To view the fairy haunts of long lost hours,
> Blest with far greener shades, far richer flowers."

GOOSE ISLAND.[*]

" Six miles lower down than Crane Island the tourist discovers the farm houses and verdant beaches of Goose Island, owned since 1876 by the Hotel-Dieu nuns of Quebec, a spot most graphically sketched by the Jesuits in 1663, as being then the inviolate sanctum[†] and breeding-ground of millions of ducks and teal, " whose loud voices made the whole island resound in the summer season, but who kept a profound silence during the spring and summer of 1663, owing to the frightful and continuous earthquakes, which caused the soil to roll and quake to such a degree that church steeples would bend to the earth and then rise up again ! ! "[‡] This last feat, from its novelty, must have

---

[*] From *Legendary Lore of the St. Lawrence.*

[†] *Rélations des Jésuites.*

[‡] It is really curious to note the care taken, both under French and English rule, to protect the game in these *preserves.* No less than two Ordinances were passed, one in 1731, and the other in 1769, to assure to the Seig-

been particularly attractive to witness, from a balloon for instance, or from the deck of a ship; from anywhere in fact, except from old mother Earth.

Goose Island is united to Crane Island by a belt of swampy ground, four miles long, shown on the map: this marsh is wholly covered by the tide, in the spring and fall, only M. de Montmagny, when Governor of the colony, obtained from the Company of New France, the grant of Crane Island and of the two neighboring Islands (Petite and Grosse Ile aux Oies) which bear the same name, as a shooting-ground. The Iroquois, in 1655, made a descent on Goose Island, and murdered M. Moyen; his wife and children were carried off, as prisoners. One of the daughters married the brave Lambert Closse, whose courage shed lustre on the early times of Montreal. An efficient game law would in a few years restore it to what it was formerly,* the best shoot-

---

neurs of Crane and adjacent islands, the exclusive privilege and right of shooting, granted them by their original title deed.

Gilles Hocquart.

"Sur les plaintes qui nous ont été portées par le Sieur de Touville aide Major des Troupes, Seigneur des Isles aux Grues, au Canot, Ste. Marguerite et la Grosse Isle, que plusieurs particuliers tant de cette ville, que des d : isle et des côtes voisines s'ingerent de chasser dans les d : isle quoique qu'il n'y ait que le *Seigneur qui ait le privilège à lui accordé par ses titres*, à quoi il nous aurait requis de pourvoir, nous faisons très expresses defenses à toutes personnes de chasser dans l'étendue des d : isles et Seigneuries sous quelque pretexte que ce soit, sans la permission du Sieur de Touville et à peine de 10 livres d'amende contre les contrevenants, et de confiscation de leurs armes et canots au profit du dit Seigneur : et sera la présente Ordonnance lue, publiée et affichée en la manière accoutumée. Mandons, &c.

Fait à Québec, 20 Mars, 1731.

(Signé)   HOCQUART.

(Archives de la Province—Registre des Ordonnances, Folio 70 Recto.

* By His Excellency, Guy Carleton, Captain General and Governor in Chief of the Province of Quebec, Brigadier General of His Majesty's armies, etc., etc., etc.

Taking into consideration the representations which have been made to us by the Sieur De Longueuil, Seigneur of Crane and Goose Islands, Canoe and Ste. Marguerite Islands, and also Grosse Isle, that by his title he has the exclusive right to shoot on these said Islands—that, notwithstanding several

ing ground in the country, for snipe, geese, ducks, teal, and all the other beach birds of which old Governor Boucher, the illustrious ancestor of the numerous Boucher family, wrote in 1663 from his capital (Three Rivers) such glowing accounts to his friends at the court of Louis XIV. Some years back, a magnificent swan was shot on these swamps and presented to the Governor General, by Daniel McPherson, Esq., then proprietor of these Islands. Not only is Goose Island a land of promise for the sportsman and the naturalist, it also has its wild legends.

More than a century, back a French officer left old for New France, as it was then called. This gentleman obtained the grant of a Fief or Seigniory, comprising a group of islands called the Ste. Marguerite Islands, to which he subsequently added the two Goose Islands and Crane Island, originally granted to M. de Montmagny in 1646. The extent of such a domain supposes rank and importance in the seignior, who chose for his manorial residence one of the most picturesque, but also one of the most

---

persons both from the city and neighboring parishes and even the inhabitants of these Islands, attempt to shoot there without leave, destroying the hay on the beaches—and catching the young ducks that they find there, thereby diminishing their numbers considerably for the next hunting season, and also removing each year a quantity of thatching grass, also using as firewood the timber on those islands, we hereby expressly forbid that any person either from Quebec, or from the neighboring seigneuries, and likewise—that any of the inhabitants of these Islands, under whatever pretence, do shoot on these Islands or any portion thereof without the express permission of the Sieur de Longueuil, under pain of legal punishment. We also forbid them to remove the young ducks, to carry away the thatching grass, to destroy the meadow hay, or burn the timber on the said Islands without the leave of the said Sieur de Longueuil, and the said Sieur de Longueuil may have this ordonnance published in the neighboring parishes.

Done at Quebec, 28th July, 1769.

(Signed,) GUY CARLETON.

Reg. I. Foi et Hommages,
Folio 226.

Modern legislation has rendered these ordonnances unnecessary by including 'Beaches' within the provisions of the Agriculture Act, and providing punishment against trespassers on property.

secluded islands of the group, and thereon built not a crenelated tower, not a baronial castle of the middle ages, but a plain massive stone house,—a prison, as it proved subsequently, either for himself or his son; tradition has failed to elucidate this point. There, for many a long year, far from the eyes of men, a solitary prisoner was immured. His keeper, perhaps his friend, his relative, for aught that can be stated to the contrary,—was a woman, a woman of rank and wealth. The prisoner, it was said, was insane. The question was often asked, " Was he born so, or, if not, what produced, or led to, his insanity ? Were there no lunatic asylums in France fit to receive him ? The replies to these queries are likely to remain for ever amongst the unfathomed secrets of the past. Dark surmises were circulated. Who was this new *Masque de Fer?* Why was he immured between four massive walls, with no sweet sounds to beguile captivity's lonely hours, save the voice of the pitiless, north-easterly storm or the monotonous murmur of the waves on the granite rock wherein he was entombed, in a living grave ? The name of the fair occupant of the manor was......Madame or Mademoiselle de Granville.* The prisoner was.....her brother : sisterly love made her his jailor—she said so.

---

* His patent runs thus :—" To the Sieur de Granville.

" Louis de Buade, &c.

" Jean Bochart, &c.

" On the petition presented to us by the Sieur de Granville, Lieutenant of a company of the detachment of Marines of New France, where he is married and settled, praying that we would grant him a new title for a tract of land, situated near Goose Island and Crane Islands, called the Ste. Marguerite Islands, together with three small islands on the south side thereof, and the beaches adjacent to the said islands, which had already been granted to him about thirty two years ago by Mr. Talon, then intendant in this country, the title-deed of which is lost ;

" We   *   *   *   *   *   *   *   *   *   "

("5th Nov., 1698.")

A Mr. de Granville (an officer in the Regiment of Carignan) had had a concession of Island du Portage in 1672—it does not appear whether this is the same man or not.

Years rolled on : the poor captive died, and

> " Perhaps, in this neglected spot is laid
> Some heart once pregnant with celestial fire,
> Hands, that the rod of Empire might have swayed,
> Or waked to ecstacy the living lyre."

The manorial residence of the seigniors was removed to the neighboring island, where it has, for half a century and more, been in the possession of the McPherson family. McPherson's house, and McPherson's shoal are equally well known to the mariner. The ruins of Madame de Granville's grim old house were standing until recently. Fresh is the legend in the memory of the oldest inhabitants of Goose Island ; but on the spot where it stood, unfortunately for the lovers of legendary lore, there has been erected a substantial modern structure. It required great efforts to disjoint the masonry of the old walls.

Who will rescue from oblivion this historical episode, ere it sinks in the shadow of the past, embodying its outlines in a brilliant narrative, throbbing with the pulse of life. Have we amongst us no Landors, no Martineaus, no Frederika Bremers, no Hawthornes ? (*Legendary Lore of the St. Lawrence.**)

° Sixteen summers have flown over since these lines were penned. *The Legendary Lore of the St. Lawrence*—a few hasty notes I had collected, as my offering towards a little work Mr. Geo. T. Cary, editor of the *Mercury*, published in 1862—has done duty in nearly every Guide Book, describing the scenery of our lordly St. Lawrence. How those scanty unpretending 33 pages have been pirated—pillaged—robbed wholesale and retail—has amused me. The coolest piece of piracy of the contents of my poor *Legendary Lore of the St. Lawrence* was perpetrated by an Ogdensburg, N.Y., writer, by name Gardiner B. Chapin, under the title of *Tales of the St. Lawrence*. Mr. Chapin put forth, in 1874, from the presses of John Lovell, Montreal, an illustrated volume of some 372 pages, purporting to be a volume of " Historical Romances ; " and whilst complaining that no enduring record then existed of incidents connected with the noble river, he undertakes to fill up the *lacuna* by his " frame work of tinted fact or flowery garlands of romance "—the reader can form his own opinion as to his success. The scene of the Goose Island *Masque de Fer* is thus transferred to the adjoining island, where certainly no tradition of that kind ever existed. Five of

SEAL ROCKS—A GAME PRESERVE.

Some miles lower down than Big Goose Island, also the property of the *Hôtel-Dieu* nuns of Quebec, and lying in the direction of *Baie St. Paul*, the eye gathers in the contour of a low, uninhabited, unadorned, rocky plateau, treeless and bare : it is known as Seal Rocks, *La Batture aux Loups-Marins*—loved by the *phocæ* of yore, though these amphibious wanderers seldom resort to it at present. A game preserve of established renown, it is leased from Government by a club of *chasseurs* from St. Jean Port Joly and Islet : the author of the *Canadians of Old*, Mr. De Gaspé, has agreeably narrated, in his *Memoirs*, the glorious sport he enjoyed here in the heyday of his youth. The Seal Rocks stand in the distance far away, some ten miles or more, from his mossy old manor at St. Jean Port Joly : his teeming fancy has woven around it a fascinating story, founded partly on fact, in which the Seal Rocks "apple tree, half sweet, half sour," holds its place.

Let us follow on the riband of white cottages, with a parish church every six or nine miles, until we shoot past the pretty villages of the south shore: St. Roch des Aulnets; Ste. Anne, with its handsome college, swathed in trees ; its model farm ; its green groves and golden wheat fields.

The establishment of a model farm by the College at Ste. Anne deserves a notice, if space permitted.

RIVIÈRE OUELLE.

Watch for the pointe of Rivière Ouelle, dear to our respected Lieutenant-Governor, the Hon. Luc Letellier, and to our literary friend, Abbé R. H. Casgrain, who has, with much ability and research, succeeded in rescuing from oblivion the early history

---

my sketches of Canadian History, some of which have cost me much research, are thus unceremoniously abstracted and perverted, transformed in what he calls "tinted fact" without any acknowledgment whatever of the source whence the materials were drawn. I was in the act of drafting an energetic protest against this literary pirate, when I heard of his death.

of his native parish. Once the crack of the musket and the loud shouts of victory resounded on this headland. In October, 1690, Admiral William Phipps attempted, in boats, a landing, but he had calculated without taking in account the bellicose old Rivière-Ouelle pastor, the Abbé Francheville,* who, after pointing out forcibly to his warlike parishioners the audacity and godlessness of *ces mécréants de Bostonnais*, for whom Canadian homes and Canadian altars had nothing sacred,—placed them in ambush under the shelter of the trees and rocks at the point; they poured in the first boat so well directed a volley that the inmates were killed or disabled, all except two, who made good their escape, on which the other boats retreated in hot haste.

Was it the memory of this repulse, asks Abbé Casgrain, which impelled Wolfe's followers to wreak such signal vengeance on this and the adjoining parishes, in 1759, by ruthlessly burning the dwellings, mills, etc. ? †

---

* *Histoire de l'Hotel-Dieu de Québec, p.* 321 ; *Opinion Publique, March* 28, 1878.

†According to a siege narrative, published in the *New York Mercury*, of the 31st Dec., 1759, Capt. Gorham and his 150 ferocious Rangers and detachments from Highlanders and Marines, in all about 300, spread terror and desolation on both shores of the Saint Lawrence. " On the 4th of August (1759) they proceeded down to St. Paul's Bay, where was a parish containing about 200 men, who had been very active in distressing our boats and shipping. At three o'clock in the morning, Capt. Gorham landed, and forced two of their guards, of 20 men each, who fired smartly for some time ; but that, in two hours, he drove them all from their covering in the wood, and cleared the village which they afterwards burnt ; it consisted of about fifty fine houses and barns—destroyed most of their cattle, etc. That, in this they had one man killed and six wounded ; but that the enemy had two killed and several wounded, who were carried off. That, from thence they proceeded to Mal Baie (Murray Bay) ten leagues to the eastward on the same side, where they destroyed another very pretty parish, drove off the inhabitants and stock, without any loss ; after which, they made a descent on the south shore, opposite Isle-aux-Coudres, destroyed part of the parishes of Ste. Anne and St. Roch, where were many handsome houses with good farms, and loaded the vessels with cattle, and then returned from the expedition."

(*From a Journal of the Expedition up the River St. Lawrence, 1759.*)

THE OLDEST COUNTRY CURÉ IN CANADA.

Would you like to witness the landing at Rivière Ouelle (in 1683) of the "oldest country curé in Canada, " ? listen to Parkman's lively description :

" On the Lower St. Lawrence, where it widens to an estuary six leagues across, a ship from France, the last of the season, holds her way for Quebec, laden with stores and clothing, household utensils, goods for Indian trade, the newest court fashions, wine, brandy, tobacco and the king's orders from Versailles. Swelling her patched and dingy sails, she glides through the wilderness and the solitude, where there is nothing but her to remind you of the great troubled world behind and the little troubled world before. On the far verge of the ocean-like river, clouds and mountains mingle in dim confusion ; fresh gusts from the north dash waves against the ledges, sweep through the quivering spires of stiff and stunted fir-trees, and ruffle the feathers of the crow, perched on the dead bough after his feast of mussels among the sea-weed. You are not so solitary as you think. A small birch canoe rounds the point of rocks, and it bears two men ; one, in an old black cassock and the other, in a buckskin coat, both working hard at the paddle to keep their slender craft off the shingle and the breakers. The man in the cassock is Father Morel, aged forty-eight, the oldest country curé in Canada, most of his brethren being in the vigor of youth, as they had need to be. His parochial charge embraces a string of incipient parishes extending along the south shore from Rivière du Loup, to Rivière du Sud, a distance reckoned at twenty-seven leagues, and his parishioners number in all three hundred and twenty-eight souls. He had administered spiritual consolation to the one inhabitant of Kamouraska, visited the eight families of La Bouteillerie and the five families of La Combe ; and now, he is on his way to the Seigniory of St. Denis with its two houses and eleven souls.*

---

* These particulars are from the *Plan Général de l'Estat Présent des Mis-*

The father lands where a shattered eel-pot, high and dry on the pebbles, betrays the neighborhood of man. His servant shoulders his portable chapel, and follows him through the belt of firs and the taller woods beyond, till the sunlight of a desolate clearing shines upon them. Charred trunks and limbs encumber the ground ; dead trees, branchless, barkless, pierced by the wood-peckers, in part black with fire, in part bleached by sun and frost, tower ghastly and weird above the labyrinth of forest ruins through which the priest and his follower wind their way, the cat-bird mewing and the blue-jay screaming, as they pass. Now the golden-rod and the aster, harbingers of autumn, fringe with purple and yellow the edge of the older clearing, where wheat and maize, the settler's meagre harvest, are growing among the stumps.

To set up his altar in a room of the rugged log cabin, say mass, hear confessions, impose penance, grant absolution, repeat the office of the dead over a grave made weeks before, baptize, perhaps the last infant, marry, possibly, some pair who may or may not have waited for his coming, catechize, as well as time and circumstances would allow, the shy but turbulent brood of some former wedlock ; such was the work of the parish priest in the remoter districts. It was seldom that his charge was quite so scattered and so far extended as that of Father Morel ; but there were fifteen or twenty others whose labors were like in kind, and, in some cases, no less arduous. All summer, they paddled their canoes from settlement to settlement, and in winter, they toiled on snow-shoes over the drifts, while the servant carried the portable chapel on his back or dragged it on a sledge. Once, at least, in the year, the curé paid his visit to Quebec, where, under the maternal roof of the seminary, he made his retreat of meditation and prayer, and then returned to his work.

---

sions du Canada, fait en l'année 1683. It is a list and description of the par-ishes with the names and ages of the curés, and other details. See *Abeille* *I.* This paper was drawn up by order of Bishop Laval.

He rarely had a house of his own, but boarded in that of the seigneur or one of the *habitants*." (*The Old Regime in Canada*, page 341.)

A CANADIAN COTTAGE.

" Do you see," writes Abbé Casgrain, " on the summit of yonder hillock that dainty white dwelling, with its thatched roof barn, furnishing such a pleasant contrast with the surrounding emerald fields. That is a Canadian cottage."

Crowning this little eminence of green sward, it seems to smile on the noble river, reflecting its graceful image, and whose ripples expire at its feet. The Canadian peasant dotes on the lordly flood, on whose banks he first drew the breath of life.

Absence will create a craving for the fond object of his youth; he feels drawn towards it; he longs to hear its great voice, in autumnal storms or in summer sunshine ; to feast his eyes on its many, wooded and beautiful isles. The stranger, unfamiliar with our Canadian farmer, and bent on assimilating him to the peasant of old France, his sire, would commit an egregious error.

More enlightened, especially more religious, the *habitant* is far above the French peasant in his style of living. Compared to the French peasant, he of Canada is a real *little prince*— quite independant in means—living on his sixty or eighty *arpents* of land, enclosed by a cedar fence—here, all his daily wants are abundantly supplied. Come, we will venture beyond this threshhold with its pleasant surroundings. I will tell you what I saw there, a thousand times. Here we are at the entrance. The porch exhibits two oaken buckets brimful of fresh water— resting on a stool ; at hand, ever ready to quench your thirst, hangs on the wall, a tin cup. In the interior of the dwelling, whilst the soup simmers at the fire-place, the housewife, sitting near the window in a rocking chair, is quietly turning her spinning wheel.

A *mantelet* of calico, a blue skirt of homespun, a neat white cap (câline) : such, her simple attire. The baby is asleep in his crib. Occasionally, the mother casts an earnest look at its fresh little face, like a rosebud, peering from under the variegated calico counterpane, made up of triangular pieces ingeniously joined together. In one corner of the room, the eldest daughter, seated on a trunk, is actively engaged at her loom, and hums a song. The shuttle, impelled by those vigorous young hands, glides along with marvellous swiftness; seven or eight ells of home-made linen represents a day's work,—materials for next year's raiment.

At the opposite end, high above an antiquated bedstead, covered with a quilt, white with blue squares, is suspended a cross between some images of saints.

That dry spruce bough is the palm blessed by the parish priest. Two or three barefooted " hopefuls " are seated on the floor, busy harnessing a pet dog."

To these truthful touches, one might add the following :

On the rafter over your head, hangs a long shot gun, which has carried death to scores of ducks and wild geese—perchance, to a stray bear or cariboo. Next to it, are suspended the snow-shoes of the farmer, ready for wood travel, when the maple sugar season arrives. Close to the black temperance cross, is the *chapelet*—the beads of the housewife—doubly dear to her should they have been brought from Rome, with the Pope's blessing, when her younger son, the Pontifical zouave, returned from the Eternal City.

There, too, is hung up the bottle of *holy water*, brought from church, on Holy Saturday before Easter. Among other properties, it is considered a specific against lightning.* Pray, do not forget to notice the traditional old eight-day clock, reaching to the ceiling, which rings with that clear, metallic tinkle, of which the secret is lost to modern clock makers.

All round the walls, are set highly-colored images of Ma-

---

* The sprinkling of holy water to guard against calamity, and scare the devil, is resorted to not only by the Canadian peasant ; I knew a family, whose respected head held a very high position in the Province ; they sprinkled the floor with *eau bénite* before every thunder-storm.

donnas, St. Ignatius of Loyola, the musical St. Cecilia, youthful St. Catherine, queen of Hungary; they surround the more commanding image of the reigning pontiff. Close by him, in plaster, on a niche, you may notice a statue of the great Napoleon, with his famous cocked hat; his arms are crossed on his chest, as if in the attitude of meditation.

In the seaboard parishes, the great Napoleon is often replaced by the burly form of a sailor, of a parrot, or of a cock in plaster.

The travelling photographer, having penetrated even in the most remote hamlet, accounts for that family album on the centre table; the leaves are well thumbed; the first picture is that of the Pope, the next that of the *curé* of the parish; then, should the family have furnished members to Holy Orders, will appear their likenesses; possibly good Governor Dufferin and his amiable Countess's picture may come next; but, of course, the church must rank before the state. The remainder of the album is a repository for the dear ones of the family circle.

KAMOURASKA.

Before the era of steamers, in fact even as late as 1850, Kamouraska was the Brighton of Lower Canada. Here, as at the other watering-places, the assembling of tourists is everywhere apparent by the increase in the number of cosy dwellings all along the beach. Kamouraska is the shire-town of the judcial district of Kamouraska, and has its resident judge and lawyers. The heights at the west end of the village are crowned by the handsomer residences of the aristocracy of the place, conspicuous among which is the picturesque villa of the high sheriff of the district, Vinceslas Taché, Esquire,—embosomed in trees, gardens and green fields. Another very attractive spot is the site of the old seigniorial manor, at the *Petit Cape,* a long antique structure, till lately inhabited by the *seigneur,* Ivanhoe Taché. The parish on the sea-shore is called St. Louis; the parish on the second range in rear, goes under the name of St. Paschal. It is remarkable for its wheat fields and delicious dairy produce; it is also a station of the railway.

" Who," asks Judge Routhier, " does not know Kamouraska ? Who does not know that it is a charming village, bright and picturesque, bathing its feet in the crystal of the waters of the river like a naiad, and coquettishly viewing the reflections of its two long ranges of white houses so near the river that from all the windows the great waves may be contemplated and their grand voices heard? On all sides, except towards the south, the horizon extends as far as the eye can reach, and is only bounded by the vast blue curtain of the Laurentides. At the north-east, the eye rests on a group of verdant isles,* like a handful of emeralds dropped by the angel of the sea. These isles are the favorite resort of the strangers who visit Kamouraska. There, they fish or bathe, or seek other amusements ; many the gay pic-nics on these charmed spots."

THE PILGRIM ISLANDS,

A few miles below Kamouraska, consist of a remarkable group of rocks, which, from their height, are visible at a great distance. These islands, in summer, scarcely ever present to the beholder the same shape for an hour at a time ; that beautiful delusion, " THE MIRAGE," seeming constantly to dwell about them. This may be due to refraction of the sun's rays, owing to the rocks being sparsely covered with vegetation.

Dr. William Kelly, a scientific gentlemen attached to Capt. Bayfield's surveying party of the St. Lawrence, read before the *Literary and Historical* Society, in 1836, a paper on " Some Extraordinary Forms of Mirage," calculated to throw light on this singular phenomenon :

" When my attention," says the Doctor, " was directed, some years since, to the different forms of objects, seen through mirage in the St. Lawrence, one of these, which I particularly remarked, was the flower-pot shape assumed by small islands when affected by the mirage, which depends on the contact of warm moist air with a surface of water colder than its dew point. Whatever the real shape of the island or rock might be, its top seemed raised and flattened ; generally extending in a straight horizontal line so far on each side as at least to equal the base in extent, often

* Isle aux Corneilles, Isle Brulée, Isle de la Martinique, Isle de la Providence.

beyond it : whilst midway between the base and distorted top the figure was contracted, having the appearance of a neck. When two islands lay close together these flattened tops sometimes met, giving the appearance of an arch from one to the other. In all other cases of mirage, depending on the same cause, the tops of objects seemed straight and horizontal in the same way, but the sides were like a wall. They frequently presented an appearance as if they were horizontally stratified.

In the paper on mirages, published by the society, in 1832, I hazarded a conjecture that these forms of arches, and flower-pots might be owing to the beach of the islands being heated by the sun, and hence acting on the air, in contact with it, in a different manner from the surrounding cold sea. I have since found that the state of the air on the beach could have no share in producing the phenomenon ; as we observed it when the islands were so distant, that the beach was below the horizon, and the refraction, consequently, was wholly owing to the state of the air over the water nearer to us. The cause of rocks and islands assuming this form was afterwards made manifest to me, as I had an opportunity of seeing the mode in which it occurred at Mingan, in July, 1832.

On the morning of the 16th July, at 9.30, the wind was light and variable, the sky clouded but bright, the temperature of the air 59,° the dew point 51,° the surface water 44°. One of the Perroquet islands, distant about 8 miles, seemed raised above the horizon, with a flattened top, and walled sides. At 10 a.m. the apparent height of the island above the water was diminished: the walled appearance of its sides, and flattened top were no longer perceptible ; but, on looking with a telescope, it was found that the horizon itself was raised, causing the diminution in the relative height of the land. At 11.30, there was a light breeze from S. W., the sky clear, and the sun bright, the Perroquet then presented a well-marked double image, the upper one being inverted. A fishing schooner at anchor to the westward of the island presented also a double image, the upper one inverted in the same way, but the whole less distinct than the images of the island. A line answering to the horizon was also seen on a level with the upper flat part of the inverted image of the island, and extending from it to a sandy point on the main. The true horizon was quite distinct, and well-marked beneath. The sandy beach between us and the point seemed raised like a wall. The two images of the island did not remain long distinct : the upper one gradually sunk, and, when both met, the island had the flower-pot shape. There was a faint return of two distinct images, about a quarter of an hour after, but it lasted only a few minutes. On the 17th, we had again an inverted image of the Perroquet, but not so distinct and well-defined as the day before. It soon presented to the naked eye nothing more than the flat top and walled sides usually seen in this form of mirage. But on examining it carefully with a telescope, in some parts of the flattened top the picture of a beach was seen above the trees ; thus shewing that this form also depended on a second inverted image lying above, and confounded with the upright one.

Since that time I have frequently observed the flower-pot shape of islands during the mirage ; and by the help of a telescope, have found certain indications of the inverted image ; the upper line generally extending as a false horizon, on the inferior edge of which, the play of the waters could be occasionally noticed. The upper portion of the flower-pot figure resembles the lower exactly in shape, as far it extends ; and the image of the stones of the beach, which is sometimes seen in it, leaves no doubt of its being an inverted picture.

All the various forms assumed by objects under the influence of this mirage seem to be the result of two or more images, alternately erect and inverted, either distinct or mingled together in a greater or lesser degree. When the objects are near, the images are usually confused ; they are so, occasionally in distant objects, but can, in most instances, be distinguished by the help of a telescope ; and sometimes they are beautifully distinct to the naked eye. The beginning of summer is the time when the contrast between the temperatures of the air and water is greatest. During the first four years of the survey, when we passed this time in the narrow parts of the river, we had no opportunity of observing more than a double image ; but in June, 1832, we went at once to the gulf ; and, in passing Point des Monts, where the breadth of the river is very considerable, we saw the three images distinctly marked, such as they have been described by Vince and Scoresby. The appearance they presented, and the attendant circumstances of both air and water, have been narrated by Captain Bayfield in a paper published in the *Nautical Magazine* for February, 1835. We have frequently since seen treble images in the estuary and gulf, but never so beautiful as on that occasion.

A telescope, if at hand, should always be employed in

observing mirages of any kind, as it enables us to detect particulars that would escape the naked eye. On one occasion,
when, to the naked eye, the hull of a ship seemed raised to an
enormous height, and the sails very small, the telescope shewed
three distinct images. Of the two lower, the second was inverted,
and its rigging and sails intimately mingled with those of the
first upright one. The third image was erect, with its hull resting
on the inverted hull of the second. The space between the
hulls of the first and second image being occupied by a confused
mingling of masts, sails and rigging, gave to the whole the
appearance of one immensely raised hull, as already stated.

By the help of the telescope we were afterwards enabled to
detect five distinct images, though the whole gave to the naked
eye the impression of only one almost shapeless mass, like that
which I have just mentioned.

We were off Metis, on the afternoon of the 14th of September,
1835. There was a light easterly wind and cloudy sky : the
temperature of the air 48° ; the dew point 40°.5 ; the surface
water 39°.5. The barometer 29.90 falling. Some light rain
fell two or three times during the afternoon, and we had very
heavy continuous rain after night-fall. Several vessels were in
sight between 3 and 4 p.m., and all presenting a variety of
appearances from refraction. The most remarkable was that in
which a vessel with all sail set, at one moment looked like an
immense black chest, no sails or masts being visible. On
observing her for a time the black body seemed to separate
horizontally into two parts ; and two sets of mingled sails occupied
the intervening spaces, with one set of very small sails above.
The figures afterwards became more distinct, and three images
were clearly discerned. Another vessel changed also from the
form of a great square flat-topped chest, to five distinct images
the upper with the sails erect, and the two lower double images
with their sails rather confusedly intermingled. A raised horizon was parallel to the upper figure of the hull. In a third case,
the chest-like figure divided into two portions, of which one
appeared much nearer than the other, the sea seeming to
be interposed. This appearance occurred afterwards in other
ships. When we first saw it we thought there really were two
hulls, and the deception was only removed by the figures gradually uniting, and forming one.* Captain Bayfield and Mr.

---

* The alternate union and separation of the different images, which often
occur within a few minutes, cause a very curious variety in the forms which
objects seem to assume.

Bowen observed five distinct images of another vessel after I left the deck.* When I first noticed extraordinary appearances, like those I have endeavored to describe, I was not aware of the advantage of employing a telescope for the examination of objects at inconsiderable distances. As the whole appeared to be a single image, it seemed extraordinary that the hull of a ship should appear to have its altitude so immensely increased, whilst the masts and sails had their height lessened in an equal, or even greater, degree.† A general increase, or a diminution, in the altitude of any object might be reconciled to optical principles, but I could think of no mode that could, in any way, account for the contrary manner in which the upper and lower parts of the same object seemed to be affected.

It seems probable that the horizontally stratified appearance, which the coast often assumes under this species of mirage, may be the effect of multiplied images of the horizon, or level sea at its base. The number of images may as well exceed five, as we find they do three, which, I believe, was the greatest number hitherto noticed by any observer.‡

The temperature of the surface water varies much amongst the Mingan Islands. Several rivers empty themselves into the sea at this place, the waters of which, in calms, float on its surface, which thus is sometimes several degrees warmer than the water at a depth of a few inches. A moderate current of air, which amongst small islands is often partial, sometimes, by agitating the water at one place, renders the surface there cold, whilst it continues warm in places sheltered from the wind. We have

---

* Since this paper was read we had an opportunity of seeing the form of a ship changed by mirage in a way we had not previously met with. Off Basque Island on the 10th September, 1836, at 3 p.m., two ships to the eastward seemed each to consist of three immense columns of irregularly formed sails, with a set of small distinct sails at the top of each column. The images seemed, not only immensely raised, but also extended horizontally (a circumstance which we had not remarked in any previous case), the space between the masts being considerable, and each column of sails quite distinct. The jibs were indistinctly erect and inverted alternately, giving some appearance of a combination of images, but there was no appearance of hull. The vessels were some miles distant from us, probably hull down. The temperaure of the air was 47°, water 39°. The dew point, found shortly after when a breeze had sprung up and the mirage disappeared, was 37°.

† On one occasion, at Bic, what appeared to be a large high boat, with two men sitting on the thwarts, turned out to be a small schooner under sail.

‡ Whatever the number of images may be, they appear in every instance to be alternately erect and inverted.

hence occasionally strange combinations of mirage. On the 16th and 17th July, shortly before the double images of the Perroquet were observed, the islands to the eastward of the harbor had their extremities apparently projecting in the air, as is usual in that species of mirage which depends on the temperature of the surface being higher than that of the air, or at least higher than its dew point. The horizon on this side was low and near—a rock, three miles distant, seemed above it. As the breeze sprung up from the S. W. the horizon receded beyond this rock, and the islands generally appeared to have flattened tops, shewing the mirage of the opposite kind. But the extreme points of the most distant island seemed still in the air, notwithstanding the island generally presented the same flat level top as the others —thus shewing, in its different parts, the opposite forms of mirage at the same time.

Something like this occurs frequently in the strait of Belle-Isle, where we saw the Labrador coast exhibiting the flattened tops, walled sides, and other marks of the mirage which is connected with a cold surface, whilst on the Newfoundland side the horizon was depressed, and the points and low shores of the headlands seemed consequently lifted into the air. Whenever we had an opportunity of examining the temperature of the water, on both sides of the strait, we found it warmer near the Newfoundland shore, and the different forms of the mirage which we saw at other times seems a proof that it is generally so.*

In these case there was no particular point which could be fixed on as shewing that there the effect of either mirage ceased. The raised horizon on the one side and the depressed horizon on the other seemed to merge one into the other; and the whole line across the strait appeared unbroken. But on one occasion near the Labrador coast, the point of junction of the two species of mirage was so well marked that it appeared like a step in the horizon.

On the 18th June, 1834, we were approaching the coast of Labrador from the central parts of the gulf. At 8.45 a.m. the temperature of the air was 46°; the dew point 45°; the surface water 43.5; the sky clear; wind S. W., light; barometer 30.12,

---

* The most remarkable mirages over water have occurred in straits : those seen by Mr. Vince at Dover, and the celebrated Fata Morgana at Messina.. In the St. Lawrence, they are most frequently observed, and present the greatest varieties in similar situations : as at Bic, Point des Monts, Mingan, and the strait of Belle-Isle.

rising. The dip of the horizon, from an elevation of 12 ft. 6 inches, was 3' 15", by the mean of three very good observations with the dip sector. As we neared the shore, the color of the water changed; the horizon towards the land seemed depressed; and the distant islands consequently elevated into the air. About the point where the water changed color, there seemed a sudden descent like a step in the horizon.

At 10.30 we had got well within the dark discolored water; the air was 47°; the dew point 46°; the water drawn from alongside 46°.5; the wind and sky as before. The dip of the horizon, from the same elevation of 12 ft. 6 inches, was 4' 11", by the mean of four very distinct equal observations."

This much for mirage, let us proceed.

CACOUNA,

In point of hotel accommodation, is doubtless the first watering place on the Lower St. Lawrence,—the abode of fashion for three months in the year, the Saratoga of Canada. It lies six miles from Rivière du Loup, and two miles from the railway station in St. Arsène. Among a number of smaller hotels is conspicuous the large structure, the St. Lawrence Hall, capable of accommodating 500 guests; the population of the village swells during the summer months to 2000 or 3000. In the village there are three churches, Episcopalian, Presbyterian and Roman Catholic. The lakes in the interior afford good trout-fishing and shooting; at the close of the season races are held, in which horses from Montreal, Quebec, and occasionally from the United States, take part. The beach is very favorable for bathing, the air very pure; several wealthy merchants and professional men have erected cottages here for their seaside holidays. Altogether, to those who wish to see life and bustle in a large watering place, we commend Cacouna.

TADOUSAC,

Is one of the most noted watering places on the Lower St. Lawrence its very name takes us back to the cradle of Canadian History. Jacques Cartier landed at Tadousac, on the 1st

September, 1535.   In 1628, Admiral William Kertk took possession of it : some years later, in 1632, Captain James Michael Kertk, a brother to the Admiral, died there, and his remains, after burial, were dug up by the Indians and given as food to their dogs.   Tadousac played an important part in our early history, as a stopping place for French and Basque vessels engaged in the fisheries.   Chauvin had founded a fishing port at Tadousac as early as 1599.   At Chauvin's death, neither Commander de Chatte, nor de Monts continued the establishment, though the fishing company, DeGuay de Monts, traded there in 1607.   It was only in 1622 that it became a regular trading post. Champlain found ships there in 1610, and remarks that their arrival dated since the 19th May, which was an earlier date for arrivals from sea than had been witnessed there for the last sixty years ; this, as the historian Ferland remarks, proves that ever since De Roberval's last voyage, in 1549, Basque, Breton, and Normand vessels had continued to trade there in peltries.   In 1648, the Tadousac traffic yielded more than 40,000 *livres* in clear profit, and the commercial transactions, in amount, exceeded 250,000 *livres* ; the weight of the fur attained at least 24,400 lbs., and there were more than 500 moose skins.   We learn by Mère de l'Incarnation that the Tadousac Fort was burnt with the dwelling quarters and church, in 1665.   In 1716, Father Delestage, a Jesuit, was charged with the spiritual care of the post of Tadousac, where more than 200 Indians were wintering.

The *Relation* of 1636 mentions that the Basques used to hunt the whale as high up and higher than Tadousac.   There seems to be some uncertainty as to the origin of the name. Tadousac in the Montagnais dialect means mounds, *Mamelons ;* others derive it from the Montagnais expression, *Shashuko*, which signifies *The Place of Lobsters ;* to some tribes, it was known under the Indian name of *Sadilege.*   It is picturesquely situated on a semi-circular terrace, fringed with mountains, on a deep and secure harbor, and overhangs a cove called *l'Anse à l'Eau*, where the steamers touch at a wharf belonging to the Messrs. Price.   A spacious hotel, founded there in 1865, by a joint stock company,* supplies accommodation to a large influx of strangers. Near the hotel, are the old buildings of the Hudson Bay Company. On the lawn, is a battery of antiquated 4 pounders. Next to the views, sea-bathing and boating of Tadousac, the great curiosity for tourists is the diminutive old chapel of the Jesuit Mission, erected in 1746, on the site of a church dating from 1615. Here botanized in July, 1792, the celebrated botanist, André Michaux.

The salmon breeding establishment, opened next to the steamboat wharf in the Hudson Bay stores by the Department of Fisheries and Marine, of late has attracted much notice. It is under the able management of Mr. Jos. Radford. In 1876, it had facilities for the incubation of 1,000,000 salmon ova, and turned out 100,000 young fish, that year. It is a curious sight to see the lordly salmon, the old ones, on a bright sunny day, disporting themselves, in droves of 100 or 200, just at your feet. Four thousand California salmon ova were introduced there last year.

The building or hatchery being lofty, one story has been devoted to a collection of the numerous sea-fowl frequenting the shores of the Lower St. Lawrence. The idea and success of the Tadousac Museum, we understand, is due chiefly to the active and intelligent agent for the Marine Department, at Quebec, J. U. Gregory, Esq.

Several elegant villas have recently been built round the bay : one of the most conspicuous, is that of the Earl of Dufferin. Let us also mention, the handsome cottages put up by Col. Rhodes, of Benmore, Mr. Powell, of Philadelphia, Messrs. John Gilmour, Willis Russell, Jas. L. Gibb and Mr. Price, of Quebec, and Mr. Radford, of Tadousac.

---

* This Company was incorporated by Act of Parliament (29 Vict. Ch. 93) and comprised the following names : Hon. D. E. Price, James B Forsyth, Wm. Rhodes, John Gilmour, Willis Russell, of Quebec ; Dr. Geo. W. Campbell, Chs. J. Brydges, Alexander Hart, of Montreal, and Joseph Radford, of Tadousac.

The St. Lawrence is here about twenty-four miles wide, and the mountains of the south shore are visible, while on clear days, the view includes the populous villages of *Cacouna* and *Rivière du Loup.*

Tadousac, as stated, is an Indian word, and means knobs or mamelons, which is illustrative of the irregular formation of the land.

"Tadousac," says Mr. Taché, " is placed, like a nest, in the midst of the granite rocks that surround the mouth of the Saguenay. The chapel and the buildings of the post occupy the edge of a pretty plateau, on the summit of an escarped height. So perched, these edifices dominate the narrow strip of fine sand which sweeps around at their feet. On the river, the view plunges into the profound waters of the sombre Saguenay; in front, it is lost in the immense St. Lawrence; all around, are mountains covered with fir trees and birches. Through the opening which the mighty flood has cut in the rock, the reefs, the islands, and south shores are seen. It is a delicious place."*— (*J. C. Taché.*)

---

* The following is culled from a correspondent of the New York *Times'* letter of a recent date : it is satisfactory as showing that our American cousins can appreciate the glories of our St. Lawrence and Saguenay.

"Tadousac is neither a town, village, nor hamlet. It is Tadousac, and the old hotel porter says, ' There ain't nothin' like it on the face of this terrestrial airth.' There is hardly soil enough in the whole place to make a decent onion bed. Perhaps the people eat manna, or are fed by ravens. But the mass of the population is present only in summer, and is quartered in about 150 little cottages set down along the road that leads from the landing into the interior. Tadousac is at the junction of the Saguenay with the St. Lawrence. The hotel and most of the cottages front the St. Lawrence, the Saguenay being visible only through a notch in the hills that make the point around which the deep waters of the Saguenay sweep themselves into the St. Lawrence. Tadousac is a place of rest and recreation. You would hardly find a lace shawl, or a pair of six button kid gloves, or a clawhammer coat the whole length of the road. The men and women and children are all of them roughing it. They make a business of enjoying everything, and they also contrive that all their enjoyment shall be of a healthgiving sort. There is bathing in the salt water of the St. Lawrence, a beach

Four miles east of Tadousac, is the harbor of *Moulin à Baude,* where are large beds of white marble. Charlevoix anchored here in the *Chameau,* in 1700, and was so enthusiastic about the discovery that he reported that " all this country is full of marble."

CHICOUTIMI.

At the head of navigation on the Saguenay, stands Chicoutimi, the capital of the county, with a population of about 700 souls : it is the great shipping point of the lumber district. The Messrs. Price here load upwards of forty vessels with deals. The trade amounts to $500,000 a year, and until lately, was managed by Senator David Price, who owns very extensive saw mills all along the St. Lawrence, and is styled "The King of the Saguenay." This much respected firm holds most of the Saguenay County. The extensive Chicoutimi mill property is now confided to the management of Jas. Scott, Esquire, formerly of Montmagny. A pier has been recently erected, and on the heights facing it is the handsome new college, of stone : near by, stands out conspicuously the large village church and convent of the Good Shepherd. Beyond the village, the court house is seen, on the dark slope of a high hill ; the swift Chicoutimi rushes past, until the flood tide intercepts its course.

---

extending about two miles, a sort of setting for the round little Bay of Tadousac. This beach is a playground, too, for the children, and at all hours of the day small boys and girls may be seen tumbling head over heels in the sand and mud. Four of the children I saw, belonged to Lord Dufferin, the Governor-General of Canada. But the little lords and ladies looked happy, and, as they trudged along the sand, Lady Helen, a miss of a dozen years, would ever and anon toss into her once white apron a bunch of sea weed or a dead smelt, while her younger brothers squabbled for the possession of a slippery, nasty piece of " kelp." Lord Dufferin's summer residence is close to the Tadousac Hotel. For older people, who do not care to bedaub themselves upon the beach, there are the crags and peaks and boulders to climb among. We were out upon the rocks this morning early, and I can honestly say that the scenery we enjoyed was the most lovely that I ever saw. Looking to the east, south and west, there was spread before us the sea of waters that forms the Lower St. Lawrence."

The ancient Jesuit Chapel and the Hudson Bay Company's post were situated near the confluence of the two rivers, and within the chapel, of which traces existed until recently, was the tomb of Father Cocquart, the last of the Jesuit Missionaries. A strong mission was founded here by Father Labrosse, in 1727.

On the high bank of the river Chicoutimi opposite, is the village of Ste. Anne du Saguenay with 200 inhabitants. Lake St. John is about sixty miles west of Chicoutimi, * and is reached by a good road, which passes through Jonquière, Kenogami and Hebertville. The *Rapids of Terres Rompues*, on the Saguenay River, are nine miles above Chicoutimi. Anglers ascend every summer in quest of the winnonish, or northern charr, a large game-fish, whose pink meat is considered as great a delicacy as brook-trout or salmon; Lake St. John was discovered, in 1647, by Father Duquen, the missionary at Tadousac, who was the first European to ascend the Saguenay to its source. Several Jesuit missionaries soon passed by this route to the great Nekouba, where all the Indian tribes were wont to meet in annual fairs : and in 1672, Father Albanel advanced from Tadousac, by Lake St. John and Lake Mistassini, to the *Mer du Nord*, or Hudson's Bay. A Roman Catholic mission was founded on the lake, at Metabetchouan, and posts of the Hudson Bay Company were also established there.

Twenty years ago, there were no settlements here, except the Hudson's Bay posts, now there are numerous villages, the chief of which are Roberval, Rivière à l'Ours and St. Jérôme.

" Mr. Price, M.P.," says Sweetser, "states that a missionary has recently discovered, high upon the Saguenay (or on the Mistassini) an ancient French fort with intrenchments and stockades. On the inside, were two cannon and several broken tombstones dating from the early part of the 16th century. It is surmised that these remote memorials mark the last resting-place of the Sieur Roberval, Governor-General of Canada, who (it is supposed)

---

* Chicoutimi, in northern Indian dialect, means " Deep Water."

sailed up the Saguenay, in 1543, and was never heard from afterwards. The Robervals were favorites of King Francis I., who called one of them ' the Petty King of Viemieu ' and the other ' the Gendarme of Hannibal.' They were both lost on their last expedition to America."

THE SAGUENAY.

" The Saguenay River is the chief tributary of the Lower St. Lawrence, and is the outlet of the great Lake St. John, into which eleven rivers fall. For the last fifty miles of its course, the stream is from one to two and a half miles wide, and is bordered on both sides by lofty precipices of syenite and gneiss, which impinge directly on the shores, and are dotted with stunted trees. Along their slopes, are the deep lines of glacial striations, telling of the passage of formidable icebergs down this chasm. The bed of the river is one hundred fathoms lower than that of the St. Lawrence, a difference which is sharply marked at the point of confluence. The shores were stripped of their forests by a great fire in 1810, but there are large numbers of hemlock and birch trees in the neighboring glens. The river is frozen from the *Isle St. Louis* to Chicoutimi, during half the year, and snow remains on the hills until June. The awful majesty of its unbroken mountain shores, the profound depth of its waters, the absence of life through many leagues of distance, have made the Saguenay unique among rivers, and it is yearly visited by thousands of tourists as one of the chief curiosities of the Western World.

" The Saguenay, says Bayard Taylor, is not, properly, a river. It is a tremendous chasm, like that of the Jordan Valley and the Dead Sea, cleft for sixty miles through the heart of a mountain wilderness...... No magical illusions of atmosphere enwrap the scenery of this Northern river. Every thing is hard, naked, stern, silent. Dark-grey cliffs of granitic gneiss rise from the pitch-black water; firs of gloomy green are rooted in their crevices and fringe their summits; loftier ranges of a dull indigo hue show themselves in the back-ground, and over all, bends a pale, cold, northern sky. The keen air, which brings out every object with a crystalline distinctness, even contracts the dimensions of the scenery, diminishes the height of the cliffs, and apparently be-littles the majesty of the river, so that the first feeling is one of disappointment, still it exercises a fascination which you cannot resist ; you look, and look, fettered by the fresh, novel, savage stamp which nature exhibits, and at last, as in St. Peter's or at Niagara, learn from the character of the separate features to appreciate the grandeur of the whole......Steadily upwards we went ; the windings of the river and its varying breadth, from half a mile to nearly two miles, giving us a shifting succession of the grandest pictures. Shores that seemed roughly piled together out of the fragments of chaos, overhung us ; great masses of rock, gleaming duskily through their drapery of evergreens, here lifting long irregular walls against the sky, there split into huge, fantastic forms by deep lateral gorges, up which we saw the dark blue crests of loftier mountains in the rear. The water beneath us was black as night, with a pitchy glaze on its surface ; and the only life in all the savage solitude was now and then, the back of a white porpoise, in some of the deeper coves...... The river is a reproduction truly on a contracted scale of the fiords of the Norwegian coast......The dark mountains, the tre-mendous precipices, the fir forests, even the settlements in Ha ! Ha ! Bay and l'Anse à l'Eau (except that the houses are white instead of red) are as completely Norwegian as they can be. The Scandinavian skippers who come to Canada all notice this resemblance." (BAYARD TAYLOR.)

" From Ha ! Ha ! right down to the St. Lawrence, you see nothing but the cold, black, gloomy Saguenay, rolling between two straight lines of rocky hills that rise steeply from the water's edge. These hills, though steep, are generally roughly rounded in shape, and not abrupt and faced with precipices. This makes the scenery differ from that with which it has been often com-pared, the boldest of the fiords of Norway. Over the rugged hills of the Saguenay, there is generally enough of earth here and there lodged to let the grey rock be dotted over with a dark green sprinkling of pine trees.   Perhaps there is hardly a spot on the Saguenay which, taken by itself, would not impress any lover of wild nature by its grandeur, and even sublimity; but after sailing for seventy miles downwards, passing rocky hill after rocky hill, rising one beyond the other in monotonously straight lines alongside of you ;......after vainly longing for some break in these twin imprisoning walls which might allow the eye the relief of wandering over an expanse of country, you will begin to compare the Saguenay, in no kindly spirit, to the Rhine ......It is a cold, savage, inhuman river, fit to take rank with Styx and Acheron; and, into the bargain, it is dull.   For the whole seventy miles, you will not be likely to see any living thing on it or near it, outside of your own steamer ; not a house, nor a field, nor a sign of any sort that living things have ever been there."   (WHITE.)

  " Sunlight and clear sky are out of place over its black waters. Anything which recalls the life and smile of nature is not in unison with the huge naked cliffs, raw, cold, and silent as the tombs.   An Italian spring could effect no change in the deadly rugged aspect : nor does winter add one iota to its mournful desolation.   It is with a sense of relief that the tourist emerges from its sullen gloom, and looks back upon it as a kind of vault—Nature's sarcophagus, where life and sound seems never to have entered.   Compared to it the Dead Sea is blooming, and the wildest ravines look cosy and smiling.   It is wild without the least variety, and grand apparently in spite of itself ; while so utter is the solitude, so dreary and monotonous the frown of its great black walls of rock, that the tourist is sure to get impatient with its sullen dead reverse, till he feels almost an antipathy to its very name.   The Saguenay seems to want painting, blowing up, or draining,—anything in short, to alter its morose, quiet, eternal awe.   Talk of Lethe or the Styx, they must have been purling brooks compared with this savage river; and a pic-nic on the banks of either would be preferable to one on the banks of the Saguenay!" (LONDON TIMES.)

MURRAY BAY.

Of all the picturesque parishes on the margin of our ocean like river, which innumerable swarms of tourists visit every summer for salt water bathing, none will interest the lover of sublime landscapes more than Murray Bay. One must go there to enjoy the ruggedness, the grandeur of nature, the broad horizons. You may not find there the waving wheat fields of Kamouraska, the shelving, verdurous shores of *Cacouna* or *Rivière du Loup* or *Rimouski:*—grateful retreats for our citizens during the dog-days, but you will enter in communion with savage, unconquered nature and view points yet more majestic than those of the coasts and walls of Bic. In the interior, precipice on precipice; impenetrable gorges in the projections of the rocks; peaks which lose themselves in the clouds, and among which the bears wander through July, in search of blueberries; where the cariboo browses in September; where the solitary raven and the royal eagle make their nests in May; in short, alpine landscapes, the pathless highlands of Scotland, a Byronic nature tossed about, heaped up in the north, far from the ways of civilized men, near a hidden volcano that from time to time awakens and shakes the country in a manner to scare, but not to endanger, the romantic inhabitants.

According to some, in order to enjoy in perfection these austere beauties, one must be at the threshold of life,—in youth, the privileged epoch of existence. If, then, you wish to taste, in their full features, of the dreamy solitudes of the shores, of the caves, of the great forests, overshadowing *Pointe a Pique* or *Cap à l'Aigle*, or to capture by hundreds the frisky speckled beauties of the remote Lake Gravel, you must own a good eye, a well nerved arm, a supple leg.

Murray Bay was explored in June, 1608, by Champlain, who named it "*Malle Baie*," on account of the furious tide running there; even though the weather is calm, the bay is greatly moved.

It is still generally known as Mal Baie, though the English use the name Murray Bay, given to it in 1782, in honor of General James Murray, who granted it to two worthy Scotch officers, captains Fraser and Nairn. These gentlemen brought a number of soldiers and followers : Warrens, McNeills, McLeans, Blackburns, Harveys, whose descendants represent large families, Scotch in name, but, in language, customs and faith, French-Canadians. Old James Thompson, one of Wolf's sergeants, in 1759, was sent by the Government here, in 1776, to superintend the erection of a depot for American prisoners-of-war in 1776. The structure was built near the Nairn manor house, the captives working themselves to the erection of the basement. One morning there was great commotion in the settlement : Arnold and Montgomery's followers, thirsting for freedom, had taken advantage of the shades of evening and a land breeze, to venture across to the opposite shore (about 30 miles) in flat *batteaux*. A reward from the British authorities soon brought back to their prison, these ill-fated patriots.

The foot of the invader, in 1759, left at Murray Bay, as well as on the remainder of the north shore, up to Quebec, a deep impress. But in these piping times of peace, this " memory of sorrow " has faded away. The descendants of the Savard and Dufour, who laid ambushes for Admiral Durell, fraternize and intermarry with the progeny of the ruthless Highlanders, who harried the Murray Bay henroosts and farmyards, a century ago and more.

Quebec, Montreal, Toronto, each summer are fairly represented, in dozens of pretty seaside hamlets, built by *les sacrés Anglais !* * who have bountifully spread their capital, at *Pointe à Pique*, and transformed it from a lone French parish to a remarkably rich, stirring and thriving settlement, during the summer months.

One smiling terrace lines the wooded heights, overshadowing the steamboat wharf, owned by W. H. Kerr, Esq., of

---

* A nick name given during the insurrection of 1837, by the French Canadian *patriots*, to the followers of Sir John Colborne.

Montreal, *batonnier* (president) of the Bar of Lower Canada, and no less distinguished as a jurist than as a thorough sportsman.

A little to the east is another row of seaside summer residences, built and occupied by W. McLimont and others. Four extensive modern hostelries line the highway, capable of accommodating 2000 visitors, and full to overflow, many weeks in the summer. An Episcopal church and a kirk were wanted by the tourists congregating here : the genial *seigneuresse* of Murray Bay, Mrs. John Nairn, having presented the site, a handsome little temple for public worship was erected, about 1872, in the very heart of the new village, so populous, so frolicsome, so English, during three months out of the twelve, placed at our doors by the *St. Lawrence* Steam Navigation boats touching there. A sketch of this favorite watering place, the Highlands of the St. Lawrence, as it is styled, would be incomplete without a mention of the numerous cottages rented to tourists and owned by Lt. Col. D. C. Thomson, late commander of the 9th Batallion Quebec Volunteers, the lessee of the Murray Bay, and other salmon streams.

One of the chief charms of Murray Bay is the numerous lakes and rivers, abounding with trout, to be found in the interior : *Grand Lac, Petit Lac, Lac Gravel,** the *Chute,* and the delightful drives all round the Bay and on both sides of the River Murray. Three miles from *Pointe à Pique,* may be seen the long and inelegant Roman Catholic Church, and, further east, two dense rows of houses styled the French village : the River Murray bridge intervenes, before reaching the court house standing sentry at the extreme end of the village, on a hill ; the main road there skirts the lofty heights, past *Pointe à Gaze,* near the old Fraser manor occupied by Lieut. Col. Reeve, and leads to a very pretty portion of the bay, named *Cap à l'Aigle,* where crowds of tourists go each summer, to recruit,—renting the farmers' houses, for a couple of months.

---

* Lac Gravel and *Lac Comporté* are owned by Lieut.-Col Reeve, Seigneur of Mount Murray.

EBOULEMENTS.

The steamers generally touch for a few minutes at the long wharf of the parish of Eboulements ; this is one of the durable though costly piers built by Mr. Francois Baby for the Government, about 1854.

There are few spots on the north shore of the St. Lawrence which have suffered more from volcanic action and earthquakes than the parish of Eboulements. Even the solid old manor of the seignior, on the lofty plateau, some three miles from the wharf, had to pay tribute ; the soil looks convulsed, upturned and crumbling from the hill sides ; the village draws its name from these extraordinary disturbances : *Eboulis* or *Eboulements*. The hilly nature of this settlement is the great bar to an influx of tourists, though once on the mountain brow or level plateau, near the church, in the neighborhood of the clouds, those in quest of mountain air, will get a supply ample and of good quality.

We have a charming pen-and-ink photo of the Laterrière manor, with its patriarchal customs and quiet rustic felicity, drawn by the Abbé Casgrain. Hon. Frs. de Sales Laterrière, the seignior, a physician of note, and for many years the respected member for the county, expired there recently, at an advanced age. With his frankness, urbanity and austere old face, he was an excellent type of the French *seigneurs*, such as we knew many in our youth—brave, hospitable and true *comme l'épée du roi*.

BAIE ST. PAUL.

St. Paul's Bay is a parish of 4,000 inhabitants of French extraction, on the North shore, about sixty miles from Quebec ; the village is clustered about the church and convent, near the Gouffre River. A tram railway leads to St. Urbain, about nine miles in the interior, to the works of an English Iron Mining Company, who, after sinking here about £80,000, has discontinued its mining operations. The place abounds in iron, plumbago, limestone and curious saline and sulphurous springs. More

than once, on the return of spring, the wild and turbulent
streams that sweep down the valley have carried away the
bridges which had been erected by the people. A detached pier
to land passengers from steamers has recently been erected by
Government, at the entrance of the bay.

St. Paul's Bay was settled early in the seventeenth century,
and has always been noted for its earthquakes and volcanic disturbances. The great earthquake of 1663, was followed by another, in 1791; as recently as the 17th of October, 1870, a
shock damaged mostly every house in the valley, and the parish
church suffered a great deal. In 1759, Capt. Gorham and his
rangers, destroyed the village. Charlevoix, writing, in 1720, says :
" Above the *Gouffre*, I have just mentioned, is the Bay of St.
Paul, where the habitations begin on the north side ; and there
are some woods of pine trees, which are much valued. Here, are
also some red pines of great beauty. The gentlemen of the
Seminary of Quebec are lords of this bay. Six leagues higher,
there is a very high promontory, which terminates a chain of
mountains which extend about 400 leagues to the west. It is
called Cape *Tourmente*, probably because he that gave it this
name, suffered here by a gust of wind."

The western promontory of St. Paul's Bay is Cape *Labaie ;*
that on the east, opposite the Isle aux Coudres, is *Cap au Corbeau.* " This cape has something of the majestic and of the
mournful. At a little distance, it might be taken for one of the
immense tombs erected in the middle of the Egyptian deserts by
the vanity of some puny mortal. A cloud of birds, children of
the storm, which continually hover about its fir-crowned brow,
seem, by their sinister croaking, to intone the funeral of some
dying man."

Between St. Paul's Bay and the upper end of Isle aux Coudres, is the whirlpool called *Le Gouffre*, where the water suddenly attains a depth of thirty fathoms, and at ebb-tide, the
outer currents are repulsed from Coudres to Cap au Corbeau in
wide, swirling eddies. It is said that formerly schooners which

were caught in these surges, described a series of spiral curves, the last of which landed them on the rocks. It was the most dreaded point on this shore. Small boats shun these chopping seas, but, latterly whether on account of the filling in with sand of the deep spot, or from earthquakes, the *Gouffre* has lost most of its terrors.

The vistas up the valleys of the *Gouffre*, and the *Rivière du Moulin* show distant ranges of picturesque blue mountains, with groups of conical alpine peaks. In 1791, the shores of the bay were shaken by earthquakes for many days, after which one of the peaks to the north belched forth great volumes of smoke and passed into volcanic state, emitting columns of flame through several days. The peaks are bare and white, with sharp precipices near the summit. The valley of the *Gouffre* has been likened to the Vale of Clwyd, in Wales, and is traversed by a fair road along the right bank of the rapid river. Ten or twelve miles from the bay are the extensive deposits of magnetic iron ore, which were explored by order of the Intendant Talon, two centuries ago.

"In all the miles of country I had passed over," says Ballantine, "I had seen nothing to equal the exquisite beauty of the Vale of Baie St. Paul. From the hill on which we stood, the whole valley, of many miles in extent, was visible. It was perfectly level, and covered from end to end with little hamlets, and several churches, with here and there a few small patches of forest. Like the happy Valley of Rasselas, it was surrounded by the most wild and rugged mountains, which rose in endless succession one behind the other, stretching away in the distance, till they resembled a faint blue wave in the horizon."

A former pastor of St. Paul's Bay, Rev. Messire Trudelle, thus alludes to the scenery:

"Nothing can be more pleasing than the landscape which may be viewed from the crest of *Cap au Corbeau*. Have you strength to clamber up the long slopes of *Cap au Corbeau*; to see the white-sailed schooners at the entrance of the bay; to compass, at one glance, the thousand divers objects at your feet ; the sinuous course of the Marée and of the serpentine Gouffre ; on the south, the antique mansions and rich pastures ; to see the church and convent and the village, the *Cap à la Rey*, the bottom of the bay ; and, farther away, the shores of St. Antoine, Perou, St. Jérôme, St. John, St. Joseph, and St. Flavien ?"

COUDRES ISLAND—*Isle aux Coudres.*

On returning from Murray Bay, the steamer, after touching at the long Government pier at Eboulements, skirts, until it reaches Baie St. Paul, the base of the rugged north shore range, with *Cap aux Oies, Cap aux Corneilles, Cap au Corbeau*, towering in the skies above. On your left, lies a low, grassy, fertile island, nearly nine miles long by four miles broad, *Isle aux Coudres*, thus designated, more than three centuries ago.

Here sojourned, on the 6th September, 1535, the venturesome St. Malo mariner, Jacques Cartier. At the west end, you can get a glimpse of the little harbor where lay the three French vessels. It is known now, as *Havre de Jacques Cartier, le Mouillage des Anglais* (the English anchorage), (hereafter we shall say why,) and the *Baie de la Prairie*, probably on account of the meadow stretching along the beach. Cartier named this inviting abode Hazel Island, *Isle aux Coudres* from the abundance of hazel bushes—*coudriers*—growing there. In few corners of new France, under French *régime*, could you have found, or could you find to this day, more fully, more agreeably preserved, the manners, *bonhommie*, patriarchical simplicity of the first Norman and Breton settlers of Canada, though the land grants are all posterior to 1720.

Everything, 'tis true, tended in this direction: the insulated position of the inhabitants, the exiguity of this sea-girt kingdom, the uneventful, even tenor of their lives, their feudal, social and religious training. During the summer months, being able to provide for all their wants, they have little communication with the mainland. No telegrams, no railways, no steamers to waft them tidings of the shifting, wicked outer world. No communists to array them against church or state. Occasionally on the eve of a general parliamentary election, a dazed politician may land on these peaceful shores, momentarily ruffling the surface of this guileless Arcadia—a passing ripple, nothing more. Cold, torpid winter has one advantage, the islanders are then safe, or nearly so, against politicians and electioneering agents. When snow storms rage, shutting out from view the frowning north shore settlements and their white-walled dwellings, like swans dosing on the sea shore, you might remain there for days a captive, though the hospitality of the natives would render it a mild captivity. 'Twould be worth the lives of the crew, for a canoe to be caught in a blinding snow storm, amidst the hummocks and field ice choaking up the narrow passage between *Isle aux Coudres* and *Baie St. Paul*, with the tide rushing past like a mill race.

To the pious of the neighboring parishes on *terra firma*, hardy enough to tempt, as pilgrims, the perils of the deep, the island possesses more than ordinary interest : a mystic, a supernatural glamour surrounds its solitary shores. Here, on the 7th September, 1535, being the *feast* of the Nativity of the Virgin,[*] was celebrated the first mass said on Canadian soil : for this incident, we have the undoubted authority of Jacques Cartier After three centuries and a half, imagination recalls to mind the brave little French squadron—the *Grande Hermine*, the *Petite Hermine*, the *Emerillon*—quietly riding at anchor in yonder

---

[*] " Le sixième jour du dit mois (de Septembre), vinsmes poser à une isle qui fait une petite baie et couche de terre. Icelle isle contient environs trois lieues de long et deux de large : il est une moult bonne terre et grasse, plaine de beaulx et grands arbres de plusieurs sortes ; et entre autres y, a plusieurs couldres franches que trouvâmes fort chargées de noisilles, aussi grosses et de meilleure saveur que les nôtres, mais un peu plus dures. Et par ce la nommâmes l'Isle es Coudres.

Le septième jour du dit mois (de septembre) jour Notre Dame, après avoir oui la messe, nous partimes de la dite isle pour aller à mont le dit fleuve."—*Voyages de Jacques Cartier.*

bay. A mellow, autumnal sun gilds the hills in rear, dispelling the haze which September's cool evenings bring forth from the surface of the heaving waters; the neighboring groves, with their graceful maple, sturdy oaks and waving pine, rustle under the morning breeze, to the decreasing notes of the retiring migratory birds. Their foliage, glistening with the dew, touched by the first chills of September, are burnished as with gold, or sprinkled with amber or tipped with scarlet—a gorgeous, a royal mantle, with sheen of diamonds and rich gems, thrown over nature by the *genus loci*, to greet the famous discoverer and sea captain.

Hark to the cadence of oars from boats bearing to the shore, French uniforms and French colors! you cannot mistake their nationality: the officers, soldiers and sailors of the gallant Francis I.; here follow the almoners of the fleet, Dom Antoine and Dom Guillaume le Breton, bearing in their hands the sacred vases, for the celebration of the sacrifice of mass.

To every son of Rome, rejoicing in religious freedom on Canadian soil, under his Protestant Queen, the spot where was offered for the first time the holy sacrifice is indeed a sacred spot. On a slight eminence close to the shore, in commemoration of the event, a wooden cross, surrounded by a palisade, was erected in 1848, by a devout islander, the Rev. Epiphane Lapointe. On the base, may be read the following inscription, calculated to mislead those unacquainted with early Canadian history:

> *Ici*
> *Fut célébrée*
> *La Première Messe*
> *Dite à l'Isle aux Coudres,*
> *Par*
> *Le Révérend Père De La Brosse,*
> 1765.*

Father La Brosse was an excellent priest—a devoted missionary. He expired on the 11th April, 1782, at midnight, at Ta-

---

o "Here was celebrated the first Mass, said in the Isle aux Coudres, by Reverend Father De La Brosse, 1765."

dousac, some seventy miles lower down. We are informed by
Abbé Casgrain, the historian of *Isle aux Coudres*, on the faith of
a pious tradition current all over the island, that the news of his
death was wafted that very night, not by telephone, be it
remembered, but by a voice which, naturally or supernaturally,
whispered into the ear of the pastor of the island, Rev. Messire
Compain, about twelve at midnight, when he had just got
through his breviary and beads, and was sitting down to study
by the gleam of his lamp. He was also told to go down next
morning to the east end of the island, where he would find a
canoe waiting to convey him to Tadousac, there to bury the
good missionary. The news was rendered more impressive by
the immediate tolling of the bell of his own chapel, and on his
entering the chapel, the bell continued to toll, though he could
discover no human agency, and no person, in fact, except himself,
was there. Though much startled, he recollected having heard
that the bells of the missions of Father La Brosse would an-
nounce the hour of his death. The next morning he accordingly
travelled to the lower end of the island, and, sure enough, a
canoe was awaiting his arrival. His first words before embark-
ing were to inform the astonished crew of his knowledge of the
death of Father La Brosse, and how he learned it. The Tadousac mariners had details still more miraculous to tell about
the good missionary's death: how he had prophesied it, long
before; how he left instructions, not to mind wind or weather,
but, without fear (he guaranteeing them against harm), to launch
a canoe and go and fetch the pastor of Isle aux Coudres, Rev.
Messire Compain, to bury him; how, in fact, they had ventured, notwithstanding the south-easterly storm raging that
morning; how, on the faith of his assurances, four expert men
had ventured out in their frail craft; how, as soon as they were
out of the bay, a perfect calm reigned round them, whilst the
waves ran mountains-high, close by ; how, conducted by an invisible hand, they soon weathered *Cap aux Oies*, Goose cape,
and arrived safe at *Isle aux Coudres*, at eleven o'clock in the
morning, to fulfil their errand.

Father La Brosse, it was said, after prophesying the hour of his death, was found at twelve o'clock at midnight, dead, with his head resting on his hands, on the first step of the altar of his Tadousac chapel.

Rev. Messire Compain landed safely at Tadousac that night.

It was currently stated afterwards that, at the churches of all the missions which had benefited by the ministrations of Father La Brosse,—Chicoutimi, Isle Verte, Trois Pistoles, Rimouski, Baie des Chaleurs,—the bells, set in motion by invisible hands, had tolled at midnight, on the day of his death.

Such, adds the annalist of the island, is the marvellous legend which all the islanders repeat, with some additions and variations, to visitors, and which now, in its main features, circulates beyond the locality. Despite the inscription on the cross, before mentioned, and the miraculous circumstances attending Father La Brosse's demise, the privilege of having said the first mass on the island must revert to Jacques Cartier's almoner.

The origin of this singular island emerging from the waters, under the shadow of the stupendous and volcanic crags of the Laurentian range, has given rise to many conjectures. Some have even asserted that at one time it formed part of *terra firma*, from which it was wrenched by a violent commotion of the earth; that the crevasse between, by the action of the tide, was worn away until it formed the deep channel now existing to the north of it. If so, it could not have been produced by the great earthquake of 1663, as old writers mention the existence of the island, prior to that year.

About one-quarter of the island is yet a forest, intersected by twelve sugar maple plantations, looked after with much care by the inhabitants, on account of the sugar and fuel they annually furnish.

A savanna covers the centre of the island—those portions of the soil not under culture. Population about 750 souls, all Roman Catholics. The church, which stands at the west end, is dedicated to St. Louis (Louis, IX.) of France.

Coudres Island is occasionally visited by violent wind and rain storms, which seem to drop down from the lofty capes across the channel, to the north of it; the western extremity faces the *Gouffre* river, and the deep gap between the capes at Baie St. Paul, acts like an outlet through which "rude Boreas," rushes across the narrow channel until his fury is spent on the green fields and sandy beaches of *Isle aux Coudres*. The annalist of the island, whilst dilating on the fertility of the soil, sets forth the rich porpoise fisheries of *Pointe à la Prairie*, which yielded in 1875 one hundred huge porpoises. There is also a whale story connected with the island, on which we shall not enlarge. We are told that the adjoining woods used formerly to be infested by myriads of bitterns, who, in this secluded spot, brought forth their young.

The bittern from its peculiar note "quac," is called, cuac, by the Canadian peasantry. The young were juicy and tender; several families used to make bittern or *cuac* pies, hence the jocular name enjoyed by the islanders to this day, "Bittern Eaters," *Mangeurs de Quacs*. The nesting place was called "Quacrie": this is the only quackery that can be charged on the honest and hospitable islanders.

If the Island produces in abundance sugar, grain, fish and oil (no mention, however, is made of *fromage raffiné*) its sandy shores yields a produce highly objectionable to strangers, if not so to the hardy islanders, whose skin is impregnated, perhaps, with porpoise oil: we allude to the robust breed of fleas, for which, says the Abbé, the isle is famous. But enough about this blissful Arcadia, though, under the guidance of such a well-informed *cicerone* as Monsieur l'Abbé Casgrain, the historiographer of the Island,* we would like to follow him in his pilgrimage, so as to examine in detail the spots he so well described, *l'Anse à l'Attente, la Pointe à la Prairie* and *l'Anse à Buttemont*, each the theatre of a shipwreck on the 27th November, 1832, where

---

* *Pélérinage à l'Isle aux Coudres*, l'Abbé R. H. Casgrain.

three Quebec home-bound ships, the *Rosalind*, *Baleckfoot* and an other vessel, were stranded, and the masters and crews most hospitably entertained.

Let us now fulfill a promise made at the inception of this sketch, respecting the origin of the name *Le Mouillage Anglais*, the English anchorage, at *Pointe à la Prairie*. It was known as such, ever since the 23rd June, 1759, when the van of the English fleet, under Admiral Durell, anchored there. The Admiral had a good reason to remember the spot, as his grandson,[*] midshipman in the fleet, and two other naval officers were made prisoners at *Cap à la Branche*, whilst riding over the island, some chroniclers say, in quest of game, others, to plant the British flag on an eminence. They had their horses shot from under them, without being themselves in any wise hurt, by two Canadian militia men, François Savard and Nicette Dufour, who had secreted themselves in an ambush, planned under the directions of Captain de Niverville, then stationed at St. Joachim or Baie St. Paul with a party of sixty Abenaquis Indians and sixty Canadian militiamen. The

---

[*] "8 June (1759), Nous apprimes que les Anglais avaient fait leur descente à l'Isle aux Coudres, et s'y étaient établis.

9. Il s'est, fait un détachement d'environ 60 sauvages Abenakis et de 60 Canadiens, commandés par M. de Niverville ; le Sieur Desrivières, qui arrivait de France, fut avec lui en qualité de volontaire.

Les sauvages s'amusèrent à l'Isle d'Orleans à manger des bœufs et des moutons qu'on y avaient laissés, l'Isle de l'Orleans ayant été abandonnée.

Le Sieur Desrivières, qui ne voulait point revenir sans rien faire, se détacha avec sept Canadiens de l'Isle aux Coudres qui s'étaient refugiés à St. Joachim, et s'en fut dans l'Isle, où il se mit en embuscade.

10. Ils ont pris trois jeunes gens, dont un, petit fils du commandant de la flotte des sept gros vaisseaux, un garde-marin et un autre officier passant à cheval par leur embuscade pour aller placer le pavillion anglais sur une éminence, qui eurent leurs chevaux tués sous eux et furent faits prissonniers.

12. Ces trois jeunes gens furent amenés à Québec, dont le petit fils du commandant ayant été tiré à part, se trouva parler bon français.

Ces jeunes gens furent traités honorablement pendant sept à huit jours à Québec, et ensuite on les envoya avec distinction au Trois-Rivières. Ils louèrent l'adresse des Canadiens d'avoir tué leurs chevaux sans leur avoir fait de mal. (*Siège de Québec*, 1759, Journal de Jean Claude Panet.)

gallant British youths praised the skill of the Canadian marksmen, were sent to Quebec, where they were closely questioned,
then transferred to Three Rivers, and finally exchanged and
released in the ensuing fall. "The Isle aux Coudres," says
Bayard Taylor, " is a beautiful pastoral mosaic in the pale emerald
setting of the river."

ST. JOACHIM.

Five miles lower down than *Ste Anne du Nord*, on the river
bank, lies the parish of St. Joachim, a village of more than 1000
souls. It recalls the great Bishop Laval, and teems with the
warlike memories of two sieges, 1690 and 1759. St. Joachim
basking peacefully, at the foot of frowning Cape Tourmente,
luxuriating in its rich pastures and natural meadows, is bounded
to the north by a range of lofty mountains, to the west, by the
river St. Anne, to the south by the lordly St. Lawrence. Several
limpid streams fecundate these fertile plains, among others,
the *Friponne*, fringed with graceful elms; the *Petite Ferme*
rivulet, which, expanding in volume, forms a goodly sheet of water,
well stocked with fish ; the river *Marsolet*, on whose bank may
yet be seen the ruins of a stone bridge erected by Champlain ;
the *Blondel* stream, accessible to flat-bottomed boats, for a certain distance from its mouth. The extensive natural meadows,
submerged each tide by the St. Lawrence, produce abundant
harvest of excellent fodder for cattle. Game is here abundant,
spring and fall, such as Canada geese, white geese and a variety
of ducks, and, for upwards of two hundred years, the eel-fishing
has been a source of wealth to the inhabitants.

It is from this fertile region that the Quebec seminary draw
a large proportion of the farm products required for their institution.

One of the most conspicuous objects at St. Joachim, is the
Petit Cap, a thickly wooded mound rising about one hundred
and fifty feet above the green meadows.

In full view of the passing steamers, may be seen the *Chateau*

Bellevue, crowning the picturesque and lovely cape. It is a roomy, two-story structure about 200 feet in length, to which access is had by a maze of umbrageous forest paths, cut in all directions by the seminary pupils during their summer holidays. Before debouching on it, the tourist meets with an eel fish crystal spring, called *La Fontaine à Bouchard*. On the façade of the *château* may be read the latin inscription :

" Eia age ! nunc salta, non ita, musa, diu."

Here, during the sultry days of August each year, you might meet a noisy bevy of seminary boys, rod or book in hand, in company with a few black-robed preceptors ; an annual pic-nic to the summit of Cape Tourmente, is never omitted, to visit the lofty cross erected there by a former generation of *seminaristes*, and to gaze at the wonderful panorama which the broad St. Lawrence and its green isles gleaming in sunshine, discloses to the view of the youthful pilgrims on a bright summer day ; the *Petit Cap* and its cool groves and river views, seems a realm of fairy land : *crede experto*.

The historian, Frs. Parkman, thus sums up his impressions after visiting the *Chateau Bellevue :*

" The *Chateau Bellevue* is a long and massive building of limestone, situated near the foot of Cape Tourmente, and surrounded by noble old forests, in which are shrines of St. Joseph and the Virgin. The *chateau* is furnished with reading and billiard rooms, etc., and is occupied every summer by about forty priests and students from the Seminary of Quebec. The neat Chapel of St. Louis de Gonzaga (the protector of youth) is south of the *chateau*.

Near this point, Jacques Cartier anchored, in 1535, and was visited by the Indians, who brought him presents of melons and maize. In 1623, Champlain came hither from Quebec, and founded a settlement, whose traces are still seen. This post was destroyed by Sir David Kirke's men, in 1628, and the settlers were driven away. St. Joachim was occupied in August, 1759, by 150 of the 78th Highlanders, who had just marched down the Isle of Orleans, through St. Pierre and Ste. Famille. They were engaged in the streets by armed villagers, and had a sharp skirmish before the Canadians were driven into the forests, after which the Scottish soldiers fortified themselves in the priest's house, near the church.

The site of the seminary was occupied before 1670, by Bishop Laval, who founded here a rural seminary in which the youth of the peasantry were instructed. They were well grounded in the doctrine and discipline of the Church, and were instructed in the mechanics' arts and various branches of farming. This was the first ' agricultural college ' in America. The broad seigniory of the Côte de Beaupré, which lies between St. Joachim and Beauport, was then an appanage of Bishop Laval, and was more populous than Quebec itself. Above the vast meadows of the parish of St. Joachim, that here border the St. Lawrence, there rises like an island a low flat hill, hedged round with forests, like the tonsured head of a monk. It was here that Laval planted his school. Across the meadows, a mile or more distant, towers the mountain promontory of Cape Tourmente. You may climb its woody steps, and from the top, waist deep in blueberry bushes, survey, from Kamouraska to Quebec, the grand Canadian world outsketched below ; or mount the neighboring heights of Ste. Anne, where, athwart the gaunt arms of ancient pines, the river lies shimmering in summer breeze, the cottages of the habitants are strung like beads of a rosary along the meadows of Beaupré, the shores of Orleans bask in warm light, and, far on the horizon, the rock of Quebec rests like a faint gray cloud ; or traverse the forest till the roar of the torrent guides you to the rocky solitude where it holds its savage revels...... Game on the river ; trout in the lakes, brooks, and pools ; wild fruits and flowers on the meadows and mountains ; a thousand resources of honest and healthful recreation here wait the student emancipated from books, but not parted for a moment from the pious influence that hangs about the old walls embosomed in the woods of St. Joachim. Around, on plains and hills, stand the

dwellings of a peaceful peasantry, as different from the restless
population of the neighboring states as the denizens of some
Norman or Breton village."

STE. ANNE DU NORD.

After shooting past the verdurous beaches of St. Joachim, the
feeding grounds of myriads of white and Canada geese, in April and
September, the steamer steers as much as possible amid-channel
in view of *Ste. Famille.* The eye catches a distant glimpse of the
new church of *La Bonne Ste. Anne,* also known as *Ste. Anne
du Nord* and *Ste. Anne de Beaupré.*

To the faithful hailing from Rome, *La Bonne Ste. Anne* is
a talisman, a spot sacred, as much as Notre-Dame-de-Lourdes
and Paray-le-Monial are to French or English pilgrims. The
miraculous cures effected here, would furnish material for a large
volume ; they have found an excellent annalist, in a brilliant
littérateur, the Abbé Raymond Casgrain. The population of
Ste. Anne is about 1,200 inhabitants. Last season 24,000 pilgrims
visited the shrine. On the anniversary of the festival of Ste.
Anne, (26th June) the numerous small inns are inadequate to
accommodate the pious crowd swarming on the piers and
beaches.

On the east of the village is the new church, of a massive
and beautiful structure of grey stone, in classic architecture.

The old building of the church of Ste. Anne is on the bank
just above, and is probably the most highly venerated shrine in
Anglo-Saxon America. " The relics of Ste. Anne are deposited
in a crystal globe, and are exhibited at morning mass, when their
contemplation is said to have effected many miraculous cures.
Over the richly adorned high altar is a picture of Ste. Anne, by
the famous French artist *Le Brun,* (presented by the *Marquis
of Tracy,*) and the side altars have paintings (given by Bishop
Laval) by the Franciscan monk, *Lefrançois,* who died in 1685.
There are numerous rude *ex-voto* paintings, representing marvellous deliverances of ships in peril, through the aid of Ste.

Anne; and along the cornices and in the sacristy, are great sheaves of crutches, left here by cripples and invalids who claimed to have been healed by the intercession of the saint; within the church is the tomb of Philippe Réné de Portneuf, priest of St. Joachim, who was slain with several of his people, whilst defending his parish against the British troops, in 1759." "Above all," says Parkman, "do not fail to make your pilgrimage to the shrine of Ste. Anne. . . . .

Here when D'Aillebout was governor he began with his own hands the pious work, and a *habitant* of Beaupré, Louis Guimont, sorely afflicted with rheumatism, came, grinning with pain, to lay three stones in the foundation, in honor, probably, of Ste. Anne, St. Joachim and their daughter, the Virgin. Instantly, he was cured. It was but the beginning of a long course of miracles continued more than two centuries, and continuing still. Their fame spread far and wide. The devotion to Ste. Anne became a distinguishing feature of Canadian Catholicity, till at the present day, at least thirteen parishes bear her name. . . . Sometimes the whole shore was covered with the wigwams of Indian converts who had paddled their birch canoes from the farthest wilds of Canada. The more fervent among them would crawl on their knees from the shore to the altar and, in our own day, every summer a far greater concourse of pilgrims, not in paint and feathers, but in cloth and millinery, and not in canoes, but in steamboats, bring their offerings and their vows to the "Bonne Ste. Anne."

"According to the traditions of the Roman Church," says Sweetser, "Ste. Anne was the Mother of the Blessed Virgin, and, after her body had reposed for some years in the Cathedral at Jerusalem, it was sent by St. James to St. Lazare, first bishop of Marseilles. He, in turn, sent it to St. Auspice, bishop of Apt, who placed it in a subterranean chapel, to guard it from profanation in the approaching Heathen inroads. Barbarian hordes afterwards swept over Apt and obliterated the church. 700 years later, Charlemagne visited the town, and, while attending service in the cathedral, several marvellous incidents took place, and the forgotten remains of Ste. Anne were recovered from the grotto, whence a perpetual light was seen, and a delicious fragrance emanated. The colonists who founded Canada brought with them this special devotion, and erected numerous churches in her honor, the chief of which was Ste. Anne de Beaupré, which was founded in 1658 by Gov. d'Aillebout, on the estate presented by Etienne Lessard. In 1668, the cathedral-chapter of Carcasson sent to this new shrine a relic of Ste. Anne (a bone of the hand) together with a lamp and a reliquary of silver, and some fine paintings. The legend holds that a little child was thrice favored with heavenly visions on the site of the church ; and that on her third appearance the Virgin commanded the little one to tell the people that they should build a church on that spot. The completion of the building was signalized by a remarkable miracle. The vessels ascending the St. Lawrence, during the French domination, always fired off a saluting broadside when passing this point, in recognition of their delivery from the perils of the sea. Bishop Laval made Ste. Anne's day, a feast of obligation ; and rich ex-voto gifts were placed in the church by the Intendant Talon, the Marquis de Tracy, and M. d'Iberville, the " Cid of New France." For over two centuries, the pilgrimages have been almost incessant, and hundreds of miraculous cures have been attributed to *La Bonne Ste. Anne.* Between June and October, 1874, over 20,000 pilgrims visited the Church, some of whom came from France and some from the United States.

The Côte de Beaupré and the site of Ste. Anne were granted by the *Compagnie des Cent Associés,* in 1636, to the Sieur Cheffault de la Regnardière, who, however, made but little progress in settling the broad domain, and finally sold it to Bishop Laval. In 1661, after the fall of Montreal, this district was ravaged by the merciless Iroquois, and, in 1682, Ste. Anne was garrisoned by three companies of French regulars. On the 23rd August, 1759, Ste. Anne was attacked by 300 Highlanders and

Light Infantry and a company of Rangers, under command of
Capt. Alex. Montgomery. The place was defended by 200
villagers and Indians, who kept up so hot a fire from the shelter
of the houses, that the assailants were forced to halt and wait
until a flanking movement had been made by the rangers. The
victors burnt the village, saving only the ancient church, in
which they made their quarters. A tradition of the country says
that they set fire to the church three times, but it was delivered
by Ste. Anne. The following day they advanced on Chateau
Richer and Ange-Gardien, burning house and barn, and cutting
down the fruit trees and young grain.

The picturesque Falls of Ste. Anne are reached by the road
to St. Joachim, as far as the rustic *auberge* at the crossing of
the Ste. Anne River. Thence the way leads up the river-bank
through dark glens for three to four miles. In descending from
the plateau to the plain below, the river forms seven cascades
in a distance of about a league, some of which are of rare beauty,
and have been preferred even to the Trenton Falls, in New York.
The lower fall is one hundred and thirty feet high.

" A magnificent spectacle," says Marshall, " bursts upon our
sight. A rapid stream, breaking its way through the dark woods,
and from pool to pool among masses of jagged rock, suddenly
cleaves for itself a narrow chasm, over which you may spring
if you have an iron nerve, and then falls, broken into a thousand
fantastic forms of spray, along the steep face of the rock, into
a deep gorge of horrid darkness. I do not know the volume of
water; I forgot to guess the height, it may be two hundred
feet. Figures are absurd in the estimate of the beauty and
grandeur of a scene like this. I only know that the whole impression of the scene was one of the most intense I have ever
experienced. The disposition of the mass of broken waters is
the most graceful conceivable. The irresistible might of the
rush of the fall, the stupendous upright masses of black rock
that form the chasm; the heavy fringe of dark woods all around,
the utter solitariness and gloom of the scene,—all aid to impress

the imagination. An artist might prefer this spot to Niagara."

The eccentric Thoreau thus lends his weird imagery to this wild glen :

"Here the river, 1,200 feet wide, comes flowing rapidly over a rocky bed out of that interesting wilderness which stretches toward Hudson Bay and Davis' Straits. Ha! Ha! Bay, on the Saguenay, was about 100 miles north of where we stood. Looking on the map, I find that the first country on the north which bears a name is that part of Rupert's Land called East Main. This river, called after the Holy Anne, flowing from such a direction, here tumbles over a precipice at present by three channels, how far down I do not know, but far enough for all our purposes, and to as good a distance as if twice as far. . . . . The falling water seemed to jar the very rocks, and the noise to be ever increasing. The vista was through a narrow and deep cleft in the mountain, all white suds at the bottom." From the bed of the stream below "rose a perpendicular wall, I will not venture to say how far, but only that it was the highest perpendicular wall of bare rock that I ever saw. . . . This precipice is not sloped, nor is the material soft and crumbling slate, as at Montmorenci, but it rises perfectly perpendicular like the side of a mountain fortress, and is cracked into vast cubical masses of grey and black rock shining with moisture, as if it were the ruin of an ancient wall built by Titans. . . . Take it altogether, it was a most wild and rugged and stupendous chasm, so deep and narrow where a river had worn itself a passage through a mountain of rock, and all around was the comparatively untrodden wilderness."

PART II.

LIGHTS AND SHADOWS

IN THE

KINGDOM OF HERRING AND COD.

I.

ON BOARD THE GULF PORT STEAMER "SECRET,"

5th June, 1877.

I CAN recall the time when the only mode of transit between Quebec and the Lower St. Lawrence, in summer, was by the medium of coasting vessels, ranging in size from forty to one hundred tons ; this, of course, takes one back to a rude, primitive era in the colony, when, according to Hon. Mr. Fabre, senator and editor of the *Evenement* newspaper, the members returned to Parliament, by the Lower St. Lawrence constituencies, came up in schooners to take their seats, boarding occasionally within these floating hotels when circumstances permitted, or else putting up at some of the *Cul de Sac* hostelries of the Lower Town

R

and dispensing *in toto* with any kind of polish on their red, beef and round-toe moccasins.*

Gaspé was then, in verity, a *terra incognita* during the long and dreary months of frost and snow. The mail service was performed monthly, and consisted of one solitary heavy clasped leather bag, strapped to the back of a sturdy Indian, who went forth on snow-shoes; when tired, he would transfer his despatches to a sledge drawn by his faithful Indian dog. Later on, rough paths having been hewn through the woods by the Government, the mail matter went through the parishes, drawn by horses, to meet the Halifax sailing packet, when not sent *viâ* New York.

Quebecers, in those days, used each morning to cast an enquiring look towards the telegraph, crowning the dizzy heights of Cape Diamond to ascertain when the long looked for letters might reach; several balls hoisted to a yard across a lofty post,

---

* "Thirty odd years ago, says Fabre, when Parliament sat during the summer, the Gulf members came up to Quebec in schooners, and lodged in them all through the session. He also says that at about the same period a *traineau*, loaded with trunks and parcels, arrived at the Parliament House, one fine day, just previous to the opening of the session, and from it descended, a stout countryman and his wife, who carefully examined the twenty-four windows of the building, and finally decided to rap at the door, which was immediately opened by one of the messengers. The countryman thereupon presented his compliments, stated that he was the member elect for the County of Berthier; that he had come with his wife to take his seat; and that he had brought his winter's provisions with him. He was consequently fully provided, but only wanted a cooking stove, and hoped that there would be one in his room. The messenger immediately saw through the primitive simplicity of his visitor, and gradually " drew him " out. He ascertained that the member for Berthier expected to find a room already prepared for him in the Parliament House, in which he and his wife could live throughout the winter, and subsist upon the provisions he had brought from his native village. The messenger grinned, you may be certain, and was finally forced to avow that there was no bed-rooms in the Parliament House for members. " The member for Berthier" thereupon gave his horse a smart lash with the whip, and indignantly and forever turned his back upon the Legislative Halls of the Province." To which, I can add, *si none vero, bene trovato.*

such was the system of telegraphing then in use. The signals were carefully repeated from headland to headland—from parish to parish—from Bic to Quebec, a distance of some 150 miles. To the simple denizen of the country a trip to Gaspesia or the Maritime Provinces was a serious undertaking, and never lightly talked of. Its duration to and through, at the shortest, covered four or five weeks. The route was not reckoned safe ; the river not lighted, nor properly buoyed. There were many dreaded spots where superstition had hung more than one wild legend— where shipwrecks had spread innumerable harrowing memories. It was not unusual for the prudent amongst the country travellers to call in the village notary to draw up, in legal form, the last will of an anxious father or of a rich uncle ; the demure official, of course, took care to add his mite to the terrors possible, or even probable, of the projected trip. Those who go down to the sea in ships witness many sights, it is well known, which are denied to timorous landsmen.

Indeed, a trip to Gaspé had trouble at its very threshold. Before inhaling salt water, one day's sail from the city plunged the traveller in the tumultuous surges of the *Gouffre*—the maelstrom, once so dreaded, between *Isle aux Coudres* and Baie St. Paul—where the hapless craft, after gyrating thirteen times or more in the baffling eddies of the *Gouffre*, if not swallowed up at once, had a fair chance of being cast ashore on the ledges of *Pointe à la Prairie*, on the west end of the *Isle aux Coudres*, or at the foot of *Cap au Corbeau*. The *Gouffre*, however, by the shifting of its sand banks, or other causes, has lost much of its terrors ; the merest tyro ventures through it, without " vowing a taper " to *La Bonne St. Anne*, the patroness of mariners, whose chapel, decorated with ex-votos and crutches, is in view from St. Joachim. Opposite to the *Gouffre*, at *St. Roch des Aulnets*, was the shallow Traverse and its mill sluice, racing tide, disclosing amongst other dreaded landmarks *La Roche Avignon*, where the Allan steamer " Canadian " came to grief about eighteen years back. No spot, however, was more feared than the en-

trance of the river *Madeleine*, lower than Matane; there, during
easterly storms, was heard the *Braillard de la Madeleine*—the
wailings of an unbaptized child, whose unquiet spirit hovered
over this rocky shore ever since the date of *Le Grand Naufrage
Anglais*,—1711. Not even the dismal shores of Anticosti, where
shipwrecked seamen have been compelled to live on one another's
flesh, and where the truculent Gamache, held undisputed
sway, caused more alarm than the idea of being becalmed, opposite to the river *Madeleine*. Then again, what could that
fantastic rock at Cape Gaspé, THE OLD WOMAN, portend, when
its quasi-human shape loomed out in the dusk of the evening
during a "stiff northwester?" Percé Rock had also its ominous
and death-presaging sights. Had not several mariners noticed
many white objects moving about, on its verdant summit at
twilight? They could not be gulls hatching there; they were
more than likely the souls of the departed, whose boats had been
shattered against this lofty rock at night during storms. Such
were some of the subjects of alarm for the honest, simple-minded
generation of fishermen, which formerly constituted the bulk of
travel between Quebec and the Lower Ports.

Of the protracted duration of one of those Gaspé trips, I can
speak from experience. In October, 1843, it took me seventeen
days to reach, in a coaster of 43 tons, the " Victoria," Capt. Basile
Cayen, of Islet, from Pointe St. Peter, Gaspé, to the then capacious
harbor of the Palais, Quebec. Of storms, bilge water, pea soup,
and junk pork I had a lion's share—of comfort, not a shadow.
On emerging from the close cabin and unwashed berth, it neces-
sitated, need I say, more than one ablution to fit a traveller for
the drawing-room. How quickly our respected fathers might
have ended their misery had a little bird whispered to them to
get up a Gulf Port line of steamers.

The idea of navigating the Lower St. Lawrence by steamships had originated as early as 1831. On the 28th April of that
year, at a cost of $64,000, the *Royal William*, steam and sailing
ship of 180 horse power and 1,000 tons burden, had been launch-

ed at Quebec, from the shipyard of Messrs. Sheppard & Campbell. This vessel, the pioneer of our early steam marine, was intended to ply, and did ply two years, between Quebec and Halifax. For many a long day, the name of the late Capt. John McDougall, her commander, was a household word amongst Quebecers.* This vessel, we are told, was purchased in London by the Spanish Government and became the *Isabella Secunda*, ship of war. It is sometimes stated that the *Savannah*, built at New York, first crossed the ocean by steam in 1819; there is here, a slight error. She did not use her engine in crossing, whereas the *Royal William* steamed all the way from Quebec to London. English as well as American books of reference ignore the *Royal William*, she was only "colonial." Let us come to a later period, about 1843. A generation still exists which can look back to the palmy days of the good ship *Unicorn* and her experienced commander, Captain Walter Douglas. The *Unicorn* was the pioneer of the Cunard fleet to Halifax, and after accomplishing the first voyage, proceeded to take her place on the route from Quebec to Pictou, which she held for several years, aided occasionally by the *Margaret*. The *Unicorn* was intended to be the connecting link between the ocean line to Halifax and Canada.

---

* Several interesting documents, including a letter from Capt. McDougall and the Quebec Custom House Register of the *Royal William*, will be found in "QUEBEC, PAST AND PRESENT."—See also appendix

II.

THE LOWER ST. LAWRENCE—ITS STEAMERS—ENCHANTED ISLES —THE PAPPYJACKS—LIGHTS AND SHADES IN THE LIVES OF GASPESIANS, &c.

WHO has not heard of the Gulf Port Steamers—those snug ocean crafts, which plough the lower St. Lawrence from May to December; and from December to May, the heated surface of the Gulf Stream, in Bermudan waters? Each season, they are crammed with tourists, jolly anglers, keen sportsmen, sallow invalids and lily-cheeked belles, in quest of the bracing sea-breeze of Gaspé, or making the fashionable *grand tour*, from Montreal to Prince Edward's Island and back.

Now the Gulf Port Steamers have to breast a storm of opposition from the Intercolonial Railway, who, in order to monopolize the freight traffic and kill off other modes of convey-ance, carries freight at half rates. May the line yet live long to bring health and comfort to the travelling community!

There were, on the 5th June, 1877, many sights, many other subjects to discuss on board of the "Secret," the staunch craft of blockade renown—for many years past commanded by Capt. Davidson—much more palatable than Mr. Brydges' recipe for mak-ing the fortune of the Intercolonial. Rapidly we were leaving be-hind Quebec, its glittering spires, bristling artillery,—monasteries and muddy streets, and edging in close to the green slopes of Or-leans, its smiling villages—the quiet home of many pilots—and their white-roofed cottages nestling tenderly, like chickens, under the wing of their maternal protector—Mother Church. Isle aux Reaux, Isle Madame, Grosse Isle—since 1832, the quarantine station—with all the gloomy memories of cholera, typhus, ship fever, *plurima mortis imago*—Ile Marguerite, one and all, we shot past, as rapidly as if Commander Wilkes was at the heels of

our blockade runner, when she bore a different name, and that
we had issued from the harbor of Charleston, instead of that of
Quebec. Soon the graceful maple fringe of *Pointe aux Pins*,
and the cosy old manor of Crane Island, open on us. Some of
the passengers being desirous of inspecting more closely the
historic shooting Box of Governor de Montmagny, in 1646,
one turn of the wheel took us inside of the Beaujeu shoal, in the
deeper though very narrow, channel, within a stone's throw from
the beach,—which bounds the ornamental grounds and flower
garden of the *seigneur*, Macpherson LeMoyne, Esq., who, after a
lapse of nearly two hundred and fifty years, has succeeded to the
Chevalier de Montmagny. Next to Crane Island, we noticed
the fertile islands so rich in pasturage and game, Little and Big
Goose Islands, the property of the Hotel Dieu nuns, of Quebec.
On we steamed, until the lofty tower on the summit of a high
rock, the Pillar light house, with its revolving moon, visible at
thirty miles, brought all hands on deck. To the south of it and
very close, lit up by the last rays of the sun, lurked that round
boulder, covered at quarter tide, LA ROCHE A VEILLON,* hard of
aspect, yea harder than the ribs of any of Sir Hugh Allan's iron
clads, as the defunct CANADIAN, if resuscitated, could tell the
tale. On this treacherous rock, we well remember seeing the
ill-fated steamer, with her bow, high in the air and her stern, sunk
in deep water. A structure now covers this insidious foe with
a reflector, to reflect the glare of the Pillar light-house. Beware,
O mariner, of *La Roche à Veillon!*

Such an avalanche of questions and comments, some passing
queer, were elicited by the fate of the CANADIAN! " Was Sir
Hugh Allan himself in command," asked a beetle-browed old
fellow, " when it was attempted to steer over this rock? I read
that Sir Hugh was one of those men who liked to come in contact with gritty substances, the harder the pleasanter." None of
us could fathom the exact inuendo here implied. " Was the

° Is it Avignon or à Veillon, antiquarians reply !

pilot mad, drunk, dazed or bulldozed by blue glass ? " inquired
an intelligent-looking Yankee, with a quid in his left jaw (some
said he was a judge, others that he was a Congress man), " in
attacking the rock ? I guess a Cap Cod or Hell Gate pilot will
do as much as any Canuck, but, by *Tiberius Gracchus !* I have
yet to learn of either attempting to climb over such a rock, with
a 4,000 ton steamship worth $500,000, rather than porting his
helm, to go round." To all, the feat of the " Canadian " remained un unsolved, an unsolvable mystery.   No one man, I
say it with pain, had the hardihood to champion the cause of
the Canadian Steam Navy. Sir Hugh's seamanship all went for
naught.

A short distance lower down, like a duck afloat, we noticed
the red hull of the " Floating Light Ship," which remains there
from April until December, each evening hoisting to the masthead,
its lantern for the guidance of the thirteen hundred square-rigged
ships sent out from Britain to denude our forests of their priceless
wealth—yea, too often priceless, in another sense of the word,
as some of our timber merchants daily find—when it reaches
British ports.   The St. Lawrence is about fifteen to twenty
miles wide at the Traverse, opposite St. Roch, though the deep
water channel for ships on the south side is not much more
than six acres, in breadth ; the tide rushes through like a mill
sluice.   In December, with the ice forming, woe to the homeward-bound ships grounding in the Traverse.   Until 1759, the
north channel was used by the French ; deeper water and, in
summer, a nearly constant up-stream current attracted inward-
bound crafts to the north shore channel. The traverse was then
made at *Point Argentenay*, at the lower extremity of the Island
of Orleans, in the direction of *St. Michel*. Admiral Saunders
and General James Wolfe sailed up in June, 1759, all the way
from Louisbourg to Quebec, without meeting with any casualty,
though the feat had been declared impossible, the landmarks,
buoys and signals having all been removed by the French
that summer.   What a capital joke the English must have

thought it! They were,'tis true, in possession of excellent French charts of the River St. Lawrence; and they also had an experienced mariner and pilot on board, in the person of Denis de Vitré, an old Quebecer, then a prisoner of war in England, whom they had brought out with them; lastly, by hoisting French colors about Bic, they succeeded in decoying some French pilots of the lower parishes. Threats of instant death rendered these " ancient mariners " particularly careful not to run the ships on shore. In those primitive days, the national rivalries burnt fiercely—a Frenchman hated an Englishman, nearly as much as a *Blue* hates a *Red* patriot, in the present day, Capt. John Knox, one of Wolfe's officers, records the fact of a French priest of the lower parishes, on witnessing through his telescope, the successful trick of the English on the French pilots, falling down dead, from a fit of apoplexy—alas!

III.

GASPÉ—BAIE DES CHALEURS—THEIR SCENERY, ROADS, SET-
TLEMENTS.

IN order to disclose at one glance Gaspesia and its sea shore, we
shall follow Mr. Pye's programme : from Cape Chatte to the River
Restigouche, round the northern side of the Bay des Chaleurs.

"The district of Gaspé," says he, " forms the eastern extremity
of the Province of Quebec.   It is bounded on the west by the
county of Rimouski, north by the River St. Lawrence, east by
the Gulf, south by the Bay of Chaleurs and the Province of New
Brunswick, and lies between the parallels of 47° 20′ and 49°
10′ north latitude, and 64° and 66° 30′ longitude west, from
Greenwich.

"From Cape Chat, the western limit on the St. Lawrence, the
sea-board extends to the River Restigouche, a distance of about
280 miles.   This district formerly constituted one county, sending only one member to Parliament, and was generally known
as the ' Inferior District of Gaspé.'   The late Mr. Robert Christie,
the historian of Canada, who was many years member for Gaspé,
often stated that ' it was a complete *terra incognita*, Kamschatka
being better known to the majority of the reading portion of the
community, even of these Provinces, than the Inferior District.'

Gaspé is now divided into two counties, Gaspé and Bonaventure, each sending a member to the Local Legislative Assembly (and one to the House of Commons). The former extends from
Cape Chat to Pointe au Maquereau, the latter from Pointe au
Maquereau to the Restigouche.   These counties united with
Rimouski form the Gulf division, which elects a Legislative Councillor (and a Senator.)   According to the census of 1861, the

total population of the county of Gaspé was 14,077 souls; this includes Bonaventure Island and the Magdalen Island group, all of which form part of the county for judicial and elective purposes.

" The population of Bonaventure, at the same time amounted to 13,092—giving a total of 27,169 for the entire district. Of this population 6,558 are Protestants, and 20,611 Roman Catholics. From Cape Chat to Ship Head (Gaspé), the coast is for the most part wild and mountainous, and so precipitous in many places that travellers must walk along the sea shore.

" There is a good carriage road from Quebec to Ste. Anne des Monts, where a point has been recently connected to Gaspé Basin, by a good road made by order of Government, in rear of the mountains which skirt the shore of Fox River. Ste. Anne is a seigniory, owned by the son of the late Hon. John LeBou-'tillier, (Horace LeBoutillier, Esq.,) who has a good fishing establishment at the mouth of the river of the same name which flows through the seigniory. There is a large tract of good land in this locality, which is well settled, the population in 1861 being 869 souls. The difficulty of access to Percé has caused this portion of the county of Gaspé to be united to the county of Rimouski for all judicial purposes, except in criminal cases, and there is also a separate registry office at Ste. Anne des Monts.

" Mont Louis is the next important settlement. This is also a seigniory, owned by Mr. Thomas Fraser, of Quebec.

" The next seigniory is Magdelaine, a small settlement; then Grande Vallée des Monts, where Messrs. William Irving & Co. have a fishing station. Fifthly, Ance de l'Etang, commonly known as Grand Etang. There are thus five seigniories between Cape Chat and Fox River. The last is owned by the Messrs. l'Espérance, of St. Thomas, who have established there a well-conducted and profitable fishery, combined with which they have a fine farm. These gentlemen, like Alexander Selkirk, may truly say that they are 'monarchs of all they survey,' and what is more to their credit is, that they are, we believe, the only French Canadian merchants who have been eminently successful in this branch of business on the Gaspé coast. Fox River is the next settlement, and here the postal road, which follows the line of coast until it reaches Restigouche, commences. The Government road, which is now open, enables a traveller to descend along the south shore of the St. Lawrence, ascend the Bay of Chaleurs, and regain the starting points, *via* the Intercolonial and Grand Trunk Railway.

"Following the line of coast from Fox River, we come to Griffin Cove, thence to Cape Rosier, that Scylla of the St. Lawrence. An excellent light-house has been erected on the Cape, to warn the mariner of his danger, and a gun is fired every half hour in thick foggy weather. The next point is Ship Head, which brings us to the Bay of Gaspé; from thence we proceed along the southern shore of the Bay, which is well settled and is known as Sandy Beach. Here, we have a neat Protestant church and comfortable parsonage, which, though standing on an eminence, are nearly concealed from view by a fine grove of trees. From this we reach Douglas Town Ferry, distant from the Basin seven miles. This is the mouth of the River St. John, a noted salmon stream, fished this year (1877) by the Earl and Countess of Dufferin. Like all the rivers on this coast, the River St. John has at its entrance a large lagoon, divided from the sea by a low sand bank, forming a safe harbor for small schooners. There is good anchorage in the bay for vessels of the largest size, and it was here that the Royal Squadron first anchored on the occasion of the Prince of Wales' visit to Canada, in 1860.

"The site of Douglas Town was originally selected by a Scotch surveyor of the name of Douglas, and intended by the Government as a place of settlement for United Empire Loyalists. The inhabitants are all engaged in the fishery, and are principally Irish and French Canadians. It is a town in name only, the sole public building being a Roman Catholic church. The high road from Douglas Town still skirts the line of coast as far as

Seal Cove, where it strikes through the forest to Belle Ance, in Malbay, a distance of about eight miles. This *portage*, the Canadian name for all forest roads, is partially towards Malbay, but the first four miles, on the opposite side, will afford the traveller a fair idea of the primeval forest.   On reaching Belle Ance, the high road joins the portage at right angles, branching off on the left to Point St. Peter's, and on the right to the mouth of the river and ferry.   As you emerge from the portage road on a fine clear day, a grand tableau meets the eye, well worthy of an artist's pencil.   The whole range of the Percé mountains rise, in all their majesty, before you, the village of Percé being partly visible.   Mount Joli and Percé form striking objects to the left, both the arch and split in the rock being plainly seen. Beyond these, Bonaventure Island stretches out, not unlike a gigantic whale, resting on the bosom of the vasty deep.   The ocean dotted with vessels and fishing boats, perhaps a steamer ploughing its smooth surface, complete the sea view, while to the right, are hill upon hill, and mountain upon mountain, crowned with the evergreen forest.

" The Bay of Malbay is a splendid sheet of water, bounded by Percé on one side and Point St. Peters on the other.   When you arrive at the mouth of the river of the same name the ferryman is again in requisition.   A few hundred yards beyond the ferry is a large Roman Catholic church.   The river is well settled along the bank a considerable distance up the stream.   The harbor is accessible for small craft only, on account of the sand bar at the mouth of the river; the lagoon is very extensive, forming a beautiful sheet of water when the tide is high.   On this river there is also good salmon and trout fishing, and abundance of wild fowl in spring and fall.   Having crossed the ferry, the road runs along the same bank which divides the sea from the lagoon, a distance of four miles, to the corner of the beach, a small settlement, consisting of a few respectable families.   Here, the road commences which winds in rear of the St. Anne range to Percé, a distance of about five and a half miles.   The scenery through this gorge is truly grand, and the contemplation of its beauties will more then compensate the tourist for the difficulties of the road.   About a mile from the highest point, you pass immediately by the base of a stupendous wall of conglomerate, which appears as though it had been upheaved by another Atlas. There are indications all around Percé that at some distant period the mountains have been rent, and vast masses dislodged from their original position by some violent convulsions of nature. A few miles out of Percé, the country assumes a level appearance ; the mountain ranges gradually disappear from the back-ground, and there is evidently a wide extent of land in the interior suited for agricultural purposes."

° It may not be out of place to state that several improvements in roads, bridges, sea and land communications have taken place since the time to which Mr. Pye alludes in his interesting volume from which we have drawn both amusement and instruction.

IV.

Pérce—Pabos—Newport—Point au Maquereau—L'Anse
au Gascon—Port Daniel—Chegouac—Paspebiac—New
Carlisle—Bonaventure—Maria—Carleton—Nouvllee
—Restigouche—A Drive All Around.

"The roads throughout the County of Gaspé are tolerably
good on the whole, for a new and sparsely settled country.
Those in the Township of Percé are decidedly the worst, and
most of the bridges are in a very dangerous state, without railings or guard of any kind to prevent the traveller from being
precipitated into the abyss below.

The court house and gaol at Percé being in a most dilapi-
dated state there is every probability that new buildings will
be erected at Gaspé Basin, which will then become the shire
town. The distance from Percé to Cape Cove is eight miles,
and ten from thence to Grand River. The land throughout this
section of the country is well adapted for agricultural purposes,
comparatively level, and well watered. All the front lots are
occupied, and the inhabitants are evidently paying more attention to their farms than heretofore.

Grand River is the only one in the district of Gaspé which
has been bridged by the inhabitants. The money was borrowed
from the Municipal Loan Fund, and it is much to be regretted
that what might have been an important public benefit bids
fair to become a public nuisance, in consequence of the dissen-
sions between the inhabitants to which it has given rise. The
harbor at Grand River is a bar harbor, accessible only to
small vessels. The seigniory of Pabos joins that of Grand
River. Little Pabos is the next settlement, with a river of the
same name, which was bridged by the Government, in 1844.

Next comes Great Pabos, where a chartered English company under the name of the Gaspé Fishery and Coal Mining Company, formerly established their headquarters, and squandered the monies entrusted to them by the duped shareholders. Under the French rule this appears to have been a well settled locality, as traces could be lately seen of what once constituted the foundations and cellar of a large house, said to be that of the Governor or Intendant. The remains of three mill-dams on the north side of the river were also visible, and the various articles found from time to time prove that a considerable number of families must have once occupied the front.

Pabos is a bar harbor, and very difficult of access. There are two rivers which empty themselves into the lagoon at a short distance from each other. A large portion of the land in Great Pabos is unfit for culture.

The Pabos as well as Grand River are the resort of large flocks of wild fowl in the spring and fall. The inhabitants are all sportsmen. The distance from Grand River to Pabos is about eight miles, thence to Newport three.

The Pabos estate may be said to be in chancery, part of the buildings have been sold and removed; the rest are going to ruin.

Newport is a snug little cove, with good anchorage for small vessels. There are two small fishing establishments here, one belonging to Messrs. Charles Robin & Co., the other to Mr. Philip Hamon, a native of Jersey, who resides here with his family. About two miles beyond are two small patches of rock called the Newport Islands, where Captain Philip Dean, of Jersey, once had a fishing stand. A mile and a half further brings us to Point-au-Maquereau, the eastern boundary of the County of Gaspé. This point marks the entrance to the Bay of Chaleurs, the Island of Miscou, distant about fifteen miles, being the boundary of the bay on the New Brunswick side. From the islands the road leaves the shore and passes through the woods, a distance of about five miles, to L'Anse au Gascon. Point-au-Maquereau is not visible from the road, so that the traveller passes the boundary between the two counties without being aware of it. The land through this portage is rocky, and scarcely fit for settlement.

Having reached l'Anse au Gascon, the country is again broken, and you have a continuous succession of hill and dale. The scenery from this to Port Daniel is bold and romantic, and when you reach the summit of the range of Devil's Cape,* (some call it Cap au Diable, others, Cap à l'Enfer), the beautiful bay of Port Daniel suddenly meets the eye, and a splendid and varied panorama lies before you. As you descend the mountain on a fine summer afternoon, an interesting and amusing scene often presents itself.

The fishing boats having just returned, men, women and children are all busily engaged in landing, splitting, and carrying the fish to the stages. At the mouth of the Port Daniel River we have again the usual lagoon and bar which prevents the entrance of vessels of any size, but there is good anchorage under the Cape. On this, the east side of the river, just at the harbor's mouth, snugly ensconced under the hill, stands the Roman Catholic church. The Gaspé Fishery and Coal Mining Company commenced an establishment and built a couple of small vessels on this river, and their so-called coal field, *a bed of shale*, is about three miles up the stream.

Crossing the ferry, about a quarter of a mile further, is another river, on which there is a small saw mill. A good substantial bridge, built by the Government, spanned this stream, but the approach from the westward being a sand bank, without protection of any kind, has been washed away, and no steps have been taken by the municipality to repair the damage.† "

---

* There is a limestone quarry on the Point of Cap au Diable, where forty or fifty vessels load annually for Prince Edward Island. It is worked by a chartered company of Prince Edward Island.

† The water mill is no more. There is a steam saw mill between the two rivers. The bridges are now completed on both rivers.

This is a thriving settlement, having many good farms in and around the bay. Port Daniel is also the name of the township which commences at Point au Maquereau. As you ascend the hill on the west side of the bay there is a small Presbyterian church, and on the level beyond, another place of worship belonging to the Church of England.

From this point the country assumes a level appearance, the land is better adapted for agricultural purposes, and the farms denote a higher state of cultivation.

An hour's drive from Port Daniel brings us to Chigouac, a small settlement, through which runs a good mill stream, with two grist mills erected on it. There is also a small Episcopal church and parsonage. This is the Township of Hope. About a mile and a half further is a small Roman Catholic chapel, which is in a settlement called Nouvelle. Beyond this we come to a small cove and river, with a small grist mill upon it. Having crossed the bridge, we come to a fine level tract of land called Hope Town. The settlers are chiefly Scotch, and the fine farms and good buildings prove that the owners are industrious and economical. The road from this to Paspebiac is perfectly level. The last three miles pass through what is termed Hope Town Woods, a fine piece of forest land owned by Messrs. Charles Robin & Co. But these gentlemen having sold or leased the lots along the road, for settlement, handsome cottages are springing up, and the forest is fast disappearing.

As we emerge from the woods, a number of vessels at anchor, and the fine white buildings on the low sandy beach, denote that we are approaching some important place. This is Paspebiac. From Paspebiac to New Carlisle is a beautiful drive of three miles. The Bay of Chaleurs is before you on the left, in all its beauty and grandeur. The adjacent coast of New Brunswick, which is now plainly seen, forms the back ground. On the right you have well-cultivated farms and neat cottages. The whole range of land, from Nouvelle River to the Great Bonaventure, is of excellent quality for agricultural purposes. From New

Carlisle to Bonaventure River, a distance of about eight miles, the road is tame and uninteresting, the only objects worthy of mention being two grist mills.

The Bonaventure is a large river, abounding in salmon and trout, and forms an excellent harbor for small vessels. Some years ago, vessels of two hundred and fifty tons could load here with timber, but the bar has increased so much of late that vessels drawing more than eight to nine feet cannot enter. An extensive business has been carried on in Bonaventure at different periods, even within the last ten years, but it appears as though some fatality attended all who have attempted to establish themselves in this locality. Nothing is done here now, and the harbor is wholly deserted, except when the coasters of Messrs. Robin or Le Boutillier Brothers come in to collect fish, or in spring or fall when a number of schooners, which winter here, are being fitted out or laid up. No extensive lumber trade could be established in this locality at present, all the rear lands from Paspebiac to New Richmond, or nearly so, being still owned by the Gaspé Company. The sale of those lands was an act of injustice to the inhabitants of the Townships of Cox and Bonaventure, who are thus almost precluded from obtaining even firewood. This river is the resort in spring of immense shoals of smelt, which enter it to spawn, and thousands of barrels are recklessly destroyed by the inhabitants for the purpose of manuring the land. Thousands of barrels of herrings, of which fabulous quantities arrive, are every spring used for the same purpose. The herring do not enter the river, but literally roll in shore along the sandy beach, which extends from here to Little Bonaventure. The inhabitants have been known to drive their cart to the water's edge and there load, by scooping the fish from the sea, with a dip net.

To the westward of the harbor, is a fine Roman Catholic Church, the largest, we believe, in the District of Gaspé. Bonaventure is a populous township, originally settled by the Acadians.

Three miles further brings us to Little Bonaventure River, a small stream scarcely deserving the name of river. In 1856, the Bay of Chaleurs was completely frozen over from the Great Bonaventure to Bathurst, the whole surface of the Bay being as smooth as a pond. Numbers of persons crossed over with horse and sleigh even as low as Little Bonaventure, from which forty persons went to Petites Roches, a distance of fifteen miles, for ash to make hoops. Though this is generally known as the Parish of Bonaventure, it is now the Township of Hamilton.

A couple of miles beyond Little Bonaventure, the country assumes a more picturesque appearance, with a succession of hill and dale. Passing Black Capes, a Scotch settlement in the township of New Richmond, a grand *coup d'œil* presents itself as you reach the highest point. The village and bay of New Richmond from the foreground, with the settlement of Maria running along the base of the Carleton Mountains, which tower aloft in the rear. To the left of these, you see the islands near Dalhousie, and the New Brunswick coast from thence to Bathurst. Having crossed the Little Cascapedia, you pass the Presbyterian Church, on your left, and soon reach what may be termed the village. Here is situated the fine property owned by the heirs of the late William Cuthbert, Esq., a Scotch gentleman, who carried on a large business in the lumber trade and ship building. Just beyond, is the Roman Catholic church. From Black Capes to the Great Cascapedia, is a good agricultural district, principally occupied by Scotch settlers. The land between the rivers is a fine level country, occupied in rear as far as the seventh concession. There is good, safe anchorage for large vessels between the two rivers. This should have been the shire town, being more central and better adapted in every respect than New Carlisle, from which it is distant about thirty miles. Both the Cascapedia rivers abound with salmon and trout.

Crossing the great Cascapedia, we land in the township of Maria, which extends along the sea-shore at the side of the Carleton Mountain range. Just as we leave the river, the road passes through a small Indian settlement of the Micmac tribe, and a little beyond is a grist and saw mill; about four or five miles from the ferry is a large new Roman Catholic Church. The land along the sea-shore of Maria is low, the road being but little elevated above high-water mark. This is a populous township, the soil being good, some three concessions deep, to the foot of the mountains.

There is nothing worthy of notice until we reach Carleton church, a large new building, about a mile from the village. There are no Protestant places of worship on this side of New Richmond.

Passing the village of Carleton we proceed through the township, which at this part is a narrow strip of land, scarcely one concession deep, until it touches the base of the mountain, which rises here with a steep acclivity. The summit is a fine table land. There, the inhabitants of the village obtain their fire-wood, which is brought to the edge and then shot down the inclined plane. A considerable extent of land has been cleared on the summit, and good hay is raised to feed the cattle which are employed in drawing the wood during the winter months.

The next township is Nouvelle, which includes the seigniory of Schoolbred. Nouvelle River is a considerable stream, abounding in salmon and trout, the latter being the finest fish we have ever seen. Meguacha Point, which is seen on the left, is about two miles from Dalhousie and derives its name from the rich color of the soil, which, in the Micmac language, means—a long time red.

We cross the river by a bridge at a distance from Nouvelle Basin. An hour's drive brings us to the township of Mann, in which is situated the Micmac colony known as Mission Point.*

---

* Pye's *Gaspé Scenery.*

V.

THE MACKEREL AND SALMON QUESTION—AN ILLINOIS JUDGE THEREON—PERCÉ—PASPEBIAC.

WE have now smelt salt water for close on thirty-six hours, the breakfast bell is just tolling merrily—glad tidings indeed. Down to the lower saloon, young and old, hurry—equal all, to the emergency. Some fat mackerel, fresh salmon and cod, which but a few hours previous were roaming heedless tenants of the "vasty deep," thanks to the art of that eminently respected individual, the cook, some in flat dishes, others in deep platters, ornament the table, flanked with French rolls, corn cake, crisp toast, spring butter, the whole rendered savory and fragrant by the steam of two huge urns of Mocha and Souchong. The bracing sea-breeze, a cloudless sky, that irresistible, overpowering feeling, which permeates those committed to the briny element, has instilled a new life. In silence, we sit; in silence, we devour. The crusty old captain exchanges a silent nod of recognition around; at one glance I take in the situation—we are there to act, not to talk. *There are others waiting for our places* at table. To my right, sits a very tall, very dignified old judge, from Illinois; thrice his plate is pushed forward for provender; thrice it returns, well freighted with that incomparable mackerel. At last, His Honor looks round complacently; some await, as if they expected from him a deeply pondered judgment on some interesting point of international law—the Fishery question,* possibly, under a new aspect; the suspense is of but short duration. The ermined sage, after stroking twice,

---

* The Halifax Fishery Commission was then discussing the indemnity we might be entitled to claim; we have since learned with what success.

in a measured manner, a bushy, snow-white beard, straightens
to its full height his herculean frame, and in a grave but silvery
tone of voice, thus addresses his neighbor: " What would the
parched-up, asthmatic occupant of an inland city give for such a
feast—for an hour of such enjoyment ? I feel transformed, I am
now a new, a better man, I hope. Sir," he added, " I feel as if
I were at peace with the whole world; a child even, might
now stroke my beard ; " he rose and disappeared up the
companion door. So impressive on us had been the dignified
bearing, fine countenance and athletic proportions of the grand
old judge that the merest familiarity with his silvery beard,
such as he intimated, even by a child, would have seemed to
one and all, sacrilege.

On we steamed, past that picturesque low, rocky ledge,
" Plato," opposite Point St. Peter; in less than one hour, the swift
blockade runner was under the lee of the frowning Percé Rock.

" The Percé Rock is one of the most remarkable objects that
meet the eye of the mariner or traveller along the entire Canadian seaboard. To the former it is an excellent beacon, and
one of those extraordinary monuments of the Omnipotent Architect, which, once seen, can never be forgotten. Its name of
Percé, properly Le Rocher Percé, or the Pierced Rock, is not derived from the hole now seen, which was very small a few years
ago, but from that which formerly existed, forming the space
between the Rock and its outward watch tower. The arch gave
way with a terrific crash in June, 1846, and this is now called
the Split. The present " Hole in the Wall " forms a perfect
arch, being about sixty feet in height by eighty in width. At low
water, you can walk through and scan its mighty proportions ;
at high water fishing boats can pass through. The rock is composed of mottled yellowish and reddish limestone (supposed to
belong to the Upper Silurian age), which is gradually yielding to
the devastating power of the elements. Its base is accessible,
at low water, on the south side, to foot passengers, who can walk
the entire length to the Split. But on the opposite side the water

is so deep that a line-of-battle ship could run stern on. It is distant some 200 yards from Mount Joli, on the mainland, and is about 300 feet high at this part. Its length is about 1,400 feet; its breadth, at the widest part, 300 feet. It is nearly perpendicular on all sides, and may, therefore, be considered inaccessible; but in 1818, Messrs. Moriarty and Duguay, two residents in the village, undertook the dangerous ascent, and having gained the summit, a strong rope was well secured thereon, by means of which the ascent was again made during several years, for the purpose of cutting the long grass which grows on the top. The grass, being made up into bundles, was lowered into boats anchored below, and as much as three tons of hay were thus obtained annually. A by-law was ultimately passed by the magistrates prohibiting the ascent, in consequence of a man having lost his life while making the perilous attempt."

A remarkable feature connected with the Rock is its being the resort, during the summer months, of vast numbers of seafowl, who make their nests on the summit; and in July and August, when the young are fledged, and the parent birds have returned in the evening from their foraging excursions, the whole surface of the rock literally swarms with thousands of birds, making a most discordant noise, which can be heard at a distance of several miles, and in dark nights or foggy weather, warns the mariner of his proximity to Percé. Our captain (Davidson,) formerly of the steamer *Lady Head*, subsequently of the *Secret*, has often gratified his passengers by firing a gun whilst passing. This causes a perfect cloud of gulls, gannets, cormorants, etc., to rise, and set up the most discordant and unearthly yells and screams imaginable. Each successive fall the feathered occupants of Percé Rock abandon their birthplace for some milder region, returning with the first indications of spring. Their arrival is always hailed with pleasure by the inhabitants of the locality, who are thus assured of the speedy disappearance of the ice and snow, by which they have been surrounded during the previous five months.

Surveyor-General Bouchette, in his topographical description of Lower Canada, published in 1814, speaking of Percé, says :—

"Very near the southerly point of Mal Baie there is a remarkable rock, rising about two hundred feet out of the water, and about twelve hundred feet in length, in which there are three arches completely wrought by nature : the centre one is sufficiently large to allow a boat under sail to pass through it with ease." (At present, one only remains).

Abbé Ferland, in his Journal of a Voyage on the Shores of Gaspé, observes that "everything would seem to indicate that in by-gone ages, the Rock and Mount Joli were united by similar arches," an opinion confidently expressed by Denys, who visited this spot more than two centuries back. At the period of his first visit, there was only one arch. But when he returned many years after, he found that the sea had scooped out two others, one of which, he says, disappeared through the crumbling away of a part of the rock. Percé is an awkward place to stop at for steamers or sailing vessels—and very difficult of access for them, when high easterly winds prevail. Elsewhere, we have described the ravages committed here in 1690. "In 1711, another naval attack was made by the British, and the French ships *Hero* and *Vermandois* were captured in the harbor. In 1776, a desperate naval combat took place off Percé Rock, between the American privateers who had devastated the shores of the Bay of Chaleurs and the British war-vessels *Wolf* and *Diligence.* Two of the American vessels were sunk within cannon shot of the Rock."

VI.

Two Invasions—The Lobster and Salmon Question at Port
Daniel—Its Practical Bearing—Port Daniel and its
worthy Mayor, "Touch not the Cat, but the Glove."

Port Daniel, 8th June, 1877.

A few words on a new industry, just sprung up at Port Daniel,
may not be out of place.

In the year 1775, there was trouble in this Canada of ours;
our worthy neighbors, the "Bostonnais," were seized with an
irresistible craving to improve our social condition. We were
supposed to be flagging, pining away, under a King—longing for
the freedom, more properly, the license, a republic brings among
other blessings. The grand panacea to cure all our colonial
evils was republican institutions. How much suffering from
cold—fatigue—hunger; how many privations, our trusty and
well beloved cousins endured in their disinterested efforts to
regenerate Canada, I shall not here rehearse; the dismal tale I
have unfolded in Quebec Past and Present. The invasion of
1775 was a *fiasco*—a very complete one; it did not pay.

One century later, the Province, at least that portion watered
by the *Baie des Chaleurs*, is again invaded; our intelligent
neighbors this time are not devastating our farm or poultry yards
—no territory, except that of the lobster and salmon, is to be
invaded; our good friends are not come to regenerate us, but to
enrich themselves—this second invasion will pay—they are
welcome.

Until last fall, the New Brunswick side of *Baie des Chaleurs*
was studded with lobster and salmon canning establishments,
worked chiefly by intelligent Americans, intent on teaching the
Blue-Noses how much hidden wealth lies imbedded, unrevealed,
profitless in the River St. Lawrence. They fished—they netted

—they trapped every living thing the beach possessed having the shape of a lobster, "provided it was nine inches long,"—without despising salmon. For some cause or other, the Americans have crossed the bay to our side, where they have leased fishing grounds and built thereon factories; at the present moment, they are spreading, in all directions, hard cash. American companies have now at least five fishing stands on the Canada side, in addition to their chief place of business and export, New Mills,* near Dalhousie, N.B. Their spirit of enterprise has found vent at Carleton, Maria, Capelin, Bonaventure, and within a few weeks, at Port Daniel, twenty miles lower down than the great centre of trade, Paspebiac. This latter establishment I was shown over by the worthy mayor of Port Daniel, who seemed to take a most legitimate pride in this new source of prosperity for the municipality over which he has presided as mayor for the last thirty years. I shall have a word to say hereafter about this enlightened civic magistrate.

The canning of lobsters and salmon at Port Daniel is worthy of some notice. The factory, a plain wooden building, provided with chimneys, ovens, ventilators, hydraulic power, etc., is 100 feet by 30—on a small point formed by a brook, whose water is pumped in the building. The internal management seemed admirable as to system, time and economy ;—no useless gossiping allowed ; no profane language ; men, boys, girls, each at their allotted task. Naturally the lighter duty devolves on the young girls, who get 40 cents per diem ; the full grown men get from $20 to $30 a month, according to their experience, knowledge and ability. Foreman, clerk and workmen all labor together ; no drones in the hive. When the clerk is not engaged at figures, he is to be seen with apron on, in the roughest work the factory offers.

Before beginning operations, the " Boss," as he is named, called on the owners of salmon nets, settled in writing with them

---

* Destroyed by fire in 1877.

the price they could sell their salmon at, viz. : 4½ cents the pound; lobsters were to fetch 2½ cents a pound, when the fishermen furnished their own traps. A lobster trap is a strange apparatus. It represents, in shape, the half of a cylinder ; light lathes—about three feet long—nailed round the halves of a hoop. At each end, there is a piece of net : in the centre, an aperture through which the lobster crawls in, tail foremost of course, with one claw lapped over the other ; this aperture forms a species of tunnel ; once inside, it is impossible for the crustacean to find his way out. The companies sometimes furnish the lobster traps, sometimes they don't : when they do, one-third of the catch is first applied to pay for the use of their traps, baited with clams, herring, capelin. On the 8th June instant, the catch for that morning amounted to five tons of lobster, representing about 2,500 individuals. None but fresh, live lobster are received ; the care with which they are prepared for canning, and the precision used in making the cans air-tight, are striking. The first boil the lobster goes through, is intended to detach the flesh from the shell ; when hermetically sealed, the cans are again immersed in hot water and boiled; each vessel contains one pound exactly, and is expected to fetch from 15 to 20 cents wholesale, and 25 cents retail.*

The only point on which we cannot chime in with these enterprising Americans, is that of passing off our delicious salmon and lobsters for United States fish, through the printed labels and trade marks attached to each can.† However, if our own folks

---

   * " The company pays 35 cents per hundredweight right out of the sea, which will come to about 2½ cents per lb. in tin. The factory during June have put up over 50,000 lbs. of lobster and salmon ; it makes shipments every week. At the end of June, 1877, a schooner took 250 boxes of 4 dozen cans in each box, to the Allan line agent, at Quebec, to be sent by one of their steamers to Liverpool ; they keep posted in the best markets, whether in Europe or the United States."

   † The labels on the cans speak for themselves, Bay Lobsters, " U. S. of America." Port Daniel is put on the outside of the box, as a private mark at which factory the fish were put up.

are lacking in the enterprise necessary to realize profit from the wealth of our own waters, it would be a kind of dog-in-the-manger policy should we object to our neighbors coming in our midst. Success, say we, to American enterprise! A canny Scot of Port Daniel, Mr. Miller, leased the company this land as a fish station, asking merely a nominal rent for the lot, provided he was allowed to have all the offal as fish manure for his meadows and potatoe fields. The lobster's offal, as a fertilizer, is said to be unrivalled, and the effluvia arising therefrom, in the dog days, after a while, gets to be less intolerable. Gaspesia is the land of loud smells: all know.

All canned fish is removed in boats to a small steamer the company owns. It may be "a joy for ever,"—it is not "a thing of beauty." This black odoriferous craft is picturesquely ugly. It strikes us, it might travel lobster fashion, stem or stern on. However, it answers its object, and that is the main point.

We alluded to the opening up of a new and valuable industry on several points on the Quebec side of *Baie des Chaleurs*, and particularly at Port Daniel. It may not be out of place to point out how it may be made to endure. For upwards of twenty years, each succeeding ministry has taken up warmly the fishing interest; we now beg to subjoin the regulations governing the capture of lobsters.

"No person shall fish for, catch, kill, buy, sell or possess any lobsters between the 10th day of August and the 20th day of September, in each year.

"Female lobsters in spawn or with eggs attached, soft shelled and young lobsters of less size than nine inches in length, measuring from head to tail, exclusive of claws or feelers, shall not be at any time fished for, caught, killed, bought, sold or possessed, but when caught by accident in nets or other fishing apparatus lawfully used for other fish, lobsters in spawn, or with eggs attached, soft shelled and young lobsters of a less size than nine inches, shall be liberated alive, at the risk and cost of the owner of the net or apparatus, or by the occupier of the fishery, on whom, in every case, shall devolve the proof of such actual liberation."

His Excellency has also been pleased to order that the regulations passed on the 24th of April, 1874, respecting "Lobster Fishing," be and the same is hereby repealed.

W. A. HIMSWORTH,

Clerk, Privy Council.

These regulations allow the lobster one month's respite in summer, as a close season; it is now stated that some doubts exist as to the period which the crustacean devotes to reproduction, as individuals are found with spawn at all seasons; if such is the fact, there stands a fit subject for enquiry. In the meantime, we think the lobster, and not his destroyer, ought to have the benefit of the doubt.

It will require all the foresight and energy of the Fishery Department, to guard against the wholesale destruction of this delicious crustacean, on the north side of *Baie des Chaleurs*, seeing what has happened on the oppposite shore.* At any place, lobsters cannot be more abundant than we

---

* CANADIAN LOBSTERS.

(From the London Globe.)

"If the evidence collected by Mr. Frank Buckland may be accepted, our English lobster fisheries have nearly followed our formerly prolific oyster beds to annihilation, through the same cause—over-fishing. Whether the evil will be stopped in time by recent legislation remains to be proved, but the people of Canada would do well to take warning by what has happened in the mother country. According to accounts which have reached us lately the lobster fisheries of the Dominion are being terribly overworked. On the third of the present month, a barque is reported to have cleared at the Miramichi Custom House £75,000 worth of lobsters on board, consigned to the London market. This is said to be the most valuable cargo of the sort ever shipped from New Brunswick, and we should imagine that the despatch of many more of equal magnitude would bring the trade to a dead stop for the want of the raw material. It is true that some parts of the Canadian coast are amazingly prolific of crustacean life. So immense is the supply provided by nature, that the Canadians may almost be excused for considering it practically limitless. But we have seen in the case of certain English fisheries that persistent overworking brings about scarcity, and so our friends

found them at Port Daniel, on the 8th June inst., when no less than 750 individuals, representing 3,000 lbs., were trapped in one night; will this continue? let us hope so. We are safe in stating that a new industry has taken root on the Gaspé coast, more valuable—though to some, less attractive —than " wrecking," such as formerly, when $400,000 of goods might float at one tide, in a sheltered bay—witness the cargo of the " Colborne," stranded in 1838. There is still another mode of achieving the prosperity of the place, viz: agricultural pursuits.

There are few localities in the Dominion combining for the tourists, as varied, as healthy pleasures, as that extensive line of sea shore, extending from Gaspé Basin to Campbellton, in New Brunswick—some two hundred miles, through groves, meadows and over rocky capes, with scenery of matchless beauty; boating; salmon and trout streams; and sea fowl in myriads, in September. The Englishman, Scotchman and Irishman is not here at a loss to make himself understood, as in the parishes round Quebec. English and French are indiscriminately spoken; the bulk of the enterprise and wealth is in the hands of the English-speaking population. Instead of a weekly mail, as formerly, the postman and his mail bags make their daily rounds, from Cross-Point to Gaspé: the mail waggon and its fast relay of horses is not only the most expeditious mode of conveyance, 'tis also the cheapest, and, in some localities, the only style of

---

on the other side of the Atlantic will probably discover if they continue this depopulating process much farther. It is said that quite baby lobsters are ruthlessly slaughtered in vast numbers for preservation in tins. Their flesh does not differ in flavor or appearance from that of adult crustaceans, so that consumers have no means of judging as to the size and age. It would be well for Canada if some one of her citizens took up the work performed in England by Mr. Frank Buckland and his coadjutors towards fish of all sorts. They were too late in the field to save our oyster beds from annihilation, but in other directions they have done a great deal for the preservation of one of the most important sources of our food supply. The Dominion has a splendid property in her maritime fisheries; she should see to it at once that they are not deteriorated by indiscriminate and reckless operations.

land transport. The Gaspesian, ice-bound during six months is a gregarious animal: he likes his fellowman; he is simple in his tastes, loquacious, full of gossip, a busy politician, especially since he has been made to believe that politics means "the cure of souls"—more concerned as a rule, in the newspapers of Bathurst and Chatham, Dalhousie, N.B., than in those of Montreal and Quebec. His hospitality is proverbial. The Scotch and English prefer agriculture to the catch of herring and cod; they form the minority, but a minority more self-reliant, with a registry certificate less burthened with hypothecs. A number of smiling parsonages peep out of groves all along the bay; but many of these dovecotes are lacking the doves. Why? it puzzled us much to find out.* Is it impecuniosity or a roving disposition which besets the divines? Does the missionary fear meeting a cassowary ready to eat him,

"Hat and boots and hymn book, too,"

in the guise of one of those fierce *Pospillats, anglice,* Paspyjacks —of former days, or else are those "praying" men to be taught the surest way to heaven, by having compulsory "fasting" added to the programme? This may work better in theory than in practice. Who will dare venture on the dreaded ground of Theology? We just now had occasion to testify to the hearty welcome awaiting the stranger, who properly accredited lands at Gaspé as a friend; one spot, however, in particular, which however free of access to all nationalities, we found a warmer greeting, a more genial shake of the hand, for those who, unforgetful of the Land o' Cakes," had a Mac in their name, and that land favored by the Gods, is PORT DANIEL, a thriving municipality, presided over for close on thirty years by a well-to-do old Scotchman, William McPherson, Esq. The Laird of Port Daniel prides himself on being a bit of a poet, as well as an orator. Under the hospitable roof of Cluny cottage, his residence, we found time slipping away unaccountably fast.

---

* I have since learned that the absence of several, was in consequence of their attendance at the meeting of the Synod, in Quebec.

THE KINGDOM OF THE PASPYJACKS—THE GREAT JERSEY FIRMS.

WE are now fast approaching the famous kingdom of the Robins and LeBoutilliers, Paspebiac.

Let us now view the chief emporium of commerce in the Baie des Chaleurs, as we recently found it. Its Indian name in Micmac means " Point of Rest "— such it was for the Micmac canoes from Gaspé, etc., frequenting the river Restigouche at the top of the bay. It is formed of two parts ; the green ridge of groves, and corn fields crowned by hand- some dwellings in rear, conspicuous amongst which are the houses of the managers of the great Jersey firms, the Robins and the LeBoutilliers ; and a triangular, low, sandy spit, four miles long—jutting out in the sea—at high water nearly an island, covered with the fishermen's cottages and lofty fish stores and outhouses of the Princes of Paspebiac, Messrs. Robin and Messrs. LeBoutillier ; the latter are less ancient, perhaps less wealthy ; the former are generally known under the mystic combination C. R. C., (Chs. Robin & Co.)   Both are deservedly respected for their honorable dealings, powerful by their accumulated wealth and compact organization.   Though at least these houses may be said to represent intelligent monopolies, still, during the dreary months of winter, they are the true, often the only friends, the starving fishermen can count on.   More than one century of success has surrounded the oldest house, C. R. C., with incredi- ble prestige in the eyes of the simple-minded fishermen.   C. R. C. is undoubtedly a tower of strength in all Gaspesia ; the firm has four fishery establishments on the coast, at Paspebiac, Percé, Grand River, Newport, and also one, at Caraquette, on the New Brunswick side, whilst the LeBoutillier firm own establishments

T

at Bonaventure Island, at Forteau, Labrador, at Ile à Bois, Straits of Belle Isle, and on the Island of Miscou. C. R. C. is indeed a powerful combination of brains, activity, method, money. To think that amongst all these bright elements of social success, there should be a dark speck! The managers and clerks are denied at Paspebiac the sweet companionship of womankind; they may own wives in Jersey, where they are generally allowed to spend every second winter, but once in the kingdom of cod and herring, strict celibacy is the order of the day; no undivided attention between family ties and business is tolerated. So was it ordained more than one hundred years ago, by the inexorable Charles Robin, the founder of the Robin dynasty; his cast-iron laws were borrowed 'tis believed, though not proven, from the edict of Draco—*De piscibus?* The historian Ferland observes that even the eatables of the clerks are regulated. Amatory food, such as eggs and oysters, have not yet, however, been " put to the index." No change either is tolerated in the mode of constructing their coasters; one and all must have round sterns. One of their ship carpenters who had dared to try an innovation on this point was threatened with a dismissal, and round sterns prevailed.

To each fishing establishment is attached a provision and dry goods store; the fishermen receive their pay, part in cash, part in goods. This is styled truck. During severe winters, when the fall fishing has failed, without the Robins' and LeBoutilliers' help there is no other alternative, for many families, but starvation. So long as the capture of cod and herring continues to supersede the tilling of the soil, the large Jersey firms must continue to retain their hold; their sovereignty will in a measure abate when agriculture shall take the lead among the natives.

The Paspyjacks, as a people, one regrets to say, neglect the tillage of the soil. Far better off than they, are the Scotch, English and Irish, with their farms; indeed, they seem a superior race of colonists. A writer has asserted of the English, that the reason why in enterprise, commerce, freedom, wealth, they surpass all other nations, is because they can be likened to a varied and lasting concrete, a mud of many nations, made up ; Ancient Britons, Romans, Danes, Saxons, Normans, all blended in one harmonious whole. One cannot say the same of the Paspyjacks : some element is wanting in the concrete. The majority had Acadian fathers : others had Jersey progenitors, some of the blacksmiths, carpenters and fishermen who came out with Charles Robin, in 1766, but for whom celibacy had no attractions. Wives were scarce on the Gaspé coast : they tamed as a substitute some spruce Restigouche squaws trapped at the Micmac settlement close by ; the offspring of these Pocahontas, bleached tolerably white ; one perverse taint sometimes remained : a craving for firewater. A marked trait of Indian character, the love of revenge, occasionally cropped out under the stimulus of the " ardent," rendering them quarrelsome. Hence why the neighbors stood off. The Frenchmen of Percé dreaded and shunned the fierce *Pospilats*, whilst the canny Scotch and law-abiding English saw little glory in fighting the bellicose Paspyjacks.

The Paspyjacks are different from other Gaspé communities ; they might inscribe on their escutcheon " Hard work and moderate intellectual developments ; " they have however much improved.

They are safe against the potato rot, and the weevill ; the Colorado bug has no terrors for them, their harvest comes from the sea. The horse epizoot, they can afford to laugh at ; they ride and drive, in boats ; they own no horses. The women occasionally do a little driving, that is when they go with oxen to fetch up the decayed herring and capelin from the beach to manure their gardens.

The great bane of their existence is the Parliamentary election. They have been told that unless they selected a candidate of the proper political stripe, why they might be " locked out of heaven." 'Tis quite a serious piece of business. An election in former days, especially in winter when the sea was sealed to them, was welcome ; it meant rum, flour, pork for the men, parasols for

the ladies ; recently, it dwindled down to bad theology, a very
poor substitute for flour, pork, parasols. Various are their tribulations. Let us discuss pleasanter topics.

THE MOVING LIGHT IN THE BAIE DES CHALEURS.

(From the Chatham (Miramichi) *Colonial Times*, of 12th Nov., 1861.)

" A phenomenon of a strange nature has been visible in the
Baie des Chaleurs for the last fifty years, and although every
inhabitant along that extensive coast is accustomed to witness
it from time to time, yet we do not remember having seen anything about it in print, or hearing of it from any individual up
to the time of our late visit to that quarter about three weeks
ago. On the night of Monday, the 17th ult., while in Caraquette, a fine settlement about forty miles below Bathurst, in
the County of Gloucester, we saw this famous light, apparently
a short distance below Point Mizzenette, but far out in the Bay.
It appeared as if the hull of some little craft was on fire, and the
devouring element was sweeping through the rigging and con-
suming everything within its reach. Such of course were the
first efforts of the imagination in endeavoring to give outline or
shape to an indefinite something that was far beyond the powers
of closer investigation. It was pointed out to us by John Mc-
Intosh, Esq., of that place, in whose company we were at the
time of its appearance. This gentleman gave us a short sketch
of its history, which was corroborated by the statements of many
others from different localities along this extensive sea coast.

" The light in its appearance and movements is totally different from the *Ignis fatuus* or ' Will o' the Wisp.' It precedes
a north-westerly storm, and is a sure forerunner of it. It is not
confined to one locality, but is seen from time to time at different
places by the inhabitants of Caraquette, Grand Ance, New Bandon,
Salmon Beach, in fact by the whole population between Miscou
and Bathurst. It is not confined to summer, nor to the open
water, but is as frequently seen on the ice during the frost of

winter.* In the summer season parties have gone out to examine
it in boats, but as they approach it, it disappears, and after they
have passed the place where it had been, to some distance, it re-
appears behind them, giving the curious but little chance of a
close investigation. What it really is, few pretend to say, but
that it is the result of natural causes, not many intelligent persons doubt; yet like all other strange sights and circumstances,
it has its tradition, which is not only current among the illiterate
but is firmly believed by many of the more intelligent inhabitants of the Baie des Chaleurs."

THE TRADITIONS.

" We have listened to many inhabitants of the Baie des Chaleurs, accounting for this strange and remarkable phenomenon ; and
also those who believe in the supernatural, while they differ in
some minor points, agree in this one, that the light originated in a
bloody tragedy committed in the Bay about ten years before it
made its appearance. It is said to be in the remembrance of
many persons now living that about sixty years ago a small
craft was cast away in the Bay—the parties in charge were
supposed to be drowned, the goods on board lost, and buried
in the water. Shortly afterwards, the bodies of the unfortunate
men were driven ashore, and from certain marks and appearances pointed out by individuals, it was supposed that foul play
had been used, and that instead of the parties having been
drowned, they had been murdered, their boat plundered and set
adrift, wherever the tossing billows were disposed to carry it.
After some time, suspicion was aroused, and rested upon certain
individuals who had been out in the bay at the time of the sad
occurrence, and were found to be in possession of articles belonging to the other boat. No legal steps, however, were taken in

---

° The writer has had this latter fact corroborated by an old *navigateur*
Capt. N. Allard, of St. Paul Street, Quebec, who stated having seen it in the
depth of winter. It blazed furiously on the ice, and seemed of the size of
a bale of merchandise.

the matter, and time passed on, the circumstances being forgotten by many, when the bay was visited by a dreadful north-west gale, such as had not occurred in the memory of the oldest inhabitants. In the morning after the gale, the boat belonging to the supposed murderers was found dashed to pieces at ——, and the individuals themselves so broken upon the rocks by the wild, dashing surges that they could hardly be recognized. Thus it is supposed, vengeance followed them, and the guilty party received a signal retribution. Since this wreck, and on the eve of every north-westerly gale, such as the supposed murderers were wrecked in, the light is visible in one part of the bay or another; and at times, approaches the shore so closely, coming into the very cove, that certain individuals whom we can name are prepared not only to assert, but also to attest upon oath, that they have seen this light, or rather this blazing craft (which it is supposed to be) so distinctly that they could recognize the individuals moving and passing through the flames! Such are the outlines of the tradition connected with this strange phenomenon."

I am not one of the fortunate visitors to whom was vouchsafed a sight of the " moving light." In explaining natural causes, there are no class of people more prone to accept the marvellous and supernatural than the hardy and storm-beaten fishermen of every country, and no portion of the Dominion, before the era of lighthouses and beacons, more famed for marine disasters than the shores and islands of the Lower St. Lawrence. On some spots, the minds of the people seem quite tinctured with tales of death, starvation, cannibalism. The Cornish wrecker hanging at nightfall, during the storm, his perfidious lantern on some jutting headland, to decoy to a horrible death the unsuspecting mariner, had once, representatives and types on the Gaspé coast. Thanks to Commander Fortin, Honbs. Theodore Robitaille, P. Mitchell, and other M.P.s, the lighthouse, the beacon, the fog-whistle, the alarm gun, and the telegraph, have been enlisted in the cause of suffering humanity, and the loss of life or of valuable merchandise rarely happens at present. I must not omit a memorable marine disaster often alluded to, but I think only described fully, in the "Transactions of the Literary and Historical Society of Quebec for 1830," page 187. I mean the melancholy shipwreck of the *Granicus* at Anticosti, in 1828. It appears to have happened thus :

"On the 29th October, 1828, the barque *Granicus* cleared from the port of Quebec, on her homeward-bound passage to the Cove of Cork, and, being wrecked on the coast of Anticosti, not far from the East Point, the crew and passengers are supposed (for their conduct subsequently, up to the period of their dissolution, is only probable surmise, founded on strong presumptive evidence, there being no living witness to the transaction) to have met, in their search along the shore, with one of the direction boards, under the guidance of which they proceeded to the north-westward, as far as Fox Cove, where a provision depot formerly existed, and where the board alluded to above, taught them to expect one still. This board, according to Godin, was brought by one of the unfortunate wretches to the place where it was afterwards found. Upon arriving at this post, they found it deserted, the provisions removed, and nothing but an empty log house and store to receive them. Into these they entered, and, yielding to deplorable necessity, they appear to have submitted themselves, gradually but deeply, to all the horrors of cannibalism ; for, what other inference could be drawn from finding the beams of their dwelling-places shambled with human subjects, half carcass, half skeleton, from which the flesh had undoubtedly been removed, to a pot which was found resting upon the ashes of the extinct fire, the whole of its disgusting contents not *quite demolished*—from the discovery of a pile of 'well picked bones' and 'putrid flesh'—from the circumstance that money, watches, and gold rings, etc., etc., were found upon the premises, together with a pencilled note, signed B. Harrington, desiring that forty-eight sovereigns in his hammock (which were found), should be sent home to Mary Harrington (probably his

poor mother) Barrick Street Cove, ' as they are the property of
her son.' This man, the only unmutilated form among them,
was found dead in his hammock, being the last to survive the
cold and the poisonous effects of this infernal feast. Some
fishermen from the Magdalen Islands, probably searching after
wrecks, were the witnesses to these closing sorrows, and, collecting them together, they were buried in a small piece of
ground adjoining, now enclosed by a wooden fence. It was
thought that the remains of three children, two women and
eight men, could be distinguished. The skeletons of two men
were also found in the woods, to which they are supposed to
have retreated with the view of avoiding such a scene, and flat-
tered by the hope of reaching a place of safety. It is said the
boat of the *Granicus* was found on the shore of Fox Cove,
when visited by the Magdalen fishermen, about the middle of
May, 1829, and hence it has been considered a subject for surprise that, when the crew and passengers found the post deserted, they did not return on their course and seek another, situated
at the East Point, not far from the spot where they appear to
have suffered shipwreck." The Island is famed for many other
shipwrecks.*

---

* Nearly two centuries ago, Anticosti and its desolation was known to
British mariners.

"One of Sir William Phipps' ships was driven on the island of Anticosti. The vessel that struck on the island of Anticosti was commanded
by Capt. Rainsford, who had with him sixty men ; when the ship struck,
they had only time to land their provisions before the vessel sunk. The
captain and his men finding that they should be obliged to winter on the
Island, built a store house and several huts to shelter themselves from the
cold, with the planks of the wreck. As they were short of provisions, they
agreed each man's allowance to be two biscuits, half a pound of pork, half
a pound of flour, one pint and a quarter of peas, and two small fish per week.
It was not long before the dismal effects of hunger and cold began to appear
among them, for, on the twentieth of December, their surgeon died, and
after him forty men, in a few weeks, and, though they were all convinced of
the necessity of keeping to their allowance unless they would at last eat
each other, yet their store houses were frequently broken open. An Irish-

CARLETON—MARIA—NOUVELLE—POINT SCIMINAC—CROSS POINT
—THE BREECHES OF AN INDIAN CHIEF—THE MICMACS OF
CROSS POINT—REV. MR. FAUCHER—INDIAN WRONGS—IN-
DIAN REVENGE.

HAVING elsewhere described Carleton and Maria, two thriving
settlements near the top of the bay, I shall not dwell further
on them; the first recalls one of our most popular early ad-
ministrators, Sir Guy Carleton (Lord Dorchester); the second,
Maria, the accomplished daughter of the Earl of Effingham, Lady
Maria Carleton, the genial hostess of the Chateau St. Louis, in
1776, at Quebec, whose kindliness of manner was commemorated
in prose and in verse, more than one hundred years ago, in that
old repository of Canadian lore, *Nelson's Gazette*, founded in 1746.
Carleton is the birth-place of two men of note—Chief Justice
Vallières and Dr. J. Landry.

The road on leaving Nouvelle—a tolerably good one—at
times skirts the sea-shore; at others, to cut off points, runs in
the interior. We met, however, with a fallen bridge—this
gave us the choice of fording the river (at low water only)
—with a spot in the centre, marked by a boulder surrounded by

---

man once got to the provisions, and eat no less than eighteen biscuits, which
swelled him to such a degree that he was in great pain and was near bursting. On the twenty-fifth of March, five of the company resolved to venture
out to sea in their skiff, which they lengthened out so far as to make a sort
of cabin for two or three men, and, having procured a sail, they shipped
their share of provisions on board, and steered away for Boston. It was on
the ninth of May, (1691), before these poor wretches arrived there, through
a thousand dangers from the sea and ice, and almost starved with hunger
and cold. Upon their arrival, a vessel was immediately dispatched away to
the Island and brought off the few unfortunate wretches that had been left
behind. (*Smith's History of Canada, Vol.* 1, *p.* 105-6.)

tolerably deep water; this deep water spot was so narrow that the
horse (if smart) and waggon was expected, so we were told, to
leap over it; or else, we had the alternative of picking our way
over a lofty and very dangerous ridge of mountains.   Our horse
not having been trained to "leaping with a waggon behind him,"
we chose the smallest of the evils, and ventured through the narrow path over the rocky ledge.   Another feature of Gaspé land-
travel, is the scow; on a calm day, and with a sober-minded
horse, there are many modes of transit across a stream worse
than a scow; but with wind and rain, and a fiery, shying horse,
the scow is not desirable—*crede experto*.   Sometimes "Rosi-
nante," being dry and blown, will persist in putting out his head,
longing for water, when a lurch of the scow may precipitate horse,
waggon and all, in the stream.   Such was the fate of a horse
shortly before we crossed.

With the shadows of evening deepening, I sought the hospitable roof of an obliging Scotchman, keeping a rude hostelry
at Point Sciminac, by name Daniel Brown.   At dawn next day,
Squire Brown was attending to his salmon nets, from which he
brought, alive and kicking, a splendid salmon, which two or three
hours later was served up, fried, piping hot, a dish fit for a king.
Five minutes' walk from Brown's hotel,

"In the zeazon of the year,"

there is excellent trout fishing, and in September, the woods
all round teem, we were told, with hares, grouse, and cariboo.
Of the feathered tribe (it was then the 9th June), we heard,
with break of day, some hermit thrushes singing right merrily.
A most romantic drive under groves of maple, spruce and
pine, skirting a declivity, with occasional glimpses of the far-
reaching bay, soon brings us to the Township of Mann; we are
skirting a natural meadow, rich in hay, periodically watered by
high tides.   Much of this moist land, we are told, belonged to
John Fraser, Esq., of Cross Point, the esteemed Warden of the
County, and formerly of Her Majesty's Customs, at Paspebiac.

Soon we debouch on the ancient, rambling, white dwelling of the worthy Warden. This was, for long years, the happy and picturesque home of our well-remembered old friend Robert Christie, the historian and renowned member for Gaspé. Mr. Christie, Secretary, in 1823, to the Commission named to investigate the claims of the Restigouche Indians, had acquired, in 1824, this homestead at sheriff's sale from Mr. Mann, who had purchased it with money borrowed from a well-to-do Scotch settler, Mr. Ferguson. With Mr. Fraser as cicerone, I enjoyed a drive through the Indian Reserve at Mission Point. The Indians have much improved their financial position through the ready sale they found at Campbellton for their canoes, baskets, and all kinds of Indian work, whilst the Intercolonial Railway Pactolus was flowing through the Metapedia Valley. The new Chief Polycarpe—whose selection was confirmed by the Department of Indian Affairs at Ottawa, resides in a very nice cottage in the centre of the settlement, amidst grassy fields; flocks of sheep are grazing in front of the house, and a double avenue of ornamental trees lead to the front door. These and other surroundings seem to indicate that the wild Aborigines of the forest have at last been transformed into civilized beings. I was complimenting my kind friend Mr. Fraser on this hopeful change, when, on looking more closely, I saw the Micmac breeches and the Micmac shirt of the chieftain, streaming to the breeze, conspicuously dependent, on the lawn, from the limbs of a graceful maple tree. Civilization had penetrated as far as the house, they had yet to reach the breeches and shirt of the venerable sachem. A civilized white man, owning the pretty cottage, would have established the laundry in rear, I thought.

Though the census returns are not encouraging for the Restigouche Mission, there is vast improvement in the place since I first saw it, in 1871. I find, in a work just published, some interesting particulars of its origin. Some fifty odd years ago, Bishop Plessis had confided the spiritual charge of the Restigouche Mission, to an energetic, devoted, and athletic missionary,

who seems to have completely won the heart of the Micmac
warriors. Various were their modes of marking their love for
their devoted and generous pastor. During his annual mission
among them, his hut each day was most bountifully provided
with salmon, venison, hares, wild ducks, grouse, etc. Life, however, was not always *couleur de rose*, with His Reverence.

" One day," says Mr. Faucher, " the spiritual ministrations
having concluded, the *patliache,* as he was styled, was preparing to return to Carleton, noticed around him an unusual and
mysterious reserve, foreboding no good. For some years past,
the tribe had loudly complained to the British authorities that
the old country colonists on the Restigouche were encroaching
on their rights and immunities; even their means of subsistence were endangered. Each season, the British, they alleged,
were in the habit of closing with their salmon nets the Restigouche
—which at the entrance was nearly one mile wide—thus depriv-
ing them of the salmon ascending the stream—their daily food.
They were consequently left to eke out an uncertain existence
on the scanty supply of game they might shoot or trap in the
forest. These complaints, although duly forwarded to the
Government, remainded unredressed. Much ill-feeling was
the result. Soon, another incident brought matters to a crisis.
A rumor got afloat that the English were taking possession of
the natural meadows created by the tide on the marshes of the
Rivière du Loup stream, in the adjoining township of Mann,
cutting and removing the hay therefrom without any regard
to the rights of the Indians.

The time was unfortunate for such a rumor to circulate.
It so happened that the warriors of the different settlements had
just met at the mission of St. Anne, on the Restigouche ; the
gathering was very large. A secret pow-pow of the chiefs had
been called, and one dark night, a unanimous vote was arrived
at, to make short work of all the English inhabiting the *Baie
des Chaleurs.* This bloody resolve once settled, an order was
issued to arm forthwith, to get the canoes in readiness, and, in

order to strike surely, to strike at once. That very night, the
sentry watching at the entrance of the council wigwam was
felled by a powerful arm, and next minute, the gigantic form of
the missionary confronted the assembled chiefs. The man of
God quietly scanned the faces of the startled warriors ; not a
muscle moved ; all stood up immoveable and silent. ' Chiefs
and warriors,' said the priest, advancing in the centre of the
circle, ' something strange and wicked must be going on here,
since you hide from me, whom hitherto you have treated as
your father. The friend of the Great Spirit, however, cannot
be deceived by those over whom it is his heavenly mission to
watch. I have come to beseech you to reveal me your sorrows, ·
so that I may unite my tears with yours, and help you to endure
troubles in a way befitting the sons of a great tribe of the
children of God.'

A deep shudder crept through the whole meeting, but no reply
was made.

' Well, Great Chief,' rejoined the missionary, crossing the
circle and placing himself before the oldest and most respected
of the tribe, ' have you nothing to say in reply to your father ?
Is your tongue tied by the spirit of obstinacy, or, rather, has the
demon of revenge become master of your heart ? I smell blood
in the very air ; your glance, usually so grave, so kind, now
darts forth the lightning of revenge. Do not forget, great
warrior, that the Deity gives old age to man merely to prepare
for his long sleep, and that before lying down to rest, it is his
duty to teach others experience and wisdom, instead of instil-
ling hatred, and opening up the way to hell. Speak, O Chief,
'tis yet time. I adjure you in the name of the living God, to tell
me what is going on here !'

The aged warrior drawing himself up majestically, with
measured and firm utterance, thus held forth : 'Father, our
patience is exhausted. The decree has gone forth. The hour
of the English has come. To-day, your place is not among us ;
stay behind. As to you, brother warriors, make ready. I have
said.'

All rush to their canoes—shove off, uttering the ominous war-whoop. The missionary remained alone, but his heart failed him not. A squaw, who knew where was the first *rendezvous* selected by the tribe, came to the missionary and told him how the work of blood was to begin at Battery Point. The man of peace, without losing a minute, seizing a paddle pushed off in a crazy old canoe considered unfit for the expedition, and paddled vigorously in the direction taken by the infuriated savages. The dread of being too late seemed to increase tenfold the agility and muscular power of the black-robed giant. The frail craft seemed to fly with wings over the silent stream; there was death hovering over so many happy homes. Soon he overtook the relentless host, when, with tears and entreaties, the missionary begged of the Micmacs to alter their resolve, promising in the name of God and of the great King of England, that justice would be rendered to the oppressed Indians.

There was so much earnestness—such manifest truthfulness in the appeal, that the chiefs began to waver.

—'Can you promise,' said one of them to the missionary. 'that within a year from this date our rights will be recognized and respected, hereafter?'

—'I do promise, my children.'

—'Well, Father, should we find ourselves deceived, the English of the Restigouche will have lived one year longer,' rejoined in a ferocious tone, the great chief, and the order was given to return.

True to his promise was the good missionary. The parliament of Lower Canada, shortly afterward, passed an Act—the 4th George IV., cap. I., to guarantee and regulate Indian rights. This law was sanctioned on the 9th of March, 1824, and it was His Excellency the Earl of Dalhousie, our Governor-General, who himself was the bearer of the good tidings, to the swarthy sons of the forest on the Restigouche, which he visited this year." Thus, adds Mr. Faucher, through the exertions of a Roman Catholic missionary, were saved the lives of many well-to-do English colonists on the banks of the beautiful Restigouche—the most noted of whom at that time were Messrs. Mann, Ferguson, and Crawford. This worthy priest was the late Rev. M. Faucher, for thirty-three years pastor of Lotbinière, who expired at Quebec on the 11th of August, 1865, and who, before dying, went to make his adieu to his cherished neophytes on the green banks of Mission Point. Thus, a promise, perhaps rashly made, but loyally fulfilled by the Earl of Dalhousie, was the means of saving many, many English lives.*

---

* From *De Tribord à Babord,*—Faucher de St. Maurice.

SCENERY ON THE RESTIGOUCHE AND METAPEDIA—THE SUGAR
    LOAF—SQUAW'S CAP—CROW'S QUILL PEAKS—BIG DAN
    FRASER.

AFTER visiting the Micmac Reserve at Mission Point, you can
now return to Campbellton by crossing the Restigouche, in the
ferryman's sail boat; taking the train at 8.30 a.m., and arriving at
Quebec, the same day at 9. 30 p.m. At the time of my first
visit to Campbellton, the Intercolonial Railway was not yet
in operation. I was therefore compelled to retain a seat in the
postman's waggon, in order to reach big Dan Fraser's house on
the Metapedia, where a regular stage, stopping at Ste Flavie, ran
daily. If this mode of transit was more tiresome, less expeditious than by rail, in its windings over hill and dale, through that
lovely valley of the Metapedia, it disclosed scenery of wondrous
beauty, denied to the traveller by the iron horse. We cannot do
better than borrow the words of a recent tourist over the same
route :

    " From this point may be seen several isolated mountain
peaks of peculiar formation, highly picturesque. The principal
are the ' SUGAR LOAF,' 'SQUAW'S CAP,' and ' CROW'S QUILL.'
At or near this place, is also ATHOL HOUSE, once the finest property on the Restigouche, but now, through financial embarrass-
ment, fallen into neglect. The mountain ranges still continue
on either side of the river, though less wild and rugged. The
scenery, like portions of the Hudson, is more beautiful than
grand, more artistic than nature. The arable lands rise higher
and higher, up these mountain slopes; whilst, from the summits,
extending many miles back, there are, it is said, rich table lands.
The valley has now widened in places, to one and a half miles
and more. The river widens also, often dividing into two
branches, and again uniting to form unnumbered islands, all rich,

many very extensive ; the recovery of one from the river, and its subduing to agricultural purposes, having cost hundreds of dollars.

Another much more extensive, beautifully shaded with elms, is devoted to common pasturage ; hundreds of horses are let loose in its luxuriant grass. As we draw near the river's mouth, the mountain ranges, as if repenting of the freedom given the waters for the last twenty-five miles, with mutual understanding seek to join their rocky ridges in a final effort to stay their progress. It is all in vain. The time to ' resist ' is in the ' beginnings.' Its voice is heard by mother ocean just beyond. The sea, ever jealous of her own, and mightier than mountains, extending to the wanderer the strong arm of the Bay des Chaleurs, takes to her bosom the returning offspring. This final attempt of the ranges at landlocking, has left one of the finest of harbors, capacious and sheltered. The Restigouche was first discovered by Jacques Cartier in, 1534. At its mouth, in 1638, Jean Jacques Enaud planted a little colony of Acadians, and laid the foundation of the fortified town of Petite Rochelle. The town has passed away, with scarce a trace remaining ; but up the river, some miles back on the table lands, clinging with tenacity to ancient Norman cap and kirtle, is a small colony of Acadians. It was interesting to me to learn these things of the people of " Evangeline." *

Since my short sojourn, in 1873, under the hospitable roof of Big Dan Fraser, the fame of the Metapedia pools has spread far and wide. The *Quebec Chronicle* of 13 Sept., 1877, mentions them as follows :

" At the juncture of the rivers Metapedia and the Restigouche, in the heart of Metapedia valley, stands the far-famed headquarters of the keen sportsmen of this continent, known as the Metapedia Hotel, whose proprietor is Mr. Dan Fraser, with whom a large number of the citizens of Quebec are well acquainted. This spot is much frequented during the fishing season by the

---

* *The Metapedia—New Dominion Monthly for Dec.*, 1869, *p.* 11.

best anglers in America, also by a number from the United
Kingdom, to enjoy such sport as can only be afforded in the magnificent rivers of the immediate neighborhood. During the
past season, the scenes for many a morning have been of the
most picturesque description ; groups of stalwart Indians, all
speaking the English language fluently, may have been observed
making their preparations for the day's work in the water with
the finny tribe, whilst their white employers were busily arrang-
ing their fishing tackle, ' eager for the fray.' So numerous have
been the visitors to the Metapedia this year, that from sixty to
one hundred Indians have found occupation as guides, etc., for
several months, and as many as thirty canoes known to leave
the hotel of a morning fully manned, a large number of them
fishing almost in sight. One gentleman during his stay killed
one hundred and three salmon—he was an expert of no mean
calibre in the piscatorial art ; others have been successful according to the length of their stay. The establishment referred to is
delightfully situated, and within fifty yards of the Intercolonial
Railway Station.

RIMOUSKI—MÉTIS—MATANE.

THE Seigniory of Rimouski and St. Barnabé was conceded
the 24th April, 1688, by the Marquis of Denonville, to the Sieur
de la Cordonnière. It now belongs to the heirs Drapeau. In
1858, the co-seigneurs were Victor Lebel, Charles Lepage, Ed.
Pouliot, Théodore Gagnon, Hypolite Lepage, Octave Rivest, etc.
Rimouski, dating from 1701, was erected as a parish in 1835,
and by act of Parliament, it was a few years back, incorporated as
a town, under the name of St. Germain de Rimouski. On the 16th
May, 1867, it was created an episcopal see, and Bishop Lange-
vin, its first bishop, took possession of his diocese, with great
pomp. It is the capital of the county of the same name, with a
population of 1500 souls. It contains several handsome private
residences, two colleges, three convents, a bishop's palace, a district jail, a district judge, a splendid cathedral, which cost up-

wards of $50,000, a good railway station for the Intercolonial. The Rimouski River, which rises in two considerable branches in rear of the seigniory, and falls into the St. Lawrence, is a great salmon stream. It is crossed at the west end of the village by a beautiful iron bridge, resting on four piers and two abutments. The scenery along the river is very pretty. There is a large lumbering establishment three miles from the town, on the river. A wharf three quarters of a mile long has been constructed by the Government, about half way between Rimouski and Father Point,* at which the English mails are landed and taken on board. A branch of the Intercolonial runs down to the wharf, so that no time is lost in despatching the mails after the arrival of the steamer in the bay.

That portion of the population which gave up their fishing pursuits for farming are thriving the most ; some, however, still stick to their boats and nets, and look after codfish and herring instead of wheat and barley. There are a number of shops and hotels.

Some twenty years ago, a most flourishing settlement was a wilderness—Sandy Bay ; now it is inhabited to the Sixth Range or Concession, and the curé has a respectable rent-roll— as a rule, a fair indication of the fertility of parishes. Some of the villages, like Ste. Luce, Ste. Flavie, Metis, Matane, are built on beautiful deep bays, in which a winding rivulet or rapid river discharges. On the majority of them, substantial saw-mills, surrounded by bright pine and spruce deals, proclaim that English enterprise dwells therein. Echo still repeats the respected name of the " King of the Saguenay," Wm. Price, Esq.

At Little Métis, a curious spectacle greets the eye—an entire settlement of Scotchmen, imported from the Land of Cakes some fifty years ago, by the Seigneur of Metis, the late Mr. McNider, numbering about 100 families. They have pushed their settlement to the Fifth Concession, and seem to prosper. I was surprised to find they could support two churches of the

---

* So called after Father Henri Nouvelle, who wintered there in 1663.

Protestant faith, a Presbyterian and a Methodist church. The children looked well clad, rosy and contented. I asked one wee lassie where she was bound for. "To see my mither, ayount the hills," she civilly replied, with charming simplicity.

They speak Gaelic, 'tis said, in the settlement. Few French-Canadians live there. Their lands are not as much mortgaged as those of the French-Canadians, and they scarcely ever inter-marry with them. I heard it stated that though they belonged to a better class, and brought several agricultural books and im-plements with them, they gradually fell back to the slow style of culture of the Canadian peasant. Some, 'tis said, have sold their farms and removed to Greenbush, Wisconsin—'tis a loss for Métis. As to scenery, nothing on the south shore of the St. Lawrence equals that of Bic, Matane, Métis. The high road, for more than forty miles, runs level like a bowling green, on the edge of the roaring St. Lawrence—so broad here, that the opposite shore cannot be seen. The back ground is diversified by hills, meadows, rivers and valleys.

I shall retain a long time the vivid impression which Métis made on me, whilst travelling through, on the 15th November, 1871. It was the first winter roads; the weather was bright and frosty. Amidst the breaking of the surf on the beach, the tinkle of our sleigh-bells was scarcely audible. Merrily, we bowled along in the solemn silence of a Sabbath afternoon, to where duty called. On our right stood the Kirk, lit up with the last rays of the setting sun, whilst a bevy of rosy-cheeked, youthful worshippers poured out of its portals, homeward bound; and far away in the blue east, a mere speck dancing on the bosom of the great river, a noble ship, the "Nestorian," also homeward bound, carrying back Lord Monck and his fortunes. One of those radiant sunsets with which autumn occasionally consoles us for the loss of sum-mer was pouring on the waters westward its purple light, whilst a pair of hardy fishermen were striving lustily at their oars, to make the entrance of the Métis bay. What a scene for an artist!

At Matane, the traveller finds a comfortable boarding-house, kept by a Scotchman named Grant, who speaks French. The Matane river, a splendid salmon and trout stream, enters the Bay of Matane. The G. P. steamers make Métis and Matane stopping places, and there is little doubt that, in addition to the Montrealers who enjoyed sea-bathing at Matane last summer, several Quebecers will deviate from over-crowded, over-dressed and noisy Cacouna, to Gaspé and the lower parishes as bathing-places. One of the greatest boons to this portion of Canada, is the opening up of the interior by colonization roads ; not those, of course, made mile by mile, such as had been previously the case—so that the first mile was rendered impassable by the underbrush which in a couple of years springs up.

The Taché road will be of undoubted service. It runs parallel to the St. Lawrence, about thirty miles inland from Beauce to Rimouski, and lower down ; cross roads are being opened towards it, from each parish.

A wonderful change has come over the Canadian peasantry since the construction of the Grand Trunk Railway, Intercourse with the cities and the United States—the spread of education—colleges, court houses, convents, opened in all the large centres—such, the spectacle which all through greets the eye, even in the remote parishes.

Rimouski, one of the largest countries of the Dominion, is one hundred and fifty miles in length. It extends from Bic inclusive, to Cap Chatte, and lower. Seventeen parishes,* of which six or eight are on the banks of the river, and the remainder in the interior, constitute this fine county, together with seven townships.†

---

* St. Simon, St. Mathieu, St. Fabien, St. Cécil, Bic, Town of St. Germain, Parish of St. Germain, St. Blandine, St. Anaclet, St. Donate, Ste. Luce, Ste. Flavie, Ste. Angèle de Merici, Ste. Octave de Métis, L'Assomption, McNider, St. Ulric.

† Township of Matane, St. Jérome de Matane, St. Félicité, Townships of Cherbourg, Dalibert, Romieu.

We are safe in averaging fifteen parishes to each county which would give one hundred and five parishes, each with a spacious parish church (sometimes two), school houses, mayor and councillors, post office, &c. Some parishes like Montmagny, since it became the *chef-lieu* (county town), with resident judge, court house, jail, &c., have sprung into importance very rapidly. The same might be said of Rimouski. The sciences taught at Rimouski college comprise a commercial course: Belle-Lettres, Rhetoric, the Classics, Natural and Moral Philosophy, Chemistry, Mathematics, Astronomy.

St. Barnaby Island opposite to Rimouski—Its Pious Old Hermit—His Romantic Sorrow and Death.

There are many picturesque isles to which scenery or association lends a charm in the Lower St. Lawrence. A low and well-wooded island, two miles in extent, facing the flourishing new town of St. Germain de Rimouski, deserves a short notice ; it still bears the name it had as early as 1629, when the Kertks, bent on capturing Quebec, rendezvoused there—St. Barnaby. A barrier against the swell of the gulf, St. Barnaby, together with the long Government pier erected there by Mr. Baby, it affords a not unnatural hope to the Rimouskites, that, at some time or other, their protected haven may become a " harbor of refuge " for vessels navigating those waters. Purveyors of romance can here find the groundwork for a pathetic tale of dissappointed love.

A letter from Col. Rivers, bearing date " Isle Barnabé, 13th October, 1766," quoted in Mrs. Brooke's interesting Novel in four volumes, written at Sillery, in 1767, under the title of the " History of Emily Montague," though silent as to the name and fate of the singular hermit who it appears, habited the island for close on half a century, sets forth in vivid language the cause of his seclusion.

Col. Rivers to Emily Montague.

Isle Barnaby, Oct. 13 (1766.)

" I have been paying a very singular visit ; 'tis to a hermit, who has lived sixty years alone on this island ; I came to him with a strong prejudice against him. I have no opinion of those who fly society, who seek a state of all others, the most contrary to our nature. Were I a tyrant and wished to inflict the most cruel punishment, human nature could support, I would exclude criminals from the joys of society, and deny them the endearing sight of their species.

(I am certain I could not exist a year alone : I am miserable even in that degree of solitude to which one is confined in a ship; no words can speak the joy which I felt when I came to America, on the first appearance of something like the cheerful haunts of men; the first man, the first house, nay the first Indian fire of which I saw the smoke rise above the trees, gave me the most lively transport that can be conceived; I felt all the force of those ties which unite us to each other, of that social love to which we owe all our happiness.)

But to my hermit and what his appearance was like; he is a tall old man with white hair and beard, the look of one who has known better days, and the strongest marks of benevolence in his countenance. He received me with the utmost hospitality, spread all his little stores of fruit before me, fetched me fresh milk, and water from a spring near the house; after a little conversation, I expressed my astonishment that a man of whose kindness and humanity I had just had such proof, could find his happiness in flying mankind. I said a good deal on the subject, to which he listened with the politest attention.

" You appear," said he, " of a temper to pity the miseries of others. My story is short and simple : I loved the most amiable of women ; I was beloved. The avarice of our parents, who both had more gainful views for us, prevented a union on which our happiness depended

" My Louisa, who was threatened with an immediate marriage with a man she detested, proposed to me to fly the tyranny of our friends ; she had an uncle at Quebec, to whom she was dear. The wilds of Canada, said she, may afford us that refuge our cruel parents deny us. After a secret marriage, we embarked. Our voyage was thus far, happy ; I landed on the opposite shore to seek refreshments for Louisa ; I was returning, pleased with

the thought of obliging the object of my tenderness, when a
lightning storm drove me to seek shelter in the bay. The storm
increased,—I saw its progress with agonies not to be described ;
the ship, which was in sight, was unable to resist its fury ; the
sailors crowded into the boats ; they had the humanity to place
Louisa there ; they made for the spot where I was, my eyes were
wildly fixed on them ; I stood eagerly on the utmost verge of
the water, my arms stretched out to receive her, my prayers ar-
dently addressed to Heaven, when an immense wave rose. I
heard a general shriek ; I even fancied I distinguished Louisa's
cries ; it subsided ; the sailors again exerted all their force ; a
second wave,—I saw them no more. Never will that dreadful
scene be absent one moment from my memory. I fell senseless
on the beach ; when I returned to life, the first object I beheld
was the breathless body of Louisa at my feet. Heaven gave
me the wretched consolation of rendering to her the last sad duties. In that grave all my happiness lies buried. I knelt by
her, and breathed a vow to Heaven to wait here the moment
that should join me to all I held dear. I every morning visit her
loved remains and implore the God of mercy to hasten my dissolution. I feel that we shall not long be separated ; I shall soon
meet her, to part no more." He stopped and, without seeming
to remember he was not alone, walked hastily towards a little
oratory he had built on the beach, near which is the grave of his
Louisa ; I followed him a few steps ;'I saw him throw himself on
his knees ; and, respecting his sorrow, returned to the house."—
" ED. RIVERS."

For the remaining links of his history, we are indebted to a
Rimouski *littérateur*, Mr. Elzéar D. Gauvreau, as appears by a
correspondence under his signature in a local journal lately edited
at St. Germain, *La Voix du Golf.* Mr. Gauvreau thus holds
forth : " The hermit's name was Toussaint Cartier ; he came to
Canada in 1723, as appears on reference to a deed executed in
1728, between him and Mr. Lepage, the *seigneur* of Rimouski.
Many times," familiarly adds Mr. Gauvreau, " my grandfather,

Charles Lepage, spoke to me about the Hermit, whom he had personally known, and who used to relate that he had been shipwrecked on the island and made a vow in consequence. He was very religious, and would spend hours in his oratory at prayers. He used to shun the sight of females." Old Charles Lepage used also to relate how the Hermit died: " One morning, it being noticed from the south shore that no smoke issued from the chimney of his cabin, he sent two young men to the island to enquire the reason. On entering they found him lying on the floor, insensible ; his faithful dog was near him, licking his eyes ; he was brought over to *terra firma*, where he died 30th * January, 1767, as appears by the Church Register. But the Hermit never mentioned to my grandfather that disappointment in love was the cause of his seclusion. Until a few years back, the remains of his hut were visible, about the centre of the island facing Rimouski, likewise the traces of a garden, such as fruit trees, surrounding his former dwelling."

On the opposite shore, a few miles to the east of the town, is Father Point, the well-known telegraph station and stoppage of the Atlantic steamers. It takes its name from the fact of a celebrated Jesuit, Father Henry Nouvelle, who having in a boat left Quebec, for a mission among the Papinachois Indians, on 19th Nov., 1663, was caught by the ice, and forced to winter at this spot where he remained until the spring of 1664.

° (*Extract of Baptismal Register of Rimouski.*)

(*Translation.*)

" The year one thousand seven hundred and sixty-seven, the thirtieth of January, died in this parish of St. Germain de Rimouski, Toussaint Cartier, aged about sixty years, an inhabitant of the said parish, after having received the sacraments of repentance, of eucharist and extreme unction. His remains were buried in the church of this parish, with the usual rites, the last day of said month of January. In testimony whereof, I have signed the day and year, aforesaid.

(Signed,   FATHER AMBROSIUS."

St. Simon—St. Fabien—Bic.

On leaving the flourishing town of St. Germain de Rimouski, the route by land lies through the comparatively new parishes of St. Simon and St. Fabien. St. Fabien is a succession of hills, mostly as steep as those of Bic. The place has been erected as a parish within a few years. The inhabitants seem industrious, but the want of railway communication, and uninteresting surrounding landscape, has kept out strangers. Rich farmers seem scarce here. Matters are mending of late.

Shut out from the river view between two mountains, St. Simon has ever appeared to me monotonous in the extreme. The road runs at the bottom of a valley, with sloping pasture lands and farms on each side, a distance of some six miles; in the centre, is the church.

At St. Fabien, a pretty lake nearly skirts the highway, and in the interior, behind St. Simon ; but more accessible from Cacouna, the lovely lake of that name, well known to all disciples of Walton, is situate amidst mountains. Its yield of trout is great, and its shores, remarkably attractive.

From St. Simon, the traveller, after a pleasant drive, strikes the mountainous and exceedingly beautiful scenery of Bic. One hill only, in this distant region, in my opinion, exceeds, in height, the hills and precipices of Bic; that is the precipitous hill, nine miles from Murray Bay, called *La Côte du Grand Ruisseau*. Amidst these Alpine heights, the Intercolonial Railway runs; at one spot, near Bic, the train glides along a mountain gorge some two hundred feet in the air. Formerly, the highway from Bic to St. Simon was located on the beach, at the base of stupendous cliffs, and was safe at low water only.

The sea washed over it during storms at a great height ; and in-
cautious travellers have found there a watery grave.

Instead of a flourishing village, at the beginning of this
century there was scarcely one house to every nine miles of
road. Tradition still points out the spot where a dreaded wayside inn existed, kept by a horrible old crone of the name of
Petit. During January storms, belated travellers seeking the
shelter of Madame Petit's roof in several instances were never
heard of again. Numerous and dark are the traditions anent
Madame Petit. M. J. C. Taché has woven some very interesting stories about Bic, in which Indian cruelty plays a conspicuous part. In early times, the chief island of Bic was named
Le Pic. It is called in the *Routier* of Jean Alphonse, *Cap
de Marbre*. Jacques Cartier, in 1535, named the harbor itself
Islot St. Jean, having entered it on the anniversary of the
day when John the Baptist was beheaded. Under French
rule, the Baron d'Avaugour, in 1663, and the celebrated engineer
Vauban, thirty years after, had planned an important part to be
played by Bic in the general system of defences contemplated
to consolidate French power, in Canada. Quebec was then to
receive most extensive fortifications. But, to the Duke of Wellington, in 1823, are to be chiefly credited the present defences of
the city. Bic was to be a harbor for the French ships of war to
be retained in these waters. It still looks forward to becoming
a winter harbor of refuge. The Trent difficulty brought it
into notice.

The Bay of Bic is of incomparable beauty. The heroine of
Mrs. Brooke,* Emily Montague, on viewing it, in 1767, exclaimed " I wish I were Queen of Bic."

The seigniory of Bic was granted by Count de Frontenac to
Charles Denis de Vitré, 6th May, 1675. In Oct., 1822, it
belonged to Azariah Pritchard, Esquire, who exchanged it for
other property with the late Archibald Campbell, N.P., of

° The History of Emily Montague. 4 volumes, London, 1767.

Quebec. Mr. Campbell, on 10th November, 1852, by *acte de donation*, transferred it to its present proprietor, William Darling Campbell, N.P., of Quebec.

The Island of Bic, Biquet, Cap Enragé, Ile Brulée, Cap à l'Orignal, especially the Cavern of Islet au Massacre: these are familiar names to the coaster or mariner of the Lower St. Lawrence, in quest of a haven during our autumnal storms.

Mr. J. C. Taché[*] has rescued from oblivion the particulars of the great Indian massacre, of which this cave was the theatre, in the early days of New France.

" L'ISLET AU MASSACRE."

AT the entrance of Bic harbor, there exists a small island. For a couple of centuries back, it has been known as *L'Islet au Massacre*, Massacre Island. A deed of blood marks the spot: tradition and history furnish the details of the horrible scene of yore, enacted there. Two hundred Micmac Indians were camping there for the night: the canoes had been beached: a neighboring recess or cavern in the lofty rocks which bound the coast offered an apparently secure asylum to the warriors, their wives and children. Wrapped in sleep, the *Redskins* quietly awaited the return of day to resume their journey; they slept, but not their lynx-eyed enemy, the Iroquois: from afar, he had scented his prey. During the still hours of night, his noiseless step had compassed the slumbering foe. Laden with birch-bark fagots and other combustible materials, the Iroquois noiselessly surround the cavern;--the fagots are piled around it;—the torch is applied. Kohe! Kohe!! Hark! the fiendish and well-known war-whoop! The Micmacs, terror-stricken, seize their arms, and are preparing to sell dearly their lives, when the lambent flames

---

[*] Col. Pelissier's feat in roasting alive, in 1845, 1500 helpless inhabitants of Algeria, the pet colony of France, recalls the infamous butchery, in 1692 of the McGregor clan, known as the Massacre of Glencoe. Between Indian and civilized cold-bloodedness, there seems little to choose.

[*] Soirées Canadiennes.

and the scorching heat leave them but one alternative, that of rushing from their lurking place. More fortunate than Pelissier's roasting Arabs,* they have at least one egress; wild despair nerves their hearts: men, women and children crowd through the narrow passage, amidst the flames; but at the same instant a shower of poisoned arrows decimates them : the human hyena is on his prey ; a few flourishes of the tomahawk from the Iroquois warriors, and the silence of death soon pervades the narrow abode. Now for the trophies: the scalping took some time,—history mentions but *five*, out of the two hundred victims, who escaped with their lives. The blanched bones of the Micmac warriors strewed the grotto, and could be seen until some years back. This dark deed, still vivid by tradition in the minds of the Restigouche settlers, is mentioned in Jacques Cartier's narrative.*

Let us close these sketches of the Lower St. Lawrence with a short summary of one of the most striking Indian legends which the Abbé R. H. Casgrain has gathered on the shores of the great river.

° Jacques Cartier obtained his information from Donnacona, the old *Sachem* of Stadacona, and speaks thus :

" Et fut par le dit Donnadona montré au dit Capitaine les peaux de cinq têtes d'hommes estendues sur des bois, comme peaux de parchemins ; et nous dit que c'étaient des *Toudamans* de devers le Su, qui leur menaient continuellement la guerre. " Outre nous fut dit qu'il y a deux ans passés les dits Toudamans (Iroquois) les vinrent assailler jusqu'au dèdans le dit fleuve, à une isle qui est le travers du Saguenay, où, ils étaient à passer la nuit, tendant aller à Honguedo (Gaspé) leur mener guerre, avec environ deux cents personnes, tant hommes, femmes qu'enfants, lesquels furent surpris en dormant, dedans un fort qu'ils avaient fait, ou mirent les dits Toudamans, le feu, et comme ils sortaient, les tuèrent tous reserve *cinq*, qui s'échappèrent. De laquelle détrousse, se plaignant encore fort, nous montrant qu'ils en auraient vengeance."

Jacques Cartier's Second Voyage, Cl. IX.

RIVIÈRE OUELLE.

RIVIÈRE OUELLE was in the 17th century the scene of one of those barbarous tragedies in which the *Iroquois* took a particular delight. The place is called after Madme Houelle, the lady of a French *Controleur General ;* she was captured with her little son, on their trip from Quebec to Rivière Ouelle : the stirring tale is brilliantly related in one of the "*Legendes Canadiennes*" recently published by the Abbé Casgrain, a young clergyman of Quebec. The Abbé has certainly succeeded in investing Rivière Ouelle, his native parish, with a romantic interest for all lovers of the chronicles of the past. No one who has glanced at the striking *tableaux* representing the career of the Ghoul of the St. Lawrence, (a diabolical old Iroquois Squaw),* but will admit that this legend is one of the most attractive of the many which cluster round Canada's glorious river. None will leave Rivière Ouelle without visiting the *three curious and inexplicable snow shoe tracks* deeply incrusted in the solid rock on the beach. Although the tide is doing its utmost to efface those foot-prints, still they are very visible at present. But another singular impression on those same rocks, has recently become obliterated : it was the marks of the anterior part of two human feet and hands.

_____

* LA JONGLEUSE ; *Legendes Canadiennes.*

DRAMATIS PERSONÆ.

THE PORT ADMIRAL, J. U. G.

COMMANDER M. of H. M. S. " DRUID."

JEAN BAPTISTE SOYER, *chef de cuisine* on board of " DRUID."

JONATHAN OLDBUCK, Antiquary—Naturalist—Discoverer.

MIDSHIPMAN EASY, R. N. Secretary to the foregoing.

JAMES CUNNINGHAM, Pilot and Sailing Master of H. M. Steamer " DOLPHIN.'

HENRY QUINN, 1st Engineer on H. M. Steamer " DOLPHIN."

R. RICHARDSON, 2nd   "   "   "   "   "

JEREMIE KEROUACK,
ELZEAR VALLEE,
LUKE MURPHY,
CYPRIEN GAGNE,   } Able-bodied seamen.
J. B. BEAULIEU,
PAT. LEWIS,
JEAN SOUCY,

    Foreign Ladies from the Kingdom of Sillery.

    The Port Admiral's dog " Shudack," a Russian.

SCENE.

    Some times on board of the " DRUID."

        "   "   "   "   "   "   " DOLPHIN."

    Time, 1.30 p.m.

I.

THE CRUISE OF THE "DOLPHIN."

> " I'm afloat ! I'm afloat,
> On the fierce bursting tide ;
> The ocean's my home,
> And my bark is my bride."

On Board H. M. Steamer "Dolphin," on the Quebec Station,

13th Sept., 1877.

From our boyhood, an indescribable charm—a freshness of existence—an exuberance of life, has ever coursed through our veins the instant we felt released from our dull shore duties and found ourselves careering amidst the rolling hills and valleys of the "vasty deep." Never yet, we say it with regret, have we succeeded in fully accepting our part of the responsibilities which the decrees of fate have awarded us as landsmen. The time was, in our rosy youth, when we longed for

> " A life on the ocean wave,
> A home on the rolling deep,"

quite satisfied to accept it, with all the hazards with which Father Neptune surrounds his adventurous sons.

Now, with the phantom of years looming across our path, we are occasionally tempted to sing the glories of old ocean, if not with the " winged words " of Byron,—Dibdin—Barry Cornwall, at least with Marryat's sober, measured prose.

Need our readers then marvel, when we tell of our readiness to form one of a party invited to the quarter-deck of H. M.

V

Steamer "Dolphin," during one of her recent cruises on the
Quebec station.

The "DOLPHIN," 1 gun, is that trim fresh water frigate, on
which Commodore Russell has hoisted his blue pendant, with
the word "Dolphin" conspicuously inscribed on it.

It was to the kind offices of our nautical friend, the Admiral
of the Port, that we were indebted for being associated to this
grand exploring expedition, in latitudes rendered famous by
scores of illustrious mariners : Cartier, Champlain, LaGalissoniere,
Cook, Bougainville, De Vauclain, St. Vincent, Jervis, Hardy,
Nelson, Boxer, *cum multis aliis.*

The "Dolphin," having coaled, provided with marine stores
and a full equipment of men, was to take us from the flag ship
the "Druid," where she was to receive her sealed orders.

To enumerate the cordial welcome extended to us by the
Commander of H. M. Steamer "Druid," the generous hospitality
showered on us, the fervent prayers of our friends for our safe
return from the hazardous voyage before us, is one of those
pleasant duties which gratitude renders still more so.

We were soon comfortably seated under the white awning
spread—to temper the ardor of a meridian sun—over the
'Dolphin's" quarter-deck. Scarcely had the boatswain's shrill
whistle died away, when from the shore was wafted the
softest strains of a city band, playing "Home, sweet Home."
This to us, leaving for a perilous and long voyage was both
soothing and melancholy ; soon our powerful engine was churning the glad waters into wreaths of foam. Off we go ! Westward Ho !

One of our first subjects of enquiry, was as to the origin of
the name of our steamer. Was she called, after Verrazano's
ship, the "Dolphin," with which the bold Florentine visited for
the first time, in 1524, the coast of Maine, etc., or could it be
after that other "Dolphin" which formed part of Sir Hovenden Walker's squadron, in 1711. So much concern was manifested that finally a promise was obtained from our gallant

Port Admiral, that the Lords of the Admiralty should be written to, for information on the subject.. The " Dolphin " is neither a turret-ship, nor an ironclad—she is a composite—built war vessel. She was launched at a time when it was fashionable in England to ignore the " colonies ;" hence, why, her name was dropped out of the navy list, though she forms a not unimportant portion of the Canadian navy. The " Dolphin " was from the beginning intended for coast defences ; by her build, draught of water, armament and general equipment, she is eminently adapted for the service.

> " On the bosom of a river,
>   Where the sun unloosed his quiver,
>   Steamed a vessel light and free ;
>   Morning dew-drops hung like manna
>   On the bright folds of her banner,
>   And the zephirs rose to fan her
>   Softly to the radiant sea."

When under a full head of steam, with her burly pilot steadying the wheel—her blue ensign streaming to the breeze, she gracefully dips her "pearly prow" into the foam-crested waves, in a " stiff northeaster," we would like to know where you would find such another perfect specimen of naval architecture. For a figure head, stands an out-stretched hand, with a formidable club—the club of the law ! Beware !

Let us now state her tonnage and the exact spot occupied by her solitary gun, which has so often belched forth destruction. Her tonnage does not entitle her to be classed with two deckers ; her one gun is neither a Krupp—nor an Armstrong—nor even a turret gun—it is precisely, however, the kind of gun a Port Admiral such as ours, takes pleasure in owning. There it crouches, loaded and primed, close to the companion ladder—a trusty double-barreled fowling piece—ever ready should ducks or other sea fowl encroach much within the nautical mile.

How oft have we watched the " Dolphin " breasting the billows, bounding with the swiftness of an antelope over Laurentian tides, in the very chops of the channel, but not beyond. We then knew, nay, we felt the harbor was secure. . . . against crimps.

The "Dolphin," if the whole truth must come out, is the Government steam launch, which, backed by the strong arm of the law (the new seaman's act), has dealt such a deadly thrust to "crimping" in the port of Quebec. Every night, it is her special province to steam round the anchorage ground, in the midst of the shipping, and each day at 1.30 p.m. the swift "Dolphin" cruises round the harbor to enforce the port regulations,—to convey to the city refractory seamen,—to board any ship flying at her main, the red or police signal—the appeal for relief.

II.

THE FRESCOED CHURCH OF ST. ROMUALD.

The "Dolphin" was headed for Cap Rouge, and skirted the wharves in succession; in a few minutes, we emerged from the dark shade of Cape Diamond, exhibiting, high up in the cliff, a black board to mark the spot from which Montgomery did not fall. The ocean steamers, huge Leviathans sleeping lazily on the waters and hugging closely the Allan's wharf, were next reconnoitered. Close by, was the indenture in the row of houses, where a portion of the cape tumbled down, in 1841, causing some forty casualties. Crowds of timber-laden ships lined the shore higher up. Here and there, a small steamer, with a raft or ship in tow, shrieked, puffed, whistled or groaned, as the fancy came over her bustling or eccentric captain.

After passing St. Columba Church and many familiar spots on the Sillery heights, the " Dolphin " edged in for St. Romuald, well known to mariners, as New Liverpool, where ships are loaded. We had just cast a prolonged gaze on *Pointe à Pizeau* and its old Indian memories,[*] when a familiar voice roused our attention.

—" Here we are, ejaculated the Port Admiral, abreast of New Liverpool, steaming over that expanse of deep water, marked out as the ballast ground. How many prows have furrowed these dark waters since this identical date of September, 1535, when the three Saint Malo crafts, the ' Grande Hermine,' about 120 tons, Jacques Cartier, master; the ' Petite Hermine.' 60 tons, Marc Jalobert, master; the ' Emerillon,' 40 tons, Guillaume Le Breton, master, were ascending the St. Lawrence, down to that 13th September, 1860, when Capt Vine Hall's Leviathan, the

---

[*] It has been surmised by some of our historians, that the tribe of Indians which Cartier had found at Stadacona in 1535, and who had disappeared when Champlain arrived, had retreated to *Pointe à Puizeau*, thus called after M. de Puizeau, who owned land there when M. de Maisonneuve wintered at Sillery, in 1641-2.

' Great Eastern,' 22,500 tons, was daily swinging to the tide, on her anchors, at this very spot.

' How balmy the air : how placid the bosom of the noble river !'

—" It is not always so," retorted the antiquary. " Let us skirt, in a southerly direction, the wharves and view the extensive saw mills, erected in 1804, on the *Rivière Bruyante* or *Etchemin*, by Col. Henry Caldwell, Wolfe's brave quarter-master General—the proprietor of the Lauzon seigniory, in 1804. They have seen several masters : Col. Henry Caldwell—his son, the Receiver-General—Sir John Caldwell ; grandson, Sir Henry Caldwell ; Messrs. John Thomson, Henry Atkinson, &c."

On a slight eminence, a little to the west, glistens the spire of the Roman Catholic Church of St. Romuald, richly decorated, thanks to the efforts of its progressive pastor.

By far the greatest curiosity which St. Romuald contains, is its ornate Roman Catholic Church. Its beauty is due to the taste of its enlightened priest, the Rev. Messire Saxe, a son of P. Saxe, Esq., land surveyor, formerly of Quebec. The decorations of the church date of 1868-69 ; the dome and ceilings remind one very much of the gorgeous Roman Catholic Church—the *Gesu*, at Montreal, where the Jesuits officiate. This portion of its interior is the work of a German artist, now settled at Cincinnati. The paintings were made by Mr. W. Lamprech, a young German, who took the first prize in the celebrated Academy of painting of Munich. This artist, 'tis said, is one of the best who ever graduated at this renowned school. Mr. Lamprech now ranks very high in the United States. He was employed to paint the principal scenes in the life of our Saviour, of the Virgin, of St. Joseph, of St. Romuald.

The subjects are thus distributed :—1st. In the chancel, the " Nativity "—" Death "—" Resurrection of our Saviour."

2nd. In the chapel of the Holy Virgin : the " Annunciation " —" Visitation "—" The Three Kings "—the " Presentation."

3rd. In the Chapel of St. Joseph : the " Marriage of St.

Joseph "—" His Flight in Egypt "—Nazareth "—" Jesus amidst the Doctors"—" Death of St. Joseph."

4th. In the dome, eight pictures represent different episodes in the life of St. Romuald. The first, when he took orders ; the last, above the altar, his " Apotheosis or Entry in Heaven."

5th. The Medallions on a gold ground, sixteen in number, portray the history of the Church, in that of Peter ; Paul ; the four Evangelists ; five Doctors of the Eastern, and five Doctors of the Western, Church.

6th. The ornaments to the ceiling of the side chapels are allegorical references to the Litanies of the Virgin, such as these : *Turris Davidica, Rosa Mystica, Sedes Sapientiæ,* etc., sixteen in number.

The pictures are like an opened Bible ; they are pregnant with meaning, even to the eye of those who cannot read.

7th. The altars were erected—on plans furnished by Mr. Schneider, who was then considered as the first architect of Munich—by a young Canadian artist.

8th. The statues are all in sculptured wood, by Rudmiller, of Munich, and copied from clay models worked by the most able artists of Munich.

Altogether, the frescoed church of St. Romuald is the handsomest temple of Roman Catholic worship in this section fo the Province ; it comes next to the famous *Gesu* of Montreal.

To those who can remember the abominable daubs on the walls of churches thirty years ago, what a pleasant reflection that progress has votaries even in country churches ? I can recollect one church picture in a remote parish that made one's hair stand on end. It depicted the narrow escape a worldly friar had of brimstone and sulphur, for ever : just when the Prince of darkness was extending his claws, to grasp the *Padre*, the latter's guardian angel, vaulting from a high horse, with a fierce look and a rapier as long as Orlando's, sprang to the rescue, cut off the devil's left whisker, and saved the penitent Padre. There was much for imagination and poetical license in this picture, but, of art, naught.

III.

THE SIEGE OF 1759—WOLFE'S FLEET AND SIGNALS—THE FRENCH GUNNER OF 1760.

—Why did you select such an historical anniversary as the 13th Sept. to make this long talked of exploration? inquired our friend the Admiral of the Port.

— Simply, illustrious mariner, to have a memorable date on which to pour into your willing ear the veracious account of the many stirring incidents of which this portion of the river was the arena, one hundred and eighteen years ago. Yes, on this day, nay, perhaps, at this very hour, on the 13th Sept., 1759, as soon as the smoke of the battle field had cleared away, this part of the St. Lawrence must have been very interesting to view with its ponderous three-deckers—frigates and transports, all flying the proud banner of England, with the Levi hospital boats, carrying the wounded of both nations, protected by their white flag. That sturdy old Highlander, Jas. Thompson, in his diary, has told us how the wounded were crossed over from the battle field to the hospital at St. Joseph—(the church.)

—Pray, most learned antiquary, naturalist and discoverer, favor us with more of your historical lore, anent the port of Quebec, retorted the Port Admiral, slightly twisting his moustache. Unroll the bright scroll of war, from the thrilling days of Phipps, down to the uninteresting era of to-day, when, instead of witnessing proud admirals opening out with shot and shell on the mural crowned city, we may shortly see this portion of the river covered with market boats conveying fat bullocks to the Exhibition.*

---

* The Provincial Exhibition was held on the 18th Sept. last, on the Cove Fields.

—Your wish, sir, has been anticipated, and my youthful secretary has there in his portfolio, a record just prepared of Wolfe's disembarkation, on the night of the 12th September, on the shores under the green groves of Marchmont. To us, the spot is known as Wolfe's Cove; under French regime, it was called *le Foulon*, on account of some fulling mills erected there and set in motion by the *ruisseau Saint Denis*, which rushes from the cliff above into the St. Lawrence. Captain John Knox, of the 43rd, serving under General Wolfe, and to whom we are indebted for the most detailed account of the campaign, will tell us, first, of the ships composing the English fleet, viz :

Neptune, 90 guns (flag ship).
Princess Amelia, 80.
Dublin, 74.
Royal William, 84.
Vanguard, 74.
Terrible, 74.
Captain, 70.
Shrewsbury, 74.
Devonshire, 74.
Bedford, 68.
Alcide, 64.
Somerset, 68.
Prince Frederic, 64.
Pembroke, 60.
Medway, 60.
Prince of Orange, 60.
Northumberland, 64.
Oxford, 64.
Stirling Castle, 64.
Centurion, 60.
Trident, 54.
Sutherland, 50.

FRIGATES.

Diana, 36.
Leostoffe, 28.
Richmond, 32.
Trent, 28.
Echo, 24.

SLOOPS.

Seahorse, 20.
Eurus, 22.
Nightingale, 20.
Hind, 20.
Squirrel, 20.
Scarborough, 20.
Scorpion, 14.
Zephir, 12.
Hunter, 10.
Porcupine, 14.
Baltimore, 10.
Cormorant, 8.
Pelican, 8.
Racehorse, 8.
Bonetta, 8.
Vesuvius.
Strombolo.

CUTTER.

Rodney, 2.

TRANSPORT CUTTERS.

Charming Molly.
Europa.
Lawrence.
Peggy and Sarah.
Good-Intent and Prosperity.

" Together, he adds, with an immense fleet of transports, storeships, victuallers, traders, etc."

You will see by the foregoing that England on this occasion meant business. The disembarking was specially watched over by Capt. Chad, of the Navy ; whilst the "General Orders" for the landing were issued on the 11th September. "The troops must go into the boats about nine, to-morrow night (the 12th), or when it is pretty near high water....As there will be a necessity for remaining some part of the night in the boats, the officers will provide accordingly, and the soldiers will have a gill of rum extra to mix with their water ; arms and ammunition ; two days' provisions with rum and water are all that soldiers are to take in the boats ; the ships, with their blankets, tents, etc., will soon be brought up.

SIGNALS.

" First.—For the flat bottomed boats, with the troops on board, to *rendezvous* abreast of the 'Sutherland,' between her and the south shore, keeping her near :—one light in the 'Sutherland's' main topmast's shrouds.

" Second.—When they are to drop away from the 'Sutherland,' she will show two lights in the main topmast shrouds, one over the other. The men to lie quite silent, and when they are about to land, must not, upon any account, fire out of the boats : the officers of the navy are not to be interrupted in their part of the duty ; they will receive their orders from the officer appointed to superintend the whole, to whom they are answerable. Officers of artillery, and detachments of gunners, are put on board the armed sloops to regulate their fire, that, in the hurry, our troops may not be hurt by our own artillery ; Captain York, and the officers, will be particularly careful to distinguish the enemy, and to point their fire against them ; the frigates are not to fire until broad day-light, so that no mistake can be made : the officers commanding floating batteries will receive particular orders from the General. The troops to be supplied to-morrow (the 12th) with provisions to the 14th. The troops ordered for the first embarkation to be under arms at the headquarters to-morrow morning at four o'clock."

An officer of the 43rd, says Knox, was sent ashore to St. Nicholas to endeavor, to procure some fresh provisions, but could not succeed......"

We shall not dwell longer here, on the incidents of the 12th September, 1759, nor on the still more important events awaiting Wolfe on the morrow ; that "morrow" fraught for him with death and glory, which he is reported to have alluded to, whilst repeating aloud, one of the sweetest of Gray's elegies and, mayhap, dreaming of the dear ones in old England, whom he was destined never again to see.

Let us follow, on the chain of time ; six months later, we can, with the mind's eye, see a solitary, helpless waif, floating over the spot, we have just left.

In April, 1760, that unlucky French gunner, dropped from Levi's boats at Cap Rouge, clinging to his solitary piece of ice was floating past the city to return with the ebb tide. Chevalier Johnstone, aide-de-camp to Lieut.-General Levi, thus relates this incident in his narrative of the siege of 1759 : "The English got the news of our army being at Cap Rouge by a most singular accident. An artillery boat having been overturned and sunk by the sheets of ice, which the current of the St. Lawrence brought down with great force, an artillery man saved himself on a piece of ice that floated down the river with him upon it, with a possibility of his getting to land, when he was opposite the city.

The English, as soon as they perceived that poor distressed man—moved with humanity and compassion—sent out boats, * who with difficulty saved him (the river being covered with fields of ice) and brought him to town, with scarcely any sign of life. Having restored him with cordials, the moment he began to breathe and recover his senses, they asked him whence he came, and who he was ? He answered, innocently, that he was a French cannonier from M. de Levi's army at Cap Rouge. At first they imagined he raved, and that his sufferings upon the

---

* From the *Race horse* frigate.

river had turned his head; but, after examining him more
particularly, and his answers being always the same, they were
soon convinced of the truth of his assertions, and were not a
little confounded to have the French army at three leagues from
Quebec, without possessing the smallest information of the fact.
All their care proved ineffectual for the preservation of life; he
expired the moment he had revealed his important secret. What
a remarkable and visible instance of fortune fighting for the
English?

Had it not been for this most unaccountable accident, M. de
Levi, to all appearances, would have captured all the English advanced posts, which were said to amount to 1,500 men, who
retired to the town immediately after setting fire to the magazine
of powder in the Church of St. Foy."

A REMINISCENCE OF THE SIEGE OF 1690.

IV.

Let us see what was taking place in port seventy years before : 1760.

Hark ! the cadenced sound of paddles in the distance : here comes, on the rush of the tide, impelled by the brave arm of Canadian *royageurs*, a light bark canoe, with the white banner of France streaming. It is sturdy old Count of Frontenac hastening from Montreal, on the 14th Oct., 1690, to give Admiral Phipps, through the "mouths of his cannon," a bit of his mind ; the historian Parkman will furnish us the particulars :

ARRIVAL OF FRONTENAC IN A BIRCH CANOE FROM MONTREAL, OCTOBER, 1690.

"A messenger arrived in haste at three o'clock in the afternoon, (of the 10th Oct.,) and gave him a letter from Prévost, Town Major of Quebec. It was to the effect that an Abenaki Indian had just come overland from Acadia, with news that some of his tribe had captured an English woman near Portsmouth, who told them that a great fleet had sailed from Boston to attack Quebec. Frontenac, not easily alarmed, doubted the report ; nevertheless, he embarked at once with the Intendant in a small vessel, which proved to be leaky, and was near foundering with all on board. He then took a canoe, and towards evening set out again for Quebec, ordering some two hundred men to follow him. On the next day, he met another canoe, bearing a fresh message from Prévost, who announced that the English fleet had been seen on the river, and that it was already above Tadousac. Frontenac now sent back Captain de Ramsay with orders to Callieres, Governor of Montreal, to descend immediately to Quebec with all the force at his disposal, and to muster the inhabitants on the way. Then he pushed on with the utmost speed. The autumnal storms had begun, and the rain pelted him without ceasing, but on the morning of the fourteenth he neared the town. The rocks of Cape Diamond towered before him, the St. Lawrence lay beneath them lonely and still, and the Basin of Quebec outspread its broad bosom, a solitude without a sail. Frontenac had arrived in time.

He landed at the Lower Town, and the troops and the armed inhabitants came crowding to meet him. He was delighted at their ardor; shouts, cheers, and the waving of hats greeted the old man as he climbed the steep ascent of Mountain street. Fear and doubt seemed banished by his presence. Even those who hated him rejoiced at his coming, and hailed him as a deliverer. He went at once to inspect the fortifications. Since the alarm a week before Prévost had accomplished wonders, and not only completed the works begun in the spring, but added others to secure a place which was a natural fortress in itself. On two sides, the Upper Town scarcely needed defence. The cliffs along the St. Lawrence and those along the tributary river St. Charles had three accessible points, guarded at the present day (1867) by the Prescott Gate, the Hope Gate, and the Palace Gate. Prévost had secured them by barricades of heavy beams and casks filled with earth. A continuous line of palisades ran along the strand of the St. Charles, from the great cliff called the *Sault au Matelot*, to the palace of the Intendant. At this latter point began the line of works constructed by Frontenac to protect the rear of the town. They consisted of palisades, strengthened by a ditch and an embankment, and flanked at frequent intervals by square towers of stone. Passing behind the garden of the Ursulines, they extended to a windmill on a hillock called Mount Carmel, and thence to the brink of the cliffs in front. Here there was a battery of eight guns, near the present Public Garden; two more, each of three guns, were planted at the top of the *Sault au Matelot*, another at the barricade of the Palace Gate, and another near the windmill of Mount Carmel, while a number of light pieces were held in reserve for such use as occasion might require. The Lower Town had no defensive works, but two batteries, each of three guns, eighteen and twenty-four pounders, were placed here at the edge of the river.*

Two days passed in completing these defences under the eye of

---

* *Relation de Monseignat. Plan de Quebec, par Villeneuve,* 1690. *Relation du Mercure Galant,* 1691. The summit of Cape Diamond, which commanded the town, was not fortified till three years later, nor were any guns placed here during the English attack.

the Governor. Men were flocking in from the parishes far and near, and on the evening of the fifteenth about twenty-seven hundred, regulars and militia, were gathered within the fortifications, besides the armed peasantry of Beauport and Beaupré, who were ordered to watch the river below the Town, and resist the English should they attempt to land.† At length, before dawn on the morning of the sixteenth, the sentinels on the Sault au Matelot could descry the slowly moving lights of distant vessels. At daybreak the fleet was in sight. Sail after sail passed the Point of Orleans and glided into the Basin of Quebec. The excited spectators on the rock counted thirty-four of them. Four were large ships, several others were of considerable size, and the rest were brigs, schooners and a fishing craft, all thronged with men."

† *Diary of Sylvanus Davis*, prisoner in Quebec, in *Mass. Hist. Coll.*

‡ 1,101 There is a difference of ten days in the French and English dates, the *new style* having been adopted by the former, and not by the latter.

THE ENGAGEMENT AT BEAUPORT 1759.

V.

WE are nearing a spot on the Beauport shore, close to Montmorency Falls, which, from noon to sunset on the 31st July, 1759, the hissing of shot and shell, and the playful tricks of the savages on British scalps must have rendered tolerably lively. Here General Wolfe paid dearly for his ill-judged attack on the French lines, which extended from the Saint Charles to the Montmorency Falls. The heights beyond the city and the city itself having been considered unassailable by water, an attempt was made by the English from their *Ange-Gardien* batteries at the Falls, with the aide of the *Centurion* frigate and boats, to capture the French redoubts opposite, and those lining that portion of the Beauport shore. No account seems to us fuller than that furnished by the historian Garneau : this defeat cost the British close on 600 men.

THE BATTLE OF BEAUPORT FLAT, 31ST JULY, 1759.

" As the left bank of the Montmorency, says Garneau, just beyond its embouchure is higher than the right, Wolfe strengthened the batteries he already had there, the gun-range of which enfiladed, above that river, the French entrenchments. The number of his cannon and pieces for shelling was raised to sixty. He caused to sink, on the rocks level with the flood below, two transports, placing on each, when in position, fourteen guns. One vessel lay to the right, the other to the left, of a small redoubt which the French had erected on the strand, at the foot of the Courville road, in order to defend not only the entry of that road, which led to heights occupied by the French Reserve, but also the ford of the Montmorency below the Falls. Cannon shots from the transports crossed each other in the direction of the redoubt. It became needful therefore to silence the fire of the latter, and cover the march of the assailants, on this accesible point of our line ; therefore the *Centurion*, a 60-gun ship, was sent afterwards to anchor opposite the falls, and as near as might be to the shore, to protect the ford which the British forlorn-hope was to cross, as soon as the attacking force should descend from the camp of l'Ange-Gardien. Thus 118 pieces of ordnance were about to play on Montcalm's left wing. Towards noon, 31st July, all this artillery began to play, and, at the same time, Wolfe formed his columns of attack. More than 1,500 barges were in motion in the basin of Quebec. A part of Monkton's brigade, and 1,200 grenadiers, embarked at Point Levi, with intent to re-land between the site of the *Centurion* and the sunken transports. The second column composed of Townshend's and Murray's brigades, descended the heights of l'Ange-Gardien in order to take the ford and join their forces to the first column at the foot of the Courville road, which was ordered to be ready posted, and only waiting for the signal to advance against the adjoining French entrenchments. These two columns numbered 6,000 men. A third corps of 2,000 soldiers, charged to ascend the left bank of the Montmorency, was to pass that river at a ford about a league above the falls, but which was guarded by a detachment under M. de Repentigny. At 1 p.m., the three British columns were on foot to execute the concerted plan of attack, which would have been far too complicated for troops less disciplined than Wolfe's.

Montcalm, for some time doubtful about the point the enemy would assail, had sent orders along his whole line for the men to be ready everywhere to oppose the British wherever they came forward. As soon as the latter neared their destination, de Levis sent 500 men to succour de Repentigny (at the upper ford) also a small detachment to espy the manœuvres of the British when about to cross the lower ford, while he sent to Montcalm for some battalions of regulars, to sustain himself in case of need. The General came up, at 2 p.m., to examine the posture of matters at the left. He proceeded along the lines, approved of the dispositions of de Levis, gave fresh orders and returned to the centre, in order to be in a position to observe all that should pass. Three battalions and some Canadians, from Trois-Rivières, came in opportunely to re-inforce the French left. The greatest part of these troops took post, as a reserve, on the highway, and the rest were directed on the ford defended by M. de Repentigny. The latter had been already hotly attacked by a British column, but he forced it to give way, after some loss of men.   The retreat of this corps permitted that sent to succor de Repentigny, to hasten back to the arena of the chief attack.

Meanwhile, the barges leaving the Point Levi columns, led by Wolfe in person, after making several evolutions, meant to deceive the French as to the real place for landing, were directed towards the sunken transports. The tide was now ebbing; thus, part of the barges were grounded on a ridge of rock and gravelly matter, which stopped their progress and caused some disorder; but at last all obstacles were surmounted, and 1200 grenadiers, supported by other soldiers, landed on the St. Lawrence strand.   They were to advance in four divisions, and Monkton's brigade, which was to embark later, had orders to follow, and, as soon as landed, to sustain them.   From some misunderstanding, these orders were not punctually executed.   The enemy formed in columns, indeed; but Monkton's men did not arrive to time. Still the van moved, music playing up to the Courville road redoubt, which the French at once evacuated.   The enemy's grenadiers took possession of it, and prepared to assail the entrenchments beyond, which were within musket-shot distance. Wolfe's batteries had been pouring, ever since mid-day, on the Canadians who defended this part of the line, a shower of bombs and bullets, which they sustained without flinching.   Having re-formed, the British advanced, with fixed bayonets, to attack the entrenchments; their showy costumes contrasting strangely with that of their adversaries, wrapped as they were in light capotes and girt round the loins.   The Canadians, who compensated their deficient discipline only by their native courage and the great accuracy of their aim, waited patiently till the enemies were a few yards distant from their line, meaning to fire at them point-blank.   The proper time came, they discharged their pieces so rapidly and with such destructive effect,* that the two British columns, despite all their officers' endeavors, were broken and took flight.   They sought shelter at first against their foes' fire behind the redoubt; but not being allowed to re-form ranks, they continued to retreat to the main body of the army, which had deployed a little further back.   At this critical time, a violent thunderstorm supervened, which hid the ruin of the combatants

---

* "Their (men of) small arms, in the trenches, lay cool till they were sure of their mark; they then poured their shot like showers of hail, which caused our brave grenadiers to fall very fast."   (*Journal of a British officer.*)

on both sides from each other, while the reverberations of successive peals rose far above the din of battle. When the rainmist cleared off, the Canadians beheld the British re-embarking with their wounded, after setting fire to the sunken transports. Their army finally drew off, as it had advanced: some corps in the barges ; others marched landwards, after re-crossing the Montmorency ford. The fire of their numerous cannons, however, continued till night set in ; and it was estimated that the British discharged 3,000 cannon balls during the day and evening ; while the French had only a dozen pieces of cannon in action, but these were very serviceable in harassing the disembarking British. The loss of the French, which was due almost entirely to artillery fire, was inconsiderable, if we remember that they were for more than six hours exposed to it. The British lost about 500 men, killed and wounded, including many officers.

The victory gained at Montmorency (on the 31st July, 1759) was due chiefly to the judicious dispositions made by de Levis, who, with fewer troops in hand than Wolfe, contrived to unite a greater number than he did at every point of attack. Supposing the British grenadiers had surmounted the entrenchments, it is very doubtful whether they would have prevailed, even had they been sustained by the rest of their army. The ground from the strand to the Beauport road rises into slopes, broken by ravines, amongst which meanders the Courville road ; the locality, therefore, was favorable to our (Canadian) marksmen. Besides, the regulars in reserve were close behind, ever ready to succour the militia men.

This engagement revived wonderfully the spirits of Montcalm's raw militia and their Indian allies, who, according to English accounts, lost no time in removing as many British scalps as circumstances permitted." (*History of Canada, Garneau.*)

"As our company of grenadiers," says a British officer, "approached, I distinctly saw Montcalm on horseback riding backwards and forwards. He seemed very busy giving directions to his men, and I heard him give the word to fire. Immediately they opened upon us, and killed a good many of our men, I don't recollect how many. We did not fire, for it would have been of no use, as they were completely entrenched, and we could only see the crown of their heads."

. . . . We were now ordered to retreat to our boats, that had been left afloat to receive us ; and by this time it was low water, so that we had a long way to wade through the mud. A sergeant, Allan Cameron, of our company, seeing a small battery on our left with two guns mounted, and apparently no person near it, thought he would prevent it doing us any mischief on our retreat, so he picked up a couple of bayonets that lay on the beach, and went alone to the battery, when he drove the points of them in the vents as hard as he could, and then snapped them off short. When the French saw us far enough on our retreat, they sent their savages to scalp and tomahawk our poor fellows that lay wounded on the beach. Among the number was Lieutenant Peyton, of the Royal American Battalion, who was severely wounded, and had crawled away as far as the pains he endured would allow. After the savages had done their business with the poor fellows that lay nearest to the French batteries, they went back, except two, who spied Lieutenant Peyton, and thought to make a good prize of him. He happened to have a double-barrelled fusil, ready loaded, and as he had seen how the savages had treated all the others that came into their clutches, he was sure that if they got the better of him they would butcher him also. Fortunately his presence of mind did not forsake him, and he waited until the first savage came near enough, when he levelled his fusil, and brought him to the ground; the other savage, thinking that the Lieutenant would not have time to reload, rushed in upon him boldly, with his tomahawk ready to strike, when Lieutenant Peyton discharged his fusil right into his chest, and he fell dead at his feet. We saw no more of the savages after that, at least on that occasion, but we saw enough of them afterwards.

While poor Lieutenant Peyton lay upon the ground, almost exhausted from his exertions and loss of blood, he was accosted by Sergeant Cameron, who had no other means of helping him than carrying him away; and he was well able to do it, for he was a stout, strong, tall fellow. He slung the Lieutenant's fusil over his shoulder along with his own, and took him on his back, telling him to hold fast round his neck. As he had a long way to carry him, he was obliged every now and then to lay him down in order to take breath, and give the Lieutenant some ease, as his wound was exceedingly painful. In this way he got him at last to one of the boats, and laying him down, said, 'Now, sir, I have done as much for you as lay in my power, and I wish you may recover." *

---

* HAWKINS' *Picture of Quebec.*

VI.

AN EPISODE OF THE SIEGE OF 1775.

—Before heading for Indian Cove, let me tell you, most worthy Admiral, of two incidents of the American Invasion of 1775 : the crossing during the silent hours of night on the 14th[*] November, 1775, of Arnold's Fire-eaters. From where we stand we might have followed the ripple of these " thirty-five Abenaquis canoes," paddled so cautiously, so noiselessly, in the darkness, in order to evade the grape-shot, or armed boats of the two English men-of-war, anchored here : the *Hunter* and *Lizard*. A few minutes more, and the frail embarcations will close in with the shore, some at Wolfe's Cove, others, a little higher up, at Sillery, and land in safety (except one birch canoe which burst asunder) their chilled but hardy warriors. On that very day, a scalping scene was very nigh being enacted in this neighborhood : the humane interference of some New England Volunteers alone saved a British scalp from Abenaquis ferocity. An eye-witness and

---

[*] " At 2 o'clock at night, assembled at a certain place, where we had for shelter some mills, when the boats were to be drawn from the cave of the Chaudière to receive us. Mr. Haulstead (previously in charge of Col. Coldwell's Mills) served as pilot. The canoes were but few in number ; therefore were obliged to cross and return three times ere the army got over. The night being exceeding dark, everything was conducted with the utmost secrecy—no lights, no noise. Captain Hatchett and Company were left as a guard at Point Levi to some effects left behind there. It was proposed to cross immediately into Wolfe's Cove, the distance a league. I went......in the Pilot boat, in which was General Arnold, Captain Morgan with some riflemen, and one boat load of savages, with others to the amount of six boats, crossed between the two vessels (the *Hunter* and *Lizard*) notwithstanding the armed barges were plying every hour from ship to ship."
—(*Journal of Dr. Isaac Senter, surgeon to Arnold's Forces*, 1775.)

actor, who lived to become a respected Pennsylvania Judge, will tell us how it occurred. Mr. Justice Henry (who died in 1824, and left a very interesting narrative of his captivity in Quebec in 1775) furnishes the name of the intended victim: a youthful midshipman of H. M. S. *Hunter*, and brother of Captain McKenzie, commander of the *Pearl*, frigate.

" A hurried and boisterous report, says Henry, came from head quarters that the British were landing to our left, at a mill, about a mile off—(at New Liverpool). Each one grasped his arms. Morgan and the Indians, who lay nearest to the commander's quarters, were foremost. The running was severe. The lagging Indians and a variety of the three companies were intermingled. Coming to the brow of the precipice, but still unseen, we perceived a boat landing, which came from a frigate lying in the stream, a mile below. The boat came ashore. A youth sprang from it. The tide ebbing, the boatman thought it better to obtain a deeper landing-place, nearer the mill, and drew off. Morgan, apprehensive of a discovery of our presence, fired at the boat's crew. A volley ensued without harm, probably because of the great space between us. They pulled off shore, until beyond the range of our guns, leaving the midshipman to our mercy.

The hapless youth, confounded, unknowing what to do, plunged into the river, hoping to regain his boat. His friends flying from him,—he waded, he swam, yet he could not reach the boat. At the distance, perhaps of one hundred and fifty yards, nothing but his head above water, a shooting match took place, and believe me, the balls of Morgan, Simpson, Humphreys, and others, played around, and within a few inches of his head. Even after a lapse of thirty years, it gives me pain to recollect that my gun was discharged at him. Such, however, was the savage ferocity engendered, in those ungracious times, by a devolution of the Ministry of the mother country from the true line of conduct towards her colonies.

McKenzie, (the name of the young man) seeing that his boat's crew had deserted him, showed a desire to surrender by approaching the shore. The firing ceased. But, a still more disgusting occurrence than the preceding followed. The lad, coming toward the shore, evidently intending to submit, salutes ; the Indian, the brother of Natanis, sprang forward, scalping-knife in hand, seemingly intending to end the strife at a single blow.

The humanity of Morgan and Humphreys towards a succumbent foe was excited. One or the other of them, it is not now recollected which in particular, by his agility and amazing powers of body, was enabled to precede that Indian by several yards. This contest of athleticism was observed from the shore where we were, with greatest interest. Morgan brought the boy (for he was really such) to land, and afterwards esteemed him, for he merited the good will of a hero. Wet and hungry, we returned to quarters. Running along the shore with our prey, the *Hunter*, sloop of war, having warped up for the purpose, pelted us all the way with balls and grape shot. It was no easy matter to ascend the bank, which was steep and craggy. Our prisoner had left the sloop, of which he was a midshipman, upon command to procure spars and oars which lay in the mill (Caldwell's Mill). He was the brother of Captain McKenzie. * * * In 1777, young McKenzie was again taken. I saw him at Lancaster (Pennsylvania), active, lively and facetious as ever. During our stay at Point Levi, Colonel Arnold was busily engaged." — (*Judge Henry—Narrative of the Siege of Quebec*, 1775, page 80).

A MEMORY OF 1792.

We are rapidly nearing a spot, amid channel, between the Church of Beauport and that of St. Joseph, Levi, always dreaded, in stormy weather, by Quebec boatmen. When the wind and tide meet, as the commander of the *Dolphin* will tell you, it requires a smart steersman and a good sea-boat, to escape being swamped by the cross-seas or "tide rip," generated here, it is thought, by the uniting of the several currents diverging round Orleans. I could enumerate many casualties : a memorable one took place here, on Monday, the 21st May, 1792, which deprived Quebec of a worthy pastor, Rev. Aug. David Hubert, and the parish of St. Pierre, Isle of Orleans, of its seignior, M. Mauvide. Twelve persons in all, that day were drowned *between the two Churches*, as the spot is called by seafaring men. The master of the skiff, a Mr Lachance, and a young man were saved ; the boat in attempting to make the Levi shore was swamped, close to the beach.

The melancholy accident is mentioned in detail by Nelson's *Gazette* of 24th May, 1792; and a suitable inscription on a marble tablet close to the altar of the *Holy Family*, in the Basilica of Quebec, commemorates the death of the good priest, as follows

Hic jacet
Rev. Augustinus David
Hubert
Hujus Ecclesiæ Parochus,
Pastor dilectus et amans,
Undis Fluvii,
Spectante et ejulante
Civitate, submersus,
Die 21a Maii,
Anno 1792.

———

Flete et orate.

—How long has our swift little DOLPHIN been shooting across from shore to shore, asked Mr. Oldbuck.

—Why, it has not taken much more time than the ice-boats do, with a fresh westerly breeze, to cross from the Napoleon wharf to Levi, when the frozen surface of the river is very smooth. It is not every winter, you know, but generally one out of three, we can calculate having this useful connecting link with the south shore, styled an ice-bridge. Nor does it entirely depend on very intense cold, though the *cold snap* in January is favorable to it; the state of the tide and wind has much to do with the preliminary to an ice-bridge, that is, the stoppage of the ice at the narrows at Cape Rouge.

—For the enlightenment of future generations, let us note here, illustrious admiral, ere it is entirely forgotten, the old style of ferrying passengers, in winter. Until 1818, the Levi ferry, winter and summer, was in the hands of Indians. In summer, birch bark canoes were used; in winter, wooden boats, scooped out from the trunk of large pines, all in one piece—hence their name, "dug-outs." In 1843, the "dug-outs" met with rivals. Messrs.

Julien & Gabriel Chabot of Levi used the first "built" canoes, made something like a long and strong whale boat. In 1827, Sir John Caldwell owned the first steam tug, the *Lauzon*, Capt. Gabriel Chabot. On week days in summer, the *Lauzon* towed rafts; on Sundays, she held the ferry. The first *horse boat* was built in 1828, by Charles Poiré, farmer of Levi, the last had to give up the ghost in 1845,* when steam superseded horseboats. The important question of a winter steam ferry was solved by the steamer *Unity*, in 1857.

Until a few years back, canoes solely were used in winter; William Howard Russell, of the *London Times*, on his visit to Quebec, in 1861, gave a very graphic description of this mode of conveyance in his Volume, *Canada and its Defences*.

---

* *Quebec Past and Present*, p. 431.

VII.

WINTER QUARTERS OF THE *Petite Hermine* IN 1535–6.—EARTH
    WORKS ON THE ST. CHARLES, IN REAR OF MR. PARKE'S VILLA.
    —THE CRADLE AND THE TOMB OF FRENCH DOMINION IN
    NORTH AMERICA.

—You certainly have furnished us pleasant glimpses of the
three memorable sieges to which the city was exposed. I never
could have conceived that so many thrilling incidents could have
taken place in the limited area over which the Dolphin has been
steaming for the last hour.

Is there anything about the St. Charles worthy of note ?

—Yes, replied Mr. Oldbuck, there is the spot where Jacques
Cartier's ship wintered in 1536, beyond the Marine Hospital. Mr.
Joseph Hamel, city surveyor, published in 1843, a useful *brochure*
on the remains of a vessel he discovered, where the Lairet stream
falls into the St. Charles—supposed to be those of the *Petite
Hermine.*

A view was lithographed, copied from an engraving
executed at Paris, the subject of which was furnished by Geo. B.
Faribault, of Quebec, retracing the departure of the St. Malo
mariner for France on the 6th May, 1536. To the right, may
be seen Jacques Cartier's fort,[*] built with stockades, mounted
with artillery, and subsequently made stronger still, we are told
with ditches and solid timber, with drawbridge, and fifty men
to watch night and day.

---

[*] "Le Capitaine fit renforcer le Fort tout àl entour de gros fossés, larges,
et profonds avec porte à pont-levis et renforts de rangs ou pans de bois
au contraire des premiers. Et fut ordonné pour le guet de la nuit........cin-
quante hommes à quatre quarts, et à chacun changement des dits quarts les
trompettes sonnantes ; ce qui fut fait selon la dite ordonnance."— *Voyage de
Jacques Cartier.*

Next comes the *Grande Hermine*, his largest vessel, of about one hundred and twenty tons, in which Donacona, the interpreter, and two other Indians of note, treacherously seized, are to be conveyed to France, for presentation to the French monarch, Francis I. Close by, the reader will observe *L'Emerillon*, of about forty tons in size, the third of his ships ; and higher up, the hull of a stranded and dismantled vessel, the *Petite Hermine*, of about sixty tons, intended to represent the one whose timbers were dug up at the mouth of the Lairet stream, in 1843, and created such excitement amongst the antiquarians of that day. On the opposite side of the river, at Hare Point, the reader will notice on the plate a cross, intended to represent the one erected by Cartier's party on the 3rd May, 1536, in honor of the festival of the Holy Cross; at the foot, a number of Indians and some French, in the old costume of the time of Françis I. So much for Jacques Cartier and his winter quarters, in 1535-6.

Two hundred and twenty-three years after this date, we find this locality again the arena of memorable events. In the disorderly retreat of the French army on the 13th September, 1759, from the heights of Abraham, the panic-stricken squadrons came pouring down Côte d'Abraham and Côte à Cotton, hotly pursued by the Highlanders and the 58th Regiment, hurrying towards the bridge of boats and following the shores of the River St. Charles, until the fire of the hulks, anchored in that river, stopped the pursuit. On the north side of the bridge of boats was a *tête de pont*, redoubt or hornwork, a strong work of a pentagonal shape, well portrayed in an old plan of the Siege Operations before Quebec. This hornwork was partly wood, defended by palisades, and towards Beauport, an earth-work—covering about twelve acres ; the remains (the round or ring field), standing more than fifteen feet above ground, may be seen to this day surrounded by a ditch ; three thousand * men

---

° It is evident that the Beauport entrenchments were to be on a vast scale. In those days of *corvées* and forced labor, when it was merely necessary to command *de par le roi*, it was easy to bring together large bodies

at least must have been required to construct, in a few weeks, this extensive entrenchment. In the centre, stood a house, still visible on a plan, in which, about noon on that memorable day, a pretty lively debate was taking place. Vaudreuil and some of the chief French officers were at that moment and in this spot debating the surrender of the whole colony. Let us hear an eye-witness, Chevalier Johnstone, General de Lévis' aide-de-camp, one of the Scotchmen fighting in Canada for the French king, against some of his own countrymen under Wolfe after the disaster of Culloden. Chevalier Johnstone's description will strike every one from its singular accuracy :—

" The French army in flight, scattered and entirely dispersed, rushed towards the town. Few of them entered Quebec ; they went down the heights of Abraham, opposite to the Intendant's Palace, directing their course to the hornwork, and following the borders of the River St. Charles. Seeing the impossibility of rallying our troops, I determined myself to go down the hill at the windmill, near the bake-house,† and from thence across, over the meadows to the hornwork, resolved not to approach Quebec, from my apprehension of being shut up there with a part of our army, which might have been the case if the victors had drawn all the advantage they could have reaped from our defeat. It is true the death of the general-in-chief—an event which never fails to create the greatest disorder and confusion in an army—may be pleaded as an excuse for the English neglecting so easy an operation as to take all our army prisoners.

---

of men. " M. de Montcalm, arrivé à Québec (from Montreal), commanda tout le monde pour travailler à des retrenchements qui furent tracés vers une paroisse nommée Beauport. Comme il pensa que ces ouvrages ne seraient pas en état avant l'arrivée des vaisseaux anglais, ce qui pouvait être d'un jour à l'autre, il envoya un ordre à M. de Lévis, qui était à Montréal, de commander, généralement, tous les hommes de ce gouvernement de descendre à Québec, et qu'on avait besoin d'un coup de main.—Il envoya à cet égard des ordres précis et conformes, dans toutes les paroisses, qui mirent tout le monde en mouvement." *Mémoires sur les affaires du Canada,* 1749-1760. Finally, Vaudreuil decided that Montreal would furnish 1500 men only for this service.

° This bake-house appears to have been somewhere at the foot of Abraham's Hill.

" The hornwork had the River St. Charles before it, about seventy paces broad, which served it better than an artificial ditch ; its front facing the river and the heights, was composed of strong, thick, and high palisades, planted perpendicularly, with gunholes pierced for several pieces of large cannon in it ; the river is deep and only fordable at low water, at a musket shot before the fort ; this made it more difficult to be forced on that side than on its other side of earthworks facing Beauport which had a more formidable appearance ; and the hornwork certainly on that side was not in the least danger of being taken by the English, by an assault from the other side of the river. On the appearance of the English troops on the plain of the bake house, Montguet and La Motte, two old captains in the Regiment of Bearn, cried out with vehemence to M. de Vaudreuil, ' that the hornwork would be captured in an instant, by an assault, sword in hand ; that we would be all cut to pieces without quarter, and that nothing else would save us but an immediate and general capitulation of Canada, giving it up to the English.'

" Montreuil told them that ' a fortification such as the hornwork was not to be taken so easily.' In short, there arose a general cry in the hornwork to cut the bridge of boats.* It is worthy of remark, that not a fourth part of our army had yet arrived at it, and the remainder, by cutting the bridge, would have been left on the other side of the river as victims to the victors. The Regiment ' Royal Roussillon,' was at that moment at the distance of a musket shot from the hornwork, approaching to pass the bridge. As I had already been in such adventures, I did not lose my presence of mind, and, having still a shadow remaining of that regard which the army accorded me on account of the esteem and confidence which M. De Levis and M. De Montcalm had always shown me publicly, I called to M. Hugon who commanded, for a pass in the hornwork, and begged of him to accompany me to the bridge. We ran there, and without asking who had given the order to cut it, we chased away the soldiers with their uplifted axes, ready to execute that extravagant and wicked operation.

" M. Vaudreuil was closeted in a house in the inside of the hornwork with the Intendant and with some other persons. I suspected they were busy drafting the articles for a general ca-

---

° It crossed the St. Charles, a little higher up than the Marine Hospital, exactly at the foot of Crown street.

pitulation, and I entered the house, where I had only time to see the Intendant with a pen in his hand, writing upon a sheet of paper, when M. Vaudreuil told me I had no business there. Having answered him that what he said was true, I retired immediately, in wrath, to see them intent on giving up so scandalously a dependency for the preservation of which so much blood and treasure had been expended. On leaving the house, I met M. Dalquier, an old, brave, downright honest man, commander of the regiment of Bearn, with the true character of a good officer — the marks of Mars all over his body. I told him it was being debated within the house, to give up Canada to the English by a capitulation, and I hurried him in, to stand up for the King's cause, and advocate the welfare of his country. I then quitted the hornwork to join Poularies at the Ravine* of Beauport, but having met him about three or four hundred paces from the hornwork, on his way to it, I told him what was being discussed there. He answered me that, sooner than consent to a capitulation, he would shed the last drop of his blood. He told me to look on his table and house as my own, advised me to go there directly to repose myself, and clapping spurs to his horse, he flew like lightning to the hornwork."

Want of space precludes us from adding more from this very interesting journal of the Chevalier Johnstone, replete with curious particulars of the disorderly retreat of the French regiments from their Beauport camp, after dark, on that eventful 13th Sept.; how they assembled first at the hornwork, and then filed off by detachments up the Charlesbourg road, then to Indian and Ancient Lorette, until they arrived, worn out and disheartened, without commanders, at day break, at Cap Rouge.

On viewing the memorable scenes witnessed on the St. Charles, the spot where the first French discoverers wintered in 1535-36, and also the locality, where it was decided to surrender the colony to England in 1759—are we not justified in considering it as both the *cradle* and the *tomb* of French dominion in the new world ?

On this land has, for many years, stood the family mansion of George Holmes Parke, Esquire,—Ringfield.

° A small bridge supported on masonry, has since been built at this spot exactly across the Main road at Brown's mills, Beauport.

—You have, Mr. Oldbuck, recalled some startling events, authenticated by our most reliable historians and enacted within the precincts of our port : you have shown us every style of naval architecture from Frontenac's tiny birch bark canoe to that modern phenomenon, the *Great Eastern :* I think we have had enough of history for to-day. Do not be vexed if I tell you, I once from my office window, witnessed a stranger sight than any you have yet described. One morning, I saw on a level with the Queen's Wharf, the huge snout of a whale.

—A whale, did you say ?

—Why, yes, a *bona fide*, gigantic whale.

—Please, explain, redoubtable admiral. I long for that whale story.

VIII.

CONCLUSION.

" On the morning of the 14th of August, 1872, I despatched one of the steamers under my control on a surveying trip to the Northern Channel, a duty annually performed by that vessel. I expected her to be absent for several days and had looked forward to this with great expectations as I would then be free to take a run out to some of the lakes, trout fishing. I had made all my preparations, looked over my flies, lines, and rods, and arranged with a congenial companion to leave early next day. Little did I then imagine the fish I was so soon to struggle with. The height of my fishing ambition was salmon and trout. I never aspired to such monsters as whales. After the departure of the steamer, I left my office in the evening for home and at the usual hour retired to bed. At about midnight I was awakened by a loud ringing of my door bell, and hurried down to see who was there. I opened the door when a young nephew, who had taken passage in the steamer, rushed into the house in a great state of excitement. As soon as he could catch sufficient breath, he informed me that the steamer had returned. This being so unexpected, I greatly feared some dreadful accident had happened—some one drowned or killed—I begged him to tell me the worst at once. In a gasping tone, he began hurriedly to say that " the steamer—the Captain—the whale," etc., etc. I really did not know what to understand, but it was evidently something about a whale.

" What do you mean? are you mad ? " said I.

" No, no," he cried. "The Captain wants to see you immediately about it. Oh! it is such a monster,—about two hundred feet long and big as a ship."*

---

* It is unnecessary to add any further testimony to the authenticity of this whale story. Hundreds in Quebec, in August 1872, hurried down to view the monster high and dry, at the slip on the Queen's wharf.—J. M. L.

I caught the young man by the shoulder, and pushed him into a seat. After a few minutes' rest, he was able to give me to understand that twenty-four miles below Quebec, and one hundred miles from salt water, they had found a large whale stranded on a sand bar, had turned back with it in tow, and the Captain wanted to see me about it. I dressed and went down to the wharf, and saw the Captain, who was full of importance and anxiety over the matter. I requested him to sit down and tell me what it all meant."

" Well, sir," he said, at once appealing to my good feelings. " Of course you are master, and can do as you wish, but I hope you will see fair play in this matter, and that I am allowed my share of the prize ; it is a fortune, and such a chance may never happen to me again. You and I can make heaps of money out of it, and afford to be generous to the crew in the bargain. Will you go half the profits and charge me with half the expenses ? I am willing to pay my share. Oh, yes, sir, I'll do the right thing, and I hope you will see to my interest. We are sure to make a great spec out of that whale ; there must be one hundred barrels of oil in that whale, and the oil is in great demand, notwithstanding the opposition made to it by coal oil."

The Captain certainly thought he had struck oil at last.

" Captain, it is a bargain," I answered. " I'll do my best for all parties concerned ; but tell me, where in the world did you get that whale ? "

" Well, sir," said he, " after leaving the wharf, everything went on quietly until, when about half way through the North Channel, the look-out man cried out : ' A schooner or barge, aground or upset on the sand bar, sir, ahead to the right of us.' Several persons being on deck at the time, all glasses were levelled in the direction of the object ; none were able to make out what it was. I stopped the steamer and sent the mate with six men in a boat to ascertain. We followed the men's movements with straining eyes, and saw them cautiously approach the sand bar, and step out of the boat ; the tide being at half ebb, left a large portion bare for a considerable distance from the object in view. The men appeared very undecided what to do next, and huddled together with evident fear ; they kept on slowly, approaching nearer and nearer, then halted, and consulted together ; finally, they set to shouting with all their might in their native tongue. We listened ; I thought I caught the words, ' *Une baleine ! une baleine !* a whale, a whale !' I could hardly believe this possible, so far up the river. However, I ordered another boat and proceeded to the scene. The men on the bar came to meet me, all very excited and speaking at the same time, saying it was a monstrous whale : two of them declaring it was alive for they had seen it wink its eyes ; another, that he saw its body quiver ; none had dared to go near ; they feared it might turn on them and, with a stroke of its enormous tail, launch them into eternity. My presence appeared to inspire confidence ; all looked to me to lead the party on, but, I can assure you I did not fancy the idea at all; so, after the men had called each other cowards, and inferred as much of me, by their looks, one Baptiste, who had plucked up more courage than the others, volunteered to go forward if all would follow and keep quite near. This was acceded to ; in single file, we started, Baptiste leading, with a boat-hook and pole in hand ; when some distance off our leader came to a dead halt, and would proceed no farther, until he was thoroughly roused to the task by the bantering tones of his followers, when, with a sudden desperation he ran forward, gave the monster a poke, and dashed back into our midst out of breath. The poor whale never stirred a muscle. This appeared to embolden Baptiste, who tried it again, with the same results. We then mustered sufficient resolution to storm the dead monster in a body ; every-one in turn struck at him with an oar or something of the kind. The whale was really dead. I stared at the great creature in astonishment. Visions of barrels of whale oil and heaps of money appeared before me. I felt I had struck oil, that prospects were decidedly bright, and the old saying, that there is a tide in every man's affairs when taken at the ebb, would lead to a fortune, was at last to be verified in me. A long consultation was held to decide what course to pursue ; next, to secure the prize and safely land it at the ancient city. After a great deal of talking, it was determined that a hole should be cut in the monster's jaw, a chain inserted, then fastened to the tail, then attached to a hawser and made fast to the steamer, and with the flood-tide, to take it in tow and return to the city. The chain was sent for and soon made fast.

"How anxiously we counted the hours and minutes which passed waiting for the ebb—that ebb-tide which was to lead to such glorious results. In due course it came, and we started with our prize in tow ; the whale swaying first to one side, then the other—at times its high mouth would open and almost stop the boat. I can assure you, I was not trolling a minnow ; it was quite the reverse of baiting with a sprat to catch a whale, and I never fancied he was running any risk of being pounced on by any cannibal fish. By dint of perseverance and a favorable tide, we at last reached the wharf near midnight; I despatched your nephew for you. Now I know you expect me to proceed again on my trip at daylight, and as I shall be absent several days, I must leave all to you, and hope you will do the best you can for me. As I said before, charge me with half of all the expenses and give me half the profits. We have got a big thing, and I would feel very anxious about it during my absence, did I not know that you will do the right thing."

—"Very well, Captain," I answered, " I'll do my very best; so make it secure."

The whale was made fast to the pier and I bade the Captain good-bye again, and proceeded home quite delighted with our prospects. I sat up nearly the whole night hunting over my books for some treatise upon the subject of whales. The only one I could find was an old copy of "Chambers' Information for the People." In this, it is stated that for every foot in length, a Right whale is calculated to give a barrel of oil. Now as the Captain told me it was seventy feet long and a Simon-pure whale, I put down the probable produce at seventy barrels —figured this up at fifty to sixty cents per gallon—smoked a pipe of peace, smiled at our good luck, and lay down to take a short rest, dreaming of whales from the one which swallowed Jonah to the one I now possessed. At an early hour I was at the wharf and found crowds of people already assembled to see it, and a large number were engaged in working it up on the rising tide in an ascent near the wharf, where at low water it could be seen nearly its entire length. The fabulous prices stated by the knowing-ones as to its value soon induced several speculators to make me offers for its purchase, but finding I would not sell, some proposed to form a joint stock company and take shares. I was deaf to all such offers, and determined that the Captain and I should be the only members of the firm. A long headed old fellow proposed to exhibit at so much per head; this struck me as an excellent idea, and I let him carry out his plan, receiving with a happy countenance the money he frequently laid on my table. During the day I was besieged with people who wanted me to relate the history of the capture. An excited individual also presented himself as a claimant of the whale, declaring that he had harpooned it some two hundred miles down the river

several days before it was found, and threatened me with all the
rigors of the law if I did not deliver it up to him at once. He
said he was sure there were marks on the body to substantiate
his claim ; upon close examination none could be found, and consequently I would not give it up to him. I had promised to
look after the Captain's interest, and intended doing so. In the
meantime, the exhibition was going on with the best of results,
and money pouring in. I came to the conclusion that if this
could continue for two or three days the result would be splendid,
especially as there was to be opened the next day an industrial
exhibition in the ancient city, and thousands of visitors would
rush to see such a great curiosity as a real whale. I can assure
you, I began to think that we had really struck oil, and something else too, and every half hour added large sums to my first
calculations of the profits likely to be divided between the Captain and myself. Whale stock kept rising, rising, and rising
again ; all these great expectations were soon to be dashed to the
ground and trouble cast its shadows before.

The weather was very warm, the sun shone fiercely, and I
don't think that big whale had been accustomed to a warm climate.
The cold North would appear to agree better with him, for the
old fellow soon began to manifest decided symptoms of suffering
from the heat. The Port physician had evidently scented that
whale, for he came to me in an excited manner and asked me
whether I intended creating some fearful disease by poisoning
the atmosphere with that whale. " We will have the typhoid
fever or cholera, sir, raging in the city before twenty-four hours,"
said he, " if you don't get rid of that whale, sir ; he must be removed
at once, sir." I tried all manner of arguments to induce him to
take a more favorable view of the matter ; it was no use. He
said, he was bound to see that whale away from the precincts of
the city, and go, it must. You may imagine this was a damper
to all my prospects. I got vexed, then cooled down a little to
become more so, and finally told the Doctor to take the whale
and do what he pleased with it.

—" No, sir," cried he in anger, " I will not have anything to
do with it. You must see to its being removed, sir ; you are the
responsible party, sir."

At last we both decided to go out and have a look at him to
see if it were not possible without danger to the health of the inhabitants, to keep it a couple of days longer. My hopes began to
rise again, but one look at the colossus lowered them like a shot.

We found him high and dry on the slip, and such a sight! he was perforated in every part of his body. He had been stabbed and stuck with knives and other sharp instruments, by numerous inquisitive visitors trying the thickness of his skin, and looked as if seriously affected with the small-pox; I had to admit that it did smell rather strong in that neighborhood. This made the Doctor more determined than ever, and about an hour after he left me, down marched an officer of police with three constables, who served me with a peremptory order from the Mayor to remove that whale at once. Now, just fancy the fix I was in. How to remove him? Where to put him? The man who owned the elephant was far better off than I was, for it was alive and could be marched off; but my monster was immovable, and could neither be coaxed, nor driven away. Not even the claimant was at hand to relieve me. Obey I must, and one trial should be made to save those seventy barrels of oil and the whale bone, which I was sure would net handsome profits. At last I decided to charter a tug steamer, and tow it off somewhere down the river. I was told that it would not float. Not knowing better, I also chartered two barges, and on the rising tide the whale was got between them, securely fastened with ropes, and off we started with the whale and barges in tow. One of the barges contained one hundred empty oil barrels, several large iron kettles, axes, shovels, and everything necessary to carry on the operations of collecting the oil. We had no idea where we could stop; we did not dare to land near any habitation. At last we espied a quiet bay, some distance from the city, and decided the steamer should give the barges good head way and run them as high on the beach as possible. The condition of the tide favoring this plan, it was carried out, and the whale was left snugly moored to some large trees and on the receding tide it was high and dry in P—'s Bay. About fifteen or twenty men were engaged to cut it up, boil it down, and barrel the oil. I then returned home, completely exhausted, bewailing the hour that made me partner in a whale venture.

I paid daily visits to my whaling establishment until I could do so no longer. The scent penetrated my clothing, got down my throat, remained in my nostrils, and prevented my eating for several days. The news of the great whale being at P—'s Bay spread in every direction, people came from miles around to see it. It was hacked and cut in pieces by curiosity hunters; some carrying away pieces of the skin to make

razor strops, or to cover old trunks. I forbade the men to say
that I had any thing to do with it; it was no use, every one
appeared to know that I was the proprietor. The newspapers
published the most ridiculous accounts of me in connection with
that whale, and for many days I got telegrams and letters from
friends all over the country, inquiring about my whale, and some
of them were very amusing. Several of my artistic friends
caricatured me; in one, I was represented in bed surrounded by
baby whales, beseeching me to return them their mamma.
Really I don't think that Barnum, as exhibitor of the Woolly
Horse, the What Is It, Mermaid, or any other great wonder,
occupied a more prominent position than I did at that time.
Presidents of Historical Societies and other learned institutions
called upon me for the history of that whale, and my name was
to be immortalized if I would donate the skeleton to their
museums; I waived all such honors until I could consult
my partner, the Captain, who I was sure would prefer turning
everything into money—and I invariably answered that he was
absent and I could do nothing without his consent.

Upon one of my visits to the whale, I observed a large barge
about a quarter of a mile below us; if was filled with country
people from the opposite side of the river, who had got up a
picnic to visit the whale. There were about sixty or seventy,
old and young, women among the rest. As there was no wharf
near, a number of strong young men carried the women ashore
on their backs. When all were landed they formed into procession to march up to the bay, but every step onward filled their
nostrils with such a scent as to nearly take their breath away.
At last they came to a halt, evidently unable to stand it any
longer. Several of the young men, not so fastidious as the
others, ventured up close to the monster and told such fabulous
tales of it that the women loudly expressed their regret at not
being able to see the sight too. One stout old dame, with broad-
brimmed straw hat, umbrella and spectacles, and apparently the
chaperone, told them that she knew how to get over the difficulty. "Just follow me," she cried. They all turned back
and went into a field, and were soon intently engaged in gathering some herbs, after which the procession was re-formed with
the old dame at the head, when on they came, shouting and
laughing with a determined air to conquer all obstacles. When
they got up near enough, every one was found to have a bunch
of wild mint under their noses, and they chuckled greatly over

the success of the old woman's plan of seeing the whale, while smelling the mint.

After several days' work I was rather astonished to find that all the men had secured was nine barrels of what they assured me was whale oil, and there was no more. This small result upset the Captain's and my own calculations with a vengeance. The man who wrote the article on whales in "Chambers' Information for the People" could not have meant such a whale as ours. I can assure you, I would have sold out my share cheap, but whale stock had lost its hold upon public confidence, and was far below par. I found that the Captain, after inquiry, had lost all interest in the speculation and did not claim any dividend. However, I was determined to bring the matter to a speedy close. I sent up the nine barrels of oil, and all the materials used in the operation of securing them. Being fond of collecting specimens of Natural History, I had the skeleton also taken up and laid out to bleach on the wharf.

The oil did not please me, there was a smell about it quite different from that of any whale oil I had ever noticed before; one would have supposed that the old whale had come back in its flesh again. So I accepted the first offer I got, before the Port-physician came around, and sold the nine barrels for thirty dollars, on condition that it was removed at once. This was done and it became the property of a dealer in junk and old stores. I was told he went off boasting of his bargain. Some days after he found a customer for it. As soon as he started the bung of the barrels to get samples, the contents pushed out and drove himself and customer away by its loud smell. Those nine barrels contained nothing more than boiled whale in a high state of fermentation. There was not an ounce of oil in the old creature's body. He had evidently been afflicted with some disease, worked himself up from the sea into fresh-water, died, and finally floated into the sand-bar where found, (to my cost). I put the best face I could on the matter; had the skeleton laid out, it soon became white, and was really a great curiosity to many, the jaw-bones being each sixteen feet long.

I now found myself proprietor of only a whale's skeleton. There is an old saying, that every man has a skeleton in his cupboard. I can assure you mine was not in a cupboard, for it was rather larger than I presume the generality of mankind are supposed to be haunted with.

I was one day quietly examining the debit and credit side of the whale account, when I found myself the loser by a considerable amount. Just as I closed the book, with much dissatisfaction, I heard a rap at my office door, and desired the person to walk in. A respectable man came in and asked me whether I was Mr. McGreevey. I answered—" No, sir, that is not my name ; " the gentleman he named was President of the St. Lawrence Steam Navigation company, a few blocks further off, but our names sound a little alike.

—" Well sir," said he, " you will probably say whether you are the person who owns a whale."

—" Oh, yes," I answered, " I am that unfortunate man. What can I do for you, sir ? "

He said, " I am one of the members of the municipal council of St. Jean, and also a church warden. You had a whale cut up at St. P—'s Bay a few miles above us ; a quantity of the offal has floated down with the tide ; settled on the beach right opposite our church, and near our homes. The atmosphere is poisoned ; we cannot remain in church, nor live in our houses, from the dreadful stench created by that horrid whale ; I am deputed by the council to call upon you and request you to have it removed before we all die of cholera or some other pestilential disease."

You may well imagine that this did not make me feel any better over my whale speculation. I managed, however, to work upon the councillor's good nature, and for a sum of money he promised to get some persons to clear the offal off the beach, and rid me of this new trouble.

In the latter part of September, a friend, who is President of a university in one of the United States, visited our city and I had many pleasant hours with him. Calling at my office, I showed him the skeleton of the whale; he was very much pleased to see it, as it was the first, and certainly a great curiosity. He gave me several gentle hints that it would add greatly to the attractiveness of his university's museum, if it was there. I told him that it cost me much trouble and considerable money. He then said that if I would have it cased and forwarded to him, he thought the trustees of the institution would allow me a fair value for it. As he offered to pay for the packing, I consented, and had it forwarded via. one of the western steamboat lines. Several months passed before I heard from him, when one day I received a letter, in which he wished to know whether I was not of opinion that that whale had been born to cause trouble to every one who ever had anything to do with it. In due course it had arrived at Chicago. Of this fact, he was notified by the agent of of the steamboat line, but perfectly dumfounded by the bill of cost ; the university being called upon to pay $225 for freight and charges, and he feared under these circumstances, my prospects of any further allowance were very doubtful indeed. So ended my adventures with that provoking old whale."

Moral : do not speculate in dead whales in the "dog days"!

Just as the Port admiral had delivered the moral of the whale story, the DOLPHIN, glided into its berth at the Queen's wharf. The shrill pipe of the boatswain, the shriller whistle of the steamer, proclaimed our safe return. One and all we tendered our hearty thanks to the admiral of the Port, whose courtesy had procured us a sea voyage, as pleasant as it was instructive.

It had just taken us two hours and ten minutes to steam round.

APPENDIX.

(Extract from my Gaspé Journal, 8th June, 1877.)

Having enjoyed a substantial repast, in which salmon, fresh from the pool, was the *pièce de résistance*, we were, amongst many tit-bits of useful or amusing knowledge, treated to a song, partly composed by the Ottawa poet, " Cousin Sandy," partly by the old " Laird of Cluny Cottage ; " it was set to the tune of " Widow Machree" with variations, and retraced some of the brightest episodes of the eventful career of a lamented literary friend of ours—alas! no more, the Hon. T. D. McGee, as follows :—

D'ARCY M'GEE.

I.

Be young Canada proud, Oh! I speak it aloud,
For there ne'er was a land, and there never will be,
But has heard of the name, aye and likewise the fame,
That's a bull—never mind that—of D'Arcy McGee.

II.

Though I say to myself all my compeers are delf,
And I am the real China, and that's true for me,
Where's the man, old or young, with a musical tongue,
That will match with this Orator, D'Arcy McGee.

III.

That spalpeen, it's true, that's from East Waterloo ; (*)
He chides me and chates me, to own it I am free,
But I'm never at fault with the great Mister Galt,
And Cartier smiles sweetly on D'Arcy McGee.

IV.

My staunch friend, J. A., can with Orangemen pray,
I soon will convince him, and that you will see,
That the priests are the hest for the folks of the West ;
As well as the Orator D'Arcy McGee.

V.

With men such as these at the antipodes,
A household word surely I am destined to be,
For the gold in the mines of Australia shines,
Through the quartz, at the mention of D'Arcy McGee.

(*) Hon. Michael Foley, since dead.

VI.

Then be aisy now, plaze, for old Demosthenese,
Had he lived in those days would have copied from me;
For the man in the moon must go off in a swoon,
When he hears the redoubtable D'Arcy McGee.

VII.

I will venture a bet that the fishes must sweat,
In the mighty St. Lawrence right out to the sea;
And my big burning words must set fire to the birds,
That fly within hearing of D'Arcy McGee.

VIII.

You all know the same, that from Ireland I came,
And I tried very hard my country to free,
With O'Brien and Meagher and Mitchel for war,
The life of Young Ireland is D'Arcy McGee.

IX.

There's no nation on earth to such genius gave birth
As the Island of Erin that lies in the sea;
Burke, O'Connell and Shiel were full matches for Peel,
And the last, though not least, that is, D'Arcy McGee.

X.

Some say I am handy at sipping good brandy,
And, with social gents, I am great on the spree;
To taste of the crathure 'tis all human nature,
And so does the Orator D'Arcy McGee.

XI.

I'll better my station by Confederation:
And be known in the future by K. C. and B.
I have made my own path up to KNIGHT OF THE BATH,
Hurrah for Old Erin and Sir D'Arcy McGee!

TABLE

Showing the distances of the various POINTS OF INTEREST from Quebec, and from each other, on the Lower St. Lawrence and Saguenay Rivers.

Miles.	Point St. Laurent.	St. John.	Ile Madame.	Cap Tourmente.	Grosse Ile.	Pillar Light.	St. Paul's Bay.	Les Eboulements.	Murray Bay.	Riviere du Loup.	Tadousac.	Ste. Marguerite.	St. Louis Islets.	Rivière aux Canards.	Little Saguenay River.	St. John's Bay.	Eternity Bay.	The Capes.	Trinity Bay.	Cap Rouge.	Cape East.	Cape West.	Ha! Ha! Bay.	St Alphonse.	Chicoutimi.
Quebec																									
Pt. St. Lawrence	12																								
St. John, Island of Orleans	5	17																							
Ile Madame (Lady Island)	6	6	23																						
Cap Tourmente, North Shore	5	11	5	28																					
Grosse Ile, (Quarentine Station)	5	16	10	5	33																				
Pillar Light-House	15	31	25	20	15	48																			
*St. Paul's Bay, N.	7	38	32	27	22	7	55																		
*Les Eboulements, N.	11	49	43	38	23	18	11	66																	
*Murray Bay, N.	16	65	59	54	49	34	27	16	82																
*Riviere du Loup, S. (Cacouna Passengers land here)	39	95	89	84	79	64	57	46	30	112															
Tadousac, N. (*Mouth of Saguenay*)	22	117	111	106	111	86	79	68	52	22	134														
Riviere Ste. Marguerite, E.	15	132	126	121	106	101	94	83	67	37	15	149													
St. Louis Islets	4	136	130	125	110	105	98	87	71	41	19	4	153												
Riviere aux Canards, E	4	140	134	129	114	109	102	91	75	45	23	8	4	157											
Little Saguenay River, W.	4	144	138	133	118	113	106	95	79	49	27	12	8	4	161										
St. John's Bay, W	5	149	143	138	123	118	111	100	84	54	32	17	13	9	5	166									
Eternity Bay, W. (Capes Eternity and Trinity)	9	158	152	147	132	127	120	109	93	63	41	26	22	18	14	9	175	175							
Trinity Bay, E	7	165	159	154	139	134	127	116	109	70	48	33	29	25	21	16	7	7	182						
Cap Rouge, E.	8	173	167	161	147	142	135	124	108	78	56	41	37	33	29	24	15	15	8	190					
Cape East, E.	7	180	174	169	154	149	142	131	115	85	63	48	44	40	36	31	22	22	15	7	197				
Cape West, W.	2	182	176	171	156	151	143	132	116	86	64	50	46	42	38	33	24	24	17	9	2	199			
Ha! Ha! Bay, Entrance.	1	190	177	172	157	152	151	133	117	87	65	51	47	43	39	34	25	25	18	10	3	1	200		
St. Alphonse, Entrance.	7	197	184	179	165	159	158	140	124	94	72	58	54	50	46	41	32	32	25	17	10	8	7	207	
Chicoutimi, *via St. Alphonse*	28	217	212	207	192	187	179	168	152	122	100	86	82	78	74	69	60	60	53	45	38	36	35	28	235

QUEBEC TO RIMOUSKI.

Quebec to Riviere du Loup.......... 112
Riviere du Loup to Rimouski.......... 66
— 178 m's.

Rimouski to Tadousac.......... 60
Tadousac to St. Alphonse.......... 72
— 132 "

Rimouski to Chicoutimi, direct.......... 142
" " *via* St. Alphonse. 160

NOTE.—In the above table the distance of any place from Quebec will be found at the top of perpendicular column under the name of the place wanted. The distance between any other two places is found by taking the name of one of the places in the left hand margin, and following its line until it intersects with the column at whose head is the name of the other places sought.

* Places marked with an asterisk are Stations of the Montreal Telegraph Company.

Quebec & Gulf Ports Steamship Company.

River and Gulf of St. Lawrence Route.

The favorite Passenger Steamer "MIRAMICHI" leaves Montreal every alternate **Monday** at **4.00 p.m.**, and Quebec every alternate **Tuesday** at **2.00 p.m.**, for Pictou, calling at Father Point, Metis, Gaspé, Percé, Paspebiac, Summerside, and Charlottetown, P. E. I., returning, leaves Pictou, every alternate **Monday at midnight**.

BERMUDA LINE.

Steamers leave New York for Hamilton, Bermuda, every **Thursday** in April, May and June, and every alternate **Thursday** thereafter.

WEST INDIA & VENEZUELA LINE.

Steamers leave New York every **Third Saturday**, for St. John, Porto Rico, St. Thomas, Laguayra and Porto Cabello, Venezuela.

A Steamer is intended to leave New York about the 1st July, and every six weeks thereafter, for Demerara, calling at St. Thomas, Martinique, Barbadoes and Trinidad.

Connections to all parts of the West Indies and South America.

For Freight or passage apply to

W. MOORE, *Manager,*

QUEBEC.

A. E. OUTERBRIDGE & CO.,

29 Broadway, New York.

G. LEVE, *Passenger Agent,*

Broadway cor. Chambers St., N. Y.

THE

1878. ST. LAWRENCE STEAM NAVIGATION 1878.
COMPANY.

A. JOSEPH,   JULIEN CHABOT,
President.   *Manager.*

This Company's Line of Steamers, plying along the North and South Shores of the Lower St. Lawrence, and on the

FAR-FAMED RIVER SAGUENAY,

Is composed of the following First-Class PASSENGER STEAMERS:—

"SAGUENAY," "ST. LAWRENCE," "UNION,"

OFFICERED BY EXPERIENCED MEN.

From the 20th June to the 10th of September, one of the above Steamers will leave the St. Andrew's Wharf every day (except Sunday) at 7 a.m., on arrival of the Richelieu and Ontario Navigation Company's Steamer from Montreal and the Grand Trunk Railway Trains from the West, which make connection for the SAGUENAY RIVER, as far as Ha! Ha! Bay and Chicoutimi, calling at Baie St. Paul, Eboulements, MURRAY BAY, RIVIERE DU LOUP, [Cacouna] and Tadousac.

☞ Connecting at Rivière du Loup with the Intercolonial Railway, for and from the Maritime Provinces and Eastern States.

After above date, until 12th October, a boat will leave Quebec for the same places, on Tuesdays and Fridays.

For TICKETS and information, enquire as follows :—

Throughout the United States at Offices Selling Northern Excursion Tickets. NEW YORK, 261 Broadway ; BOSTON, 197 and 240 Washington Street.

In CANADA, at all principal Offices of the Grand Trunk and Intercolonial Railroads.

At all Western Offices of the Richelieu and Ontario Navigation Co., and on their Passenger Steamers.

In MONTREAL, Nos. 133 and 177 St. James Street, 228 St. Paul Street, and on the Richelieu Pier.   A. MILLOY, *Agent.*

In QUEBEC, at the General Ticket Agency of G. LEVE, opposite the St. Louis Hotel, where State Rooms can be secured.

And at the Company's Office.

For further information, apply to   A. GABOURY, *Secretary.*

Or to **H. F. BELLEW, Freight and Passenger Agent,**

ST. ANDREW'S WHARF, QUEBEC.

Quebec, 1878.

ST. LOUIS HOTEL,

ST. LOUIS STREET,

QUEBEC.

This Hotel, which is unrivalled for Size, Style and Locality in Quebec, is open through the year for pleasure and business travel. It is eligibly situated in the vicinity of the most delightful and fashionable promenades, the Governor's Garden, the Citadel, the Esplanade, the Place d'Armes, and Durham Terrace, which furnish the splendid views and magnificent scenery for which Quebec is so justly celebrated, and which is unsurpassed in any part of the world.

The Proprietors in returning thanks for the very liberal patronage they have hitherto enjoyed, inform the public that this Hotel has been enlarged and refitted, and can now accommodate 500 visitors, and assure them that nothing will be wanting on their part that will conduce to the comfort and enjoyment of their guests.

THE RUSSELL HOTEL COMPANY, *Proprietors.*

WILLIS RUSSELL, *President.*

1878

SALMON FISHING

IN THE

River Ste. Marguerite.

Which is about sixty miles long, and contains six separate stations, each affording ample fishing for two rods.

A TRIBUTARY OF THE RIVER SAGUENAY, CANADA.

ROBERT HARE POWEL, Esq., 424 *Walnut St., Philadelphia.* ⎫ *Lessees.*
WILLIS RUSSELL, Esq., *St. Louis Hotel, Quebec.* ⎰

Summary of Catch by the undersigned for the Season of 1877.

	Days.	Fish.	Weight.	Average.
Messrs. R. H. Powel,	17	74	999½	13½
" W. Russell,	1	9	145	16
" Streit (New York) & Green (New Jersey),	36	489	13⅛	
" Walter M. Brackett (41 Tremont Street, Boston,)	5	31	449	14½
" E. V. Clark (New York,)		7	98	14
" Col. Rhodes, Quebec,		2	44	22
Total......................		159	2224½	14

THE POOLS OF THE MARGUERITE.

From "Sketches of the Lower St. Lawrence," by J. M. LeMoine, Esq., late President of the Literary and Historical Society of Quebec.

Picturesque scenery, combining exercise and healthy repose with moderate charges, during the languid days of July and August, has, no doubt, contri. buted, in no small degree, to attract, for some years past, pleasure-seekers from every corner of the continent to the watering-places on the Lower St. Lawrence. Two spots in particular—Chicoutimi, at the head-waters of the Saguenay, and Tadousac, at its outlet—are famed places of resort during the "leafy" months. Of late, a new source of attraction has sprung up between these two points—that is, the opening up to tourists of a piscatorial turn, of the Salmon-Pools of the MARGUERITE, which, until recently, were held in reserve by the proprietor, for self and friends.

The MARGUERITE, a tributary of the Saguenay, after taking a short turn, near its entrance, runs parallel with its big brother for some seventy miles. It is distant fourteen miles from Tadousac, and one hundred and twenty, from Quebec. Steamers leaving Quebec at seven a.m. reach Tadousac the same day at seven p.m.

This river has all the rugged beauty of the Saguenay on a smaller scale. Hidden amidst the silence of the forest primeval, far away from the haunts of civilized man, it rejoices in some of the most magnificent scenery on the continent ;—its eddies and roaring rapids, wheeling occasionally around perpendicular capes as lofty as those of Eternity and Trinity, are varied by a succession of deep, quiet pools, in which the lordly salmon, fresh from the briny billows of the St. Lawrence, disports himself at leisure, carefully guarded from poachers by vigilant overseers.

The proprietor of this noble river has completed arrangements, at several of the pools, calculated to add much to the comfort of anglers de-. sirous of enjoying a few days' salmon-fishing, at a rate of remuneration which will certainly place it within the reach of many. Six plain Gothic. cottages, 30 x 24 feet, with verandahs, have just been erected—one at each of the pools. They are provided with beds, linen, blankets, crockery, cooking stoves, and utensils, and also ice-houses for cooling drinks ;—in fact, all the indispensables requisite for a well provisioned disciple of old Izaak, located for a week in the depths of a Canadian wilderness, with a *compagnon de route*, or help mate,—if a benedict, his wife—that is, provided she has a taste for rusticating, and can enjoy fresh salmon cooked in twenty different ways. Some brave ones have, last summer, followed their lords to the tranquil pools of the *Marguerite*, and added roses to their cheeks by "roughing it in the bush."

There are no other habitations in this wilderness but those recently put up by the proprietor. The intercourse from one pool to the other is by means of birch bark canoes, or by paths cut out, at some expense, through the virgin forest. It is nature in its wildest graces. However, to many

> " There is a pleasure in the pathless woods;
> There is a rapture on the lonely shore ;
> There is society where none intrudes."

o   •   o   o   o   o   o

Each cottage can accommodate several persons. The Quebec line of steamers passes daily up and down the Saguenay. Sail or row-boats are at all times available at Tadousac, fourteen miles lower down, to convey the tourist, his provisions, wardrobe, etc., to the elysium of the lovely *Marguerite*.

Previous to the improvements on this estuary, the fly-fishing had attracted considerable notice, having been patronized by His Royal Highness Albert Edward, of Wales, Lord Lisgar, and his popular successor, Lord Dufferin, Governor-General of the Dominion. Some of the salmon caught have attained 38 lbs., but, as a rule, they do not average more than 16 lbs. The following items, as to the capacity of the six chief Pools, were obtained from the proprietor himself :

The Lower-Forks Pool

Suffices for four or five Rods. The Station has a large cottage furnished with kitchen detached.
The next station is four miles above, and is called

Home Pool :

Four Rods, etc. ; cottage furnished throughout.

The Chateau :

Three miles above, for four Rods; also, has a cottage, etc.

The Sand Pool :

Four miles higher, with same accommodation ; a cottage furnished. Two Rods.

Bardsville :

Six miles above; has a cottage furnished. Four Rods.

Upper-Forks Pool :

Six miles higher ; has a cottage furnished. Three Rods.

Academy

of

Jesus-Marie,

ACADEMY OF JESUS-MARIE.

ACADEMY OF JESUS-MARIE.

HIGH above the umbrageous groves of *SOUS-LES-BOIS*, for many years the attractive Villa of Errol Boyd Lindsay, Esq., looms out the majestic *ACADEMY OF JESUS-MARIE*, an institution for the education of young ladies. It is owned and conducted by the French Nuns of Jesus-Marie, well known for the excellence of their teaching. The system followed in that Convent is that of Father Lacordaire, which is well suited to develope the reasoning and judgment of the pupils, who are not required to learn anything by memory, but exclusively by analysis. All the subjects comprised in a classical course of studies are taught in this Convent, in English and in French.

As to sanitary arrangements, this Academy is one of the best institutions in Quebec. Ventilation and airing in every room is perfect, and the place where the Convent is situated is one of the healthiest around the City. The ground occupies an area of several acres, and is ornamented with trees, walks and gardens, giving a rural appearance to the place and a great deal of comfort and amusement to the pupils.

This Convent is about three miles from Quebec, on St. Louis road, to the north of the parish church of St. Colomban of Sillery. It is a lofty white brick building, roomy, and built with all the modern improvements, under the direction of Rev. Mr. Audet, member of the Board of Arts and Manufactures. From the roof of the building, one may enjoy one of the grandest views of Quebec, the Plains of Abraham, the St. Lawrence and the surrounding country.

ESTABLISHED IN 1841.

THOMAS ANDREWS,

No. 1 ST. JOHN STREET

QUEBEC,

Importer and Dealer in

English and American House Furnishing,

Building and Cabinet Hardware.

FISHING TACKLE.

A SUPERIOR ASSORTMENT OF

Salmon and Trout Rods, Fishing Baskets, Landing Nets, Gaffs, prepared Silk Lines, Double and Single Casts, Spoon Baits, Artificial Minnows, Marana Gut, Fly Dressing Material, &c.

FLIES.

The best selection of Salmon and Trout Flies, made expressly for the Lakes and Rivers in the vicinity of the Lower St. Lawrence.

TO SPORTSMEN.

Double and Single Fowling Pieces, Scott's, Webley's and other celebrated makers; Rifles, Revolvers, Shot Belts, and Pouches, Powder Flasks, Shot, Wads, Central and Pin Fire Cartridge Cases ; Curtiss & Harvey's Diamond Grain Powder.

Constantly on Hand

Paints, Oils, Turpentine, Varnishes, Painters' Brushes, Window Glass, Putty, Nails, Spear & Jackson's Files and Edge Tools, American Ship Augers, Blind Staples, Wrought Iron Gas Tubes and Fittings, Globe and Check Valves, Steam and Water Gauges, India Rubber and Hemp Packing, Lift and Force Pumps, Sinks, Wash Hand Basins, &c.

—ALSO—

A great variety of Cooking Stoves, Kitchen Ranges, Fancy, Hall, Parlor, Box and Coal Stoves; Cooking Utensils, Fire Guards, Fire Irons, Coal Scuttles, Bronzed and Wire Fenders, Cocoa Matting, Door Mats, Wool Rugs, Chamois, Brushes, Sponges, Refrigerators, Water Coolers, Ice Cream Freezers; and

AGRICULTURAL IMPLEMENTS.

Jos. Rodgers & Son's, Westenholm's, celebrated Scissors, Razors, Pocket and Table Cutlery.

Orders for Tin and Copper Work, Plumbing, Gasfitting, Bell Hanging, will be attended with neatness and despatch.

Steam and Hot Water Apparatus. Special attention is given to this branch.

WORKS

PUBLISHED

By J. M. Le Moine.

ENGLISH.

*LEGENDARY LORE OF THE LOWER ST. LAWRENCE, (1 vol. in-32).. 1862

*MAPLE LEAVES, (1st Series) (1 vol. in 8o)........... 1863

*   "   "   (2nd Series) (1 vol. in-8o)........... 1864

*   "   "   (3rd Series) (1 vol. in-8o)............ 1865

*THE TOURIST'S NOTE BOOK, (1 vol. in-64) by Cosmopolite.. 1870

*SWORD OF BRIGADIER GENERAL MONTGOMERY, (A Memoir) (1 vol. in-64)...................... 1870

*JOTTINGS FROM CANADIAN HISTORY, (Stewart's Quarterly)... 1871

*TRIFLES FROM MY PORTFOLIO, (New Dominion Monthly)... 1872

MAPLE LEAVES, (New Series)........................... 1873

QUEBEC, PAST & PRESENT............................. 1876

THE TOURIST'S NOTE BOOK (second edition)....... 1876

FRENCH.

*L'ORNITHOLOGIE DU CANADA, (2 vol. in-8o)..... 1860

*LES PECHERIES DU CANADA, (1 vol. in-8o)....... 1863

*MEMOIRE DE MONTCALM, VENGEE, (1 vol. in-32).. 1865

*L'ALBUM CANADIEN.. 1870

NOTES HISTORIQUES SUR LES RUES DE QUEBEC.. 1876

TABLEAU SYNOPTIQUE DES OISEAUX DU CANADA, à l'usage des Ecoles............................. 1877

For sale at Messrs. DAWSON & Co., Lower-Town, Quebec.

* The works marked with an asterick are very scarce.

CONTENTS.

PART I.

CHAPTER VI.

CHAPTER VII.

CHAPTER VIII.

CHAPTER IX.

CHAPTER X.

CHAPTER XI.

CHAPTER XII.

CHAPTER XIII.

CHAPTER XIV.

CHAPTER XV.

CHAPTER XVI.

CHAPTER XVII.

CHAPTER XVIII.

CHAPTER XIX.

CHAPTER XX.

CHAPTER XXI.

THE ROUND TRIP TO MURRAY BAY — CACOUNA — TADOUSAC—CHICOUTIMI AND INTERVENING PLACES.

PART II.

LIGHTS AND SHADOWS IN THE KINGDOM OF HERRING AND COD.

THE CRUISE OF THE DOLPHIN.

NOTE FOR PAGE 111.—Since I prepared, chiefly from the French narrative of
Mr. Faucher, in *Tribord and Babord*, the short summary I gave of Father Crespel's
sufferings on Anticosti, I have learned that an English translation of this interesting document had been made in New York, by John G. Shea, Esq.

To Abbé Ls. Bois of Maskinongé, I owe thanks, for having placed at my disposal his narrative of this shipwreck ; and to Mr. Faucher, for the use I made of
several passages of his volume, notably of that relating to P. E. Island ; to Chris-
topher O'Connor, Esq., of Quebec, for a copy of Sir Hovenden Walker's *Journal*
—a very rare work.